The publisher gratefully acknowledges the generous support of the General Endowment Fund of the University of California Press Foundation and the Chairman's Circle of the University of California Press Foundation, whose members are:

Stephen A. and Melva Arditti
Elizabeth and David Birka-White
Michelle Lee Flores
Gary and Cary Hart
Michelle Ciccarelli Lerach
Judith and Kim Maxwell
James and Carlin Naify
William and Sheila Nolan
Barbara Z. Otto
Ajay Shah and Lata Krishnan
Ralph and Shirley Shapiro
Peter J. and Chinami S. Stern
Howard Welinsky and Karren Ganstwig
Lynne Withey

Joyce Goldstein

with Dore Brown

Inside the Food

CALIFORNIA STUDIES IN FOOD AND CULTURE

Darra Goldstein, EDITOR

California
Revolution

Thirty Years That Changed
Our Culinary Consciousness

University of California Press   BERKELEY LOS ANGELES LONDON

University of California Press, one of the most distinguished university presses in the United States, enriches lives around the world by advancing scholarship in the humanities, social sciences, and natural sciences. Its activities are supported by the UC Press Foundation and by philanthropic contributions from individuals and institutions. For more information, visit www.ucpress.edu.

University of California Press
Berkeley and Los Angeles, California

University of California Press, Ltd.
London, England

Library of Congress Cataloging-in-Publication Data

Goldstein, Joyce Esersky
    Inside the California food revolution : thirty years that changed our culinary consciousness / Joyce Goldstein ; with Dore Brown.
        pages   cm. — (California studies in food and culture ; 44)
    Includes bibliographical references and index.
    ISBN 978-0-520-26819-7 (hardback) — ISBN 978-0-520-95670-4 (ebook)
    1. Cooking—California—History.   2. Restaurants—California—History.   3. Cooking—California style.   I. Brown, Dore, 1956–   II. Title.
    TX715.2.C34G65   2013
    641.59794—dc23   2013014798

Manufactured in the United States of America

22   21   20   19   18   17   16   15   14   13
10   9   8   7   6   5   4   3   2   1

The paper used in this publication meets the minimum requirements of ANSI/NISO Z39.48-1992 (R 2002) *(Permanence of Paper)*.

CONTENTS

Preface   vii

Introduction   1

1   Thirty Years of Food Revolution: A Historical Overview   15

2   One Revolution, Two Ways: Northern versus Southern California   39

3   Defying Kitchen Convention: Self-Taught Chefs and Iconoclasts   62

4   Women Chefs and Innovation: The New Collaborative Kitchen   84

5   New Flavors: Upscale Ethnic, Eclectic, and Fusion Food   109

6   New Menus: The Daily Menu and the Story behind the Food   130

7   Restaurants Reimagined: Transformations in the Kitchen and Dining Room   154

8   A New World of Fresh Produce: Reviving the Farm-to-Table Connection   187

9   Custom Foods: Chefs Partner with Purveyors and Artisans   224

10   Merging the Worlds of Wine and Food: Common Cause   262

Afterword: The Continuing Evolution of California Cuisine   299

Acknowledgments   321

Sources   323

Index   331

In the mid-1970s, a handful of innovative, mostly self-taught chefs and restaurateurs in California felt driven to create a dining experience very different from what prevailed at the time. Their new approach, featuring fresh, seasonal ingredients and creative interpretations of flavor themes from cuisines around the world, captured people's attention. Eventually labeled "California cuisine," it engendered a revolution in Americans' relationship with food through the 1980s and into the 1990s. Styles of restaurants broadened from formal and ceremonial to more democratic and casual. Kitchens that had been hidden were opened up to become part of the dining room. Chefs who had toiled behind closed doors in anonymity became stars. Ingredients such as arugula, baby greens, and goat cheese, virtually unknown previously, became household items for many. Today, in large part because of the influence of California cuisine, both restaurant and home cooking inhabit a radically new world. People now have expectations for freshness, flavor, variety, and healthfulness that are very different from those of the previous generation.

Many people currently working in restaurant kitchens or shopping at farmers' markets are unfamiliar with the early chefs, farmers, and artisans who brought about the California culinary revolution. Apart from recognizing the names of a few celebrities, they do not know very much about the pioneers of California cuisine whose efforts and persistence have made life in the restaurant and culinary worlds easier and more gratifying for us today.

They are not aware of the work it took to get to where we are now, to our easy familiarity with terms like *fresh*, *seasonal*, and *local*. They don't give much thought to the fact that forty years ago most of this was just a dream. That is why I wrote this book.

What I found most interesting and exciting about the California cuisine revolution was that it was led largely by autodidacts. I was amazed at how many of the

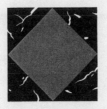

■ DAILY SPECIALS ■

Fettuccine al funghetto – mushrooms, prosciutto, tomatoes, lemon
and cream $10.00

Linguine with grilled tuna, lemon, capers, onions and olives $11.00

Grilled pork brochette with Indonesian peanut sauce, served with
coconut rice and snow peas $14.00

Grilled rib eye steak with sauce poivrade (mirepoix, red wine and
pepper), served with potato gratin with gruyere cheese $15.00

Grilled swordfish with charmoula (cilantro, parsley, lemon, garlic,
cumin, paprika and cayenne), served with roast potatoes and grilled
zucchini $16.00

Paella – saffron rice with lobster, clams, chicken, chorizo, peppers,
artichokes, tomatoes and onions $18.00

Lamb noisettes a la grecque – with tomatoes, cognac, feta cheese,
oregano and garlic, served with roast potatoes $18.00

Baked salmon with tarragon shallot butter, served with grilled
zucchini $15.00

All wines served by the glass are selected as accompaniments to the menu of
the day. Please ask your waiter for suggestions.

August 31, 1985 .   DINNER

Beginning September 8, Square One will be open for dinner on Sundays from
5 – 10 PM

Lunch: Monday–Friday 11:30–2:30
Dinner: Monday–Thursday 5:30–10:30   Friday–Saturday 5:30–11:30
Closed Sunday

An eclectic selection of entrées from Square One, August 1985.

participants at all levels (chefs, artisans, farmers, winemakers, produce company owners, seafood buyers, ranchers, and managers) were self-taught. They were not embarrassed to have learned by trial and error. Their creativity, fearlessness, and generosity impressed me. They not only tirelessly pursued their passions but were willing to share what they learned so that we all could benefit and progress. It was a collective and contagious high.

In writing this book I feel a deep sense of responsibility to do right by the people whose work brought California cuisine to national and international prominence and influenced our collective American palate. I want to give credit to those who contributed to our growing knowledge, skills, and education, who made change happen, who affected how and what we eat now. Together we learned how to run restaurants with collaborative kitchens, how to write menus to entice, educate, and tell a story, and how to build connections with farmers, artisans, and our communities.

Once a revolution has run its course and the changes it has wrought begin to be taken for granted, it's time to tell its story. I have been an active participant in the development of California cuisine since its early days. I taught classic French, Italian regional, and Middle Eastern cooking classes in San Francisco from the mid-1960s through the 1980s, starting with small groups in my kitchen and moving on to open the California Street Cooking School in 1972. I worked as a chef at Chez Panisse Café from 1980 to 1983, and then opened Square One restaurant in 1984 at the age of fifty and ran it for twelve years. I was also a founding member of Women Chefs and Restaurateurs and a recipient of a James Beard award for Best Chef in California.

Over the past forty years I have developed personal connections with most of the chefs and restaurant owners associated with California cuisine and many of the purveyors who supplied their restaurants. In preparing this book, I recorded the stories of more than 190 of them. They shared inspiring accounts of success, provocative revelations, enlightening facts, intriguing points of view, and a few angry tirades. Unfortunately, space considerations meant that I couldn't include everyone, and I apologize to those whose stories don't appear in these pages.

While I was conducting the interviews, I quickly realized that it would not be easy to get to the bottom of some of the stories. Who came up with the label "California cuisine"? Who created California pizza? Was Chez Panisse Café inspired by Tommaso's Restaurant in North Beach or a trip to Italy? In these cases, there were several legitimate claims to the truth, and I gave each the benefit of the doubt. In the face of conflicting claims and gaps in the record, I dug deeper and talked to more people, but there will continue to be discrepancies as memories fade and myths grow.

This is not a tell-all filled with juicy gossip about affairs, drugs in the kitchen, or accusations of culinary plagiarism. Those titillating tales have already been told, or are, in the broader history, trivial aspects of an important time in California's culinary development. You won't find recipes from famous chefs in this book, either, though sample menus are included. Most of the chefs who are part of this history have written signature cookbooks and you can find their recipes and philosophy there.

What you will find in this book is a community of passionate, openhearted, and talented people who together discovered a new way to appreciate food. I feel proud to have been among them.

Introduction

Like the rest of America, California is unformed, innovative, ahistorical,
hedonistic, acquisitive, and energetic—only more so.
—Wallace Stegner, Saturday Review, 1967

Perhaps because California has no past—no past, at least, that it is willing
to remember—it has always been peculiarly adept at trailblaʒing the future.
—Rebecca Solnit, River of Shadows, 2003

When you go to a supermarket today in many parts of the country you are not surprised to find twenty kinds of extra virgin olive oils, some made from California olives. A plethora of mustards and salsas in the condiment aisle is to be expected. The produce section has bags of salad-ready baby lettuces and bins filled with radicchio, arugula, golden beets, haricots verts, and bouquets of fresh herbs. You could get lost in the cheese department while making up your mind what to buy. You can select pastured eggs, grass-fed beef, and old-fashioned pork from a Berkshire pig that bears little resemblance to the commodity-raised "other white meat." When you go out to a restaurant, you don't consider it odd to find goat cheese or smoked salmon on a pizza that was cooked in a wood-burning oven, or to be served soft polenta with a stew of just-harvested chanterelles or a Moroccan spiced lamb *tagine* on a bed of couscous. You have come to expect diversity of ingredients and flavors, and above all, you expect the ingredients to be fresh, seasonal, and to a large extent locally grown.

In the 1960s, things were very different. Supermarket produce selections were limited, and what little there was often had been shipped from far away, tasting a bit tired by the time it arrived. Bags of assorted lettuces or arugula did not exist. Herbs were packed in small jars, dried, their perfume lost. Most mushrooms were canned, and wild mushrooms were unknown to all except for a few hobbyist foragers. In homes and even in high-end restaurants, many ingredients came from cans, jars, or the freezer, and rich, heavy sauces compensated for their lack of flavor. What caused the landscape of food to change so radically during the last quarter of the twentieth century? Many of us eat very differently than people did in the 1960s because of a new approach to cooking called California cuisine. It changed our expectations and opened up a new world of possibilities.

What Is California Cuisine?

The restaurants that I really like are the ones that don't try to make you believe that you're somewhere else. They tell you this is it, this is California.
—Chef Mourad Lahlou, Aziza

The world's classic cuisines, such as Chinese or Italian or French cuisine, developed and evolved over centuries as part of a traditional culture. These cuisines are not monolithic—they are in turn broken down into many unique regional cuisines. Their recipes are rooted in the specific culture and environment in which they developed.

California cuisine, in contrast, developed recently and grew rapidly. For the most part it was unfamiliar, innovative, and electrifying, and yet, like traditional cuisines, it reflected its setting. It shares with classic cuisines a crucial feature: it is the food and cooking of a particular, unique *place*. In chef Paul Bertolli's poetic rendering, "A cuisine is based in a place where food is wedded to people and soil and what can grow there and what can be made there from the natural resources, the land." The state of California is extraordinarily diverse geographically, culturally, and ethnically, and California cuisine is a cuisine of diversity, open to multicultural cooking styles, flavors, and traditions. Our chefs may cook food of other cultures, but their ingredients come mostly from the same larder, stocked with the produce, fruits, and grains grown in our fields, the animals grazed in our pastures, and the fish pulled from our waters. California cuisine is the product of the state's geography and climate, its abundant ingredients, its history of immigration, its support for entrepreneurs, and the ingenuity of its chefs.

Those who are interested in food will recognize its components: Baby vegetables. Gathered greens. Goat cheese. Pizza. Salsa. Other characteristics are equally familiar: Fresh. From the farm. In season. Local. Organic. Pasture-raised. Ingredient-based. Live-fire cooking. Open kitchen. Daily menu. Eclectic menu. Fusion cooking.

All of these are aspects of California cuisine, but most are not requirements. To belong to the California cuisine community, chefs do not have to have an open kitchen, although many do. They do not have to use a wood-burning oven or mesquite grill, although many consider that equipment essential to their cooking. They do not have to change their menu every day; they can change one or two things or just the sides. They can choose to list all of their suppliers and farmers on their menu, or not. They can focus on the Mediterranean, Asia, or Latin America, all of these, or none. They can spoon a Mexican salsa on an Asian fish. They can use Parmesan cheese from Italy instead of California and not find picketers outside their restaurant. California cuisine is a cuisine of options. It has wide parameters and no rigid rules. The one common element is that California cuisine uses fresh, seasonal ingredients, preferably raised nearby.

Unlike traditional cuisines, which have their roots in the home and community, California cuisine originated in restaurants. "There was no California cuisine at somebody's house," said Gary Jenanyan, who headed the kitchen at the Great Chefs program at the Robert Mondavi Winery. "No one said, 'We're going to Joyce's house for California food.' No one asked, 'Are we going to have Italian or Californian tonight?'" Instead, California cuisine arose gradually, set in motion by a group of pioneering and passionate chefs who wanted to run new kinds of restaurants. Many were self-taught, while others had the finest European training. An unprecedented number were women.

In 1978, Sally Schmitt opened one of the first restaurants to offer what would become identified as California cuisine—the original French Laundry in the Napa Valley. This history is about people as much as food, and in these pages they share their stories.

SALLY SCHMITT

French Laundry, Yountville

Today anyone who loves food has heard about the French Laundry. But there was a French Laundry well before Thomas Keller bought the building and turned it into one of the most famous restaurants in the country. In 1967, Sally and Don Schmitt moved to Yountville to manage a new real-estate development called Vintage 1870. Their little café had the first espresso machine in the Napa Valley, to the delight of the local Italian community. Sally offered a simple menu of hamburgers from the grill and a couple of sandwiches. It was hard to get people off the highway in those days because the Napa Valley and Yountville were not known for food, but Sally's delicious cooking led to a line out the door, and the Schmitts realized they needed a second restaurant to accommodate the hungry diners. When a space became available in the main building at Vintage 1870 in 1968, they opened the Chutney Kitchen, a lunchroom that quickly became the hottest spot in the Napa Valley. Soon Sally was cooking regularly for the St. Helena Ladies Luncheon Group. "They took me under their wing. They taught me how to set a lovely table and that the salad could be served after the main course. I owe them a huge debt."

Next Sally and Don added a once-a-month dinner series that grew to twice a month. There was one menu and one seating, by reservation only. "We ended up cooking for seventy," recalled Sally. "I don't know how I managed. I was young and had more energy, but the thought of cooking a five-course dinner for seventy people frightens me today. We have five children, and the two oldest girls were able to help in the kitchen and serve, and [our son] Johnny, who now runs the Boonville Hotel, was the designated omelet man. The menus were all hand done, one for each table, with nice little drawings on them. Our daughter Cathy was very good at that."

Sally was a locavore before the term was even coined. "I remember some-body was bringing people from France over, wanting me to do a special dinner and suggesting that I make French food for them. But my idea was to have Dungeness crab and artichokes, because that's California." She had grown up on a small farm, so it made sense to her to source food from as close to the restaurant as possible. However, there were few small farms that could provide quality ingredients back then. Neighbors would come to Sally and inquire, "What would you like me to plant?" but they wouldn't follow through. She asked one man if he could supply her favorite beans, Kentucky Wonders. "I loved the flavor. That was before we ever had heard of haricots verts. He said, 'Oh, anything you want,' and then he dropped out of sight."

Ten years later, after a dispute with their landlord, Sally and Don left Vintage 1870 and, along with a good friend, purchased a building that had previously housed a French laundry. The people of the community continued to refer to the building as "the French laundry," so the Schmitts kept the name. They worked hard to maintain the property's charm during the restoration. As Sally said, "It was a simple building, built by people who did not have any money. In our restoring it, we respected that and didn't gussy it up, partly because of our belief that simple is better, but also because we couldn't afford it. It turned out to be lovely."

The French Laundry opened in 1978. Sally wanted to offer a single daily menu, but at first she wavered about the concept. "I talked this over with my family and said, 'Maybe we should have a little steak in case somebody can't eat what we present, or maybe offer them one choice.' My children and Don said, 'No, stick to your plans.'" She did, and her menu consisted of a selection of appetizers, a soup, a main course, salad and cheese, and a choice of desserts. The appetizers always included one fish, one vegetable, and perhaps a pâté, "so if anybody couldn't eat lamb or was a vegetarian, we could substitute an appetizer for the main course or make them an omelet—that was the secret weapon. We tried to make the French Laundry as much as possible like entertaining at home. You don't get a choice when you go to someone's house for dinner; you are served whatever the lady of the household is preparing."

Sally had one part-time assistant, who cleaned during the day and then went home, changed her clothes, and returned to wait tables at night. "We operated with a tight staff and our own girls. The French Laundry is on two floors, so we had one waitperson on each floor, one person to help me in the kitchen, a dishwasher, and Don to greet people and pour wine. We served mostly Napa Valley wine, although we snuck in a few outsiders, like a couple of Chalone wines that we particularly liked." Of course, there weren't very many wineries in the region at that point, so the French Laundry represented almost all of them.

The Schmitts ran the French Laundry nonstop for seventeen years, then decided to sell because, as Sally said, life in the Napa Valley was getting fancier and that was not their style. When Sally and Don read Thomas Keller's proposal to gather investors and learned about the vast array of kitchen equipment and the anticipated number of staff, Sally was astounded. "It was night and day. I thought it could never happen in this small building, but he loved the building as much as we did." Thomas's transformation of the French Laundry into a world-renowned three-star dining destination put the tiny town of Yountville on the map. The Schmitts moved to Boonville and opened the Apple Farm in Philo. Today Sally and Don have retired to Elk and their children run the farm.

While most of the established restaurants in the 1960s and early 1970s were content to cook with generic commercial ingredients, supplemented with canned and frozen products, the new chefs wanted to serve fresh, seasonal food that could be cultivated locally, ideally by people who shared their passion for flavor and quality. Although the majority of restaurants had not been sourced this way in the past, it was not a wild or impractical dream. California had the rich soil and ideal climate to grow a wide variety of ingredients. But to change the existing supply chains, wherein restaurants were limited to a standard array of commodities offered by large producers, chefs had to first find and then support like-minded small farmers and ranchers.

Driving the produce revolution forward required the efforts of a diverse group of individuals working in different corners of the state's food system. The pioneers included Georgeanne Brennan, who imported seeds from Europe so farmers could raise specialty produce; growers such as Warren Weber, Rich Collins, Lynn Brown, Bob Cannard, and Jeff Dawson, who slowly built up alternatives to produce grown on an industrial scale; Jameson Patton, Steve Walton, and Sibella Kraus of GreenLeaf Produce, who helped create a distribution network that could get local produce into the hands of chefs quickly; and Bill Fujimoto of Monterey Market, who connected growers and buyers and educated both groups in the process.

Chefs supported ranchers and poultry farmers who raised animals sustainably and humanely, and they encouraged artisans to revive the traditional arts of making cheese, curing meats, and baking bread by hand. A few artisans went to Europe to observe time-honored techniques. They longed to learn from cultures that had a rich history of experience, although their reverence was usually accompanied by the California desire to tweak the original. John Finger studied oyster aquaculture in Ireland, France, and Spain, and Cindy and Liam Callahan researched the making of sheep's milk pecorino in Italy. Laura Chenel, one of the most widely respected early artisans, briefly apprenticed to a cheese-making family in France.

LAURA CHENEL

Laura Chenel's Chèvre, Sebastopol

Goat cheese producers around the country refer to Laura Chenel as the mother of them all. Laura Werlin, the author of award-winning books on American cheeses, thought that "Laura Chenel's goat cheese was the start of the artisan movement." Her initial effort yielded a soft, creamy fresh cheese, and as her skill grew, her offerings included olive oil–marinated *cabecou*, aged *crottin*, and ash-coated *taupinière*.

Laura Chenel was born and raised in Sonoma County. Her interest in the back-to-the-land movement led her, in the 1970s, to start a small farm in Sebastopol with bees, chickens, a couple of goats, a vegetable garden, and fruit trees. "The idea was that if the world was going to come to an end, I wanted to be able to produce my food. I made kefir and yogurt and all that stuff. I fell in love with the goats, a deep connection that exists to this day."

Her goats provided so much milk that Laura decided to make cheese. "I mailed away for the government pamphlet on how to make cheese. It never worked out—it was horrible. I kept trying and trying." One day someone brought her a piece of French goat cheese, and as soon as she tasted it she knew that this was what she aspired to create.

Laura went back to school to learn French and then wrote for advice to Jean-Claude Le Jaouen, who had recently published *The Fabrication of Farmstead Goat Cheese*, his now-classic book for artisanal cheese makers. He invited her over, and she found somebody to take care of her goats in California while she undertook a brief apprenticeship, or *stage*, in Europe.

"Jean-Claude got me a *stage* in the southwestern part of France in a little mountaintop village. I was there for about a month with some really nice people who had about eighty to one hundred goats. We took them out to graze, and milked them, and made cheese. I was avid in wanting to learn, and they were grateful to have me, because the work is 24/7. From there I went to a second family in the Loire. When they knew I could make cheese, they took off for Italy. They hadn't had a vacation in who knows how long." In all, Laura lived with four families, and she recalled that by the time she left, she wanted "to stay and do this forever."

Flying back to America in tears, she told herself, "I'm going to give this about a year and if it doesn't happen, I'm going to come back." But it did work out and, starting in 1979, Laura was making cheese daily. One day Helen Allen, co-owner of the Wine and Cheese Center near San Francisco's Jackson Square, introduced her to Alice Waters. "I thought, 'A restaurant? What's a restaurant going to want with cheese?'" But that encounter changed her life. After she started selling to Chez Panisse, cheese shops and chefs from all over California started ordering her products. In 1981, while I was the chef at Chez Panisse Café, we would send someone to the bus station every day to pick up a dripping-wet box of fresh goat cheese for our signature salad. Soon Wolfgang Puck was using Laura Chenel's chèvre on his pizza. Square One wrapped it in phyllo and baked it to serve with a pear, endive, and walnut salad. Others bundled it in grape leaves and grilled it. The impact of Laura Chenel's cheese was felt as far away as New York, where chef Larry Forgione at the restaurant An American Place incorporated it into a strawberry cheesecake. The ubiquitous goat cheese became a symbol of California cuisine.

Laura would visit restaurants to train the staff how to use and store goat cheese, giving them samples of a range of cheeses, from mild and young to sharp and aged. In 1983, when she went to Cindy Pawlcyn's Mustards Grill to show the staff her cheeses, she brought a newborn goat with her to win them over.

Laura inspired others to try their hand at cheese making, especially women. "I think that aspect was critical," she remarked. "Cheese had been a very traditional male-dominated [business]." She paved the way for Mary Keehn at Cypress Grove, SoYoung Scanlon at Andante, Cindy and Liam Callahan at Bellwether Farms, and Jennifer Lynn Bice at Redwood Hill Farm.

In 2006, after thirty years of making cheese, Laura sold her company to a French business. "I knew the man's father when I'd been to France, so I respected the company. I didn't have it for sale, they just called. It was time. I was tired." She said that the transition was gradual. "I ended up spending almost four years side by side with them making cheese and tending my goats. The goats just this spring [2010] went to their new home, built from scratch for them. So they're happy and I'm now going, 'Okay, who am I? What am I going to do?'"

While respect for custom and convention helped Europeans preserve their culinary practices, it also made them less open to the food of other cultures. Californians, on the other hand, embraced multicultural cooking. According to Harvey Steiman, editor-at-large of *Wine Spectator* magazine, home cooks had begun to explore "diverse cooking perspectives" as early as the mid-twentieth century. "Pick up any issue of *Sunset* magazine from the 1950s and you will find Mexican, Italian, Russian, Chinese, Japanese, and other cultures represented not just by their own dishes but by new dishes that incorporate ingredients and techniques from those cultures." However, it wasn't until California chefs picked up these cultural threads and started to weave them together that California cuisine was born.

It took time for this diversity to be fully accepted. Food writer Janet Fletcher observed that for some white California residents in the 1940s through the 1960s, this was "the food of the *other*, whether it was Southeast Asian or Indian or Mexican or Japanese. Eventually California became so multiethnic, so diverse—you lived next to people from other countries, you worked with them—that there was no longer that sense of the other, and this became our food too." Instead of an awkward intrusion into the cultural status quo, California's multicultural diversity became an enrichment that contributed to the development of its cuisine. Some chefs, such as Barbara Tropp at China Moon, focused on foods from a specific culture, faithfully honoring those recipe traditions. Others, like Mary Sue Milliken and Susan Feniger at City Restaurant in Los Angeles, served traditional dishes from many cultures on one eclectic menu. Still others, like Roy Yamaguchi at 385 North in West Hollywood, experimented with fusion cooking.

California cuisine was further distinguished by an emphasis on techniques and equipment that were not part of the European-style restaurant kitchen, such as live-fire cooking on a grill or in a wood-burning oven. Chef Tony Gulisano, who did a stint behind the grill at Prego in Los Angeles, asserted that "the whole start of the California food movement was that wood grill." At Prego, "the grill was full for hours straight. That was the distinct component that differentiated it from the past. It was attractive to the general public as well—smelled good." The open kitchen, another signature of California cuisine, permitted customers to watch chefs at work, a dynamic that changed a restaurant's atmosphere, style of service, and dining experience.

Only in California

I'm not sure it could have happened anywhere else on the planet. You needed this amazing confluence of circumstance—this collection of people, the land, the climate.
—Chef Judy Rodgers, Zuni Café

The conditions that led to the growth of California cuisine were the result of happenstance and a gathering of talented, well-traveled, and intelligent people who were in the right place at the right time. But these people needed raw materials, and California, the nation's largest food-producing state, had them in abundance. California agriculture encompasses not only fruits and vegetables but dairy, livestock, and poultry. Dry in the south, wet in the north, cool on the coast, and warm in the inland valleys, the state's microclimates give chefs year-round access to fresh produce. Variations in weather and soil permit California farmers to grow or raise almost anything imaginable, from cool-climate greens to tropical fruits: avocados and heirloom vegetables in San Diego County; lettuce, artichokes, and strawberries in Monterey County; rice in Sutter County; grapes in counties up and down the coast and in the Central Valley; pears, asparagus, and corn in the

Sacramento Delta; dates in the desert. The San Joaquin Valley offers the greatest fecundity and diversity, producing dairy products and beef, as well as nuts, citrus, stone fruit, and melons.

This plenitude had a seductive pull on chefs. Chef Corey Lee came to cook at the French Laundry in the Napa Valley, planning to return later to his native New York to open his own restaurant. But after four and a half years as *sous chef* and then *chef de cuisine*, Corey told Thomas Keller, "I don't think I'm going to go back to New York." "He had become so accustomed to the quality of the vegetables in California," said Thomas, "that he couldn't see himself being as successful outside of the state. That is significant, when somebody who has all his life wanted to open a restaurant in New York realizes that he will be happier here because of the products. There's no place I've been in our country that has the raw products that we have here in California, and we're blessed."

But the entrepreneurial climate of California may have been as important in the genesis of California cuisine as the accommodating weather. Cookbook author and former Cocolat owner Alice Medrich, who grew up in Los Angeles, thought historian Kevin Starr, in his book *Coast of Dreams*, captured the state's spirit. "Basically he says that California is to the rest of the country, and especially the eastern establishment, as the New World was to Europeans. People who didn't have prospects, or who had a sense of adventure, came here with all these dreams, and so this is the birthplace of all the crazy ideas that have now become very mainstream."

Californians chose not to emulate the static, orderly societies of the East Coast and Europe. In the relatively young and developing region they felt at liberty to pursue their ambitions, and by virtue of their enterprise the economy began outperforming that of the rest of the nation. This attracted more innovators, who came to share in the opportunities and bring their visions to life. Creative Californians developed such whimsical commodities as fortune cookies, Popsicles, Barbie dolls, blue jeans, boysenberries, and white Zinfandel wine. The state also produced two radically different models of eating: California cuisine and what might appear to be its very antithesis—the hamburger fast-food joint, which began when Ray Kroc bought his first McDonald's restaurant in Southern California in the 1950s. By 1970, California had become the most populous state in the union, and its prodigious appetites fueled both ways of eating.

The permissive restaurant culture allowed for many culinary points of view. While the East Coast continued to be Eurocentric, the wide parameters and flexible rules of California cuisine gave chefs the freedom to cook in ways that reflected their individual predilections and cultural bent. When chefs cooked traditional food—based on flavors, ingredients, and dishes they had tasted and wished to eat again—they were cooking the food of memory. They had a benchmark for flavor imprinted on their palate. Their goal was to try to match the original dish: the beef daube they ate in France, the *spaghetti alla carbonara* in Italy, the *romesco* sauce in Spain, or their family's version of Vietnamese *pho* or Moroccan *tagine* of chicken with preserved lemon and olives. While they could not reproduce it using ingredients cultivated in the original country's *terroir*, they sought the best ingredients they could find and used tried-and-true techniques to get as close as they could to what they remembered. They might put their personal imprint on the recipe, but it was still recognizable. The resulting dish could be predictable and boring, right on the money, or sublimely inspired, depending upon the chef's larder and skill at the stove, and the accuracy of his or her memory.

Other chefs wanted to break away from cooking traditional and predictable food, wanting instead to create dishes they had never tasted but only fantasized about—the food of dreams. Yet they could not work in a vacuum, so they took familiar and available ingredients and combined them in unusual ways or tried out innovative techniques to make a dish with their personal imprint. They had no flavor benchmark or taste memory to match, but ventured into the unknown with every dish. Their success was dependent upon their technical skills, culinary experience, and creativity in transforming an idea into an edible reality. The resulting dish could be anything: confused, terrible, challenging, interesting, or pure magic.

Chefs took chances either way, but that freedom to take risks was one of the keys of California cuisine. California celebrated iconoclasts, which enabled often inexperienced newcomers to open restaurants, create new artisanal food products, and make wine. "They could start up a business and not be slapped down because they didn't fit into a mold," said Bob Long of Long Vineyards. "They could experiment and try their ideas out. And they had a relatively accepting audience because the people here were saying, 'Well, okay, why not?'"

At a time when upscale European and North American restaurant culture was dutifully following the classical conventions and recipe strictures of the influential French chef Georges Auguste Escoffier, Californians were doing their own thing. In the 1970s and 1980s, said restaurateur Narsai David, "you'd have had a hard time in a French restaurant finding fresh ginger. Escoffier taught that ginger is this powdered stuff you put in spice cake. California cuisine made an impact because we were not bound by the traditions of the French. Here on the West Coast, we were open to ideas. We just did the things that were appealing to us."

Although in many respects California cuisine was beholden to European know-how, "California itself, as the end of the western ideological expansion of America, represents the getting away from the status and class system of Europe to celebrate the idealization of individualism and the power of the individual," according to chef Mark Miller. "California cuisine, by its nature, has to be revolutionary in terms of not only its fashion, its style, but also its culinary ethos. It cannot be a repeat. The Chinese have a saying, 'you can hold on to the past or you can create the future,' and California was about creating the future. It was America's frontier."

The Revolutionary Years

This history focuses on the years 1970 to 2000, which were the most transformative in the development of California cuisine. The movement had repercussions in agriculture, the wine industry, and restaurant design. Developments during those thirty years had an enormous impact on the quality, freshness, availability, and diversity of the raw materials at chefs' disposal. The California restaurant wine list became a model for restaurants all over the country. The open kitchen allowed a more casual but still professional style of service. By the late 1990s, California cuisine had begun to influence every aspect of the food universe: home as well as restaurant cooking, what was grown, how it was grown, how fresh it had to be, and where it could be purchased.

Calling California cuisine a revolution implies a note of finality, as if it's over and the changes are accomplished and goals achieved. But it continues to evolve. This history stops at 2000 because in the years that followed, food writers and food entrepreneurs, competing in an increasingly dense and crowded arena for the attention of diners and consumers, have tended to make every little change, every new chef or restaurant trend, every novel farm or ingredient seem important and groundbreaking. This has obscured the fact that the pace of change in the culinary world has slowed since the turn of the millennium. Compared to the revolutionary changes in the 1970s, 1980s, and 1990s, what's happened in the culinary world over the past fifteen years or so has been mostly evolutionary, with variations on and extensions of earlier innovations.

Over the years, California has influenced the rest of the country. In the early 1980s, when California chefs Nancy Silverton and Mark Peel were hired to revamp Maxwell's Plum restaurant in New York, pickings were slim for seasonal vegetables. Today, the selection at the Union Square Greenmarket is much improved, although it still seems limited compared to the abundance and variety found at the San Francisco Ferry Plaza or Santa Monica farmers' markets. In 1998, Suzanne Goin of Lucques reported that, after four days of dining out in New York, she despaired of getting a decent salad or seeing any vegetables on the plate. "They weren't part of the dining culture. It was protein and sauce, protein and sauce," a reflection of the lingering European influence on East Coast cooking.

For years it drove East Coast chefs crazy to visit California, see the markets, and listen to their California counterparts rhapsodizing about ingredients, especially when they had to place orders with California produce companies to tide them over during the months when their walk-in refrigerators were bare. Even as recently as 2009, David Chang of New York's Momofuku made the calculated press-grabbing remark that "fuckin' every restaurant in San Francisco is just serving figs on a plate," implying that California chefs lacked culinary chops. We don't need Freud to recognize produce envy. But I suspect that by now Chang has forgiven us for flaunting our figs. Because today, thanks to the California culinary revolution, chefs all over the country have closer connections to farms and ranches. Farmers' markets have expanded. We are all eating better, fresher, and more varied food.

1

Thirty Years of Food Revolution

A Historical Overview

*California has always been as much of a state of mind as a state of the
Union. . . . Other places have decent organic produce, or so they say. But
California promises something more: transformation. The state is the repository
of America's frontier spirit, the notion that a better life is possible for anyone
who wants it regardless of the circumstances of her birth. You can leave your
past at the border and reinvent yourself here.*

—Peggy Orenstein, "The Coast of Dystopia," *New York Times*, January 15, 2010

On May 9, 1984, I was waiting for the electrician to turn on the power so we
could cook our first dinner at my restaurant, Square One. Although the official
opening was not until May 14, we had invited friends to come for a few trial meals
to help us get used to the kitchen and refine our timing. Square One's manager,
Max Alexander, had hired more waiters than we needed because he knew that
not all of them would make the grade. I was still learning their names and their
handwriting, because in those days before computer ticketing systems, the orders
were handwritten in duplicate.

Sous chef Paul Buscemi and I had been in the kitchen prepping like mad with
our staff. Barbara Haimes and Amaryll Schwertner had followed us from Chez
Panisse, as had pastry chef Craig Sutter. We had made pea and lettuce soup, a
tuna and white bean salad, gorgonzola- and ricotta-stuffed ravioli with sage butter, and saffron fettuccine with clams, onion, and basil. We had grilled halibut
with *charmoula* (a Moroccan sauce made with fresh coriander and spices), lamb
chops with mint aioli, *ossobuco alla milanese,* and pork with housemade mango
chutney. The bread baker, Thomas Solis, was making whole-grain loaves. Craig
Sutter and Diane Dexter in our pastry department were preparing macadamia
cake with crème anglaise and poached kumquats, puff pastry pecan tarts with
bourbon whipped cream, and flan with the first of the season's strawberries.

We held our breath as the orders came in. We hadn't slept for days. I had lost fifteen pounds from stress. But our guests were smiling and coming up to the line to thank us and wish us well.

•

I had come a long way from my childhood in Brooklyn, when I was the problem eater who pushed away food because I didn't like it. We had bad cooks on both sides of the family: the vegetables were overcooked, the lamb stew was gray, the roasts were shriveled—even the brisket was dry! We ate Birds Eye frozen peas and carrots, and yes, even Jell-O. A good night was a rare filet mignon and a baked potato.

With both my parents working, we ate out at least twice a week. Restaurants saved my culinary life and showed me that good food was possible. I realized that to eat well I would have to learn to cook. In graduate school, when I finally had my own kitchen, I taught myself from books and my taste memories. I pored over Irma Rombauer's *Joy of Cooking*, Craig Claiborne's *New York Times Cookbook*, and Elizabeth David's *Book of Mediterranean Food* and *French Provincial Cooking*. Whenever I tasted a new dish, I would look it up in a few cookbooks and try to reproduce it at home, adjusting the recipe as I went along to match my recollection of the flavor.

But it was in Italy that my taste buds were truly awakened. After a brief visit in 1957, I went with my husband to live in Rome from 1959 to 1960. We had no refrigerator in our rented apartment so I shopped daily. I also ate out as often as possible to learn about Italian cuisine and ingredients. I gained twenty-four pounds in my quest to find the perfect version of *spaghetti alla carbonara*, which ended euphorically at Pier Luigi's. I compared the bite-sized fresh mozzarella *ovolini* and all manner of *salumi* at five neighborhood shops. I tasted the difference between baby goat chops and diminutive lamb chops. I learned to love assertive and bitter flavors and began adding radicchio and arugula to my salads. Italy changed forever the way I cooked.

Back in the 1950s and 1960s, a generation of aspiring cooks like me, tired of the dreary and predictable food landscape in the United States, avidly consumed the food writing of Elizabeth David, M. F. K. Fisher, Waverly Root, Ada Boni, and Julia Child. Along with providing recipes, these writers gave us a sense of place. We dreamed of dining at the French country inn described by Roy Andries De Groot in *Auberge of the Flowering Hearth* or of eating *cacciucco* at a seaside restaurant in Livorno, as brought to life by Elizabeth David in her book *Italian Food*. We were eager to discover new foods and to learn more about the history and culture of the countries they came from.

Julia Child's *Mastering the Art of French Cooking* appeared on the scene in 1961. By the midsixties I was teaching cooking classes to middle-class housewives, and it was the era of the competitive dinner party. My students were buying Chuck Williams's imported French cookware at the newly opened Williams-Sonoma store and then killing themselves making Julia's Veal Prince Orloff, seafood quenelles, and cassoulet for eager guests. Long before the movie *Julie and Julia* appeared, there were women who cooked their way through Julia Child three times. *Mastering the Art of French Cooking* brought the fundamentals within reach of a generation longing to become more worldly and sophisticated.

The 1960s was a decade of burgeoning affluence, and with the new affordability of jet travel, many more Americans went abroad. Arthur Frommer's *Europe on Five Dollars a Day*, published in 1957, enabled even frugal families to experience the Old World. Many future California cuisine chefs first learned to appreciate food while vagabonding in Europe after or in place of college. Their ensuing approach to cooking "had so much to do with reading and traveling," said *Los Angeles Times* restaurant reviewer S. Irene Virbila, known to her friends as Sherry. "Once you traveled and tasted better food, you wanted to replicate that. What if Alice Waters hadn't gone to France!"

At the same time that Californians were being exposed to other parts of the world through travel and literature, they were defining their own identity and establishing a distinctively western way of life. *Sunset* magazine laid the foundation. The quintessential regional lifestyle publication, sold only on the West Coast, *Sunset* combined articles on cooking with advice on gardening, travel, homes, and do-it-yourself projects. Who didn't dream of building a deck on which to host lavish parties, wowing the guests with the bread you had baked in the adobe oven you had constructed from scratch, accompanied by the vegetables that *Sunset* had shown you how to select and cultivate? Jerry Di Vecchio, food editor for over forty years, said, "The gardening column helped Californians turn to local because we grew all these foods and told you how to cook them. Everybody had artichokes. We grew *fraises des bois*, avocados, persimmons, mandarins, Meyer lemons, and so on. California just had different foods to work with than the East Coast." *Sunset* was a powerful determiner of California cuisine, according to Caroline Bates, restaurant reviewer for *Gourmet* magazine for thirty years. It "focused on western life and shaped how we all cooked, entertained, and ate on the West Coast. It had a very eclectic approach, because its [definition of] California cuisine embraced [the foods of] Mexico, Asia, the Middle East, and many other cultures." With travel and food literature whetting Californians' appetites for greater variety in what they ate and the restaurants they dined at, change was inevitable.

The Continental Restaurant Scene in the 1960s

These newly educated and passionate food enthusiasts didn't find much excitement in the world of restaurant dining. Sacramento food and wine retailer Darrell Corti has been in the family business for most of his life. Highly respected for his extensive knowledge about food and culinary history, he remembers this era all too well. "In the 1960s, there really wasn't anyone who was interested in food per se. The concept of 'foodie' didn't exist. When you went to a restaurant you wanted to eat something that was relatively familiar. Restaurants in San Francisco in 1960 were either French-named with Italian cooks or French-named with French cooks." For special occasions, diners in the Bay Area patronized one of the elegant upscale restaurants, such as Ernie's, the Blue Fox, La Bourgogne, L'Etoile, the Ritz Old Poodle Dog, or Alexis on Nob Hill. Jack's was the place to go for a veal chop and Celery Victor; Vanessi's and New Joe's served good but not authentic Italian food; Alfred's was known for steaks, and Tadich Grill and Sam's for seafood. These last three restaurants, which specialize in basic meat and seafood preparations without cultural pretensions, are the only ones on this roster still open for business.

Los Angeles had Chasen's, a West Hollywood hangout known for its chili, themed places like Don the Beachcomber and the Brown Derby chain, some formal French establishments, and a few expensive Continental restaurants, such as Perino's and Scandia, where it was important to be recognized and seated at a good table. While the Bay Area prided itself on its fine cuisine, Los Angeles promoted drama and exclusivity.

Writer and editor Colman Andrews was born and raised in Southern California. His parents were avid restaurant-goers, so from an early age, Colman came to know all the better places to eat in the LA area. "When people first started talking about California cuisine, I remember thinking that it didn't have much to do with the food that I'd grown up eating in the very European-oriented restaurants of my youth—Chasen's, the Brown Derby, hotel restaurants, and places like that." But even back then, some places did things differently. Colman described these renegades as the "forgotten ancestors" of today's California cuisine restaurants. "One that I know had influence, because I've talked to chefs who used to love it as much as I did, was Trader Vic's. Vic Bergeron was the first person to popularize kiwifruit and green peppercorns. At the same time that Chez Panisse was serving sweetbreads and cream sauce with mushrooms, poached trout, and old-fashioned French food, there were places like Cafe Four Oaks in Beverly Glen, and Alan Hooker's Ranch House in Ojai, which opened in 1956. They were run mostly by people who had traveled in Europe. The Ranch House wasn't exactly California cuisine as we know it, but this guy used 'extra virgin' olive oil back in the days when that phrase could still provoke titters. He used fresh herbs, and not just the conventional ones, but lemon verbena and salad burnet. They were out of the mainstream of the traditional Italian, French, Middle European cooking that almost all the other good restaurants were serving. I think of these as distant inspirations for what became California cuisine."

In the sixties and early seventies the variety of fresh fruit and vegetables available in grocery stores was limited, and most restaurants in both Northern and Southern California used commodity produce from wholesale markets or flew in food from Europe that arrived in less than pristine condition. Chasen's, Perino's, Ernie's, L'Etoile, La Bourgogne, and even the famed Pot Luck in Berkeley, known for its regional French dinners, resorted to serving canned and frozen foods. Fortunately for them, culinary technique and complex sauces concealed a multitude of sins.

The original Pot Luck was opened by Ed Brown in 1954. He gave it that name because diners literally took pot luck—whatever he happened to feel like cooking that day. Wine maven Henry (Hank) Rubin bought the restaurant in 1962 and brought in Narsai David as the kitchen manager. At the time, it was considered the most sophisticated place to dine in the East Bay. Chef Mark Miller was an admirer: "Pot Luck was doing regional French menus on Monday nights way before Jeremiah Tower or Alice Waters did. The food was better, and the menus were more interesting."

People still talk about Pot Luck with reverence, so they may be surprised to learn the inside scoop from Narsai David. "The soups were made with hundred-pound drums of chicken soup base. We used dehydrated onions and powdered garlic. I could not use raw garlic because customers, particularly the lunchtime customers, were angry the first couple times when they went home and their wives complained about the garlic smell in their breath. The main course was served with rice and a vegetable, using frozen vegetables. We dumped two-and-a-half-pound boxes into a large sauté pan with some Kaola Gold margarine." That Pot

Luck was able to draw a devoted following in spite of these shortcuts is evidence of the talent and experience of Narsai's kitchen staff. But by 1972, when Narsai opened his eponymous restaurant, his five-course menu was prepared with fresh ingredients. "There was not an ounce of chicken base in the house, or dried garlic or onions. Absolutely everything fresh," he said. One force behind this growing interest in freshness was a new culinary movement from France.

The Influence of Nouvelle Cuisine in the 1970s

Nouvelle cuisine freed French chefs from the strictures of classic cuisine, which had been codified by Escoffier in the early 1900s. The fad seems passé today, but it had a revolutionary effect at the time and was an important precursor to California cuisine. It was introduced to the general public in 1973, when French food critics Henri Gault and Christian Millau published "Ten Commandments of Nouvelle Cuisine" in their publication, *Le Nouveau guide*. Several practitioners of this new style of cooking—Paul Bocuse, Roger Vergé, Alain Senderens, Alain Chapel, and the brothers Troisgros—became the world's first superstar chefs.

But established French chefs were swept up in the movement as well and began to fundamentally change their approach to cuisine. The commandments urged chefs to be modern and inventive, to not drown the flavor of foods in marinades or heavy sauces, and above all, to begin with fresh, quality products and not overcook them. As a result, cooking times were greatly reduced. *À la minute* preparations were preferred over long, slow cooking. Vegetables were no longer thoroughly cooked—crisp and crunchy became de rigueur. Recently harvested, premium products replaced canned or frozen ingredients.

Chefs bid adieu to béchamel and *sauce espagnole* and started to make greater use of broths and vegetable purées. This was done not for dietary reasons but to make food taste brighter and more vibrant. Sauces were still enriched with copious amounts of butter. More attention was paid to dietetics, meaning that on the whole the food was lighter than that of classic cuisine and portions were smaller. (Because it hit the press at the same time, *cuisine minceur*, a style of low-calorie cooking created by chef Michel Guérard at his spa in Eugénie-les-Bains, was occasionally confused with nouvelle cuisine.)

Fresh, in the parlance of the time, did not necessarily mean seasonal or local, however. While chefs in some fine-dining restaurants in France shopped at neighborhood markets every day, many did not. And with respect to seasonality, traditional haute cuisine training advised the professional chef that once he had created a dish, he should perfect it by cooking it the same way 365 days a year. Disciples of nouvelle cuisine still followed this principle, so if a chef was making a dish with asparagus, where formerly he might have used the canned version in the winter, now he had it flown in from South America. Fresh, yes; seasonal, no.

Highly stylized plate presentations showed off the new dishes. Paul Bocuse and Pierre Troisgros had taught at the École Technique Hôtelière Tsuji in Osaka and drew inspiration from Japanese aesthetics. Large white plates displayed small, dramatic food vignettes, and creative food combinations were encouraged. Yet one of the downsides of nouvelle cuisine was that for a while portions were absurdly small and the food was overly arranged. Dishes such as fanned duck breast with three raspberries and three snow peas artistically arrayed on an oversized plate became a target for parody and complaints.

The era was also infamous for producing some bizarre and unfortunate food combinations in the name of creativity, and ingredients such as kiwifruit and raspberry vinegar overstayed their welcome and became culinary clichés. However, regardless of its sins, the movement was liberating for French chefs, enabling them to break away from the constraints of French haute cuisine.

Nouvelle cuisine entered restaurant kitchens in California via French-trained chefs and restaurateurs based here. In Los Angeles, many followed the movement's doctrine to a T, but others created their own interpretations, such as Michel Blanchet at Jean Bertranou's L'Ermitage, Gerard and Virginie Ferry at L'Orangerie, Bernard Jacoupy at Bernard's, and Wolfgang Puck at Ma Maison. Given LA's interest in style and presentation, nouvelle cuisine met with a warm reception there, and by the early 1980s, its precepts had become associated with California cuisine.

In a 1982 article in the *New York Times,* food columnist Marian Burros wrote that Wolfgang Puck might be "the link between nouvelle cuisine and this new California cooking, between the formal and the informal. The new California food, he says, 'is Schramsberg and pizza with grilled Santa Barbara shrimp instead of caviar.'"

WOLFGANG PUCK

Spago, Beverly Hills; Chinois on Main, Los Angeles; Postrio, San Francisco

Wolfgang Puck was born in Austria, apprenticed in France, and worked at the three-star restaurants L'Hôtel de Paris in Monaco, Maxim's in Paris, and

Raymond Thuilier's L'Oustau de Baumanière in Provence. In 1973, he emigrated to the United States. After two years at La Tour in Indianapolis, he moved to Los Angeles to become chef at Patrick Terrail's nouvelle cuisine restaurant Ma Maison. The rest is history with a capital *H*. "For the first six months at Ma Maison we were so poor, I used to buy lobster shells to make lobster soup base," said Wolfgang, but once the restaurant started attracting the who's who of the entertainment industry, he could afford to buy whole crustaceans and began turning out warm lobster salads topped with caviar along with other luxury dishes, such as salmon soufflés with mustard sauce, trout fillets in puff pastry with beurre blanc, and veal medallions with onion marmalade.

After a few years in Los Angeles, Wolfgang became fascinated by the city's ethnic enclaves. "I got very excited. This is such an interesting city with so many different cultures, so many different cooking styles. You could eat at a lot of restaurants. And I was thinking, 'You know, our food should reflect *a little bit* the cultures we have.'" At Ma Maison, the *salade niçoise* was made with canned tuna, which Wolfgang thought was crazy. He bought fresh tuna at the Japanese fish market, marinated it, and served it rare, either grilled or poached in olive oil. People would eat the vegetables but skip the tuna because they thought it was not cooked. They told him he didn't know how to prepare fish. Of course, "now you cannot go to a restaurant where they don't serve some kind of raw tuna," he added.

In 1981, Wolfgang left Ma Maison and opened Spago on the Sunset Strip. It was an instant sensation and a magnet for celebrities, who came to have Wolfgang cook something special for them. Spago did things differently. The cooks wore baseball hats instead of chefs' toques. You could see them because Spago had one of LA's first open kitchens, and its giant grill and wood-burning oven were visible the minute you walked in the door. After Ruth Reichl wrote a cover story for the *Los Angeles Times* about Spago in the early 1980s, every restaurant in town wanted a pizza oven, a grill, and its own version of California pasta, where angel-hair noodles were tossed with goat cheese and broccoli or used as a bed for squab or trout, combinations that no Italian would consider.

Wolfgang followed his growing culinary curiosity, taking traditional recipes and tweaking them to suit his palate. "What is great about California is that it's new and there's not much tradition, so if I'm going to make pizza, I can give it my own twist that reflects what I like. Instead of having pepperoni we made duck sausage and put it on. And we put goat cheese on pizza, which at that time was completely new. Even sun-dried tomatoes were new. It's crazy to think how many things have become everyday staples that were completely out of this world at that time."

Wolfgang bought a smoker to air-dry his version of Peking duck but wound up using it to make cold-smoked salmon. "I put it on a pizza and sent it out to Joan Collins. She said, 'Oh, that's my pizza!' Robin Lynch, who at the time had the *Lifestyles of the Rich and Famous* show, said Spago and Le Cirque were the two most important restaurants in America. We made the smoked salmon pizza and he called it the 'Lifestyles of the Rich and Famous Pizza.' The funniest thing is that I went to Lyon to hang out with Paul Bocuse and went to one of his restaurants, his brasserie. He had a partly open kitchen, and I saw a smoked salmon pizza. I said, 'Paul, what is that?' He got the menu and it said, 'Spago's smoked salmon pizza.'"

When Wolfgang opened Chinois in 1983, it was the first fusion restaurant in the country. He wanted to bring Asian influences into his cooking, but as he had done with pizza, he created his own interpretations. "To me, cooking is an evolution, and as I grow, my cooking style changes. I am bored very easily, and I don't want to be boxed in with one thing."

Michael McCarty was another important restaurateur whose culinary foundation and technique were French. At his namesake restaurant, which he opened in Santa Monica in 1979, he presented dishes inspired by those he had eaten at his favorite places in France. His early cooking was based on nouvelle cuisine, with its emphasis on freshness, simplicity, and lightness. "Almost all of my recipes are prepared quickly," he wrote in his 1989 *Michael's Cookbook*, "showcasing the natural quality of the ingredients I use, many of which come from or have been popularized by the innovative food suppliers and cooks of California." The cookbook is illustrated with nouvelle cuisine–inspired plate presentations: elaborately fanned vegetables with slices of grilled meat, and pasta topped with hieratically arranged strips of seafood and geometrically placed dollops of caviar. The nouvelle look to the food eventually evolved into simpler plating.

Self-taught chef Bruce LeFavour was originally influenced by the French three-star chefs who popularized nouvelle cuisine, according to an interview he gave Marian Burros in 1986. But when he moved to the Napa Valley to open Rose et LeFavour, he became "bored with France" and more taken with California. "There are more exciting things going on here, more ferment, more eclectic cooking," he said. Rose et LeFavour was a jewel of a restaurant that opened its doors in 1980 in St. Helena. There Bruce offered a single five-course menu each evening that was French in conception but Californian in its incorporation of fresh, local ingredients and ethnic touches. On the entry hall table there might be a basket of *fraises des bois* from Napa farmer Lynn Brown, a hint of the deliciousness that was to come inside. On April 24, 1985, guests dined on Muscovy duck breast in a salad of local greens, a Thai-style soup with Monterey squid, gray sole with spinach, chives, and basil, steamed New Zealand venison with morels and wood ear mushrooms, a cheese tray, and a sweet from the dessert cart.

BRUCE LEFAVOUR

Rose et LeFavour, St. Helena

I still miss chef Bruce LeFavour's tiny, personal, and idiosyncratic restaurant in the Napa Valley. Bruce opened Rose et LeFavour in 1980 with the charming Carolyn Rose at the front of the house. Cindy Pawlcyn, who later opened Mustards Grill, was his first *sous chef*. The French-inspired California food was so wonderful that we would drive all the way from San Francisco to St. Helena just for dinner.

In the late 1950s and early 1960s, Bruce worked in American Army counterintelligence, stationed in eastern France. On weekends he would go down to Burgundy or Alsace or into Paris to see the sights and, of course, sample the regional cuisine. In 1961, he came back to the States and got married. Three years later, he opened a restaurant in Aspen, Colorado, called the Paragon. "I had never really worked in a restaurant before. But our rent was $300 a month, so we could afford to make mistakes." Bruce served his interpretation of nouvelle cuisine in a series of private rooms, where guests could sit in their own little dining room with a curtain. The restaurant was very successful. "We got a pretty good reputation, but as Aspen started to grow, it wasn't a place I wanted to bring my two kids up in by the time they were eight and nine."

He sold the Paragon and moved his family to an isolated two-hundred-acre ranch on the Salmon River in central Idaho. They were fairly self-sufficient. The growing season was short, but they were able to cultivate lettuce, broccoli, and other cold-weather crops. In addition, they had about a hundred chickens, eighty ducks, some lambs, and two Jersey cows. They made their own butter and had wonderful heavy cream. Bruce said he'd probably still be there if he and his wife hadn't gotten divorced and been obliged to sell the ranch.

After the divorce Bruce came to Northern California and looked for a place to open a new restaurant. He settled in the Napa Valley because "all my experience had been that you need a fairly sophisticated audience to do the type of cooking that I was doing at that time." He met Carolyn Rose, and in 1979 they became partners in the intimate Main Street site that they named Rose et LeFavour. Carolyn, known as "C," ran the dining room with warmth and quirky authority. Bruce didn't have enough land to grow anything aside from herbs, but he found that he didn't need to. "I realized that in California you don't need to raise it yourself. You have everything here that you need." He drove an hour to Berkeley to buy seafood from Paul Johnson at Monterey Fish and fruit and vegetables from Bill Fujimoto at Monterey Market. He also had a close relationship with Lynn Brown and Pete Forni of Forni-Brown Gardens in Calistoga, and they supplied him with produce a few times a week. They grew what he asked for, so he'd bring seeds to them and patiently await the results: little *fraises des bois* and unusual varieties of carrots and beans.

"We changed the menu every day and set the menu that day. We just rolled with whatever looked good. Carolyn always handwrote the menu with her elegant script." The menu was terse, and Bruce didn't list most of his sources, since the practice was not yet common. He did mention a certain Mrs. Herb. "Mrs. Herb was a retired detective from Chicago who raised snails. She was a tiny lady, maybe 5 foot 2 inches in sneakers and thin as a rail. She would make her rounds in town. If you didn't use poisons in your garden, she would ask if she could come into your property early in the morning and pick snails. She had a big greenhouse in the back of her house and she'd raise the snails, purge them, and deliver them in strawberry boxes to the restaurant." Bruce had a standing order with her, and her name always appeared on the menu.

Bruce bought Carolyn out in 1986 and renamed the restaurant Rose et LeFavour Cafe Oriental. He switched to an à la carte menu that offered light French food with an Asian twist. But he tired of cooking the same things every night and felt burdened by the paperwork and other responsibilities of sole ownership. In 1987, he sold the lease to a man in town and retired.

As a whole, the new restaurant chefs in Northern California did not embrace nouvelle cuisine. Unlike their counterparts in Los Angeles, most of whom were formally trained, chefs up north were largely self-taught and independent and did not readily buy into any doctrine. There was a period in San Francisco when classically trained French chefs such as Jacky Robert at Ernie's and Hubert Keller at Sutter 500 practiced this new style of cooking, but they were in the minority in a world of traditional French restaurants, old-fashioned Continental and Italian

Rose et LeFavour · Restaurant Français

8 March 1985

Fresh Duck Foie Gras with
Mâche, Roquette & Wild Watercress
Dressed in Champagne

—

A Soup of Fresh Snails
from Mrs. Herb's Garden

Grapefruit Sherbet

Roast Leg of Sonoma Lamb
with Chanterelles & Garlic Sauce

Cheese Tray

—

Dessert Cart

$50.00

Rose et LeFavour menu from March 8, 1985,
featuring local foie gras and snails from Mrs. Herb's garden.

family places, and the budding new California establishments. At this time, cooks at Chez Panisse, Bay Wolf, and Narsai's were still recreating classic French recipes, and their plating style was straightforward, direct, and traditional.

Naming It: California Cuisine in the Early 1980s

According to Victoria Wise, the first chef at Chez Panisse, "The tipping point for California cuisine began in the late 1970s. By the eighties, it was on the road. I had a conversation with a journalist from the *London Observer* along about 1988 who asked the question, 'Do you think there's such a thing as California cuisine?' I said, 'Yes, there certainly is.' He looked a little startled because at the time, many others, including Alice [Waters] and Jeremiah [Tower], were denying this. I guess it was too scary to name yet." Maybe not so much scary as premature. Most chefs were saying it did not exist and did not want to be labeled or pigeonholed. (In fact, until recently, Chez Panisse did not identify itself as a California cuisine restaurant.)

While *Sunset* was exemplary in depicting how we ate in the West, offering multicultural recipes made with ingredients grown in the region, it did not brand these recipes as California cuisine. *Bon Appétit,* the only other mainstream food magazine published in the state at the time (though it relocated to New York after the demise of *Gourmet* in 2009), was the first to raise the topic of California cuisine with chefs when interviewing them for restaurant profiles. Barbara Fairchild, the longtime editor of *Bon Appétit,* said that around 1980, "we used the term 'California cuisine' in the magazine, and riffed off that as a new way of cooking. I don't remember using it with regard to Wolfgang Puck, but I do distinctly remember talking to Michael Roberts about it when I wrote an article about him at Trumps. And he said, 'There's no such thing,' which is, of course, what we all said."

Trumps was an idiosyncratic LA restaurant that occupied a former gas station with concrete floors and polished concrete tables. In keeping with a Southwestern design theme, the waiters wore string ties along with European-style long white aprons. A formally trained chef with broad-ranging tastes, Michael served dishes such as beet and watermelon soup, sweet pea guacamole, fried plantains garnished with sour cream and caviar, seared tuna with mint, dill, and cilantro pesto, Asian chicken salad with grapefruit, and buckwheat noodles with potatoes and smoked salmon. In other words, his California cuisine menu was all over the culinary map; it was multicultural, eclectic, and personal.

Barbara Fairchild thought that applying a label got people to talk and think seriously about California cuisine. For her, the term "California cuisine restaurant" conjured up "food with a dreamscape lifestyle behind it." The image was of casualness, ease, warmth, and leisure—attractive people sitting outside, perhaps around a pool, eating something off the grill and sipping California wine. Restaurants such as Michael's, Mustards, and West Beach Café enabled people to slip into these fantasies.

Clark Wolf is a restaurant consultant now based primarily in New York. I call him "Mr. Soundbite" because he always says something eminently quotable. Clark lived in Northern California during the early years of California cuisine, first opening a pioneering cheese shop and then managing the San Francisco Oakville Grocery. For him, California cuisine was best exemplified not downstairs at Chez Panisse in the 1970s, but upstairs at the Café, which opened in 1980. "It was at Chez Panisse Café that California cuisine got a focus in the nomenclature. Downstairs was experimental and emotional and metaphorical; it was too intellectual, it was university. It was based on French structure and codification. At the Café, cooks thought, 'I'm going to make a simple salad but every time I touch these leaves, they will be special.'" Upstairs worked from the produce sheet, whereas downstairs worked from a concept of French food.

"I always say that restaurants are one of two things," added Clark. "They make you feel either very much where you are or very much someplace else. Downstairs was taking you away to someplace else, a magic France land, and upstairs was so much of where you were in a particular way, and that's what got translated to what people called California cuisine. It came to New York, oddly, as a concept, with quotes around it and capital letters. It sailed instantly and permeated totally.

"When I moved to New York in 1982, if you wanted a great piece of grilled fish and a great salad, the only choice was the Grill Room at the Four Seasons, and lunch was 160 bucks for two. Fresh food was simply not in New York. I used to joke—and it's still very much true in a lot of cases—that things percolate and develop in the Bay Area, and when it's named by New York media, it becomes a trend. Sometimes it goes to LA to become a business."

Indeed, it was the *New York Times* that applied a label to California cuisine and gave it official status, and Marian Burros gets the credit. She wrote about California cuisine in the *Times* first in 1982 and then again in 1984. She identified several trends: "grilling, especially with mesquite; combining cuisines that scarcely had a nodding acquaintance before, such as Japanese and French;

FRIDAY, OCTOBER 30, 1981

:CHEZ:PANISSE:CAFE:

1517 SHATTUCK AVENUE, BERKELEY, CALIFORNIA 94709 :: 548-5525
OPEN 11:30 AM TO MIDNIGHT :: MONDAY THROUGH SATURDAY :: NO RESERVATIONS

APPETIZERS, SALADS, & LIGHT ENTREES

Mixed green salad vinaigrette with croutons $2.75
Four salad plate with mint-chick pea salad, tapenade crostini, red
    cabbage vinaigrette and fennel with oil and pepper $4.50
Smoked trout and salmon with onions and capers $5.50
Duck liver mousse with green salad and croutons $4.00
Cold brisket of beef with potato, eggs, pepper and salsa verde $5.00
Baked Sonoma goat cheese with green salad $4.25
Spinach soup with lemon cream, bread and butter $3.75

FROM THE BRICK OVEN

Calzone with goat cheese, mozzarella, prosciutto and herbs $8.00
Pizza Messicana with our own chorizo, hot and sweet peppers, onions,
    cilantro, fresh and dry jack cheese $7.00
Pizza with artichoke, prosciutto, onions and parmesan $7.00
Pizza with mushrooms, porcini, fontina and mozzarella $6.50

PLATS DU JOUR

Chicken lasagna with porcini, mushrooms, cream and parmesan $7.50
Fettuccine al Dolce Forte with sweet, sour and spicy meat sauce,
    raisins, pine nuts, wine and tomatoes $6.50
Lamb stew with fennel, carrots, chick peas, lemon and garlic $7.50
Cod baked with Belgian endive, walnuts and walnut vinaigrette $7.50
Steamed Tomales Bay "Supreme" mussels with rouille and croutons $7.00

DESSERTS

Genoise with coffee buttercream $2.50
Pear sherbet $2.00
Pineapple sherbet $2.00
Coconut ice cream $2.00
Pears poached in red wihte with cognac cream $2.50

CONDIMENTS   Garlic, .50   Anchovy filets, three, .75   Italian Parmesan cheese, $1.00
Virgin olive oil, 4 oz. pitcher, $2.00

Minimum table service per person, $5.00, 11:30-3:00 & 5:00-10:30. We do not accept credit cards.
* *While available.*

Chez Panisse Café menu from October 30, 1981,
with the iconic Sonoma goat cheese salad.

replacing stock-based sauces with compound butters or no sauce at all; using baby vegetables to garnish almost every plate; serving fish, chicken, squab, and quail rather than red meat; and elevating country food to the status usually reserved for truffles and caviar. Freshness [is] always the cornerstone." Some trends came and went, like the use of baby vegetables and compound butters, while others became lasting characteristics of the cuisine. She noted that in America, "there had been nothing like it before. We finally learned that cooking and eating were important. We did French, then nouvelle cuisine, and then *cuisine minceur*, but it was still very French-oriented. Here were people taking the ingredients they had, and cooking with those ingredients, and making something that was unique to California. It was something that gave the rest of the country an idea [of] how to make uniquely American food, whether you were using French techniques or not."

In 1983, Marian gave an example in the *New York Times* that demonstrated how things were changing. The president of the United States at the time, Ronald Reagan, had come to California to fete the queen of England. A dinner was held at the St. Francis Hotel, which had a German Swiss chef by the name of Norbert Brandt, who had been hired in 1979 to replace the hotel's ossified Continental cuisine with the new California style of cooking. "The White House social secretary described the dinner as a 'toast to the cuisine of California,' and said that it was 'California nouvelle cuisine internationalized,' using only fresh and local fruits and vegetables. Salmon poached in zinfandel, lamb salad with lentils, radicchio and enoki mushrooms with raspberry vinegar and walnut oil dressings, sweetbreads with hot mustard sabayon, and balsamic vinegar shallot sauce." The dinner featured many ingredients that were so overused in the early days of California cuisine that they became clichés: raspberry vinegar, walnut oil, and the newly available imported balsamic vinegar, which were poured with impunity on everything.

One of the first cookbook authors to make the newly emerging California cuisine accessible to home cooks was Diane Worthington. In her 1983 cookbook, *The Cuisine of California*, she praised California chefs and their food. "They are youthful, daring and inquisitive in their attitude; they have created a spirit that has resulted in an identifiable cuisine. This movement toward freshness, simplicity, and originality defines itself by the use of the freshest local produce, herbs, fish, and dairy products; lighter marinades and sauces; California wines as both ingredients and accompaniments and an astounding array of ethnic and indigenous ingredients."

In her 1994 follow-up book, *The California Cook*, Worthington noted that chefs in both San Francisco and Los Angeles were experimenting with new ethnic ingredients and combinations while continuing to use classical techniques. She also observed that grilling had become prevalent. She mentioned Zuni Café and Chez Panisse in Northern California, and Spago and West Beach Café in Los Angeles. "Although California cuisine is in its formative stages, it rests upon several fundamental principles: First, brief cooking releases fresh flavors while retaining the desired textures. Vegetables are briefly cooked so that they still have some crunch when served. Second, combinations of ingredients are chosen so that natural flavors are heightened and balanced rather than masked. Third, the simple and elegant presentations that began with 'nouvelle cuisine' continue as California chefs bring their varied and eclectic training to bear on interpreting regional ingredients."

In some kitchens, creativity and freedom combined to give rise to a new subset of California cuisine: fusion. A fusion dish results when a chef borrows flavor combinations, signature ingredients, or techniques from one culture's cuisine and applies them to a dish where they are not part of the original flavor profile or even part of the culture from which the dish is derived. Russ Parsons, who has written about food for the *Los Angeles Times* for many years, said that some people thought that *all* California cuisine was fusion, and this perception gave the movement negative connotations. He described the fusion cooking of the early 1980s, especially as it was presented at Wolfgang Puck's Chinois on Main and John Rivera Sedlar's Saint Estèphe, as "the period equivalent of molecular gastronomy today. It fit with the general California reputation for more is more, but also 'the land of fruit and nuts.' You know, we're wacky out here. We can do anything we want, and frequently we shouldn't, but we still do."

Chef Mark Miller, on the other hand, rejoiced in fusion cuisine's inventiveness. According to him, "California cuisine was born when Chinois opened in 1983. It was definitely the keynote speech—times had changed and they were never going back. California cuisine was taking Chinese things, cooking them in an Italian oven, and putting French sauces on them. It was a mastery of multiplicity, fashion, form, design, flavor, everything." Like it or not, fusion in its various forms became part of the movement.

After the cuisine was named, chefs and restaurants would become famous for preparing it. Chefs in the California cuisine movement did not go into cooking to reap fame and never really dreamed of financial reward. Cooking in the United States up to the 1980s was not considered a prestigious profession, and most entered the trade simply because they were passionate about food. Chef Gary Danko, who attended the Culinary Institute of America in New York in the mid-1970s, said, "It wasn't the most highly revered profession, but a lot of us went because we loved to cook. We loved to eat. We loved the whole feeling about it. It wasn't like we were going to be famous."

But as food became a hot topic in the United States, many chefs did indeed become celebrities. Gradually they and their food became the focus of restaurant dining. There wasn't the full-blown worship of today, but there was a growing spotlight on newly famous California chefs and the restaurant world in general. By the 1980s the names Alice Waters, Wolfgang Puck, and Jeremiah Tower were familiar to the dining public.

JEREMIAH TOWER

Chez Panisse and Santa Fe Bar and Grill, Berkeley; Stars, San Francisco

Flamboyant, hedonistic, and blessed with an amazing palate, Jeremiah Tower came to Berkeley in 1972 after graduating from the Harvard School of Architecture. He was born in Connecticut but spent much of his childhood abroad, attending schools in Australia and England. Through dining out with his parents and relatives, he developed a highly refined sense of taste. The timing of his arrival at Chez Panisse in 1973 could not have been better: he was broke and the restaurant was in need of a cook. He read the want ad in the paper and prepared eighteen sample menus, as requested. When he came into the restaurant, he presented his menus and asked Alice for an immediate interview. She ordered him to taste and adjust the day's soup. He stepped up to the pot, added some wine and cream, and was hired on the spot.

Both Jeremiah and Alice were committed to using the best-quality local ingredients, but stylistically and philosophically their paths diverged. She wanted rustic and simple food, while he wanted boldness and drama. In the battle of egos, only one could be the winner. It was clear to both of them that Chez Panisse would always be "Alice's restaurant." Jeremiah needed his own place, where he could be the star.

He left in 1978 to pursue numerous ventures. He opened Ventana Inn at Big Sur, taught at the California Culinary Academy, and consulted at the San Francisco watering hole Balboa Café. In 1982, he took over the Santa Fe Bar and Grill in Berkeley. Then, in 1984, in partnership with moneyman Doyle Moon, he opened Stars, a grand brasserie near the San Francisco Civic Center. Stars was an instant sensation.

"The food was very California-driven, very seasonal, and done in a big way,"

DINNER MENU

JULY 9, 1988
On Thursday, July 14th we will be featuring a special a la carte menu to commemorate Bastille Day, as well as Stars' fourth year anniversary.

Jeremiah Tower

APPETIZERS

SIX OYSTERS ON THE HALF SHELL WITH SHALLOT-BLACK PEPPER SAUCE .. 7.25
HAWAIIAN TUNA CARPACCIO WITH CILANTRO-CHILI VINAIGRETTE, THREE
    OYSTERS & GINGER CREAM 9.25
DEEP FRIED BLUE CRAB CAKES WITH CHINESE BLACK BEAN SAUCE &
    SAFFRON-GINGER AIOLI 10.00
HOUSE SMOKED STURGEON WITH GRILLED HERB BRIOCHE &
    HORSERADISH CREAM 9.00
FRESH PASTA WITH SALMON GRAVLAX, SMOKED TROUT, MUSHROOMS,
    ROAST BEETS & DILL CREAM FRAICHE 8.75
GRILLED CALAMARI WITH BLACK OLIVE PASTA, AVOCADO SALSA &
    RED BELL PEPPER ROUILLE 8.75

SALADS & SOUP

STARS' MIXED BITTER GREEN SALAD WITH CREAMY BLUE CHEESE
    VINAIGRETTE, TOASTED PECANS & RED BELL PEPPER TOASTS 8.25
JEREMIAH'S STEAK TARTARE WITH A BAKED RADICCHIO SALAD,
    ROAST CHILIES & ROSEMARY AIOLI 8.75
WARM SPINACH & FRISEE SALAD WITH ROAST DUCK CONFIT, SHIITAKE
    MUSHROOMS & HAZELNUTS 8.75
SWEET WHITE CORN & MUSSEL CHOWDER WITH BACON, ONIONS &
    SAGE CREAM 7.00

GRILLS & MAIN COURSES

ROAST SEA BASS WITH ROAST JAPANESE EGGPLANT, OVEN-DRIED TOMATO
    VINAIGRETTE & BASIL PESTO 18.75
SAUTEED ALASKAN SPOT PRAWNS WITH A FENNEL-ARTICHOKE SALAD,
    GARLIC, BASIL & TOMATOES 19.00
GRILLED SALMON WITH MUSHROOM DUXELLES, ONION CONFIT, CUCUMBERS &
    SAGE HOLLANDAISE 18.75
SAUTEED CHICKEN BREAST WITH A POTATO-HERB GRATIN, RADICCHIO-
    CHILI SALAD & MARJORAM AIOLI 18.00
BAKED HOUSE CURED HAM WITH BLACK BEANS, MANGO-CHILI SALSA &
    LIME SOUR CREAM 18.75
GRILLED BRAISED SWEETBREADS WITH POTATO PUREE, ROAST RED &
    YELLOW BELL PEPPERS, LITTLE ARTICHOKES & ROSEMARY AIOLI 19.00
GRILLED AGED NEW YORK STEAK WITH ROAST FIRE ONIONS,
    FRENCH FRIES & TOMATO SALSA 25.00

SEE OUR DESSERT MENU FOR TODAY'S DESSERT SELECTIONS.
PEERLESS COFFEE .... 1.75   ICED ENGLISH BREAKFAST TEA 1.50
TEAS .... 1.50   EVIAN WATER 2.00

STARS' OYSTER BAR IS NOW AVAILABLE UNTIL MIDNIGHT, MONDAY THROUGH
THURSDAY, AND UNTIL 12:30 a.m. FRIDAY & SATURDAY

Stars, July 9, 1988, with French, Asian,
and Latin American flavors on the menu.

said pastry chef Emily Luchetti. "With fancier restaurants, if you wanted good food, you had to sit for a three-course meal. At Stars, you could go for oysters, hot dogs, and dessert, or for a martini and oysters, or just the martini, or you could get a full-fledged dinner. You could have it your way. "

Jeremiah had a purist's love of fine ingredients. "For me, it's always been about quality. I don't care where it comes from as long as it's properly raised, healthy, and of the quality that I want. In the Chez Panisse days, you couldn't get anything unless somebody brought it to you from their garden. It had to be local; anything else was supermarket food that had survived shipping across the country or being flown in."

He felt that it was essential for cooks to travel and taste to develop their palates and establish a benchmark for the dishes they would make. "If you've never had the best of anything—the perfect olive oil or white truffle—how would you know what you're supposed to be doing?"

Gradually Jeremiah moved out of the kitchen, entrusting Stars's day-to-day culinary activities to his talented chef Mark Franz and a dedicated kitchen crew. Jeremiah became the host with the most, a glass of champagne always in hand, throwing a great party every night in the spectacular tiered dining room, which seated a huge number of guests.

But even the grandeur of Stars was not enough for Jeremiah. He began to expand his domain, opening Stars Café, an upscale bistro adjacent to Stars, in 1988. "In his mind he was going to serve all the most important socialites, artists, designers, opera singers—everyone from Yves Saint Laurent to Pavarotti," said former Stars Café chef Loretta Keller. Jeremiah opened branches of Stars in the Napa Valley, Palo Alto, Manila, and Singapore. But after the 1989 Loma Prieta earthquake, which closed off Civic Center and forced the opera and symphony to relocate, Jeremiah lost heart. Overextended both financially and emotionally, he sold his interest in Stars to a financial group from Singapore led by Andrew Yap. It closed after two difficult years. Jeremiah first relocated to Manila and then New York before finally settling in Mérida, Mexico, where he enjoys a less stressful life restoring old houses and scuba diving.

Imitating It: Food for the Masses in the Mid-1980s

Not everyone could afford to eat in the hallowed halls of Chez Panisse, Spago, Michael's, and Stars. But people who read about these places wanted a taste of this new cuisine. Seizing this opportunity, Robert Freeman, Mosen Aminifard, and James Benson, owners of the Victoria Station restaurant chain, formed the private California Café Restaurant Corporation in 1979. They opened the first California Café in Walnut Creek in 1983, followed by restaurants in Los Gatos in 1985 and Palo Alto in 1986. These were bistro-style places serving what the owners considered "idiomatic" California cuisine to the general dining public. Their eclectic menu offered interpretations of dishes that had become California classics, such as the Chez Panisse baked goat cheese salad and the grilled fish with a side sauce that Patricia Unterman was doing at Hayes Street Grill. Their simplified—some might say dumbed-down—presentations defined California cuisine for many people. By 1997 the California Café Restaurant Corporation had successfully established twenty cafes, and in 1993 it added the Napa Valley Grille to its portfolio.

In the mid-1980s, two lawyers who knew a good thing when they saw it, Richard Rosenfield and Larry Flax, jumped on the California cuisine casual-dining bandwagon in Los Angeles. I first encountered Rosenfield and Flax while I was chef at Chez Panisse Café, where they took notes and questioned me about the value of a wood-burning as opposed to a conventional oven. They went on to hire Ed LaDou, who had worked for Wolfgang Puck at Spago and had created unusual pizzas at San Francisco's Prego. In 1985, Rosenfield and Flax opened the California Pizza Kitchen. CPK, as it was known, offered some multi-ingredient fusion pizzas that would have turned any Italian's hair white, including Thai chicken pizza and Jamaican jerk pizza. The chain is still in business, with over two hundred restaurants in the United States and almost a dozen abroad.

These mass-market restaurants served all the nouvelle cuisine clichés that had been adopted by California cuisine in its early years. Chef David Gingrass describes how he was particularly irked by "hazelnut oil, raspberry vinegar, and rare duck breasts with raspberries and hazelnuts. These subsequently spun off into the California Café–type garbage where you had macadamia-nut-crusted things and every manner of salsa you could ever imagine."

The wild success of both these chain restaurants gave negative associations to the term "California cuisine," and many in the business shied away from using it. When Patricia Unterman wrote restaurant reviews in the 1980s she avoided using the label because she saw it as slightly derogatory. "It was associated with fusion, food not based in logical technique. When the California Café and the California Pizza Kitchen opened, I saw that as a terrible trend. I think that California then meant some kind of unfettered experimental cooking that had no foundation or roots and really wasn't very good."

Hiro Sone and Lissa Doumani of Terra in the Napa Valley refused to identify their cooking as California cuisine because, according to Lissa, "it was permission to do anything. It was the more, the better—twenty ingredients in a dish. Just because you can doesn't mean you should, and that's what happened. The people who were really cooking California cuisine weren't promoting it. The press and writers were. But when the chains saw that there was business to be done, they adopted the name."

Expanding It: The 1990s

The 1990s was a decade of over-the-top creativity and odd juxtapositions. Fusion cooking thrived. Chefs dreamed big, and fifteen ingredients on one plate were not too many for some of them. Press coverage spurred chefs to be expressive with their cuisine, and the dining public got caught up in the enthusiasm of the moment.

At this adventurous time, genuine Asian food also came into the spotlight, and soon other types of ethnic restaurants entered the arena. As diners became more accepting of regional and authentic cuisines, chefs could present their food as it was served in their country, without having to make compromises to please timid diners. Indian restaurants no longer needed to tone down their flavors, Asian restaurants didn't need to serve bread, and at Mourad Lahlou's Kasbah, he didn't have to offer ketchup as a condiment alongside *harissa*.

MOURAD LAHLOU

Kasbah, San Rafael; Aziza, San Francisco

Mourad Lahlou came to the Bay Area from Marrakesh to pursue a PhD in economics. "I had no plans to cook. I was going to be somebody who had a degree, then go back home and make everybody proud—the typical immigrant story."

Living so far away from where he had grown up made Mourad nostalgic for Morocco and homesick for his family's food. "I would go home to my apartment and miss getting together around a table, everybody yelling, the kitchen all upside down. It was quiet, there was no smell. There was nothing that made me feel alive, so I started to cook." Working from the memory of his mother's *kefte* with tomato sauce, he bought some tomatoes and paprika and started experimenting. Soon he was cooking for others, and after he got his master's degree, he decided to start a small restaurant with his brother while he worked toward his PhD. They found a space in San Rafael and financed Kasbah by putting $300,000 on Mourad's credit cards. On opening night, there were no menus. Mourad told the servers, "Go to the table, tell them to give us $40, and we'll cook for them." He improvised, and the guests were happy. The restaurant was busy from day one. Within four weeks it started getting rave reviews. After one year he realized he was in it for the long haul.

Mourad initially intended to make recipes that he remembered from home: his mother's chicken with lemons, his aunt's lentil soup, the *bastilla* his family served at special events. But when he could not manage to make his food match his memories, he started to doubt his abilities as a chef. A visit to Morocco revealed the reason for the differences. "Our Moroccan chicken took an hour and a half to cook; here it takes thirty-five minutes. It's not the same tomatoes; it's not the same lamb; it's not the same spices. It's not the same hands. This is not made by somebody who made it for thirty years, over and over again."

It dawned on Mourad that people who were able to recreate dishes from the past were considered the best cooks in Morocco. Nobody talked about innovation or about tweaking recipes. In the United States, traditional ethnic restaurants rarely evolved. "I was getting bored making couscous the same way. I remember thinking, 'I can't do just this for five years.'" He decided that there were enough restaurants serving standard Moroccan cuisine. "That stuff was not going to be endangered if I didn't do it anymore, so I thought I might as well take a chance, see where it was going to go."

He began eating out to see what other chefs were doing. He went to Chez Panisse and Zuni Café. He realized that the chefs at those restaurants were cooking with a wide variety of ingredients. "But when I went to the market, I was just looking for tomatoes, carrots, beans, stuff that I recognized from Morocco. I began adding arugula, cress, and goat cheese to Moroccan food and cooking it in a way that still had some link to the foundation, but at the same time was branching out.

"Moroccan food has layers of flavor. It's a stew that takes six hours, a *tagine* that takes twelve hours, a couscous that needs five or six steamings, pancakes that have to be proofed three times." The problem was that these methods robbed individual ingredients of their unique flavors. Mourad was investing in quality products—lettuce from Annabelle Lenderink at Star Route Farms, chickweed from Jesse Kuhn at Marin Roots Farm, rabbits from Mark Pasternak, chickens from Hoffman Game Birds, lamb from Niman Ranch, and produce from GreenLeaf—but when cooked in traditional Moroccan fashion, "what you taste is the spices, so the flavor of the carrot is masked by the cumin, the flavor of the rabbit is like paprika, the flavor of the chicken is merely preserved lemons and cracked olives. Why was I spending this much money on produce if people couldn't tell the difference?"

He began to simplify traditional Moroccan preparations so that the flavors of his ingredients would stand out. "Not as much cumin, not as much spice. We don't need to put seven vegetables in the same pot and cook them at the same time. Why don't we cook them one at a time so we can have each one perfect and then put them together? It was the Chez Panisse influence; you go there and get a garden salad that tastes like a salad, it tastes like lettuce. My role is to know when to stop, to show restraint, and not to spoil the taste of the carrot."

Mourad's goal was to find a middle ground where he maintained the integrity of the ingredients without sacrificing the flavor of the dish as a whole. "I would be lying to people if I said I'm making Moroccan food. I'm making food that is a compilation of everyone who has influenced me, including you, Joyce, and Judy Rodgers and Alice Waters and Paula Wolfert, and more recently Pierre Gagnaire, Michel Bras, and David Kinch. I try to understand what they do and apply it to what I'm doing. Food that has an idea behind it and food from the soul—that's what I try to do. I try to find a place in me where that food resides."

People came to California from all over to taste this distinct and special cuisine. It was difficult to define, yet people were eager to experience it. It had iconic dishes—Chez Panisse's goat cheese salad, Wolfgang Puck's California pizza—but it was characterized by its ever-changing, all-encompassing nature. This is a story about how communities evolved and the kitchen culture shifted. How immigrants arrived and created California versions of cultural staples. How growers and artisans made their way to the table. All of this took place in the context of a productive push-pull between Northern and Southern California.

2

One Revolution, Two Ways

Northern versus Southern California

You can always tell the difference between a San Franciscan and a person from LA because the San Franciscan cares about what's on the plate and the LA person cares who's sitting next to them.

—Restaurant publicist Andrew Freeman

In my many years of living and working in the Bay Area, I looked forward to slipping away to sample the food in Los Angeles and see what my colleagues were up to. On one trip, I was dazzled by a visit to Chinois on Main, with its dramatic open kitchen, fanciful dining room, and glorious wall of orchids. Wolfgang Puck's Asian fusion food—the famous tempura tuna sashimi that remained raw in the center after deep-frying, the rich Shanghai curried lobster—was bold and original.

On the same trip I luxuriated in the gorgeously restored 1928 art deco building in downtown LA that housed Mauro Vincenti's Rex. The glamour was backed up by a serious menu that offered the first *alta cucina*—Italian high cuisine—on the West Coast. Rex's chef, Filippo Costa, had brought many dishes with him from celebrity chef Gualtiero Marchese's eponymous restaurant in Milan, where he had trained before being hired to work in California. I had the chilled lobster with a purée of red peppers and the veal medallions in Vernaccia. While the flavors were familiar, the presentation of the food was modern and elegant. It proved to me that Italian cuisine did not always have to be rustic.

Northern California restaurants did not have such high-style design concepts. Nostalgia and tradition were our vernacular. We had better ingredients to cook with, but our plate presentations remained simple and direct. LA gave me a respite from the rustic and a glimpse into an exciting new dining culture.

•

As far back as the 1850s, critics have suggested that Northern and Southern California be divided into two states to reflect the regions' political and cultural differences. The chasm was particularly broad in the sixties and seventies, when Californians elected the charismatic and conservative Ronald Reagan in 1967 followed in 1975 by the liberal Jerry Brown, who was derided by Republicans as "the granola governor, appealing to flakes and nuts." Reagan came out of Tinseltown, Jerry Brown from UC Berkeley. The Hollywood/homespun dichotomy prevailed in California cuisine as well.

In Northern California, in the formative years of the new cuisine, politics was on the plate. People took their food seriously. Using fresh, local, "politically correct" produce and artisanal products and having a philosophy behind the food were of primary importance. Restaurant publicist Andrew Freeman, comparing dining in Los Angeles and San Francisco, said, "When people dine out in Los Angeles there's a chance that there's something else going on in their evening, and that dining out is a *part* of the experience. In San Francisco dining out *is* the experience."

In Southern California, the film and music industries dominated, so glitz and appearance determined which places were popular. Diners wanted restaurants to be showy and to confer social status. Because the quality of the food did not determine success, LA restaurateurs cared less about getting their hands on the best raw materials and were slower to join the crusade for better ingredients. While fine-dining restaurants in Northern California tended to be traditional in format and based on the classic flavors of the Mediterranean, Southern California restaurants offered a broader array of ethnic flavors and were more concerned with style and innovation.

The North: Food as Politics

In Northern California, the cooking of the 1960s grew out of the counterculture. Barbara Haimes, an instructor at San Francisco City College Hotel and Restaurant School, observed that at the time, "the people who had an understanding of food's place in culture were part of the hippie movement and the communal farms, going back to the land and eating together. You had the beginnings of the food collectives, the co-ops, health food, organics, and recycling. Thinking of food in a political way came out of the 1960s, and coming into a kitchen was desirable as opposed to being just a job."

Rachel Carson's authoritative 1962 book *Silent Spring* alerted the public to the dangers of pesticides in food. In 1971, Frances Moore Lappé's *Diet for a Small Planet* awakened Americans to the costs of industrial meat production, urging people to do what was best for the earth as well as themselves. In the face of these warnings about the despoiling of the land and water, people were eager to be "part of the solution." Many eco-conscious eaters became vegetarians, and many farmers switched to organic practices. Progressives and intellectuals promoted ethically raised "natural" foods and rebelled against big business and mass-produced convenience foods, which had become ubiquitous following World War II.

A university town like Berkeley served as a perfect locus for a new kind of cooking—adventurous and fresh. Berkeley's constantly changing population of professors and students, many of whom had traveled or come from abroad, contributed to a vibrant environment for the exchange of culinary ideas. This community nurtured the shops that made up the Gourmet Ghetto, which included the first Peet's Coffee in 1966 and the Cheese Board Collective in 1967. "The first week I got to Berkeley," said restaurant critic Sherry Virbila, "I met some anthropology graduate students who made what I thought were incredible dinners. It seemed like an incredible dinner when somebody didn't use a packaged mix to make spaghetti sauce or use that little seasoning mix for the salad dressings. You asked yourself, 'What is the point of all this convenience food when it's so easy to make it from scratch and it tastes so much better?'"

The person who brought change from the home into the restaurant arena was Alice Waters. "There always has to be a catalyst," said wine writer Gerald Asher, "someone who starts things off, and Alice Waters got things started up here. She [had] a political interest in food. Tying [it to] politics had a lot to do with getting the thing going." What followed was an active crusade to promote the cultivation of local ingredients, preferably grown without pesticides (organic certification would come a few years down the road, with organic practices codified in 1979 by the California Organic Food Act). Not only was there a high regard for natural foods and ingredients per se, but to be morally and politically correct many restaurants later put a statement on the menu that said, "We serve organic or sustainable food whenever possible."

According to *Los Angeles Times* writer Russ Parsons, "There's a certain reverence that goes with Northern California, a conservatism, which is a funny thing to say about Northern California. When you go to Chez Panisse, you need to bow at the knee when you approach. Chez Panisse comes out of the 1970s—what's political is personal, what's personal is political."

ALICE WATERS

Chez Panisse Restaurant and Café, Berkeley

Alice Waters founded Chez Panisse, an influential, world-famous restaurant that has been running successfully for forty years. She is not a chef and doesn't claim to be one, but rather works closely on menu concept with the chefs she hires. She has an impeccable palate, and if you pay attention when she critiques your cooking, you will learn about balance and flavor.

I worked for Alice as chef of Chez Panisse Café for three years and came to know her predilections and passions well. Though not the most practical person I've ever met, she is a visionary. Her genius is that she inspires people to help her realize her dreams, and those dreams are big ones. Underneath a whispery voice and flirty manner lies a will of steel. She has stayed on message for forty years, driven not by money but by an unflagging commitment to make better food available to all. In 1996, for the restaurant's twenty-fifth anniversary, Alice created the Chez Panisse Foundation, whose mission is to teach, nurture, and empower young people. The goal of "cultivating a new generation" led to the development of the Edible Schoolyard Project at a nearby school, which includes a garden and teaching kitchen. Alice serves as a public policy advocate at the national level for school lunch reform and universal access to healthy organic foods. In 1997 she received the Humanitarian of the Year award from the James Beard Foundation.

"The big movement that we're all a part of is local, organic, sustainable, and seasonal. I don't think anything touches a buffalo mozzarella like I've had in Naples, but I'm not going to bring in buffalo mozzarella from Italy even if I think it's better. Our goal should be to try to produce our own versions of these things. We've succeeded in a gigantic way in terms of bread; I think we have in this country the best bread on the planet. And we have some of the great wines of the world. The olive oil is getting really good. It's just that we haven't had three hundred years to perfect them—we've got work to do."

The few exceptions to sourcing local products, according to Alice, "have to do with friendships—that's the bottom line for me." One example of this is her tie to Chino Farms, a small specialty produce grower in San Diego County. Founded by Japanese immigrants Junzo Chino and Hatsuyo Noda in 1969, the farm is now run by their children, headed by Tom Chino. Alice buys from them because of the extraordinarily high quality and variety of their produce, but also because of her personal connection with them. "We are bound to them. We have such admiration for the way they work with their interns, the way they stay small at their stands, the artisanal way they make *mochi* every New Year. It's an inspiration to me to see them doing their thing against the tide of industrial farming.

"I think California cooking is a philosophy and a way of living your life. It isn't just about the food. It's about all the values of the culture—the artist and production, the *terroir*, the rituals of the table. That's the beauty of being around for forty years. You can see that we have succeeded in a certain way. It's beautiful to see this next generation of kids—they're completely committed, they're going to do it right, [whereas] the French and the Italians, they're having a hard time holding on to their hats and hoes these days." (Ironically, although in the early days many California cuisine chefs looked to Europe for inspiration, today long-standing cooking traditions there are being eroded by common market regulations and fast-food restaurants such as McDonald's and Wendy's, which are replacing cafés and tavernas.)

Although Alice admired Old World values, she had a modern belief in job sharing and allowed chefs to split their duties, starting in 1987 in the Café, when David Tanis and Catherine Brandel shared the chef position, each working three days a week. Later Tanis and Jean-Pierre Moullé divided their responsibilities from 2004 to 2011, each working in six-month stints. Alice wanted her staff to be able to live well-rounded, balanced lives, but she toiled tirelessly herself. "When you're talking about being there from 7:00 in the morning, you don't have any other life. I never left Chez Panisse, and I never knew what was going on in the world, I never went to a movie. All I got to see were Carrie's flower arrangements and everybody's tired faces."

I did not set out to write an encomium to Alice, but I've got to hand it to her. She drove the train of the ingredient revolution. I cannot tell you how many times her name came up while I was interviewing farmers, artisans, and chefs whom she supported and pushed to do more and better. We all have profited from her persistence and passion. She's stuck to her guns despite criticism that she's overly idealistic and elitist: "I think people have criticized me about being uncompromising, and I don't regret it for one single second."

Under the influence of the counterculture and the back-to-the-land movement, the 1970s saw the emergence of several best-selling vegetarian cookbooks, including the *Tassajara Bread Book* (1970) and later *Tassajara Cooking* (1986), both by Edward Espe Brown of the San Francisco Zen Center, Anna Thomas's *Vegetarian Epicure* (1972), which became the bible for many vegetarians, and *Laurel's Kitchen*

(1976), by Laurel Robertson, Carol Flinders, and Bronwen Godfrey. Macrobiotic diets were in vogue, especially in the new communes of the era. Health food stores and food cooperatives opened, followed by small vegetarian restaurants. One of the first was the Shandygaff restaurant on Polk Street in San Francisco in 1970, where Mollie Katzen trained before moving to Ithaca, New York, to help found Moosewood Restaurant. Dipti Nivas was opened in 1973 by Deborah Santana, the then wife of legendary guitarist Carlos Santana, and her sister Kitsuan. At most of these places the food was earnest and well-meaning but rather heavy, combining grains and legumes to make complete proteins, garnished with nuts and seeds and accompanied by heaps of steamed vegetables sauced with tahini and tamari. Greens Restaurant, which opened in 1979, departed from the brown-rice-and-veggies model by serving elegant vegetarian food in a beautiful setting on the San Francisco Bay.

ANNIE SOMERVILLE

Greens Restaurant, San Francisco

Annie Somerville has been the chef at Greens, a groundbreaking vegetarian restaurant at Fort Mason, for thirty years. The restaurant was opened in 1979 by the San Francisco Zen Center with Deborah Madison as the chef and medita-tion students as the staff. Initially, Greens served only lunch, but within a few months the restaurant had proved so successful that it began serving two prix fixe dinners that changed nightly. Annie was brought on to assist Deborah in 1981 and became executive chef in 1985 after Deborah left to do a rotation at the Tassajara meditation retreat. Annie hadn't planned to become a chef, but she grew to love the work.

"In the early days, if we had polenta, the menu would say in parentheses, 'A northern Italian staple,' or for phyllo, if it was a savory phyllo dish, it would say, 'Not a dessert.' We had to let people know that these dishes were something other than what they might expect. Over the years the cuisine has evolved, but many of those original dishes are still on the menu, like the wilted spinach salad, because it's so popular."

Much of Greens' produce came, and still comes, from the Zen Center's Green Gulch Farm in Marin, which has been farmed organically since its founding in 1972. The remainder is purchased from neighboring farms and markets. Annie declared, "For me, California cooking is seasonal, local, and organic as much as possible. I think the big part is buying from people I know, [witnessing] the cycle, the web of life. It starts with the person planting the seed, growing the produce, producing the olive oil, producing the cheese. We help support that effort, the wineries as well. Our goal is to cook with the produce of as many small local growers as we possibly can."

The first Tasting of Summer Produce, a trade show for specialty crop growers and retail and restaurant buyers, was held at Greens in 1983. Eventually the event grew so big that in 1986 it moved to the Oakland Museum. "The phrase 'farm to table' is recent," said Annie, "but we have been doing it for a long time. We know these growers and are connected to them and committed to buying from them and supporting them even when it hasn't been the best crop."

Like many Bay Area chefs, Annie did not go to cooking school but instead learned on the job. As she put it, "I've gone to cooking school at Greens Restaurant. As my husband says, this is where I got my PhD. And I'm still working on it. One of the great things that you said to me, Joyce, was, 'Working in the restaurant keeps you young,' because you're working with great young people. All of these super young people, that's the lifeblood of the restaurant."

Rather than being shaped by cooking school or experience abroad, Annie's culinary ideas come from living in the Bay Area. "I'm not a big traveler," she said. "While I love the idea of spending time in Italy and France and other countries, I don't do much of that. My inspiration is focused on learning from what I read about what other chefs are doing and what I experience other chefs doing when I go to their restaurants."

Annie is also energized by her visits to the farmers' market, as much by the people she meets there as by the produce. "One of the wonderful experiences I have every week at the Ferry Plaza farmers' market is with Stan Keena of Petaluma Farms—Stan the egg man. I always call him 'your egg-cellency.' I ask his egg-cellency how he is, and he says, 'I am egg-static to see you.'

"What's also fun about going to the farmers' market is talking to home cooks, the shoppers who are passionate about buying leeks or carrots from a particular grower. What I try to do every day is to impart that enthusiasm and excitement for these ingredients to our staff. Our diners expect to be challenged a little bit, [to get] excited about something they may not have seen before. These days that's getting harder because there's so much exposure to food."

Annie sees Greens as much more than a vegetarian restaurant. "At Greens we've been very fortunate to be in this location in continuous operation all these years, a part of the whole food culture. What we're doing here is nothing new in the world. This is the real way to eat. The cuisines of the world produce beautiful

DAILY SPECIALS   SATURDAY, OCTOBER 6

SOUP
    "Mayorquina" --A Catalan-style vegetable soup
    made with leeks, savoy cabbage, sweet red
    peppers, tomatoes, and other vegetables.
        Cup: .75   Bowl: 1.35

PASTA
    Eduardo's egg pasta with cream, gorgonzola
    (an Italian bleu cheese), and parmesan
    cheese.   4.50

CHINESE NOODLE SALAD
    Thin fresh noodles in a sauce with ginger,
    green onions, Chinese parsley, and garnished
    with cucumbers, mung bean sprouts, and
    charcoal-grilled tofu.
                                         4.00

SALAD
    Romaine hearts with bleu cheese, new fall
    apples, walnuts, served with country French
    bread grilled over the coals.
                                         4.00

DESSERT
    Thompson seedl ss grapes with creme fraiche
    and walnuts, erved with a shortbread cookie.
                                         1.75

Green Gulch Farm is in between plantings so there
is no lettuce available from Green Gulch this week.

Specials at Greens Restaurant, October 6, 1979,
at a time when gorgonzola still had to be identified for the diner.

dishes made with vegetables [that aren't] necessarily called vegetarian. I think what we've done is to make that accessible to the dining public, whether people are vegetarian or not."

Counterculture cooks in Northern California cared about quality, connecting with local farmers and ranchers, and supporting sustainable agriculture. "Small is beautiful" was part of the zeitgeist. In his book by the same name, published in 1973, E. F. Schumacher opposed mass production and argued for "a new orientation of science and technology towards the organic, the gentle, the non-violent, the elegant and beautiful." The book helped promote a return to smaller-scale production and traditional values. Proponents of the new California cuisine cooked "more like our grandmothers than our mothers," said chef Gary Jenanyan. "My grandparents, for example, grew chickens and vegetables and fruits, and had a cellar, so when we wanted tomatoes in winter, we had tomatoes, but they were preserved. We were seasonal whether we liked it or not. They made cheese, they made all that stuff. We did it all at their house."

Given Northern California's produce obsession, a few restaurants attempted to maintain their own gardens, but most could not provide a large, steady supply. Mudd's in San Ramon was opened by Virginia Mudd in 1981 with a "romantic idea about creating a garden and a restaurant that would fuel itself both inspirationally and contextually with things that were grown in the garden," said chef Amaryll Schwertner. "And, in fact, many beautiful things were grown there, primarily herbs." Although the restaurant had ten acres of land, "nobody understood the quantities that would be required to supply a restaurant," so the garden produced mainly garnishes, or, at certain times of year, massive tomato harvests. "There were a couple of weeks when there were full-out tomatoes everywhere. I coupled up very quickly with Green Gulch down on the coast, because we had hot weather in the San Ramon area, and they had the cool-weather crops, and we quickly figured out that we could have more diversity on our menus if each of us contributed, so the cars were going back and forth."

In addition to raising their own crops, people were interested in old-time skills such as pickling, canning, curing meat, and smoking fish. They wanted to avoid the preservatives and additives in commercial foods and to exercise control over the flavors and quality of these products. Sherry Virbila reminisced, "It was an extraordinary generation in that everybody learned from everybody else. [They] shared information. An entire generation of cooks was learning a lost art from scratch. Nobody wanted to cook the way a commercial restaurant cooked; that was a blind alley to go down. So it meant you had to learn how to do it from scratch, the way the older people used to do it in the country. When Pig-by-the-Tail [a charcuterie in Berkeley] opened, I was amazed. It was a bizarre notion that somebody would open a place and make sausages from scratch."

Sherry remembered eating wild fennel for the first time, and tasting mussels and oysters harvested by the "eccentric local forager Dr. Jerry Rosenfield. That was a fascinating moment when you discovered that your own land had things that were unexploited. You could go out and find authentic ingredients of place." Foraging has become hip today, but it was still a largely untapped market when Connie Green made a business out of it in the late 1970s.

CONNIE GREEN

Wine Forest Wild Foods, Napa

Connie Green began foraging for mushrooms in the early 1970s and turned her hobby into a commercial business in 1979, when she found herself gathering more mushrooms than she could eat. She approached restaurants to see if she could trade mushrooms for dinners.

"One day I took baskets of chanterelles into San Francisco. I decided to go to Nob Hill because at that time you had Fournou's Ovens, L'Etoile, the Fairmont. I'm sitting there with baskets full of beautiful chanterelles, polished within an inch of their life, not knowing which way to turn." A Swiss gardener working outside one of those hotels spotted her baskets and came running up. "He took me to the chef at L'Etoile, who looked at me and said, 'Those are not chanterelles. They don't grow in America.' He wanted to show me what chanterelles were, and he opened a can. He said, 'These are chanterelles. They're small, they're perfect'—and they were canned. I said, 'But these really are chanterelles; they grow differently in America.' And he said, 'But no, they're not French.' He wanted nothing to do with them, and that place was closed in two years."

Udo Nechutnys at Miramonte was one of the chefs who did snap up Connie's mushrooms when she appeared at his kitchen door. Connie remembers that he "almost got tears in his eyes" when he saw them. Bruce LeFavour of Rose et LeFavour in St. Helena also "was all over it. He was a self-educated man with deep knowledge and went through great trouble to get good ingredients.

"A tiny bit later, Masa Kobayashi was at Auberge du Soleil. I knew that this was an internationally famous dude, and I polished some chanterelles and took them up there. He went over the moon and made everybody in his kitchen stop and look. Then he paraded them through the dining room. He honored me to a degree I had never experienced. These are very important people who remain locked in my heart."

Connie also approached Thomas Keller at the French Laundry. "I left a note at the kitchen and he called me up giggling—this is a man who doesn't giggle—and asked me to come down right away. He was so excited that I was a mushroom hunter—he was just on fire."

Chefs who want to order a steady supply of mushrooms have to be taught that the wild varieties are strictly seasonal. Connie warns people who want to order fresh porcini for a set menu that they may be available for only a few weeks. "There are chefs that are locked up, and then there are nimble chefs—people like Todd Humphries [of Campton Place] and Staffan Terje [of Perbacco]—who can turn on a dime because they have deep levels of creativity.

"Back before California cuisine, this place was filled with Italians, Napa in particular. People would be speaking Italian in the grocery store. Gardens were everywhere; everybody had tomatoes and beans. Even a little 20-by-30-foot backyard was filled with vegetables. There were certain dishes on every menu that you never see anymore that I really miss. Everybody had malfatti, cannelloni, and seafood stew. Europeans understood how to deal with wild mushrooms. But in 1981, a lot of the prep guys, and some of the chefs, had never dealt with this stuff. I'm selling chanterelles for $13 a pound and here's the prep guy cutting the tops off and throwing the stems in the garbage bin. And I was like, 'Don't throw those away! That's my favorite part.' People had to learn from rock bottom about what they were cooking."

Connie still hunts mushrooms and sells about five thousand pounds a week, mostly in San Francisco.

With the support and encouragement of new restaurants, Northern California foragers, farmers, and artisans began to provide chefs with the quality and variety of ingredients they were seeking. Warren Weber of Star Route Farms personally observed the evolution of agriculture in Northern California. "When I came out in 1974, Marin County was dairy and animals, because it grows grass and is a cool climate and doesn't have the deep soils that we like to farm real [mass-market] crops in. When we started it was the Zen Center [at Green Gulch Farm] and us. The kids on the ranches would go to Davis or Cal Poly and never come back home. They'd become veterinarians or something, but there was no place for them and the dairy industry was slowly going out. Now we have a lot of vertical integration in the dairy business—people making cheese, doing all kinds of stuff. We have horizontal integration where we have guys doing strawberries on the dairies or leasing the ground out to somebody who's doing vegetable crops. We have sheep and sheep cheese and milk and goats and some fifty organic farms in Marin County. It actually looks like the thing that we wanted to see when we started, and it took that long for it to happen."

The South: Food as Fashion

Historically, "Los Angeles never cultivated an image of fine cuisine," said Russ Parsons. "People didn't think of Southern California as a place to go out to eat. When the first good restaurants opened up—when Michael McCarty opened up, Michael Roberts, Wolfgang Puck, Mary Sue Milliken and Susan Feniger—it was a shock. I remember the 1984 Olympics, and all of a sudden we were on the cover of every magazine, and it was like, 'Oh my god, there's actually food to eat.'"

Jonathan Waxman arrived at Michael's after working at Chez Panisse. He recalled that "at Michael's, it was Southern California sensibility versus Northern California. The flavors were much bolder. We were less afraid of making mistakes than Chez Panisse. The clients were so excited. People like Lillian Hellman, Ronald Reagan, and Mel Brooks were coming in, and Hollywood people, politicos, musicians like the Eagles. You would go to the table and they would grasp your hand, and they would say, 'Thank you, that was delicious.'

"LA was much more receptive to change than Northern California was. When I got to LA [in 1979], LA was ready to go. Michael's opened up at the right time, in the right situation, and it allowed Wolfgang to open, it allowed everybody, it was a springboard for everything."

MICHAEL MCCARTY

Michael's, Santa Monica

The first time I met Michael McCarty, he was wearing red snakeskin boots, had his hair slicked back like a 1940s movie star, and was talking about his "little Latinos" in the kitchen. I was with Barbara Tropp of China Moon, and we asked each other, "Who is this guy?"

When Michael opened his eponymous restaurant in Santa Monica in 1979, the dining world took notice. Jeremiah Tower said, "If there really is a California

GOLDSTEIN, JOYCE ESERSKY.

INSIDE THE CALIFORNIA FOOD REVOLUTION: THIRTY
YEARS THAT CHANGED OUR CULINARY CONSCIOUSNESS.
                              Cloth   348 P.
BERKELEY: UNIV OF CALIFORNIA PRESS, 2013
SER: CALIFORNIA STUDIES IN FOOD AND CULTURE; 44.

HISTORICAL STUDY OF DEVELOPMENT OF CALIFORNIA
CUISINE FROM 1970S-2000S. A CHAIRMAN'S CIRCLE BOOK
LCCN 2013-14798
  ISBN 0520268199   **Library PO#** FIRM ORDERS

		List	34.95	USD
8395 NATIONAL UNIVERSITY LIBRAR	**Disc**	14.0%	
App. Date 4/16/14 SOC-SCI 8214-08	**Net**	30.06	USD

SUBJ: 1. COOKING--CALIFORNIA--HIST. 2. RESTAURANTS
--CALIFORNIA--HIST.

CLASS TX715.2   DEWEY# 641.59794   LEVEL GEN-AC

YBP Library Services

GOLDSTEIN, JOYCE ESERSKY.

INSIDE THE CALIFORNIA FOOD REVOLUTION: THIRTY
YEARS THAT CHANGED OUR CULINARY CONSCIOUSNESS.
                              Cloth   348 P.
BERKELEY: UNIV OF CALIFORNIA PRESS, 2013
SER: CALIFORNIA STUDIES IN FOOD AND CULTURE; 44.

HISTORICAL STUDY OF DEVELOPMENT OF CALIFORNIA
CUISINE FROM 1970S-2000S. A CHAIRMAN'S CIRCLE BOOK
  LCCN 2013-14798
  ISBN 0520268199   **Library PO#** FIRM ORDERS

		List	34.95	USD
8395 NATIONAL UNIVERSITY LIBRAR	**Disc**	14.0%	
App. Date 4/16/14 SOC-SCI 8214-08	**Net**	30.06	USD

SUBJ: 1. COOKING--CALIFORNIA--HIST. 2. RESTAURANTS
--CALIFORNIA--HIST.

CLASS TX715.2   DEWEY# 641.59794   LEVEL GEN-AC

style, it's Michael's. Michael's was all beige and umbrellas, waiters in pink shirts and chinos, the garden, the sunlight, the light food, and modern art on the walls—it was style."

"In 1978," said Michael, "if you asked any hotel concierge in any major city, 'What's the best restaurant in town?' the response would be a classical French restaurant or an Italian restaurant serving Continental food. Our revolution was creating modern American food and modern American restaurants. I think one of my most important contributions was the creation of a modern American restaurant that embodied many different components."

From an early age Michael knew he wanted to be a restaurateur. He grew up in Briarcliff Manor, New York, in a family that valued fine food and the good life. In 1969, he enrolled in the Cordon Bleu. "Before I left [for Paris], my father, my mother, and I went to Laurent, a classical French restaurant—art deco, everybody dressed to the nines, great scene. We're having this great meal, and the owner walks in the door. The electricity level in the room just ratcheted up. I had an epiphany. It was like one of my parents' parties, where the mix of people was perfect, they're all eating and drinking and enjoying it. It was this pure moment of light. And then, within two or three minutes, the captain brought over the bill. That's what a restaurant is, the whole experience, which is always what drove me here at Michael's. That's why I don't own ten restaurants and places in Dubai."

Instead, he owns the original Michael's restaurant in Santa Monica and Michael's New York. "I love my New York, I love my LA. The crowds that I get in both places are the people I want to talk to, and that's a very important part of what we do."

Michael didn't waste a moment of his time in Paris. "I went to get the *grand diplôme*, and the pastry *diplôme*—every *diplôme* they had [at the Cordon Bleu]. At the same time, I enrolled at the École Hôtelière. Steven Spurrier and Jon Winroth were starting the Académie du Vin. I did everything simultaneously, and it was such a wonderful experience to live the first half of the seventies in Paris. Les Halles was still there, and it was just switching over to Rungis market."

One of Michael's instructors sent him to restaurateur René Lasserre. "I worked at Lasserre one night and said, 'I want to come back here for dinner. This is how I'm going to learn.' It was faster and more efficient to eat in all these restaurants than it was to go to school, [because] in those days, you spent the year in the kitchen as a slave. So I'm absorbing all of this. I'm learning the old, the new, the Escoffier, the Gault-Millau. We're down at Bocuse, and at Les Frères Troisgros, and it's all fabulous.

"Then I come back and go to the Cornell School of Hotel Administration for the summer program. Cornell was a very good program because it Americanized you. You could learn everything from business and tax law to how the Americans cut their meat differently to Vance Christian's California wine class."

After Cornell, Michael moved to Los Angeles and made a connection with Jean Bertranou at L'Ermitage. Together they invested in a duck farm in the high desert north of LA. "We took the Peking duck and mated it with the Muscovy duck to create the moularde. We [used the] legs and thighs for confit, the breast for magret, and made foie gras in my house in Malibu in the basement."

Michael spent over a year looking for a site where he could open his own restaurant. "I finally found this beautiful, funky old California bungalow built in the 1930s, with a huge backyard that was totally overgrown. I wanted to make it look like a house. It was all part of what we were trying to accomplish here. A big part of it was eating outdoors, and having that indoor-outdoor feel. My wife was a painter, so we became very involved in the art community. There were all these artists in Venice; we started to build our collection." Michael bought paintings from Richard Diebenkorn, Jasper Johns, David Hockney, Jim Dine, and Frank Stella. Their works, along with paintings by his wife, Kim, adorned the restaurant walls.

Every aspect of the ambience was carefully considered. "I said to Jerry Magnin, 'I don't want [our staff wearing] tuxedos. I want a modern American designer. Who do you have?' This guy named Ralph Lauren. I go over to his shop. He's got the pink shirts, khaki pants, Top-Siders—that's our uniform."

Michael went on to assemble an all-star kitchen staff. "Ken Frank came to me and said, 'I've heard a lot about this place. I'm in between gigs.' Billy Pflug comes in. The next day Mark Peel walks in. The next day Jonathan Waxman walks in. And I go, this is it, we've got enough, I've got my line designed here. Then Jimmy Brinkley walks in. There's my opening team. Phil Reich, our sommelier, worked the floor for a long time, until he could no longer deal with humans." "Michael created a magnificent stage," said chef Jonathan Waxman. "And he was smart enough to let me and the boys and the girls go and cook while he did his thing in the front."

"In those days," said Michael, "we wanted to do modern American with French influences because that's where our roots were, but we wanted to change it. We wanted to use more California greens. My wife was a salad nut—a very big influence on the salads and vegetables here. We continued to bring in most of our greens from France. We were the exact opposite of the locavore program, but still to this day, I do both. I'm still gonna have my Dutch white asparagus every season."

DINNER

M A I N S

Mixed Grill of Seasonal Vegetables, Red and Yellow Peppers, Baby Red Potatoes, Asparagus, and Sweet Onions with Extra Virgin Olive Oil and Balsamic Vinegar	22.50
Atlantic Salmon Salad with Roma Tomato Vinaigrette, Roasted Red and Yellow Sweet Peppers and Grilled Sweet Onions, Extra Virgin Olive Oil and Balsamic Vinegar	23.50
Shelton Farms' Chicken and Montrachet Goat Cheese Salad with Roasted Red and Yellow Sweet Peppers, Grilled Sweet Onions, Roma Tomato Vinaigrette, Jalapeno, Cilantro, Lime, and Extra Virgin Olive Oil	24.50
Nicoise Salad with Seared Hawaiian Tuna, Nicoise Olives, Giant Spanish Capers, Roasted Peppers, New Potatoes, Grilled Sweet Onions, Reggiano Parmesan, Tomatoes, and Hard Cooked Egg with Tarragon Vinaigrette	24.50

***

Atlantic Salmon with Lake Superior Whitefish Caviar	23.50
East Coast Sea Scallops with Watercress and Guss Bacon	24.50
West Coast Swordfish with Tomato Basil Vinaigrette	24.50
French Turbot with Fava Bean, Sweet Corn and Chervil	24.50
Hawaiian Ahi Tuna with Hudson Valley Foie Gras and Crispy Sweet Onions	24.50

***

Shelton Farms' Grilled Chicken with Tarragon and Frites	19.50
Chicago Sweetbreads with Lemon, Giant Spanish Capers, and Parsely Butter	23.50
Carpinteria Squab and Hudson Valley Duck Foie Gras with Pinot Noir Cassis, Ginger and Scallions	24.50
Thuel Farms' Duck Breast with Figs and Neiport Port Sauce	24.50

***

Grandma Moses BBQ Guss Pork Tenderloin with Jalapeno Cilantro Lime Salsa	23.50
Dutch Valley Veal with Shiitake Mushrooms and Fresh Herbs	25.50
California Prime Lamb with Cabernet Cassis and Currants	26.50
Superior 28-Day Dry-Aged Prime New York Steak with Frites	26.50

***

"B I G   E A T S"

"BIG EATS" Superior Veal Porterhouse with Oregano and Frites	28.95
"BIG EATS" Guss Lamb Porterhouse Chops with Rosemary, Frites	28.95
"BIG EATS" Superior Beef Porterhouse with Garlic and Frites	29.95
"BIG EATS" 2-lbs. Maine Lobster with Basil Butter and Frites	29.95

***

Please Note a 15% Service Charge will be added to all food and beverage items. Sales tax is then added to this total.

Michael's menu from the 1990s, listing the provenance of every item and the ingredients for every dish.

Although professionally trained chefs and restaurateurs like Michael McCarty dominated in Southern California, this did not result in a more rigid or formulaic cuisine. To the contrary, Lucques's Suzanne Goin remarked, "in LA, I feel that there's a little more freedom, more influences, more people going off in different directions than in Northern California." A few years ago when cooking at the Napa Valley wine auction, Suzanne observed a certain uniformity in the approach to cooking in Northern California that was perhaps stifling creativity: "Focusing mainly on the ingredients contributes to this sense of sameness. Down here I feel like there are more people following the beat of their own drum. A lot of the LA chefs are into supporting the markets and local farmers too, but they're going in different directions rather than echoing each other."

Food columnist Marian Burros applauded LA's creativity as early as 1984, in a story about California cuisine in the *New York Times*. "These days the focal point of culinary innovation in California has shifted from San Francisco to Los Angeles, where foods are combined with wild abandon." She quoted Julia Child, who lived in Santa Barbara in the winter, as saying that San Francisco cooking was now "hidebound." Julia asserted, "We're adventurous; they are a bit self-satisfied. We don't have to worry about standards as much." "Julia always exaggerated a little," laughed Marian in our interview.

On the other hand, too much creativity and freedom could produce some clunkers, as the *New York Times* article went on to point out. "Judging by some of the combinations recently sampled, however, Los Angeles could use some standards. There should be no place for lobster salad with watermelon pickle on the menu at Trumps, where the chef, Michael Roberts, is supposed to have a good palate. And sole garnished with ginger, three kinds of caviar, and a shrimp sauce spiked with vodka at Wolfgang Puck's Chinois on Main cannot be assimilated in one mouthful." Even the most talented chefs can create ill-conceived dishes in their desire to be original and imaginative.

Mark Miller, food scholar, chef, and critical diner, observed that "California symbolizes, in the American psyche, everything new, young, fresh, multiethnic. It also has to embrace the idea of style and lifestyle above form and above what I would call content." Southern California, in particular, was all about *now*, as it still is. In a 2012 essay in the *New York Times Magazine*, novelist Michael Chabon characterized LA as "the capital of the eternal American present."

Mark Miller thought LA's chefs were the cream of the crop. "When you look at Southern California, you have Wolfgang Puck, Michel Richard, and later Joachim Splichal at Patina—the three best and most experimental chefs all in one city at the same time. [In] Northern California, there was nobody equaling what they were doing." It's no wonder that East Coast chefs relocating to the West Coast initially tended to gravitate to LA. Southern California was viewed as more modern and permissive, while the Bay Area seemed more closed to outside points of view.

Restaurateur Piero Selvaggio of Valentino, an Italian immigrant who moved to Los Angeles via Brooklyn, suggested that "California was the laboratory of new ideas. Chefs felt that they had to be here to be part of this process, not necessarily from an economic viewpoint, but as an evolutionary moment." Piero saw LA as the embodiment of "the new great West, the land of opportunity for culinary genius."

But a restaurant scene fueled by fashion and novelty makes for inconstant customers. Readers of winemaker Randall Grahm's newsletters know that he is fearlessly outspoken and not easily flustered, but he acknowledged that the capriciousness of LA diners unnerved him. "There is something about Southern California that freaks me out. The restaurant patrons are infinitely more fickle. They are into novelty, and dining is a form of entertainment in the extreme. Dining is also far more of a social statement about where you rank in social class, so being able to secure reservations at a particular place—getting the right table—is a major status thing."

This flightiness caused Michel Richard, former owner of Citrus in LA, to close his doors and move to Washington, DC, in 1998 to open Citronelle. "Los Angeles was a great town. But the life of a restaurant is very short there, except for Wolfgang. Or McDonald's. Very trendy. You're good, you're busy, and then, when a new restaurant opens, say good-bye to your business."

MICHEL RICHARD

Citrus, Hollywood

Michel Richard was born in Brittany and worked his way up through the apprentice system in France, beginning as a baker at the age of fourteen. He advanced to train as a pastry chef under the famed Gaston Lenôtre and in 1974 moved to New York to open Lenôtre's Chateau France pâtisserie. When it closed in 1975—"Americans weren't ready for Lenôtre's pastries," said Michel—he moved to Santa Fe to run The French Pastry Shop in La Fonda Hotel. In 1977, he made a last move, to Los Angeles, where he opened a bakery of his own. When he found that selling dessert was not enough to sustain the business, he built an adjacent café, where he offered salads, terrines, and a few other dishes. He went on to launch his restaurant Citrus in 1987.

"At first I was very French. While I was cooking in my pastry shop, I would have conversations with my guests. Most of them were not very happy about French food; they were telling me it was too creamy, too rich, had too much butter. When I opened Citrus, I didn't use cream or butter." Michel labeled his cuisine "French in California" and described it as "a combination of simplicity, lightness, and tasty food."

"Los Angeles is my Provence. It's hot, and people want to eat lighter food. And I've been thinking about what is California food. Fresh, fresh, fresh. More vinaigrette. More spice in the food. In most of my sauces, I stopped using stocks. I was using roasted chicken jus or miso. The miso was like consommé—it had a lot of flavor. I used to love that umami."

Part of Michel's menu changed every day, but not all of it, because he thought the cooks needed time to perfect a new dish. The dishes he served were his ideas, but today he says he welcomes input from his staff, whose diverse backgrounds and life experiences enrich the restaurant's offerings. "I was in Paris last year, talking with Joël Robuchon. And I was thinking of a great thing we had in California: most of my chefs in the kitchen, they're college educated. It's a big change. When I left school, I was fourteen. Most of the young people working in my kitchen, they start to work in a kitchen at twenty-two."

Citrus was a dramatic white space with umbrellas and a glassed-in kitchen. "The decision to have an open kitchen was mine. The [design of] the entire restaurant was mine. In LA, every French restaurant was dreary and dark. I managed to create a restaurant that would make you feel like you're in Provence—bright, open, green, unpretentious. I remember going to the Troisgros restaurant in Roanne. It was real good, but the kitchen—it was spectacular. So gorgeous, but nobody was able to see it. At Citrus, I came up with that nice open kitchen." Because his kitchen was installed in what had been an outdoor patio, it had to be enclosed in glass due to building code requirements.

"To succeed you have to be the owner," said Michel, "and you have to work all the time. You have to introduce new things. When I go to a market, I harvest not only the vegetable, I harvest ideas. And it's exciting for me. I need to go to a market two times a week and see what's going on. And I'm proud—and I just love my profession. Sometimes I feel like I'm a kid when I go back to my kitchen and create a new dish."

Restaurateur Michael Dellar, who grew up in Los Angeles, was critical of the pomp at restaurants such as Citrus and St. Germain, where he found the food "very overdone, very over-manipulated." But chefs were trying to impress, and this was true at all the better restaurants, which were "places to see and be seen. Southern California people didn't care about the food as much. They cared much more about the pretense."

This apathy toward quality food and ingredients demoralized some chefs. Wendy Brucker worked at Square One and Stars before going down to Los Angeles to cook at City Restaurant in 1990. She found that the fish and meat were as good as what she was used to, but the produce was another story. "LA was about ten years behind as far as produce. And not just produce, but the sensibility about how to treat the ingredients—really taking care of the food. Ingredients were not nearly as important as they were up here. In terms of popularity of restaurants, it was really about who went there. It was all about being seen. The quality of food did not have much to do with whether a restaurant was successful because there were a lot of really crappy restaurants that did tremendous business. I think that people who live in LA don't know nearly as much about food, and don't care. Everybody's on a diet of some sort."

Jeff Jackson, a former chef at Hotel Nikko in Beverly Hills, admitted that cooking there was disheartening for a professionally trained chef. "In LA, everyone eats out every meal of every day, it seems. No one cooks. Consequently, people tend to eat very light, too. I've never made so many salads in my life. I was coming from classical French kitchens in Chicago, and here I was making Caesar salad with a chicken breast on it, and I was pulling my hair out. It's all how you look, the car that you drive, and all of that stuff."

"We've got good restaurants, but they're still places for entertainment," Russ Parsons said of LA. "Chez Panisse has a completely different ethos than Spago, which is basically 'Come on in, have a great time. You're gonna see amazing people, and yeah, the food's gonna be great.'"

Mark Miller was more impressed by the playfulness and daring of Los Angeles than what he saw as the conservatism of Northern California. "Southern California has no history, no ritual, no heritage. It's Hollywood. Southern California embraces food as fashion, food as lifestyle." Mark sees Wolfgang Puck as the quintessential California chef. He believes that one of Wolfgang's important contributions was to take popular dishes and elevate them. People liked pizza, so Wolfgang added prestige by topping his pizzas with costly ingredients like smoked salmon and caviar. Expensive ingredients were essential to pleasing the status-hungry LA audience.

MARK MILLER

Fourth Street Grill and Santa Fe Bar and Grill, Berkeley

Mark Miller is one of the most intelligent, well-traveled, and opinionated people I know. We did not work at Chez Panisse at the same time, but over the years we have taught and cooked at some of the same venues and have become friends.

Mark was interested in food from his early days as a student at UC Berkeley, and he ate at Chez Panisse the week it opened. He knew Victoria Wise, the opening chef, and after dining at the restaurant he would hang out in the kitchen, trading gossip and food stories. He was hired at Chez Panisse by chance several years later. He had been writing a food newsletter, "The Market Basket," and said, "Alice was aware that I was knowledgeable and passionate about food, and that I was what I would call a good home cook." In 1977, Alice asked if he could fill in at the restaurant for two weeks, even though, as he recalled, "I had no background in the restaurant business besides my prep school summers scooping ice cream in New England."

About his time at Chez Panisse, he explained, "I liked the restaurant—it was easy to. Alice was always interested in people having a passion for foods she didn't know about. She wanted to learn, and if you pursued your passion, she saw that as a good thing. In 1977, it was Jean-Pierre Moullé, Alice, and I. The format was always one cook did one course all night, 120 guests, two seatings. Tom Guernsey was basically running the restaurant as the general manager and maître d'. Jerry Budrick was around. Lindsey Shere was doing desserts."

In those early days, the food at Chez Panisse was not yet the California cuisine that the restaurant would become known for. "It was simple French bistro food. It wasn't any different from bistro food in San Francisco or stuff that I had had in Europe. I do not believe that Chez Panisse as a restaurant—the structure and food—has ever been revolutionary. To me it's always represented *cuisine bonne femme*, the woman who cooks home-style food in a small Provençal restaurant and is the center of community life. It's never been a commercialized restaurant business."

Mark said that Chez Panisse opened after the ideological philosophy of the time had already been set. "Alice became an acolyte of what was going on in Berkeley at the time: the free speech movement and political activism of the 1960s. To me, San Francisco is conservative, wanting to preserve the past and [concerned with] history and status. The food in Northern California has always been ideologically based. It's not been based on setting new precedents, new styles, new fashion, new restaurants, and it's not based on commercialism. Alice is the ideological person who represents Northern California and its arts and crafts and its sort of purity."

Mark found greater inspiration in the innovative restaurants of LA. "Wolfgang Puck is the most important chef in the history of the world. He is the revolutionary. He has more business than any other chef ever has done or does today. So why do people think that California cuisine is Alice Waters? This is where you have to get a little philosophical and psychological. The American people want to have safe, good, pure food; they don't want to have really, really great food. They are puritans at heart, and the ideological argument of pure, good food that's locally sustainable is an ideological message that they find they can identify with. Michael Pollan is a minister of pure food; he is not a chef, he doesn't represent culinary history, he doesn't represent the complexities or understand what is possible or the meaning of cuisine, of ritual, of flavor, of mythology. He wants to take that away and have pure food, and so do most Americans. People are motivated to make an ideological choice."

Mark departed from Chez Panisse in 1979. "Susie Nelson was the hostess, and she had found this site on Fourth Street in the redevelopment and rail yard area. She wanted to leave Chez Panisse and open her own restaurant because she thought Chez Panisse was getting too snooty, and I wanted to leave, so she said, 'Why don't we become partners, fifty-fifty, and open the restaurant together?' So I opened Fourth Street as a 50 percent partner, and it cost us $70,000. I put up half of it, the restaurant was a hit, and we paid off our investors in four months."

At Fourth Street Grill, Mark was able to cook his own food. He changed the style of food frequently. For a while he was doing Moroccan, Italian, English, American, and regional dishes, and then he turned to Southwestern food. Two years later, he and Susie Nelson opened a second Berkeley restaurant, Santa Fe Bar and Grill. "I decided to do no more European food, only Cajun, Caribbean, and Southwestern. That was a big success. I wanted to do big-flavored food of everyday life and explore ethnic flavors in their richness and kaleidoscope of intricacies."

In 1985, Mark had been in Berkeley eighteen years, and "it was time to go." He left both the Fourth Street Grill and Santa Fe Bar and Grill, moved to Santa

Fourth Street Grill

Dinner

Pastas

```
Pasta with parsley, garlic, olive oil & cheese....3.50
Pasta with fresh herbs & seasonal vegetable.......3.50
Puttanesca, pasta with anchovies, garlic, tomatoes
      capers, olives & tuna.........................4.00
Green pasta with four cheeses.....................4.00
```

Grilled Specialties

```
Hamburger, made with choice chuck, served on an
      egg roll with chips & pickles................2.85
Cheeseburger, with swiss or cheddar...............3.10
Louisana hot sausages, served with shoestring
      potatoes....................................3.50
Italian sausage, served with polenta..............3.50
Grilled chicken, served with shoestring potatoes..4.25
Steak sandwich, served with shoestring potatoes...4.75
Extra thick loin pork chop, served with potatoes
      & homemade applesauce........................5.25
Extra thick top sirloin, served with potatoes.....6.00
Double loin lamb chop, marinated in wine, herbs,
      & olive oil, served with potatoes............6.75
New York steak, served with potatoes.............8.00
```

And please ask about the grilled fresh fish of the day!

Salads

```
Letťuce, with vinegar & olive oil dressing........1.50
Mixed greens, with garlic croutons................2.50
Cesar salad, wtih garlic croutons.................3.50
Carpaccio, paper thin slice of raw steak, served
      with mustard sauce or anchovy sauce..........3.50
Steak Tartar, minced raw steak served with egg,
      capers, shallots, mustard, parsley, anchovies
      and fresh ground pepper......................6.00
Greek salad, spinich, red onions, feta cheese,
      garlic croutons & house dressing.............4.00
```

Beverages

```
House coffee....................40
Espresso........................70
Double Espresso.................95
Cappucino.......................90
Cafe Latte....................1.20
Espresso Decaffeinated.........95
Pot of Tea.....................65
Milk...........................60
Mexican Hot Chocolate..........75
Mineral Water..................75
```

We offer also: Soup of the Day (bowl-1.50, cup-.90)

The opening menu at Mark Miller's Fourth Street Grill, 1979, featuring classics and shoestring potatoes, with a nod to Mexico in the hot chocolate.

Fe, New Mexico, and opened Coyote Cafe, where he again concentrated on Southwestern cuisine. Today he does consulting work for restaurant companies and travels widely to study diverse cuisines. He believe his life's work is to raise the level of ethnic food to where it receives higher esteem.

Word about the innovations occurring in California's restaurants was traveling eastward. Danny Meyer, who had just opened Union Square Cafe in New York City, decided to come out and see what was going on. He traveled to California with Ali Barker, his chef. "We went to Los Angeles first. We got off the airplane and went to Michael's for lunch. We went to Trumps. We went to Piero Selvaggio's place, Primi. We went to Angeli Caffe. We went to Spago. We got a taste of what Los Angeles meant, and it was, because of the clientele, a flashy version. It was a big party.

"Then we went to San Francisco. We went to Square One, Washington Square Bar and Grill, Hayes Street Bar and Grill, the Post Street Bar and Grill—everything was a bar and grill. I even went to Perry's to try to understand the San Francisco ethos. And I found that San Francisco was more focused on food.

"Stars was a bridge for me between the party of LA and the food of San Francisco. Stars and Spago pushed the boundaries. They were the first places I had gone to in this country where the party did not mean that the culinary experience had to be dumbed down. The experience I had had in my early twenties in New York was that the people who knew how to do really good food didn't know how to have fun, and the people who knew how to have fun didn't know how to do really good food. I was trying to piece it all together: the club, family, fun, excellence. I can say that in the absence of California, there could never have been a Union Square Cafe. What a refreshing gift that California gave the country, gave the world."

3

Defying Kitchen Convention

Something we have here [in California] that they don't have in a lot of other areas is that entrepreneurial spirit, the passion. Passion can overcome a lot of shortcomings. As the people with the passion gain the skills and knowledge, look out, because they will set new highs.

—Winemaker Michael Mondavi

I was forty-seven years old when Alice Waters asked me to fill in for Steve Sullivan, the bread baker at Chez Panisse, while he took a six-week vacation. Although I had taught cooking classes for eighteen years, I had never worked in a restaurant. Suddenly I found myself making thirty loaves of bread, four buckets of pizza dough, and thirty pounds of pasta a day. When Steve came back, Alice asked me to stay on to cook in the Chez Panisse Café, where I later became chef. As word got out about the good food at the café, our volume of business increased dramatically. We went from serving 45 lunches and 80 dinners daily to 150 lunches and up to 340 dinners.

Three years later, I left Chez Panisse to open Square One. Today it's hard to imagine that someone would enter the demanding restaurant field with so little experience. But in California, from the 1970s through the early 1990s, passion-ate amateurs, many of whom hadn't gone to cooking school or even worked in a restaurant, jumped eagerly into the business. How did so many of us dare own and manage restaurants with so little practical knowledge? All I can say is that ignorance is bliss. We had no idea what we were getting into.

•

The model for the kitchen brigade was developed by Georges Auguste Escoffier in the late 1800s. For the next century, the typical restaurant kitchen, both in

Europe and abroad, was run by trained culinarians who had either gone to cooking school or come up through the ranks of the brigade, with its specialized stations for prep, fish, seafood, meat, pastry, and so on. In the 1970s, however, a door opened for enthusiastic innocents, and scores of newcomers walked through it. According to Emily Luchetti, the early years of California cuisine presented unique opportunities. "When I took over at Stars as the pastry chef," she said, "I had no pastry training. But Jeremiah Tower knew me, I knew him, we agreed on the style of food, and the rest I figured out. If you had a restaurant like Stars today, you would never put someone in there as pastry chef who did not have pastry training." Ironically, Jeremiah himself would not be hired by most restaurants today due to his lack of professional culinary training.

The California cuisine revolution occurred at a time when the restaurant world was not as competitive as it is now. Before the modern phenomenon of the celebrity chef and the constant media focus on restaurants, being a cook was not considered an impressive career, so there were fewer highly trained culinary students. This helped make California in the 1970s a fertile ground for iconoclasts. Some cooks had formal training or restaurant experience, but others were completely inexperienced. Many skipped the slow and predictable career climb and clambered straight to the top to run their own kitchens or become chef-owners. They were caught up in the spirit of the revolution, which saw more unique restaurants open and their seats fill with appreciative diners. As chef-owners, they could cook a more personal type of food and develop their own culinary style. Responsible only to themselves and their investors, eventually they became celebrities in their own right.

Self-Taught Chefs

Back in the 1980s and early 1990s, a lot of the chefs weren't trained. That was freeing. You weren't tied down to a set of rules and told, "You have to go this way." No, I don't, because I don't even know what those rules are.
—Tom Worthington, chef and partner at Monterey Fish Market

Many of us early California chefs were food-obsessed college grads or dropouts from other fields. We read cookbooks voraciously, dined out frequently, and cooked constantly. Since we did not have any formal training to rely upon, we would make mistakes, but we learned from them and kept going, trusting our palates and passion to guide us.

Culinary instructor Barbara Haimes described the diversity of these new chefs' backgrounds. "Back then, people came to cooking with college degrees, with some intellectual curiosity. People had traveled, and that sensibility came with them into the kitchen. Not everybody went to cooking school. A lot of people came in from other careers. They were smart people who had a range of knowledge. It wasn't the European model of you're fourteen, you go through an apprenticeship. It was a really different model, and it was more of a West Coast thing than an East Coast thing because the East Coast was still impacted by the European model. It was the usual California thing—the Wild West. You just do your own thing."

It was a remarkable phenomenon, with lawyers, nurses, brokers, and artists moving into cooking. Mark Miller was in anthropology, Jeremiah Tower came from architecture, Alice Waters taught at a Montessori school, Bruce Marder was in dental school, and I was a painter who had studied with Josef Albers. The common bond is that we all were crazy about food.

Despite our initial naïveté, we persevered, and those of us who succeeded did so by dint of single-minded devotion and determination. California applauds and supports rebels and entrepreneurs, especially those willing to work ridiculous hours to accomplish their goals. We autodidacts were driven by our love of food and flavor.

Catherine Pantsios, former chef-owner at Zola's, took no offense when a reviewer called her restaurant "amateur." She explained that the word *amateur* comes from the Latin *amāre*, "to love." "I probably had more restaurant experience than a lot of people. But at the time people just jumped in because they really wanted to do something. They didn't want to open a restaurant and sell a predictable kind of food. They wanted to create a particular environment, a particular type of experience." These amateur lovers of food and cooking made homes for themselves in the new California cuisine movement. One passionate novice was Margaret Fox, who raised the culinary bar in rural Mendocino, 150 miles north of San Francisco, when she gave up her academic career plans to run a rural café.

MARGARET FOX

Café Beaujolais, Mendocino

Margaret Fox liked to bake and cook from an early age and in her teens would throw dinner parties at the drop of a hat. Her mother was a self-taught cook whose creative recipes were published in *Sunset* magazine. Margaret remembers her mother telling her, "If you can read, you can cook."

Despite her early interest in food, Margaret was expected to go to college. She graduated from UC Santa Cruz with a degree in psychology, "fully intending to go to graduate school." But what she did instead surprised everyone. She decamped to Mendocino, hoping to find a job in a bakery, and wound up taking over the drowsy Café Beaujolais with friends who knew even less about the restaurant business than she did. "My mom burst into tears when I told her I had done this. But I was twenty-four and full of spunk, and you don't know what you don't know, which turned out to be a very good thing. My mom did at one point say something like, 'For this we sent you to college?'"

Like many other Northern California chefs at the time, Margaret had no formal experience, but she was wholly committed to baking and had the stamina to succeed in a tiny coastal town that was not on anyone's fine-dining radar. "It was a slow beginning," she recalled. "It was like, if an omelet is made in the forest, does anyone hear it? I was in this remote place and I was doing breakfast, which was really unusual. People weren't used to going out for that."

She started off serving breakfast and lunch. Little by little, the news got around, and Margaret was able to buy out her partners in 1977. However, it was still somewhat slow going, and to drum up business she launched a weekend summer cooking series with guest chefs. Marion Cunningham, longtime assistant to James Beard and author of the *Fannie Farmer Cookbook* and *Fannie Farmer Baking Book*, was one of her first guest instructors. Alas, it was the year of the gas crisis, and only about five people showed up in the dining room, three of whom were friends. These were hard times, and Margaret admitted to feeling "disheartened."

Then, in December 1983, Ruth Reichl came to Café Beaujolais on assignment for *New West* magazine. At the time she was writing the "Best of California" column, and she included Café Beaujolais in her list of the best breakfasts in the state. When a photographer called to ask Margaret if he could come do a photo shoot, she was taken by surprise, since no one had told her about the article. After that, as she put it, "the flood gates opened." People would drive up for the weekend to sample her coffee cake, muffins, and egg dishes.

In 1984, Chris Kump came on as executive chef. In the late 1980s, Margaret and Chris began to host a farmers' market on their property, which introduced them to an expanding number of local growers and prompted them to start putting the names of farms and farmers on their menu. At that time this was an unfamiliar practice and people would ask why they did it, to which Margaret would respond, "We're proud of getting what they're proud of selling and we want to pass that on to you." In 1989, they invited well-known oven builder Alan Scott to give a workshop, and the outcome was a fantastic outdoor brick oven on the property. In this showcase oven Margaret and Chris baked bread and pizzas and roasted tomatoes that they then froze for the winter. They offered daily specials based on freshness, availability, and seasonality and a menu that changed every month or so. Not every item changed, though. "We had certain things, like that darn baked goat cheese salad, you never could take off."

Margaret marveled that forty years after the start of the California cuisine movement, "you still see this amazing energy and enthusiasm and celebration of ingredients. People who have grown up in more recent years probably take this as a matter of course, but we who have been around for longer look at it and say, 'Oh my god.'"

Like Margaret Fox's, many parents were shocked when their children selected careers in the restaurant industry. They hadn't sent their kids to college to become kitchen workers. Barbara Haimes, one of the rare chefs who studied in a culinary training program, said, "My parents cried—sat in front of me and cried for hours when I told them. 'My god, what are you doing with your life? It's manual labor. It's blue-collar stuff.'" Barbara disagreed, and went on to a successful career cooking at Mudd's, Chez Panisse, Square One, and China Moon. "I think people were so intelligent and well read that it didn't come out as blue-collar food. It came out as way more than that, which was a mixed blessing, because it came out pretty elitist, and a lot of people weren't happy with that either. But then we had more sophisticated diners."

When she was in the kitchen at Chez Panisse, said Barbara, she observed that "a lot of really good people were not trained and, in some ways, weren't interested in being trained. To some extent at Chez Panisse, there was no respect for technique because they were anti culinary training. You couldn't possibly have a palate if you had technique; if you were technically good there was something wrong with you. They were interested in the sensual experience of something that reminded them of something else. They considered ingredients more important than technique." The Chez Panisse staff put down technique because most of the culinary school alumni they tried out or worked with had no sense of food history and were taught only to execute, not how to taste and explore ingredients. Most trained chefs did not understand how to put flavor first, which had become the mantra of California cuisine.

Janet Fletcher worked on the line at Chez Panisse Café in 1982 and is now an accomplished reporter and prolific cookbook author. She credits Alice Waters for much of the sea change in the public's perception of restaurant work. "Cooking became a respected profession partly because of the kinds of people Alice had in that kitchen. Until then, most professional cooks and chefs had come up through the apprenticeship system. Alice not only disregarded it; she disdained it. She was looking for cooks with an educated brain and some exposure to a broader world, someone who knew the history of food and culture. So that kitchen became a very stimulating place to be. I think it reinforced the notion that this is an exciting profession and a profession of prestige."

In the early days at Stars, said Emily Luchetti, "PhDs were prepping three cases of tomatoes and were thrilled. These were bright, educated, artistic, creative people with raw enthusiasm and passion. Their overall goal was producing great food." Many big-name chefs learned their craft on the job, including Loretta Keller, Mark Miller, Nancy Oakes, Catherine Pantsios, and Amaryll Schwertner in Northern California and Ken Frank, Octavio Becerra, Suzanne Goin, Evan Kleiman, and Nancy Silverton in Southern California.

A daring few opened their first restaurant with no restaurant experience at all, including Sally Schmitt, Bruce LeFavour, Daniel Patterson, Alice Waters with Victoria Wise and Lindsey Shere, Michael Wild, and Jesse Cool. They were ardent home cooks with refined palates who took great pleasure in cooking for others. This intrepid band also includes several chefs who were born abroad: Charles Phan and Mai Pham from Vietnam, Mourad Lahlou from Morocco, and Hoss Zaré from Iran. They taught themselves to cook because they missed the flavors of their homelands and then opened restaurants to share their culinary heritage. They embraced entrepreneurship and the do-it-yourself model. All four also saw their cooking styles evolve over their years in California. Like many foreign-born chefs, they incorporated new local ingredients into their basic dishes. Both Mai and Charles began to expand beyond the repertoire of traditional Vietnamese cuisine, Mai reaching toward Korean and Indian food, Charles adding Mediterranean tastes. Mourad became interested in mastering new cooking techniques, with his food taking on a more modernist California style. Hoss started delving more deeply into his native cuisine, introducing more Persian-inflected dishes to his menu.

HOSS ZARÉ

Zaré at the Fly Trap, San Francisco

Hoss Zaré grew up in Tabriz, a region in northern Iran famous for Persian rugs, agriculture, and hospitality. "We had a farm about ten to fifteen minutes' walking distance from our house, and from the beginning of spring to the end of fall, we had all kinds of fruits and vegetables. We had chickens, lamb—everything grew there. When I tell people we had forty-five kinds of grapes and fifteen kinds of apricots on one farm, they can't believe it. My mouth is watering just thinking about it." Before dawn store owners used to go to the farm, pick the ripe fruit, pay, and by 9 o'clock, all the stores were stocked with produce. Every herb was cut the morning it was sold. Hoss grew up with freshly harvested seasonal produce.

He was twenty-three years old when he came to California in 1986. "The first few years I was unhappy because the food wasn't good. Everything was picked too early. The big supermarkets put green tomatoes in the stores. Everything was money, money, money—big and cheaper products. I was used to eating a tomato like an apple, but here I lost interest in tomatoes in the market. The flavor was not there."

Hoss went to Skyline College and then UC Davis, where he took pre-med classes. While attending school, he hung out at the Billboard Café in San Francisco, which was run by his brother. "My passion for cooking started there. I had no idea about cooking before. I was watching and learning." He started working at the Billboard, and then moved on to the Fly Trap, an old-time San Francisco restaurant. "For a year and a half, I commuted an hour and a half every day to the Fly Trap. It was a battle between going to school and cooking. Cooking took over."

Eventually Hoss bought the Fly Trap and renamed it Zaré at the Fly Trap. He was nervous about changing the menu because the restaurant was a San Francisco landmark. "It's been there a hundred years, and it was an Italian immigrant's story. I thought, why not do my best to make it another immigrant's story?"

He described Zaré as a Mediterranean restaurant with a Persian influence, a combination he felt comfortable with because Mediterranean cuisine is widely accepted in San Francisco. Hoss borrows flavors from the Mediterranean and incorporates them into his Persian food. "Some spices I mix, we didn't have in Iran, and I'm enjoying it. Persians, they never use spicy food—spices, but not spicy. But *charmoula* and *harissa* are my favorite tools right now. I make buckets of *harissa* fresh. It gives a nice subtle heat but doesn't overpower."

At the same time he is teaching himself to cook more authentic Persian dishes. "I'm learning from myself actually, from taste memories of my childhood. Even though I have the cookbooks and recipes, if it doesn't taste the same as my mom used to make, I don't like it. I do it again. I am taking the backbone of the cuisine that I have, and twisting it a bit with the others, as long as it works. When I did a traditional dish like *gormeh sabzi*, a stew with beans and vegetables, to make it more appealing, I put a braised short rib on top. The presentation was beautiful, people saw the meat, and underneath was stew. It started selling. But if I had put just the *gormeh sabzi* and rice, it would be a hard sell. Or the *fesenjoon;* I did the chicken separately, flavored it, put sauce on the bottom, and added a timbale with the wild rice. I introduced people to *fesenjoon* and later, when I did it the traditional way, it worked."

Hoss could give a primer on how to acquaint people with unfamiliar foods. "When I try a new dish, I give it to my staff first, and a small audience next. Then I put it on the menu. For example, with rosewater, no matter how much you try and train Americans, it's hard. You have to go very subtle. Like yogurt, I put it in barely. I don't want to give up, but I put it on the side. But some other flavors, I try and incorporate them into my dishes so I can bring in more authentic Persian flavor.

"It's fascinating to me that if you compare California and Iran, it's the identical climate and agriculture. Bergamot is in the north of Iran near the Caspian Sea, where we have oranges, tangerines, like California. You can get drunk from the smell of citrus when you're driving there. So for me California is coming home, but in a different way."

Professionally Trained Chefs

In traditional culinary schools in the United States and abroad, students learn the basics that will prepare them for their profession. Not all of them go into the restaurant field. Some become food writers, stylists, caterers, and private chefs. In the classroom they study food safety, business practices, and food history. In the kitchen they learn knife skills: how to butcher meat and poultry, fillet fish, turn vegetables to create even surfaces for cooking, cut foods into uniform dice for mirepoix and *brunoise,* and chop herbs into tiny fragments. They study cooking techniques: how to poach, steam, braise, roast, sauté, and grill. In recent years *sous-vide* cooking has been added to the curriculum. Students learn to make clear and flavorful stocks and master the sauces: *espagnole*, velouté, béchamel, mayonnaise, hollandaise, and aioli. (In contrast, in the early days of California cuisine, some self-taught chefs avoided complex sauces that required stock, and instead used compound butters and salsas.) Students take turns working at all of the kitchen stations in the traditional brigade: *commis* (prep), *garde manger* (cold station), *entremetier* (vegetables and sides), *poissonier* (fish), *rotisseur* (roasts), *saucier* (sauces), and *tournant* (a rotating position). They also learn how to bake bread and make pastries and desserts. Some schools have basic classes in wine.

Finally, as part of their studies, culinary students apprentice at an approved restaurant, usually one run by a graduate of the school. If their school has a restaurant on the premises, they work there in both the back and front of the house. Their training is rigorous, usually of two-year duration, with a codified curriculum. In the United States and Europe in years past there was no in-depth study of "foreign" cuisines, such as Asian or Italian. Nor was there any attention to creativity or originality. For years, culinary school was a highly regimented and competitive environment dominated by men.

The Culinary Institute of America in Hyde Park, New York, produced many notable graduates, including Northern California chefs Michael Chiarello, Gloria Ciccarone-Nehls, Gary Danko, Todd Humphries, and Bradley Ogden and Southern California chefs Susan Feniger, Anne Gingrass, David Gingrass, Jeff Jackson, Joe Miller, and Roy Yamaguchi. The CIA, as it is known, opened in 1946 as the New Haven Restaurant Institute, with fifty students, many on the GI Bill, and three faculty members: a chef, a baker, and a dietician. In 1972, the thriving school, now called the Culinary Institute of America, moved into a larger campus at the former St. Andrew-on-Hudson Jesuit novitiate in Hyde Park, where it grants associate and bachelor's degrees in the culinary arts, baking and pastry arts, and culinary science. In 1995 the CIA opened a West Coast campus at Greystone, the former Christian Brothers Winery in the Napa Valley, which offers a global cooking program and in-depth studies in wine.

While the CIA is perhaps the best-known culinary school in the United States, a host of other schools taught notable chefs as well. David Kinch of Manresa studied at Johnson and Wales in Providence, Rhode Island. Bruce Marder attended Dumas Père cooking school in Illinois. Emily Luchetti went to the New York Restaurant School. Mark Peel of Campanile studied in the hotel and restaurant department at California Polytechnic University at Pomona. Others studied abroad. Michael Roberts attended the École Jean Ferrandi in Paris, and Cindy Pawlcyn went to both La Varenne and Le Cordon Bleu after finishing hotel and restaurant school in Wisconsin. Michael McCarty did stints at the Cordon Bleu, the École Hôtelière, and the Académie du Vin in Paris and rounded off his education at the Cornell School of Hotel Administration in upstate New York. Wendy Brucker was one of several women who attended culinary programs before opening places of their own, along with Suzette Gresham, Heidi Krahling, Jennifer Millar, and Maria Helm Sinskey. Wendy graduated from the California Culinary Academy and then extended her training through jobs at Ernie's, Square One, Eddie Rickenbacker's, Stars, and City Restaurant before finally opening a place of her own.

WENDY BRUCKER

Rivoli Restaurant, Berkeley

Like many California chefs, Wendy Brucker was inspired by travel abroad. "I grew up in Berkeley, and my father was an Italian historian, so I spent a lot of time in Italy and France eating really good food. There was a lot more good food in Berkeley than probably almost anywhere else in the country, with maybe the exception of New York."

She spent several aimless years before deciding to pursue a career in food. "I went to cooking school at nineteen, sort of by happenstance. My brother worked in the same building as the California Culinary Academy. I was a high school dropout, cleaning houses, painting, not going anywhere, but I had started cooking at home and doing dinner parties for wealthy ladies at the Berkeley Tennis Club. My brother said, 'Wendy, you should check out this school.' And I loved it. I asked my dad, 'Would you send me?' I think he was so happy that maybe I would find a career that he was like, 'Hell, yes!'"

The standard culinary school curriculum was still firmly entrenched at that time, even in California. "When I started in 1980, all of the chefs at the CCA were European, predominantly Swiss or German, and the food was very old-school Continental, not a hint of nouvelle anywhere. They had all been cooking since they were ten and were bitter and unhappy people. First semester, most of them were fired, and the second batch was European and classically trained but younger and more open-minded, a breath of fresh air. Nouvelle cuisine was the big thing then, so we were doing carrot mousse and scallops in beurre blanc. Flour-thickened sauces were a thing of the past. They started getting in really good chefs to do six-week classes, including Wolfgang Puck, Jeremiah Tower, and Ken Hom."

After graduation, Wendy landed a job at Ernie's in San Francisco and fell under the spell of chef Jacky Robert. "He became one of the great influences in my cooking career because he was the first chef to hire women at Ernie's. He did not care if you were black, white, male, female, Asian—he had the most diverse kitchen I have worked in to this day in terms of experience and age and sex. He was an amazing teacher because he knew how to do everything and was really, really talented. You didn't get to work on the next station until you knew how to do the first one. So by the time I left, I had done all the stations, which included prep, pastry, butchering, sauté, and grilling."

During her time at Ernie's, the restaurant was changing over from traditional French to nouvelle cuisine. "It was real old school/new school," said Wendy. "We used orange juice concentrate in the sauce for the classic duck à l'orange. We were getting gorgeous Dover sole from France and freezing it, yet we also got in gorgeous fresh scallops and served them as they came in. The food went from the ridiculous to the sublime. The favorite nouvelle cuisine [dish] was seared scallops in a vanilla beurre blanc, and each scallop was topped with a slice of kiwi. Some of the old dishes were lovely, like we did a beef Wellington that was exquisite. So it was a funny, in-between thing."

Wendy worked at several restaurants over the next few years, each of which gave her new insights. "Square One opened my eyes to another kind of cooking and food and sensibility. Ingredients had not been a big deal in the restaurants that I worked at up until that point. Baking the bread, getting fresh seafood from Monterey Fish, the menu changing every day, pastas—that was an amazing experience.

"When I left Square One, I worked one year at Eddie Rickenbacker's, which was a nightmare. I learned a lot about organization and writing menus, but it was a crazy place. Then I went to Stars, which was another revelation. Square One was doing authentic food, which was a great grounding for me, and at Stars, we had a lot of leeway, and dishes would be more vaguely Asian, or Moroccan. Then I worked at City Restaurant for Susan Feniger and Mary Sue Milliken. Again, a very different cuisine. They were true to each dish, they were doing international, not fusion."

In keeping with her sundry cooking experiences, Wendy opened two stylistically different restaurants. Her first was Rivoli, a special occasion restaurant that she established in 1994 with her then husband, Roscoe Skipper. At Rivoli,

Wendy started out serving Mediterranean standards but then broadened the focus to offer an eclectic menu. Wendy said, "Right now I've got a pot roast with potato pancakes, blue cheese, and bacon and a quail dish that is Italian-ish—it's got a hazelnut stuffing and we're doing it with farro and mustard greens and a Bing cherry sauce. I've got an appetizer that's kind of southern—a corn spoonbread soufflé but with prosciutto instead of southern ham and succotash and a grilled peach. We do what I think of as truly California cuisine. It isn't Mediterranean, because you wouldn't see pot roast or spoonbread soufflé."

Corso, which Wendy and Roscoe opened in 2008, is based on the Italian trattoria, a more casual place where you get a carafe of water on the table to pour yourself. "It's very straightforward. Order a whole grilled fish, you get whole grilled fish. They don't bone it for you; you're going to bone it yourself."

The two restaurants illustrate two different styles of California cuisine: one eclectic and inventive, the other more orthodox, using local ingredients. "Rivoli has a smaller menu and is more about presentation. We're going for whatever I feel like cooking. Corso is more about trying to recreate a kind of food that I know and love, and the dishes are very traditional. Our classic meat *sugo* came from a tenth-generation Florentine man, and it tastes like when you go to a trattoria in Florence."

In the 1970s and 1980s, American restaurants, hotels, and country clubs decided it would add prestige to their establishments to bring in foreign-trained chefs. Highly skilled professionals could land good positions in the United States, and many of them leaped at the chance to leave their predictable career paths behind and take advantage of these overseas opportunities for advancement. Most thought American food meant hot dogs and hamburgers, but they were willing to come and elevate our cuisine and have an adventure too.

The majority arrived from Europe—primarily France, Germany, and Scandinavia. Some had endured a lengthy apprenticeship from a very young age, in which they were often treated harshly, but they learned how to work hard and fast. Those who attended culinary school were trained in the manner of the rigorous Escoffier brigade.

European chefs who settled on the East Coast generally retained a European culinary point of view, whereas those who came west found that their cooking evolved. In California, chefs were exposed to diverse cultures and gained access to local and seasonal ingredients, and soon they were putting more vegetables on their plates. Their food became lighter and healthier. Ethnic influences made their mark on chefs who had essentially grown up in a monoculture, and California's unfettered restaurant milieu allowed European chefs to break away from culinary traditions and rules and enjoy increased creative freedom. Their cuisine could become more individual.

In Southern California, almost everyone who opened a restaurant had either worked in restaurants or gone to cooking school or both. Michel Richard, Joachim Splichal, and Wolfgang Puck had started working in European kitchens as teen-agers, although in keeping with the entrepreneurial spirit of California, Michel Richard trained in pastry and later reinvented himself as a restaurant chef and became a master of technical ingenuity. His clientele were delighted by his fried shrimp "porcupines" wrapped in *kadaif* pastry, thousand-layer salmon terrine with caviar sauce, and phyllo-wrapped white bean "belly dancer" rolls.

In the early 1980s, Joachim Splichal was representative of many European-trained chefs working in fine-dining establishments. Chef Traci Des Jardins, who joined the staff of his Max au Triangle at the age of seventeen, noted that the restaurant "had a very extensive menu, a lot of fancy ingredients—foie gras, truffle, lobster, John Dory, sole—all imported from Europe. We were using the best ingredients, but I don't know that we were paying as much attention to season as we were to luxury. I can remember menus where we would have asparagus in December, and they were beautiful asparagus, but they weren't from California, and they weren't seasonal."

It was a major departure for a classically trained European chef to step back from the premise that a recipe, once perfected, doesn't ever change, and instead decide to use something else or alter the recipe if the prime ingredient is not in season. It took Joachim a while, but he eventually adopted the philosophy of California chefs such as Mark Peel, whose credo was "the best dish today is going to be made with the best ingredients today." Joachim narrowed his list of menu items and shifted from imported goods to local.

JOACHIM SPLICHAL

Max au Triangle, Beverly Hills; Patina Restaurant, Los Angeles

Joachim Splichal is the chef of Patina Restaurant Group and runs a culinary empire that includes pizzerias, the Nick and Stef's steak house chain, the Pinot bistros, and his flagship Patina Restaurant, which has reopened in the Frank Gehry–designed Disney Concert Hall in LA. Born in Germany, Joachim began his training on the international hotel circuit. In his early twenties he moved to

France to work at La Bonne Auberge in Antibes and the legendary L'Oasis in La Napoule, and then he spent four years on the Côte d'Azur under the tutelage of famed chef Jacques Maximin at the Chantecler Restaurant in the Hotel Negresco.

Joachim came to the United States in 1981, when he was hired to serve as executive chef for the Regency Club in Los Angeles. He stayed for three years but felt frustrated because the LA clientele never warmed up to what he liked to cook. His cuisine, which included such Provençal-derived dishes as vegetable napoleon, stuffed zucchini blossoms, shrimp ratatouille, and salade niçoise, may have been too authentically Mediterranean for diners who were used to heavy cream sauces and classical French fare, so he was forced to compromise and offer a few more familiar dishes on his menu. Initially he shipped in ingredients from France, including truffles, olive oil, and fish. "But then I met a couple of guys from Santa Barbara who brought fish to my doorstep and I went away from the European imports.

"When I first came [to the United States], I was shocked. You went to the supermarket, you had big carrots, ugly produce, and there was not much there. I was amazed because, for example, people threw the zucchini flowers away. Everything was a size too big. There was a lot of produce I was used to in the Mediterranean that I couldn't get. That became better very rapidly; within five or eight years we had a tremendous amount of progress. First the variety was better, and then there also was a direct connection between farmer and chef. I didn't know any other way because wherever I worked in Europe, mostly in France, you went to the market, you knew the farmer, you ate tripe early in the morning with him. Then he came to the restaurant. There was a strong connection between farmer and restaurant or restaurateur or kitchen."

Joachim built his own network, because at the time the Santa Monica farmers' markets weren't in full swing. In the 1990s, new produce companies started up that acted as brokers between the farmers' markets and the chefs. "You could call and ask, 'What's really looking good?' If they said 'tomatoes,' you could say, 'Bring me two cases of tomatoes.'"

After leaving the Regency Club Joachim opened Seventh Street Bistro in downtown LA, then Max au Triangle in Beverly Hills in 1984. Patina opened in 1987 to great acclaim. By then LA was ready for Joachim's inventive cooking. Diners loved his innovative lasagna made with thin slices of potato, duck liver with rhubarb, lobster minestrone, corn blini with salmon, and squab with bacon sauce atop spiced bread.

"When you're in Europe, you eat in French bistros, Italian trattorias—typically the food of that country. When I came here, I started to eat at sushi places, Korean places, Indian places, Chinese places, and that influenced my cooking. I used some of their ingredients, some of their vegetables, and incorporated them into the food I did. In my opinion, everybody was influenced by ethnic cuisines because it's Southern California and that's the way we live. It's totally different from Europe." Joachim became enraptured by California's bountiful ingredients and never stopped exploring and sharing what he discovered.

"The basic approach I took was French, and I added a twist to it, and people loved it. People really appreciated variety. When I came here, [the food] was basically French, heavy and super heavy. The restaurants at that time—L'Hermitage, L'Orangerie—did that old-fashioned cooking. I was taught under nouvelle cuisine—light, the vegetable stock sauces, really letting the quality of the produce and the protein speak and not bothering with some sauce. Early on I was doing vegetarian menus.

"If I had stayed in Europe, I would have been most likely part of the group of people who took nouvelle cuisine to a different level. I think it was better that I made the decision to come here and elevate the cuisine in California. I saw my food evolving from a very traditional, nouvelle cuisine standpoint, and now I feel my approach about food is ten times more casual. I incorporate all elements, the pizza oven as well as the grills. My food, I want it light. It's all about the product. It's all about the connection with the farmers and the fishermen."

Although Northern California was shaped in large part by its preponderance of self-taught chefs, it also had its share of the professionally trained. Foreign-born chefs René Verdon, Jacky Robert, Hubert Keller, Masa Kobayashi, Jean-Pierre Moullé, Udo Nechutnys, Julian Serrano, and Staffan Terje had received classical training in Europe, along with a legion of hotel and country club chefs.

Roland Passot illustrated a typical progression from France to the United States. He grew up in Lyon and at the age of fourteen apprenticed at Les Trois Dômes at the Hôtel Sofitel Bellecour. He then went to work for Jean-Paul Lacombe, whose restaurant Léon de Lyon was a one-star Michelin establishment transitioning from classical to nouvelle cuisine. Roland emigrated to the United States in 1976 and after several restaurant ventures opened the elegant La Folie in San Francisco in 1988. After more than twenty-five years in California, Roland still cooks his "root French cuisine," but being here, he said, "has liberated me, because I feel like I can cook whatever I want." In fine-dining restaurants in France, he was taught that seasonality was not important; in California, he rejoices in feeling "in

Patina's Classics

Appetizers

Corn blinis with fennel marinated salmon, crème fraîche and red bell pepper sauce $13.00
Santa Barbara shrimp with mashed potatoes and potato truffle chips $15.00
Potato roll of scallops with brown butter vinaigrette $13.85

Main Courses

Gratin of lamb with mashed potatoes and garlic $24.95
Peppered tournedos of tuna with bok choy and ponzu sauce $24.75

Fish

Lasagna of large pieces of buttery potato plaques with basic salmon
and little neck clam juice $24.50
Seared whitefish with French fries "not fried", roasted garlic cloves and brandade $24.50
Maine lobster à-la-Thai   Market Price

*Our philosophy is to use the freshest fish...so please forgive us, if the fisherman
didn't catch the fish today for the chef.*

Meat

Chicken with carrot rounds and fresh thyme lemon sauce $23.75
Roasted rabbit with polenta gnocchi, roasted shiitake and everything from the rabbit $25.95
Buttery potato chips with high cholesterol foie gras and squab $25.00
Unfashionable pepper steak $24.50
Roasted medallion of rack of lamb with carrots, pearl onions, garlic, chanterelles
and roasted yukon potatoes $26.50
A roasted piece of a pig called suckling with a basic polenta gnocchi
only available on Wednesday $23.50
Medallion of venison with celery root pancakes and butter pepper sauce $24.75

The Garden Menu will be back on the first day of Spring!

Chef's Menu

A five-course menu based on the freshest market ingredients available
$59.50

Inquire about our upcoming special events:
Valentine's Day Dinner on February 14, 1995
and
Truffle Dinners on February 15 and 16, 1995

*For special entertaining, Patina Restaurant offers three beautiful private dining rooms
and the services of our catering division for off-site functions.*

*In downtown Los Angeles, visit our new café, Patinette at the Museum of Contemporary Art, for classy take out breakfast and lunch. Also,
watch for the opening in early February of Café Pinot, an exciting brasserie-style restaurant located next to the Los Angeles public library.
Complimentary shuttle service will be provided to the Music Center.*

January 13, 1994

Joachim Splichals's menu at Patina Restaurant, January 13, 1994,
with the famed potato lasagna and Asian touches on the
French-inspired cuisine.

tune with the seasons. I know when corn is coming; I know the first peach. I may not get the first one if I don't think they're good yet, but I know they're here."

Roland's friend and former *sous chef* Gerald Hirigoyen is another European-trained chef who embraced the California produce-centric approach to food. Unlike Roland, who had worked in Michelin-rated restaurants with fine fresh ingredients but no commitment to changing food according to the time of year, Gerald grew up in a family of good cooks who always followed the seasons. "When I first came [to California], we didn't quite have seasonality. I've seen the evolution of the product and of seasonality. When I worked at Lafayette restaurant, I was very limited in what I could use—I had spinach and carrots and frozen foods." As a professionally trained chef, he simply made the best of what he had.

GERALD HIRIGOYEN

Le St. Tropez and Fringale, San Francisco

Gerald Hirigoyen started out as a pastry chef in his hometown of Biarritz. His father told him, "Pastry is going to give you some discipline. Once you know pastry, you can switch to the other side and do both." When he was only thirteen, Gerald moved to Paris on his own. "When I look at my boys at thirteen, I can't believe I was working at this age. But it gives you a good perspective. You go through all the emotions and the difficulty. In Paris, I caught the infectious disease of wanting to cook and wanting to learn. It was perfect for me."

At twenty-one, Gerald was at a crossroads in his career. Should he stay with his boss in Paris, where he was getting rudimentary kitchen training along with the pastry work? Or should he follow his heart and go to California? A Basque friend and mentor set him up with some contacts on the West Coast, and Gerald seized the opportunity. When his intended job in a commercial bakery on the Peninsula did not pan out, he came to San Francisco with suitcase in hand. At the first French restaurant he approached, he was told to go to Le Castel, where there was a new young chef, Roland Passot. "Roland was a driven young man," recalled Gerald, "and he's driven to this day, like we all are, very dedicated to his profession. We had a five-minute interview. He asked me what I wanted to do and I said, 'Listen, I'll do anything for you. I can cook. I can do desserts.' I was a perfect candidate for him. It was only the two of us in the kitchen, plus the helpers, so he used to do the meat, and I used to do the fish, and that little restaurant got some attention. We tried to elevate it and do something different.

It was a fun experience, and I felt like I was back into that groove of being professional and wanting to do my best."

The stint at Le Castel lasted only about a year, and then the owners sold the restaurant. After a brief tenure at a new restaurant, Le Vaudeville, which folded, Gerald tried but failed to get a job at Chez Panisse. Jean-Pierre Moullé was already there, and Gerald suspected that Alice Waters was wary of hiring another French-trained chef, preferring someone with a less structured approach to food. He was hired instead as chef at Lafayette on Pacific Avenue. It had a tiny kitchen and an even tinier budget, but Gerald managed to cook excellent food there. That brought him to the attention of restaurateur Jean-Baptiste Lorda, who was in need of a chef. He partnered with Gerald at Le St. Tropez on Clement Street and later at the very successful Fringale, where Gerald served bistro fare along with a few Basque dishes from his heritage.

Gerald credits his parents for his passion for cooking and exemplary ingredients. They were avid cooks and canned their own vegetables and fruit. "My uncle had a farm, and I grew up with seasonality. We didn't eat green beans in winter except [for] the canned ones that my father was so proud to have [put up] in the summer.

"I'm very conscious of the freshness of the product, like everybody else. I am moving away from the heavy sauces. In France, people are used to eating in certain ways, and they're more difficult to change. Here, people don't necessarily have a foundation [in technique], which can be difficult because they don't understand certain things, but the good thing is that they're open to anything. European chefs are sort of restrained, and they know not to put crazy stuff together. Here you can evolve because you know that if you try to do certain things, it probably will work, because in the end it's good food."

In spite of an abundance of fresh produce in European markets, Gerald found that much of it didn't show up on the plate in restaurants. "In Europe you get fish and a potato, but you don't get a lot of vegetables. Spain is even worse—you get unripe tomatoes. In California, no matter what you order, you've got vegetables on that plate. It's funny, because my vegetable bill is more than my fish bill.

"In California we include the vegetables in the profile of the dish. When you compose a plate, you think about what the vegetable is going to be, and how its flavor works with the other things. All my dishes have different vegetables. The lamb comes with braised fennel and little confit potatoes. The chicken comes with parsnips. The sea bass is with Brussels sprouts right now. You work with the season, then balance the flavors. It's a whole composition. Fruit's also important to the composition throughout the season."

After years of running classic French restaurants, in 2002 Gerald returned to his roots and opened the Basque-inspired Piperade. The cuisine has been a part of California's culinary landscape for a long time, mostly associated with Basque immigrants who opened casual family-style restaurants to feed their communities. Gerald's goal was to raise Basque cooking to the level of fine dining. "It was interesting for me to put [a cuisine] like that on the map, to revive it and keep it alive. People were intrigued. There's a generation of older people who grew up with their parents going to the Basque dinner, and to this day, they're still coming. It's funny because when I go to the Basque regions in Spain or France, I look forward to coming back here, where there's a healthy way of eating. California has been a great place for me."

A small but significant contingent of chefs trained in Asia. Kazuto Matsusaka, Hiro Sone, and Udo Nechutnys studied in Osaka at the esteemed culinary school École Technique Hôtelière Tsuji. There they received impeccable training, especially in knife skills. They learned the Asian cooking techniques of stir-frying, grilling, frying tempura, preparing sushi, pickling, and preserving. They were taught the traditional ingredients and plating styles of Japan and the fundamentals of the rich and varied cuisines of China, Singapore, and Thailand. Given the status of French cooking in the culinary world, they were instructed in European cooking techniques and recipes as well.

While most European chefs who came to California became established in Eurocentric restaurants, usually French or Italian, Asian chefs often did not end up in traditional Asian restaurants. Kazuto Matsusaka worked with Michel Blanchet at Jean Bertranou's L'Ermitage and with Wolfgang Puck at Spago and Chinois on Main before opening Zenzero and then Beacon, where he served Asian fusion food. Alex Ong, who undertook a formal apprenticeship at the Shangri-La Hotel in Kuala Lumpur, trained in French cuisine at the Ritz Hotel chain, and then brought his knowledge of Asian flavors to Stars. Hiro Sone collaborated with Wolfgang Puck at Spago before he opened the eclectic Terra in the Napa Valley.

HIRO SONE AND LISSA DOUMANI

Spago, Beverly Hills; Terra, St. Helena

Hiro Sone owns Terra in St. Helena with his wife, Lissa Doumani, whom he met while working for Wolfgang Puck at Spago in 1983. Hiro studied in Japan at the

École Technique Hôtelière Tsuji, where he trained under Paul Bocuse, Pierre Troisgros, and Joël Robuchon. For Lissa, the restaurant life was "bred in." Her father, Carl Doumani, was owner of Stags' Leap Winery as well as two Mexican restaurants in Los Angeles, and she always knew she would have a restaurant of her own someday. She moved to LA and talked Wolfgang Puck into hiring her when Spago was only a couple of months old. "The first day, I peeled a case of asparagus, and the next day I went to work with Nancy Silverton, making desserts and pastries, and that's where I stayed."

Hiro was cooking at an Italian restaurant in Tokyo when a friend introduced him to investors planning to open a Japanese branch of Spago. "They explained that Spago's cooking was called California cuisine. That was first time I heard of it. They told me the chef was from Austria but had been working at three-star Michelin restaurants in France. I didn't know what California cuisine was, but the background sounded French, and I had experience with that, so I thought maybe I could cook it."

Hiro was brought to California for training at the original Spago. To educate himself, he asked everybody what California cuisine was, but nobody could give him a clear answer. He started studying what they were cooking and what products were available in the kitchen and at the market. Like Wolfgang Puck, Michel Richard, and Joachim Splichal, Hiro began eating out in LA, and not just in restaurants featuring California cuisine. "I tried Thai restaurants, Vietnamese restaurants, Mexican restaurants, understanding the culture and background of each, and kind of melding everything on a plate. I started understanding what's going on here, but I still didn't know how to explain California cuisine."

After training at Spago LA, Hiro returned to Japan to open the restaurant's Tokyo outpost, but he found that California cuisine could not be transplanted to foreign soil. "Wolfgang used to make angel-hair noodles with goat cheese sauce," said Hiro. "He used goat cheese from Laura Chenel. When I tried to do exactly the same food in Tokyo, that goat cheese was not available, so I had to use French goat cheese. Then I asked, 'Is this California cuisine?' Even if the recipes are exactly the same here and over there, the availability of ingredients is different."

"It's the purveyors that aren't available, the little growers," said Lissa. "There aren't farmers' markets and things like that. So if you think of California cuisine as farm-to-table, and pairing with your purveyors, in this case, your purveyors are Japanese, and what you're doing is not California cuisine because you're not in California."

After getting Spago Tokyo off the ground, Hiro returned to the States to become chef at Spago LA. In 1988, he and Lissa, then married, left to open their own restaurant, Terra. "We found this location in St. Helena," Hiro recalled, "and the minute we looked at the building, we said, 'Wow, this is a great spot.' We told Wolfgang, 'We are leaving.' We had a really short time to move from Los Angeles to St. Helena."

"Everybody told us to do pizza," said Lissa. "And we were saying, no. It's been done. We don't need to do it just because we're both from Spago." Hiro added, "At Spago, everything is fresh, basically a showcase for ingredients. A simple way to prepare vegetables, very *à la minute,* just sauté quickly, then add a simple sauce. Instead I want to do *ragù* because it cooks a long time—a classic approach. More rustic, too." Lissa chimed in, "We wanted bigger flavors, more developed, because the other side had been like a grilled veal chop with baby vegetables with a very light sauce, which was delicious, but we had moved on from that. We wanted more depth to what we were making."

That style of cooking suited Terra's Napa Valley clientele. "The Napa Valley has many immigrants from Italy," said Hiro. "They ate mom's cooking, so Italian cooking was great for us to do. *Ragù,* innards, tripe, tongue, sweetbreads—they loved those things." Lissa added, "Napa was much more open to that than people would've been in Los Angeles, probably even at that time, in the late 1980s."

When Terra opened, only a few dishes on the menu had Japanese elements, because Hiro didn't want Asian flavors to dominate his Napa Valley cooking. "Hiro is Japanese," said Lissa, "so some of that comes into the food. He might know if you put soy sauce here, even though it's a Western dish, it's going to develop a deeper flavor. He did an eggplant dish where you deep-fried it, then blanched it with water to take the oil out, and then cooked it again with the sauce. It created a lighter eggplant, the way they do it in Japan. That went with the veal, and people were crazy for it."

Restaurant guides and newspapers had trouble categorizing Terra's cooking. "Each year, we were in a different category," they laughed. "One year was best Italian restaurant. (Good friends of ours in Los Angeles said, 'Congratulations?') Then one year was fusion. Also best California or best American. Mediterranean a couple times. We've been just about everything."

In the days before California cuisine, once a French restaurant, always a French restaurant. Whether they were professionally trained or had forged their own path, the new California cuisine chefs resisted labeling. They did not want their restaurants to be categorized and constrained. Stars started off serving hamburgers and andouille-infused gumbo alongside French- and Italian-inspired dishes, added salsas from south of the border, and eventually assimilated more Asian ingredients as Jeremiah Tower expanded his restaurant domain into Singapore and Hong Kong. Conversely, at Square One we opened with a California menu with global touches but over the years focused more on the Mediterranean. Our restaurants were a work in progress, a voyage of discovery, and our customers were delighted to come along for the ride.

4

Women Chefs and Innovation

The New Collaborative Kitchen

In California no one said to a woman, "You can't run a restaurant—you're a woman." Look how many women chefs we had here.

—Sherry Irene Virbila, *Los Angeles Times* restaurant reviewer

At Square One, my staff and I began our day at 7 A.M., gathered around a central table. Unlike in the conventional kitchen brigade, where a prep crew did the drudge work required to execute the menu, we worked as a group. Together we chopped hundreds of pounds of onions, made buckets of mirepoix, peeled endless heads of garlic, and trimmed caseloads of artichokes. While we prepped we talked about food and the menu of the day. Then we would break up, go to our stations, and continue the prep for our own *mise en place*. Working together energized us. Tasting together allowed us to establish the benchmark flavors—the common palate of the restaurant. It was a style I had learned at Chez Panisse, and I thought it worked well.

There was no real pecking order. Cooks rotated to different stations according to their skills and training. When hiring, I aimed for a balance of men and women in the kitchen. Too many women and the pace slowed down with conversation; too many men and things overheated as competition took over. When writing the weekly schedule, I took into account child care issues for both sexes. I had been a mom with young children and knew that cooks would stay with the restaurant longer if their schedule supported their home needs. A nonmacho and noncompetitive work environment made for harmony and longevity. As a result of this we had very little turnover in the kitchen and on the floor. We were a workplace family that tolerated individual quirks and idiosyncrasies because we were bound together in the mission of producing and serving great food.

Challenging Male Domination of the Cooking Profession

When Alice Waters opened Chez Panisse as a "country French" restaurant, she had never worked in a restaurant and was unaware of how the classic French kitchen was organized. But this naïve move by a passionate amateur changed the way many kitchens were run in California. Alice hired Victoria Wise as her first chef in 1972, and then she hired more women for Chez Panisse Café in 1980. "Alice was really interested in hiring women in the restaurant," said her partner and pastry chef Lindsey Shere. "She made a point of doing it whenever she could, and I think that's one of the things that made Chez Panisse such a different kind of place to work, a much more comfortable place." Men and women worked side by side, hired for their palate rather than their gender.

Although there had always been *mammas* in restaurant kitchens in Italy and women who ran small family restaurants in France (usually called La Mère something or other), the classic restaurant kitchens and cooking schools were inhospitable to women. The standard *brigade de cuisine* emulates a hierarchical military model: the head chef, or *chef de cuisine,* is followed by the *sous chef* (subchef), the *chefs de partie* (line cooks who work the designated stations), and, at the bottom, the *commis* (junior chef, aka prep slave). In these rigid and regimented domains overseen by men, the instructors and chefs were often abusive, even to other men. Extreme competitiveness was promoted, along with mastering technique and building physical endurance and speed—a "chop 'til you drop" mentality. Chef Gary Danko was "appalled" by the macho behavior he witnessed at the Culinary Institute of America: "The chefs were teaching how fast you could bone a chicken. It was a speed race, a competition, not like the women's cooking I had come to know, which came from the heart." Authority was not questioned. Innovation was not encouraged. There was a right way and a wrong way.

Linda Carucci, culinary instructor and former chef-director of the International Culinary School at the Art Institute of California, was one of the few women who attended the California Culinary Academy in its early days. All the chef-instructors were men and either were French or had trained in France. As she recalled, "They came up through an apprenticeship system, so they didn't know how to treat us. In *garde manger,* the first lesson on mayonnaise—I will never forget this—we were told, 'And for the girls, when you have your period, you do not create the mayonnaise. It will break.' We looked at each other, just incredulous. This was 1983. You'd have thought it was 1883.

"When we did butchery and made steak tartare, or when we had raw oysters, some of the chefs would pull the men aside and make some mention about how it gives you a stiff erection. And the women would be, 'What are these guys talking about?!'"

These were not Linda's only experiences of sexism in the kitchen. She explained how the male chefs called all the women "Mommy": "I was twenty-seven; I didn't have children; I wasn't even involved in a relationship. I was there on a Saturday helping them with a special dinner, and executive chef Jean-Luc Chassereau said, 'Mommy, are you gonna make lunch for us?' I didn't pay attention, and he came right up in my face and said, 'Mommy, are you gonna make lunch for us? Start slicing the meat!' And I said, 'Why did you call me that?' and he said, 'Well, you're a housewife, right?' There was this classification: either you're serious or you're a housewife. It was very, very strange, especially in light of the fact that a woman, Danielle Carlisle, was the president of the California Culinary Academy."

Every Friday the students would prepare a classical buffet, reminiscent of those served on old-fashioned cruise ships and in *grand luxe* hotel dining rooms. The hors d'oeuvres were displayed on a mirrored surface for a glitzy presentation. Linda's *garde manger* instructor told her to make the mirror platter with pâté and slices of elaborate stuffed-meat dishes such as *galantine* and *ballotine*. She said, "Chef, I've done the *galantines* and *ballotines*. [But] I wasn't exposed to Japanese food till I came to California. For the next project, I would really like to make a sushi mirror." He replied that sushi was never included on the grand buffet. Linda volunteered to pay for the ingredients and promised to do a spectacular job. She begged him to reconsider, but again he said no. One of the male students overheard this conversation and afterward confided that he also wanted to do sushi. He approached the chef the next day and said, "Linda and I want to do this together." Because he was a man, they were allowed to do it.

Linda navigated the sexist environment of the California Culinary Academy with the help of a few understanding and encouraging instructors, including Robert Jorin and Lars Kronmark. She praised Lars, who now teaches at the Culinary Institute of America in St. Helena, as "a fabulous instructor, and a gentleman." As for that sushi mirror, Lars now teaches contemporary seafood charcuterie at the Culinary Institute of America—including sushi, *boquerónes*, cured salmon, salmon pastrami, and tuna confit.

LARS KRONMARK

California Culinary Academy, San Francisco; Culinary Institute of America, St. Helena

Lars Kronmark was one of the early instructors at the California Culinary Academy in San Francisco, which opened in 1977, and he has been on the faculty of the Culinary Institute of America's St. Helena campus since its founding in 1995. He emigrated to the United States from Denmark in late 1979 and took a job as a country club chef in Sacramento in order to get his green card. In 1981, he started teaching at the Culinary Academy. He witnessed major changes in culinary education and observed and participated in the evolution of cuisine in California. Despite his strict training in Europe, he recognized that California was a burgeoning culinary environment and was open-minded and collaborative with his students.

"My first class taught me a lot about food. The students challenged me. Why do we have to do it this way? Why do we have to call it fricassee? Why do we have to use a sauté pan? Couldn't we grill it? At first I was answering from my classical training. Then in 1982 or 1983 we snuck in originality. Students from New Orleans would bring in okra. They would bring in tasso. My students and I were not afraid to experiment. Ken Hom would take our students on walking tours of Chinatown. Many times I tagged along, and it was eye-opening.

"We started using more Italian ingredients because they were so tied in to Northern California. Carlo Middione showed me the Italian part of San Francisco, and we brought in good coffees, sausages, fennel. To discover all those ingredients in Northern California was great. It was the first time I ever tasted a grilled peach or had mango cilantro salsa. I was called 'cilantro chef' at the CCA because I loved cilantro."

Lars met Laura Chenel in 1982 or 1983, when she came to the Culinary Academy to present her goat cheese. "Even though we had Vella cheese and Marin cheese, this was the first goat cheese, and it was handcrafted. Laura Chenel started something new and showed you could do it without having a family who'd done it for two hundred years.

"These changes brought discomfort to some of the French chefs I worked with. They were screaming and squirming. They were not happy to see bok choy and ginger and whatever else the students [brought back]. I was young enough to join the group that wanted to do new, interesting, and fresh stuff.

Some French chefs didn't want to do that. A lot of people had to leave because they would not change their way of being. I was at the Culinary Academy right at the pivot of change."

Lars moved up to St. Helena when the CIA opened. It offered a different teaching climate and a global food curriculum, including Mediterranean and Asian food, small plates from many parts of the world, and international grilling. The program reflected what was happening in the country and broadened the approach to food beyond classic French training. It studied what was selling in restaurants.

Lars said he has come full circle. "It was a big move for the CIA to put a school here and say it's not happening just on the East Coast—we need to be in the Napa Valley. When we started in 1995, this school had a vision about organic food, about pure ingredients and complete openness to food as long as it was good and authentic. And we started with such an explosion of good things that it's still kind of settling. You know why I didn't go back to Denmark? When I came to San Francisco in 1981, people appreciated my classical training because I knew how to cook mussels, but what I didn't know was that I could add Italian or Asian flavors to the mussels, or put in curry. I had the foundation, and many of the talented people there didn't have that background, but they had the nose for flavor. I learned so much and could not go back."

Lars stayed in California because he thrived in the multicultural, cooperative environment. When presented with a new idea, he always said, "Yes, let's try it." That generous spirit extended to his treatment of his colleagues and students. Man or woman, he figured that if they were in culinary school, they were serious.

In a delicious irony, Linda Carucci eventually went back to the California Culinary Academy—as the dean. She became dean of students in 1989 and the next year was made registrar and dean of the academy. At that point, a quarter of the students were women, but there were still no full-time female instructors. Linda said, "Surely, there are women qualified to teach here." And the president said, "Bring 'em on." So she hired a few.

"It got better," Linda reported. "There would be some kooky women—not that we didn't have our share of kooky guys—but the women would be held up as examples. 'You see what happens when you bring one in.' I'm so glad those days are over, and now, jump ahead to 2008, and I'm hiring the first faculty at the Culinary School at the Art Institute. I say to the dean, 'I don't know how to tell you this, but it could be that all the first faculty we hire in our culinary program are women.' And she said, 'I have no problem with that.' So much has changed."

From 1986 to 1993 I wrote a regular column for the *San Francisco Chronicle* under the heading "California Cuisine." I covered timely food topics and behind-the-scenes restaurant stories, pre–Anthony Bourdain, minus the expletives. In 1992 food editor Michael Bauer asked me to write about the upsurge in the number of women chefs in the Bay Area. I discovered that my sister chefs and I were fortunate to be in San Francisco, a permissive and progressive culinary environment where women were able to be entrepreneurial and succeed. Despite the growing number of women in cooking schools and professional kitchens, there were very few recognized female chefs in New York, Los Angeles, Chicago, and New Orleans, and even fewer in cities with small but burgeoning restaurant communities, such as Atlanta, Seattle, and Boston.

"In 1985, the dominant chef culture in New York was French," said Danny Meyer. "It was male, macho." In the 1980s, most of the recognized, and rare, female chefs in New York were chef-owners: Anne Rosenzweig at Arcadia, Josefina Howard at Rosa Mexicana, Zarela Martinez at Zarela, and Sarabeth Levine at Sarabeth's Kitchen. Debra Ponzek at Montrachet had been the *sous chef* under Brian Whitmer and inherited the chef position when he left, although she cooked unannounced for months. Lidia Bastianich ran the kitchen at Felidia and partnered with her husband and later her son and daughter as well to open additional restaurants.

Even as chef-owners, women faced obstacles. In cities as competitive as New York or Los Angeles you had to make a giant splash when you opened a restaurant to get any media coverage. It could be a very expensive proposition. Traditionally, men had an easier time raising capital to fund a restaurant than women, so fewer women owned restaurants.

In Los Angeles, there was a boys' club led by European chefs, which spurred Elka Gilmore to leave the city and move to San Francisco to open Elka in 1992. As in New York, the few women chefs in LA succeeded mainly because they owned their restaurants. In the 1980s the only well-known women chefs in LA were Mary Sue Milliken and Susan Feniger of City Restaurant and Border Grill; Nancy Silverton of Campanile, which she owned with her former husband, chef Mark Peel; and Evan Kleiman at Angeli Caffe. The Caffe, and later Trattoria Angeli and Angeli Mare, were all started with a male partner to help with fund-raising. A few women worked at Citrus, Patina, Trumps, Chianti, Chasen's, 72 Market, Maple Drive, Chinois, Spago, Celestino, and Valentino, but the head chefs were men. Today Suzanne Goin and Suzanne Tracht have joined the intimate community of women chefs in Los Angeles.

Mary Sue Milliken began her professional career in Chicago at the esteemed Le Perroquet, though initially chef-owner Jovan Trboyevic told her "she was too attractive a woman to work in the kitchen and she should get herself a job as a hat-check girl." After she commenced a letter-writing campaign to win her job, "She convinced me she could handle herself and the job in the kitchen," Trboyevic told the *Chicago Tribune*. According to Ruth Reichl, "They made her kill, like, a hundred lobsters. But she ended up running the kitchen." Experiences like this in male-dominated restaurants fueled Mary Sue's and Susan Feniger's determination to open City Café on their own. "We had this conversation [about sexism] a million times and thought, fuck that, we're not gonna stay working for these guys even if we have to make a lot less money and start out with a peanut of a restaurant. We're going to call our own shots."

Catherine Pantsios found East Coast kitchens so suffocating that she eventually packed her knife kit and moved to San Francisco. She was tired of working in restaurants that barely tolerated women: "It was very discouraging. At that time I could think of three women chefs in New York, but San Francisco seemed very female dominated. There were female role models. You could say, 'it worked for them, it'll work for me.'"

Northern California in the mid-1980s was a welcoming environment. In the Bay Area you could open a low-profile place on a shoestring budget and still get press coverage and a clientele eager for food rather than froufrou. You did not need Baccarat glassware, Limoges china, and $600 chairs to succeed. There was competition, but the theatrical one-upmanship that prevailed in other cities was kept to a minimum. There was no old boys' network to fight, either; the Bay Area restaurant community was and remains wide open and liberal.

Women chefs hired, mentored, and promoted other women. Judy Rodgers, Patricia Curtan, Amaryll Schwertner, Peggy Smith, Catherine Brandel, and Barbara Haimes all passed through Alice Waters's kitchen at Chez Panisse. Hayes Street Grill's Patricia Unterman had Jacqueline Buchanan in the kitchen, and Catherine Pantsios worked there before she opened Zola's, where she cooked with Rachel Gardner. Elka Gilmore worked with Traci Des Jardins and Elizabeth Falkner at her eponymous restaurant, Elka. At Square One, I hired Wendy Brucker, Barbara Haimes, Amaryll Schwertner, Heidi Krahling, and pastry chefs Diane Dexter and Jennifer Millar, along with a number of other talented women. Many in turn went on to run their own kitchens, including Heidi Krahling at Butler's in Mill Valley and Amaryll Schwertner at Mudd's in San Ramon and Boulette's Larder in San Francisco.

In the Bay Area, you could oversee the restaurant without having to own it. At Greens, Deborah Madison and Annie Somerville led the kitchen. Also running but not owning restaurants were Donia Bijan and Maria Helm Sinskey at Sherman House, Gloria Ciccarone-Nehls at Big 4 Restaurant, and Rick O'Connell at Rosalie's, all in San Francisco, Alison Negrin at Bridges in Danville, and Patricia Windisch at Chateau Souverain in the Alexander Valley. Others did own and head up their kitchens, including Biba Caggiano of Biba Restaurant in Sacramento, Regina Charboneau of Biscuits and Blues, Suzette Gresham at Acquerello, Bette Kroening of Bette's Oceanview Diner in Berkeley, Donna Scala at Bistro Don Giovanni in the Napa Valley, and many chefs mentioned elsewhere. Women who owned their restaurants often hired other women for important positions, not relegating them exclusively to the pastry or pantry departments, which were the traditional places for women in fine-dining restaurants. Of the stars in pastry, Lindsey Shere was a role model in Northern California.

LINDSEY SHERE

Chez Panisse, Berkeley

Pastry chef and founding partner Lindsey Shere was the only person in the kitchen who was my age when I began work at Chez Panisse. The rest of the staff were just kids. In that sea of chaos and melodrama, Lindsey was an island of calm and concentration. Judy Rodgers called her "the rock." Her quiet demeanor was accompanied by an intuitive sense of how to balance flavors and integrate dessert into the menu rather than leaving it as a disconnected after-thought at the end of a meal. Once you tasted Lindsey's signature almond tart or her Meyer lemon and peach ice creams, you never forgot them. She mentored pastry chefs David Lebovitz, Diane Dexter, Craig Sutter, and Mary Jo Thoresen, as well as chefs Deborah Madison and Mark Peel. Lindsey's book *Chez Panisse Desserts* was first published in 1985 and is still in print.

Lindsey was born in Chicago but moved with her family to a ranch in Healdsburg, in Sonoma County, when she was twelve. "The years on the ranch were formative because it seemed like coming to paradise from where we had been. You could pick oranges off the tree in the winter. That was mind-boggling."

She married musician, journalist, and critic Charles Shere in 1957 and had three children. While working at the Bay Area radio station KPFA in the mid-1960s, Charles met David Goines, who was Alice Waters's boyfriend at the time. "We used to visit a lot with one another and dined together often. At that time,

Alice was doing recipes for the *San Francisco Express Times*. The 'Thirty Recipes Suitable for Framing' print series [designed by Goines] came out of those."

When Lindsey's youngest child was eight, Alice asked Lindsey if she would make desserts for a restaurant she was thinking of opening. "I said, 'What the heck. Not really doing much of anything else at this point, all the kids are in school.' I had no idea what I might be getting into. I was making desserts in that little cottage behind the building and ferrying them into the restaurant. I remember years of trying to keep one step ahead of what we needed, trying to figure out how to make something that I'd never made before."

Lindsey had no professional culinary training and drew her inspiration from recipes by Elizabeth David, Ada Boni, James Beard, Richard Olney, Robert Courtine, and Waverly Root. She had been fascinated by baking since she was eight or nine years old. "It was something I loved to do. My sister says that they had to eat cake all the time. They were experimented on a lot. So I had a lot of hands-on experience, but nothing like restaurant experience. I had to learn by the seat of my pants every day."

Lindsey went to Europe in 1974, visiting France, Italy, Holland, and Austria. She spent a week at the Auberge of the Flowering Hearth in France, made famous by Roy Andries De Groot's book of the same name, which had been published the previous year. "It was this charming little hotel with a wonderful old-fashioned dining room. I had a pear tart with crème fraîche and pepper. It was so delicious and interesting, not like anything else I'd ever had."

At Chez Panisse, she was allowed creative freedom. "Alice pretty much left it to me. If there were problems, she said what she thought, and we talked about them. But in general, I tried to do things that I thought she wanted, and the kinds of things that she liked. I don't think there was ever much friction between us.

"I mostly worked with fruit because it seemed to me that after a big dinner you didn't want heavy, rich desserts." She shopped at the Monterey Market and obtained special items from her family. "I used to get violets from my father, and plums from my mother. My father got other stuff for me too, because he had a lot of connections, they both did, around Healdsburg. People were still growing Gravensteins then, and there were lots of different kinds of apples. We got stuff from David Eichorn, who had blackberries growing in Berkeley, and Meyer lemons from people's backyards.

"Chez Panisse was probably different from many places in that there was constant tasting of things, and constant trying to figure out how to improve them. Most of the people in the kitchen knew something about the history of food and had read important people like Elizabeth David." It was a stimulating environment that fostered culinary dialogue and experimentation.

Lindsey's quietly elegant desserts did not need over-the-top presentations to make a memorable impression. They had flavor and finesse. To this day I and many others turn to her cookbook for inspiration.

Without the efforts of so many women chefs, California cuisine would not have evolved as it did. Many of us had worked together in various kitchens, and we shared a sensibility about food based on how it nurtured our families, our community, and the people we loved. We served more vegetables on the plate and didn't try to disguise the natural flavors of the food with too much technique. In Northern California in the 1980s, other than Jeremiah Tower, Mark Miller, and Bradley Ogden, men weren't associated with the newer California restaurants. The few European imports—Hubert Keller, Roland Passot, and Julian Serrano—were operating classic French restaurants but didn't dominate the scene. Even at Jeremiah's Stars, Noreen Lam, Loretta Keller, and Emily Luchetti had a major impact. It was largely a woman-run food community.

To keep the momentum going, in 1993 Barbara Tropp of China Moon founded Women Chefs and Restaurateurs, an organization dedicated to promoting the advancement of women in the restaurant industry. I was a founding member on the board, along with Barbara Lazaroff, Mary Sue Milliken, Elka Gilmore, Anne Rosenzweig, Lidia Bastianich, and Johanne Killeen. Emily Luchetti soon joined. Barbara was convinced that women starting out in the business needed support from their peers, especially those who had succeeded in opening their own places. The group held dinners to raise money for awards, scholarships, and organizational expenses and hosted conferences where women could share their experiences and knowledge, helping women advance in the food world.

Boy and Girl Food

California cuisine has a feminine touch to it at its best. I don't know that guys can cook California [cuisine] quite as well as women.
—Restaurateur Danny Meyer

The female sensibility in Northern California manifested itself in the style of the food being created and served. Most women chefs were cooking the traditional and communal food of memory—*cuisine bonne femme*, or home-style cooking. In 1985, chef Evan Kleiman began offering authentic *cucina casalinga della nonna*, or grandma's home cooking, at Angeli Caffe in Los Angeles. "At the beginning I got a lot of attitude from the Italian guys in town, except for Piero Selvaggio," she said. "I think Piero was taken aback by how successful I was, but he really got it. A lot of the other guys were trying to legitimize Italian food by presenting it as a high-end experience. They didn't have a frame of reference for understanding why we'd be cooking mom and grandma food, and why people were responding to it."

EVAN KLEIMAN

Angeli Caffe, Trattoria Angeli, and Angeli Mare, Los Angeles

Evan Kleiman is an only child of a single mother who started teaching her to cook at the age of nine. Since Evan grew up in LA, it was not surprising that she wanted to pursue a career in the film business. While studying Italian literature and film at UCLA, she had the opportunity to spend time in Italy, where she became fascinated with the home cooking of Italian women. After graduating magna cum laude, she began a graduate program in arts management, but she soon realized that her true calling lay in cooking and catering.

Evan started her restaurant career at Mangia in 1982 as the night chef and kitchen manager. Her talent and work ethic were recognized, and she was recruited by Verdi Ristorante di Musica in Santa Monica to be executive chef. After a year at Verdi she took time off to write her first cookbook, *Cucina Fresca,* published in 1983, followed by *Pasta Fresca* and *Cucina Rustica,* all written with former Mangia colleague Viana La Place. The books became instant classics.

When Evan decided to open a restaurant of her own, she initially wanted it to be an American diner. But she partnered with John Strobel, who "wanted to do Italian. I was like, 'Well, I can do that with my eyes closed. Let's do that.'"

She observed that the high end of the northern Italian restaurant scene had started to fill in after Valentino opened in 1972 and then Rex il Ristorante in 1981. What was missing was the bistro segment of the market. "Everything inexpensive was either an ethnic dive or a chain or a mom-and-pop Italian restaurant, which is not what we think of now when we think of Italian food." So Evan launched what she calls "the first hipster, low-cost, affordable Italian café."

She loved modern architecture and design and had a specific vision for her restaurant. She didn't have much money, but luckily her college classmate Thom Mayne was a brilliant young architect-to-be. Evan approached him, saying, "I have 1,000 square feet that I'd like to set up like a little Italian church, with niches, and with the pizza oven as the altar." He took the job. After designing Angeli Caffe, Thom went on to cofound the influential design firm Morphosis.

Angeli opened its doors in December 1984 and was a sensation. "People would wait in line for two hours to eat salads, antipasti, pizza, and sandwiches," said Evan. "We didn't even add pasta or entrées onto the menu until we were open for a couple of months. I wanted to take it really slow. What I discovered, and what everybody else then discovered thereafter, was that the Italian *gioia di vivere* was totally synchronous with how we saw ourselves then in California." Californians came to Angeli to imbibe the spirit of Italy, of enjoying life, and the restaurant soon expanded from twenty-four to sixty-four seats.

Evan was one of the few women chefs in LA and the first to introduce casual trattoria dining to an audience accustomed to Italo-Continental fare. Ruth Reichl wrote in the *Los Angeles Times* that Evan brought a "whole new character" to the LA restaurant scene: ethnic authenticity "filtered through such sophisticated sensibilities." Chef and author Faith Willinger described the cooking at Angeli as Italian rustic cuisine from the region of California. Angeli quickly became the most copied Italian restaurant concept in LA, serving what we now consider the beloved essentials of Italian food—pasta, pizza, and antipasti—all on one menu.

In the early days, many ingredients were difficult to source. Evan struggled to find fresh basil, flat-leaf parsley, and Italian cheeses. Mozzarella had to be flown in from Italy, along with Parmesan and even pasta. Change came step by step. "Soon after I opened Angeli, a couple of guys from Puglia who had moved here came knocking on my door. They were making cheese. It was incredible. All of a sudden I had great ricotta and no longer had to make my own."

In 1987, Michele Saee, an acolyte of Morphosis and Evan's boyfriend at the time, designed Evan's cutting-edge second restaurant, Trattoria Angeli. "Michele and I had the private room like a floating cube in the middle of the space. We didn't want a drop ceiling; we wanted the trusses to be exposed. We built a catwalk that went to the wine storage area, and in the front of the building, like all the restaurants, was this piece of sculpture made basically of quartz and steel." Unfortunately, hassles with the health and building departments prevented her from putting in an open kitchen.

Next she and John Strobel opened Angeli Mare in 1989, but both it and Trattoria Angeli closed within a few years, victims of the recession in 1991 and

1992. Angeli Caffe, however, was a mainstay on Melrose Avenue for twenty-seven years, until it closed in 2012.

An important mover in the LA food community, Evan started the city's first Slow Food chapter and was on the board of the Hollywood farmers' market. Since 1998 she has been the host of KCRW's *Good Food* program. *Los Angeles Times* restaurant critic Jonathan Gold called Evan "a connector. She has everyone on her speed dial, and everyone is willing to do what she wants at the drop of a hat, including me."

The terms "boy food" and "girl food" are shorthand in the industry for two distinct styles of cooking. The division is readily acknowledged by many in the restaurant profession—not to trivialize what we do, but to show our sense of humor in recognizing that there are differences in food cooked by men and women. To generalize, those practicing the male style are competitive and look for the latest thing to give their cooking an edge—*sous vide*, foam, complicated butchering techniques, elaborate plating, whatever it takes to show off their technical and professional prowess. Seeking recognition, they will invent dishes based on intricate techniques and are not afraid to show off their creativity by deconstructing classic dishes and using those dishes' components to present familiar foods in new ways—taking them apart and arraying the individual ingredients on the plate. They push the limits with lengthy tasting menus, employing as many methods and tools as possible to demonstrate their training and skill. Equating money with success, many do not hesitate to open multiple locations in order to promote their "culinary brands," leaving others in charge of their kitchens and reputations and not losing sleep over it.

Those cooking "girl food" are in general less inclined to expand their territory, preferring instead to stay at a single restaurant, bonding with staff and regular customers. (This may have contributed to the fact that most of the Bay Area restaurants that have been in business for over thirty years, including Flea Street Café, Chez Panisse, Greens, Zuni Café, Hayes Street Grill, and Mustards, are headed by women.) These cooks are more apt to consider their restaurant an extension of home. They want to put their personal imprint on the food they serve, and they want to be there to taste it. Women are in professional kitchens today for the same reason that they were inspired to make food ten thousand years ago—because they want to feed people, nourish them, and make them feel good. Of course, women chefs must also pay attention to the bottom line, but they tend to measure their success and satisfaction in the happiness of their staff and the looks on the faces of their patrons when they taste their food.

Women chefs typically feel less need to reinvent the wheel in a culinary sense. They do not value innovation and creativity for their own sake, and they rarely substitute one thing for another purely for the sake of novelty. They are not interested in deconstructing traditional recipes unless goaded to do so for a TV show (out of the need to garner good press for their restaurant). Rather than focus on technique, they focus on ingredients. Culinary instructor Barbara Haimes noted, "When women went into the kitchen, there was less 'Let's turn this into something else' as opposed to 'Let's see what's in this—what this ingredient says to us.' The spirit of the kitchen changed." Instead of starting with a dish concept and then finding ingredients to use, women start with the ingredients and then select a dish that uses them well. For the most part female chefs rely on simple plating— no dots of sauce or smears that might remind them of baby diapers.

Chef Chris Lee, formerly of Chez Panisse and Eccolo, believes that it was the influence of women chefs that caused California cuisine to shift attention toward quality ingredients and produce and away from the traditional European entrée, which featured only protein and a starch, and maybe baby carrots as a colorful garnish. "I think I might be taken to task for saying this, but that there were so many women involved is a very important part of what happened here. It went in that [lighter] direction, not just because it was the taste of women, but because they were leaders at that time." California women chefs were the first to give equal value and attention to produce as part of the plate concept, not as a mere embellishment but as a presence in a dish's total flavor profile. Over the years it became a signature of California cuisine to feature produce on the plate, often in the form of bigger salads, soups, and vegetarian pastas.

Setting gender aside, it would be safe to say that there are two types of chefs: those who aim to nurture, and those who aspire to awe. Rather than being purely gendered divisions, I suspect that they are based on a combination of personality and philosophy. A few women, notably Elizabeth Falkner, author of *Demolition Desserts,* and Dominique Crenn, the first female chef to win two Michelin stars at her restaurant Atelier Crenn, are happiest when creating cutting-edge haute cuisine. And many men, for their part, want to please their guests, cook ungimmicky food, and base their cuisine on communal culinary traditions. Craig Stoll at San Francisco's Delfina once teased me by saying, "Hey, Joyce, I hear you say I cook like a girl," and he smiled when he said it.

The Collaborative Kitchen and the Palate Community

[One] element that comes from the collaborative kitchen is a desire to educate the staff, both in the kitchen and in the front of the house, about the food. Letting the staff taste the food. In old-style restaurants, you just sell the food, you don't taste it.

—Chef Catherine Pantsios, Zola's

Perhaps the most significant difference between the new California kitchens and conventional kitchens was that the California kitchens were collaborative rather than hierarchical. Women introduced a cooperative ambience. Catherine Pantsios recalled, "I worked for male chefs who would scream and swear and throw things. But I felt that you didn't need to do that to run the kitchen. To get it done, you talked to people. I felt like I got a lot of respect from the people who worked for me, and that was why they did what I asked them to do. I consciously set about creating a different kind of atmosphere. I wanted the kitchen to be collaborative, and to work with somebody that I felt I could have an equal exchange with."

The fact that Alice Waters hired so many women at Chez Panisse was pioneering, and her kitchen setup was also iconoclastic. She abandoned the hierarchical titles of the *brigade de cuisine* and referred to all the members of her staff simply and democratically as cooks. They rotated and did all the jobs in the kitchen. Men and women worked together and equally in the kitchen, and the women were not segregated in pastry. This was revolutionary.

Judy Rodgers told me that "employees appreciated the nonmacho kitchen, very much a product of women running the show. It wasn't a disruptive, threatening revolution, challenging the powers that be—that wasn't Alice's thing. Delicious was her thing; it was to seduce people." Judy's first formal restaurant job was at Chez Panisse, and her experience there helped influence how she would run the Union Hotel and Zuni Café.

JUDY RODGERS

Zuni Café, San Francisco

When she was sixteen years old, Judy Rodgers went to France as an exchange student. As luck would have it, she was placed with the family of three-star chef Jean Troisgros. There she learned, along with French, the language of cuisine. While she admired the elegant food served in the family's restaurant, Les Frères

Troisgros, it was the everyday food prepared at home that became her model for style and flavor. "The Troisgros food was very simple. It was just the beginning of nouvelle cuisine. Most of the plates at Troisgros were four elements at most, maybe five, with a lot of butter and cream. I watched, and paid attention, and wrote down every single thing I saw and everything I ate.

"[But] Jean was never so happy as when we drove down the block to the schlocky café and had the steak frites. He honestly loved that better than going to a three-star restaurant. It was pretty clear, the food you eat every day is the most important food. This is what we do at Zuni."

Back in the United States, Judy hoped to reproduce the dishes she had eaten in France, but she found it impossible to do so without top-notch ingredients. When she moved to the Bay Area in the fall of 1974 to study art history at Stanford, she thought the situation would be improved, since restaurants had been part of the social fabric of San Francisco since the gold rush. She was disappointed to find that it was "not a food town, [but] a restaurant town. Huge distinction." It took the advent of California cuisine, according to Judy, and the emphasis on quality and authenticity, to raise San Francisco to the status of a food town first and foremost.

When Judy first dined at Chez Panisse around the time of her graduation from Stanford in 1978, she realized that "the restaurant's approach to putting the meal together reminded me of going to dinner at Jean's sister's house. I was so bereft of the spirit and the experience of France that I wanted to be around whenever Chez Panisse would let me. I spent two weeks there. Then Alice wanted to take a leave of absence and needed somebody to do lunch, and she asked me if I would do it. There was no real training—it was that era. At the beginning I was doing 20 to 30 lunches. By the time I left, we were doing 100 to 120.

"I left Chez Panisse thinking, 'OK, this was great, but do I think staying in food is the sensible thing to do with my life? I have no real training.' I went to Europe and landed at a restaurant in southwest France in a town of maybe thirty people and thousands of ducks. The chef, Pepette Arbulo, cooked just with what was grown nearby, a perfect example of the sustainability idiom. It was the pure traditional cooking of one small area of the Landes region, a cuisine tethered to a specific place. You cooked the best you could with what you had."

When Judy came home from France, she was hired as chef for the Union Hotel in Benicia on the recommendation of Marion Cunningham. There she aspired to follow the local cuisine model that she had admired under chef Pepette. "Naïve as I was, I thought I was going to discover this full-blown American cuisine. And the owners of the restaurant were going, 'American cuisine is milkshakes and Reuben sandwiches.' They actually wanted Jell-O. I was thinking, 'No, I want to corn my own beef.' And they were OK with that. But in that era, 1980 or 1981, the notion of a regional American restaurant was pretty new.

"When they said, 'We want hamburgers,' I thought, 'We're going to have the best. We're going to make a hamburger the way Michel Guérard makes puff pastry, or with the same kind of affection and care that you would give for high-ticket foie gras.' There are problems with making hamburgers that way. You can't charge enough for them because they're labor-intensive. But for me it was a really great thing."

Over time, Judy realized that the New England repertoire that they were cooking from was too limiting, and she left for a sojourn in Italy. When she returned to the States in 1986, upon Mark Miller's recommendation, she was hired to open Yellowfingers restaurant in New York. It was originally conceived of as an American restaurant in the manner of the Union Hotel. The savvy owner, Dr. Joe Santo, quickly recognized that Judy's heart was in Italy, and he let her run with it.

During the six months that she was in New York, Billy West, the owner of Zuni Café, visited innumerable times to beg her to come to Zuni. Once she saw the space and felt the general funky vibe, she thought, "I'm on. Kathi Riley had been here for a couple years. She had been my *sous chef* at the Union Hotel, so some of the cooking principles were in place. The Caesar salad was already here, the hamburger was already here. Billy wanted Mexican. I told them what I do was going to be more Italian with some French traditional. I love Mexican, but it's not my idiom.

"I started pretty tentatively. When the health department took away the *molcajete* [a stone Mexican mortar and pestle used to make guacamole] because it wasn't a smooth, cleanable surface, it simplified a coherency problem, because it was always difficult to do a coherent menu. What is the weather? Today feels like Liguria, or Liguria with some Rome, and the menu will all be of a piece. But then I would have the guacamole and chips, and it made me crazy, that lack of coherence, and it was important to me at that time to not be eclectic. I saw value and virtue intellectually in the coherence of it all. That's again my idiom of Pepette.

"What I see going on in California cooking now is that things that once were scattershot have been massaged so they can coherently coexist. A French dish

SUNDAY DINNER   AUGUST 27, 1989

PLEASE CONSULT OUR OYSTER LIST

House-cured anchovies with celery & Parmesan 6.00
Whole garlic braised in red wine with thyme & pancetta 5.00
Piccolo fritto: deep-fried onions, radicchio & lemon with anchovy mayonnaise 6.50
Antipasto: prosciutto with Zante currants 8.00

Mesclun lettuces with garlic chapons 5.00
Minutina salad 5.00
Caesar salad 8.00

Bowl of warm polenta with mascarpone or Parmesan 4.25
Soup: tomato & onion tourin with a poached egg 4.50
Corn & lobster chowder with pesto 8.00
Penne pasta with fresh shell beans, greens & pecorino 9.50

"Arista": standing rib roast of pork stuffed with thyme, garlic & rosemary; roasted figs 15.50
Deep-fried "poussin" with summer greens, sweet 100's & beets 14.00
Chicken for 2 roasted in the brick oven; warm bread salad with currants & pinenuts 25.00 (40 Min)
Yellowfin tuna grilled rare with marvel-striped tomatoes, herbs & tapenade toast 16.00
Niman-Schell New York steak with grilled radicchio, fennel & toasted breadcrumb salsa 22.00
Hamburger on grilled focaccia bread 6.75 (Available after 10 PM)
    with Gruyère 7.25   with grilled onions 7.75   with roasted peppers 7.75

Ratatouille 4.50

Bintje potato baked in the brick oven
    with mascarpone 4.00

Gravenstein apple tart
  with Calvados cream 4.50
Raspberry-peach trifle 4.50
Gâteau Victoire chocolate cake 4.50
Pistachio-sultana biscotti 2/1.25

Espresso granita with whipped cream 4.25
Nectarine sherbet 4.25
Fig ice cream 4.25
Chocolate pot de crème 4.75

APERITIFS		WATERS			BEERS		COFFEE & TEA	
Cinzano	2.75	Calistoga	1.50	2.75	Miller or Miller Lite	1.75	Coffee	1.25
Dubonnet	2.75	Perrier	1.50	3.25	Anchor Steam	2.25	Espresso	1.25
Amer Picon	2.75	Badoit	2.75	3.75	Sierra Nevada Porter	2.50	Cappuccino	1.75
Campari & Soda	3.00	Evian	2.50	3.50	Beck's Light	2.25	Macchiato	1.25
Punt e Mes	3.00	Levissima		3.50	Samuel Smith's Pale Ale	3.00	Caffe Latte	2.00
Lillet	3.00	San Pellegrino	1.50	3.50	Guinness Stout	2.50	Mocha Latte	2.00
Kir	4.25				Pilsner Urquell	2.50	Mexican chocolate	2.00
Pernod	3.25				Moretti Pilsner	2.25	Hot cocoa	1.75
Ricard	3.25				Aass Bokk	3.00		
Bitter San					San Miguel Dark	2.25		
Pellegrino	1.25				Dos Equis	2.50	Tea	1.75
					New Castle	2.50	Iced tea	1.25
					Non-alcoholic beer	1.75		

*While we prefer payment in cash or personal check, we do accept major credit cards. A gratuity of 15 per cent will be added to groups
of six or more. Art work on display is for sale, please inquire with the host.*

Z U N I   Cafe & Grill   1658 Market Street, San Francisco, California 94102   Tel. 552-2522

Zuni Café dinner menu, August 27, 1989, with Judy Rodgers's beloved
wood oven–roasted chicken for two.

like a bouillabaisse can be on the same menu with a southern Italian fish stew, but there are little tweaks that the chefs do so they don't feel eclectic. The ingredients are the defining characteristic of the cooking, not the cultural antecedents. The sensibility that embraced that fish dish could just as thoughtfully on the same day embrace a vegetable *tagine* and a raw shredded artichoke salad from Nice. What's important is the sensibility and the generosity and the [awareness that] this tastes good today."

Although Judy taught herself to cook, she learned from the Troisgros brothers and the Chez Panisse chefs. In turn, at Zuni Café she provided a launching pad for many other women chefs, including Kathi Riley, Gayle Pirie, Kelsie Kerr, and Marsha McBride. Judy mentored her staff by cooking with them, showing them what she wanted, and tasting with them. I respect her as a gifted, intelligent chef with a great natural palate.

For Judy, Chez Panisse was a forum that attracted like-minded people who could then work things out together. "Bless her heart, Alice let them do that for the most part. Not every person every time, but it was an atmosphere where things could be checked out. Initially modeled after the traditional French idiom, it was a laboratory for things to get thought through and tried out with the daily changing menu that is so distinctive."

Mark Miller compared how different it was to work with Jeremiah Tower, during his tenure at Chez Panisse, as opposed to Alice Waters. Jeremiah chose the recipes, planned the menu, and expected the staff to follow it. On the other hand, Mark said, "Alice was always allowing us to be collaborative. We sat down every Thursday night, Jean-Pierre, Alice, and I; the format was three courses and we'd each have our input. If I had a special dish or something I wanted to do, I'd say so. She had veto power, but everybody had input." Lindsey Shere added, "I would know what was at the market, what kind of fruit was there. I would make a list of ten ideas, and then we would sit down and talk about the menus that the chefs had made and figure out what was wanted for which dinner. Sometimes my ideas would work without any changes, and sometimes we talked about how we could do things a little differently."

The collaborative kitchen evolved out of the daily changing menu. Each day brought different ingredients, and they in turn brought their own questions: How did they taste today as opposed to last week? How were they going to be handled? What if the ingredients the chef had planned to cook did not come in? Everyone talked about the food, tasted together, and arrived at food and flavor decisions through consensus, as opposed to a dictatorship where the chef mandated the standards and delegated the work. It was, as Judy Rodgers aptly labeled it, a "palate community," or what Kelsie Kerr called "culinary camaraderie." Kelsie, who worked at Mudd's, Square One, Zuni, and Chez Panisse, loved that the chefs at these restaurants—women all—offered a certain amount of guidance but left the cooks free to taste the ingredients and discuss their options and concepts.

Working cooperatively came naturally to many chefs. Nancy Oakes of the San Francisco restaurant Boulevard said, "I've always been collaborative. When you allow yourself to be collaborative, the food may evolve in a slightly different direction. If it's delicious and looks good, I've always been for it." She has worked with Pam Mazzola for twenty-five years, so Pam's palate has had an influence on the cuisine at Boulevard. "Then Ravi Kapur was a profound influence. He was there eight years, had strong curiosity, and brought in all the new trappings. When you employ young cooks you almost owe it to them and yourself to keep up and at least examine the trends. You can reject them, but you should know how to operate a *sous-vide* circulator."

The collaborative kitchen model extended to male chefs who were willing to break with the accepted hierarchical kitchen structure. Michael McCarty was an open-minded chef-restaurateur. "It was a great community effort. I would write the draft menu, give it to the team, and they would say, 'Why don't we do this? Why don't we update that?' I would lay out the grid of the items. I still do it to this day. Here are your proteins, this is when we want to use them, these are the ones we change, these are the ones we keep. I'd determined early on that I couldn't be in the kitchen because the people out in the dining room, they'd never seen arugula before, they'd never seen fresh sea bream from France, or chèvre. It worked out perfectly." Michael knew that his starring role was to work the dining room and schmooze with guests. He trusted his kitchen staff to do their best while he played host.

The liberal spirit of California also must have impressed Wolfgang Puck, because he was one of the first conventionally trained male chefs to permit some menu collaboration. According to Anne Gingrass, Wolfgang would let the staff come up with dishes. "He took your idea and worked with it. Unless it was really bad he never said it was bad, he was always very supportive of your creativity. Still, he brought it down around to the way he wanted to have it done. I can see now that maybe he wasn't sure how it was going to go, but if he did it himself then he'd say, 'Yeah, that's what I want to do,' and then you would say, 'Okay, that's what we're going to do now.'"

L'Avenue

APPETIZERS

FRESH MARYLAND SOFT SHELL CRAB served with crayfish remoulade   8.25
& mesclun greens

SKILLET CRISP SKATE served with mesclun greens, salsa verde &   7.25
tomato vinaigrette

SEARED JUMBO SEA SCALLOP served with roasted corn vinaigrette,   8.25
crispy slaw and roasted red pepper aioli

ROASTED EGGPLANT WITH FRESH ITALIAN MOZZARELLA CHEESE, lemon,   7.75
basil & garlic served with Sicillian tomato relish

PROVENCALE TOMATO TART with arugula & basil salad & shaved   7.50
Parmesan

CRISP SWEETBREADS served on a bed of warm swiss chard & shiitake   8.25
mushroom salad with sherry vinegar beurre blanc

FRESH SONOMA FOIE GRAS sauteed & served with grapefruit vinai-   10.75
grette on a bed of mesclun greens & arugula

FRESH WILD MUSHROOM NAPOLEON: layers of garlicky mashed potatoes   9.75
& crispy potato galette with roasted porcini, morel,
& oyster mushrooms with a natural sauce

JUNE SALAD: pan roasted squab breast (boneless) served with mesclun 8.25
greens, fresh blackberries, toasted pistachios & blackberry
vinaigrette

ROMAINE SALAD with anchoide, garlicky bread crumbs & shaved   7.50
Parmesan

WARM GOAT CHEESE SALAD with fresh figs, pears toasted walnuts   7.50
& walnut croutons

ARUGULA, ROASTED BEETS & ROQUEFORT CHEESE SALAD   6.75

ENTREES

GRILLED AHI TUNA served on a bed of warm baby spinach salad &   17.50
skillet potatoes with onions, olives & herbs with roasted
tomato relish

PAN ROASTED CALIFORNIA SEA BASS topped with crispy calamari served 17.75
on a bed of swiss chard & Phipps Ranch cannelini beans, roasted
peppers & roasted garlic nage

SONOMA DUCK LEGS SLOWLY ROASTED WITH HERBS & GARLIC served with   16.50
fresh white corn spoon bread, sauteed green chard, apples,
crispy onion rings & an apple cider sauce

PAN ROASTED RABBIT (boneless) stuffed with Aidells spicy-herb   16.75
sausage served with buttermilk mashed potatoes, stuffed fresh
morel mushrooms, asparagus & a morel mushroom sauce

OVEN ROASTED LAMB SIRLOIN served with a potato-artichoke cake;   17.75
haricots vert, yellow wax beans, roasted peppers, portobello
mushrooms & a claret sauce

GRILLED BONELESS QUAILS STUFFED WITH MAUI ONIONS & PANCETTA   17.25
served on a bed of roasted new potatoes, shiitake mushrooms,
& young garlic with arugula, mizuna, & asparagus

GRILLED RANGE FED VEAL T-BONE served with fresh porcini mushrooms, 19.75
smashed yukon gold potatoes, assorted spring garden vegetables
& a rich, natural veal jus

Nancy Oakes's May 14, 1993, menu from L'Avenue—
a forerunner of Boulevard—celebrates California seasonal ingredients.

David Tanis and Jean-Pierre Moullé split chef duties at Chez Panisse until David left in 2011. Both collaborated willingly with their staff. "I was always more interested in having it be a great dish than having it be my idea," said David. "In fact, you have to give it to the cook at a certain point. You can't just have it be your concept. Even if we have the menu meeting every day before the meal, I know the dish is going to get translated through somebody else's eyes because I can't stand there and do it. Their vision will come in. I'm going to push back a little, but I'm also going to stand back a little bit to see where they're going with it. There's a lot of trust."

Jean-Pierre Moullé was successful in the collective kitchen because he was open-minded despite his rigid classical training, did not let his ego get in the way, and embraced the spirit of California. A passionate cook, he knew the food came first.

JEAN-PIERRE MOULLÉ

Chez Panisse, Berkeley

Jean-Pierre Moullé retired in 2012 after thirty-five years at Chez Panisse. Today his hair is gray, but he's still handsome and he still cooks delicious food. "California is the best place to be," he said. "I'm not saying it is paradise, but it's pretty close. Sometimes Alice gets in trouble because she says, 'Wow, it is salad all year round.' Tell that to the people on the East Coast! We have to understand that California is a special place, and everybody's looking at us because we are pioneers. It's easier for us because we have access to everything.

"In France now, it's more technique. There are three-star places where you have a beautiful dish, but sometimes you don't even have one vegetable for your dinner or lunch! That's the strength of California. Here, the amount of vegetable and fruit we serve is enormous. That's what distinguishes our food: the seasonality, and the beauty of these vegetables and fruits. There are a few things that we still import, capers, anchovies, Parmigiano, black truffle, spices, of course.

"A French chef could do something decent with some really bad stuff because of the techniques. Here we start with incredible things, but we don't work the ingredients as much. The 1970s, 1980s, it was really a switch, a revolution. It happened at a certain time because people were ready; you had the actors in place, it just happened."

Though he spent his career in Northern California, he admired his resourceful colleagues in LA. "California cuisine grew fast because of creative people. I have some classical training. If you don't have any training, if you have no rules, it is better for creativity. You have the handicap of not knowing how to do it, but you don't have the bias of 'No, you can't do that.' In France, we had lots of rules. In Los Angeles, they are blessed. For me, Los Angeles is really what California is about. You tell them that to build a restaurant you have to have four walls—they could not care less. What happened is that you have open places, all those beautiful things because they could. No limits, no rules."

Jean-Pierre saw the value in structure, however, and felt that his culinary training provided a constructive counterpoint to the freewheeling experimentation in the Chez Panisse kitchen. Jean-Pierre was young but experienced when he interviewed with Alice and Jeremiah. After Chez Panisse's rather chaotic beginning, they realized that they probably could benefit from hiring someone with a restaurant background. Jean-Pierre's training helped them execute the food, and, in turn, working with them changed Jean-Pierre. "I started to drop my sauces. I call it unlearning. I started to be more flexible. It took a few years to unlearn rigid stuff and to be less rigorous, more playful with the food. After all, we're doing that twelve or thirteen hours a day, so might as well enjoy it. I went through school to get a job, to get a paycheck, and slowly it became interesting, and after that, a passion, and it's much better that way, right?"

Sometimes it drove Jean-Pierre crazy to be the only trained chef at Chez Panisse and to watch everyone else bumbling around. "I kept thinking, 'What are they doing? Why do they do it this way?' To get from point A to point B, they went from A to Q to B. I think that's why I worked well with Mark Miller. He had a really creative mind, and [there] was a good combination of the technician—myself—and the artist. The two were essential for the birth of that movement."

Jean-Pierre provided the discipline that kept collaboration from degenerating into disorder. "For the architect to build the house, you have to have the solid base, the foundation. And I was the foundation. I was the base for people like Jeremiah and Alice. I didn't know how to make a menu, but I knew how to do all kinds of things technically, and that was used to go ahead." Jean-Pierre gave them skills and they gave him freedom to break the rules. It was a good deal all around.

By the time Jeremiah Tower left Chez Panisse to open Stars in 1984, he had modified his approach and taken up a collaborative working style. He gave his *chef de cuisine*, Mark Franz, and the staff responsibility for composing the menu. He offered critiques but let them develop the dishes. Mark, not Jeremiah, had the final say, because he was in the kitchen and had to make it happen. Bruce Hill cooked on the hot line at Stars in those early days and explained how it worked: "The menu was constantly changing. I was blessed to be part of that inner circle that sat in the office after the shift at night and wrote the menu outline for the next day. It was a team effort between Mark Franz and the chefs working that day. Before we opened, to make sure it worked, we made one of everything, and everyone tasted it and gave their opinion. Dishes weren't ever scrapped and started over; things were tweaked and changed. It was a daily style of food, which was very exciting."

Collaboration on the menu worked successfully at Stars because there was a common aesthetic, and Mark vetted the menu after the group tasting. He held the kitchen together with his palate. This philosophy didn't work as well at Jeremiah's next venture, Speedo 690, a hip restaurant down the street from Stars. There less experienced cooks were making up dishes, but none of the food had a common culture or collective point of view.

Bruce Hill, who went on to work at Aqua before becoming chef at Oritalia, the Waterfront, and finally Bix, where he was chef and co-owner, said that Stars was his first experience with collaboration. "It opened my eyes to how much easier it is to make food that way. And how much more fun it is. At my restaurants I have what I call the circle of trust. When you make a new dish, you're in a vulnerable place. You don't want to spend all this effort just to get shot down in a second— 'Oh, that stinks. Start over.' You want to adjust it, to salvage it. I'm always trying to get people to understand that in the circle, you're safe, and you're safe failing in that circle too, because without the failure, we're not going to get anything done.

"I may help my guys solve a problem with a dish that needs to be completed, but for the most part, my relationship is all about letting them come with their own inspiration. My role has changed so much that I don't create new dishes that often. I want my guys to create the dishes because I feel like they're going to care more and they're going to own it more if they create it themselves."

One of the hallmarks of the collaborative kitchen is having the cooks taste the food. Chefs know how important it is to make the waiters taste the food because they have to sell it, but many restaurants neglect to prepare another dish for the cooks to taste. Bruce described how this works at Bix. "We typically do that between 5:30 and 6:00, right before it gets busy. We make at least two dishes, especially if there's a new person. It's a team way of having the cooks school the new person, and not in a judgmental or a harsh way. You have the new person make the dish on their station and bring it to the experienced cooks and say, 'How does this taste? Is this to our specifications?'"

Eventually more men began organizing their kitchens in a collaborative manner. They realized that this would help them survive in the long run, because the top-down, autocratic regime wears you out. They learned from experience how draining it was to have all the responsibility. Sometimes the well runs dry, and a little fresh input and energy are needed.

When he was chef at Rakel and Checkers, Thomas Keller created the menu and the recipes and implemented everything. The system he established at the French Laundry liberated him because no single person was responsible for everything. He said, "I've learned from my mistakes. When we opened the French Laundry, it was with a different point of view. It's a collective effort, and through those efforts we have been able to achieve great things, things that I would never have been able to achieve by myself. It's that collaboration that allows us to continuously evolve, and evolve in a collective way that has given me the strength to be able to continue and do other things. As a team we can execute at a much higher level than any individual can."

According to chef Daniel Patterson, today some European kitchens are starting to function in a more collaborative way, although in his opinion their model was the much-admired El Bulli. But in the 1970s in the United States, "who else was running a kitchen like it was run at Chez Panisse? Nobody. I mean, nobody."

5

New Flavors

Upscale Ethnic, Eclectic, and Fusion Food

Opening an American restaurant featuring Mediterranean cuisine in 1984 was a challenge. Diners did not even know what the term "Mediterranean" meant. The phone would ring and someone would ask, "What kind of food do you serve?" We'd reply, "Mediterranean," and there would be dead silence on the other end of the line. Then we'd add, "You know, from Italy, Spain, France, Greece." A sigh of relief would be heard and a reservation made.

Square One's menu could be intimidating to those who had not traveled abroad, and we had to educate and entice our customers to make them comfortable with our food. Although we cooked traditional dishes—the food of memory—they were from *my* memory rather than the customer's, for whom they were often totally new. Writing the menu in a clear but tempting manner was daily wordplay.

Many of the dishes we served are commonplace on restaurant menus today, but in the 1980s they were unfamiliar to the average restaurant patron. We offered meat and seafood in a *charmoula* marinade from Morocco; grilled asparagus, baby leeks, and shrimp with *romesco* sauce from Catalonia; fish couscous from Sicily; *skordalia* from Greece; *muhammarah* from Syria; tapas from Spain; and *mezze* from the Middle East and North Africa. Although our daily menu might feature Italian pasta, Greek moussaka, French beef ragout, and Turkish lamb kebabs, we did not fuse or combine multiple cultures on one plate. Each dish was faithful to its country of origin.

Because Square One was an upscale establishment, these ethnic dishes received a certain cachet. Up until the 1970s, high-end ethnic restaurants were scarce and often relied on gimmicks to bring in customers: diners sat on the floor and watched belly dancers while eating Moroccan food; they dodged flaming shashlik skewers at Russian places; or they were entertained at Benihana by joke-telling, knife-wielding teppanyaki chefs. Places like Joe Baum's La Fonda del Sol in New York City and Vic Bergeron's Señor Pico in San Francisco were popular during a culturally naïve period in American restaurant dining. These restaurants offered more theater than authenticity, but they set the stage for the newer cuisine emerging in California, which changed the way ethnic dishes were presented and perceived.

Ethnic Goes Mainstream

Nearly all cuisines introduced to the United States from other countries were considered ethnic upon arrival, with the exception of French, which initially came to the attention of Americans in the late nineteenth century through luxury hotel restaurants such as the Savoy, the Waldorf-Astoria, and the Ritz and dining establishments like Delmonico's in New York. In the 1960s, ethnic food was typically served in an informal and casual environment. Neighborhood ethnic restaurants in California—which chiefly served Italian, Mexican, Chinese, and Japanese food—were well patronized, but to satisfy the tastes of American diners and to promote sales these restaurants often Americanized their food, making it less authentic. The label "ethnic" tended to imply second-tier, moderately priced food that was not particularly worthy of critical culinary attention.

Today ethnic food is taken seriously from the point of view of cuisine. Square One was the first upscale restaurant in the United States to elevate Mediterranean cuisine; Cecilia Chiang's Mandarin did the same for northern Chinese food; Border Grill in 1985 later highlighted pan–Latin American cuisine. These restaurants aspired to give diners a new experience of these less-familiar foods and to bring their vibrant tastes and dishes to a broader dining public. The shift to move authentic ethnic food into contemporary fine-dining restaurants happened mainly in California.

California chefs took different paths to create their menus. Some, such as myself, chose an eclectic approach, offering many dishes from different cultures at a single restaurant, but preparing each as authentically as possible, using quality ingredients. Other chefs chose a more focused approach, concentrating on the food of a single country or region: Italian restaurants delved into Sicilian, Tuscan, Neapolitan, and Ligurian food, while the familiar French repertoire was expanded to encompass the cuisines of Provence and Alsace as well as Paris. Still others chose a fusion approach, selecting and blending elements from multiple cuisines.

Traditional Food and the Pursuit of Authenticity

Not every new California chef sought to pioneer new culinary territory. Some were well versed in and passionate about one country's cuisine and aspired to prepare its traditional recipes with the best ingredients possible. In the early days, obtaining the right ingredients was challenge enough.

The focus on preparing foods of memory as authentically as possible continued to dominate in the Bay Area. In Northern California, Chez Panisse and Zola's concentrated on country French food. In Southern California, Jean Bertranou's La Chaumière, and later L'Ermitage and L'Orangerie, served classic French fare until Ma Maison, Michael's, and Citrus set the standards for a new, modern approach to French cuisine.

California's Italian restaurants in the 1950s and 1960s were for the most part old-fashioned red-sauce joints: Italian American–inspired and inauthentic. Change began first in Southern California due to the pioneering efforts of Piero Selvaggio at Valentino, Evan Kleiman at Angeli Caffe, and Mauro Vincenti at Rex in the 1980s. There the flavors of regional Italian cuisines made their first appearance, along with newly available imported Italian ingredients. While these were part of the collective food memory for these chefs, they were foreign to the average LA diner. Some presentations were rustic and traditional; others mimicked the high style of the *alta cucina*, Italy's version of haute cuisine. This was Italian food cooked in California with California and Italian ingredients. The menus presented a single culture, but in greater depth.

Piero Selvaggio was born in Sicily and immigrated to the United States at the age of eighteen. In 1972, he opened Valentino in Santa Monica. At the time, he said, "LA was a wasteland. The competition was little Italian American restaurants serving cliché Italian American food—baked shrimp, lobster *fra diavolo*, clams *arreganatta*, *fusilli filetto de pomodoro*, steak Sinatra, and *salsa pizzaiola* everywhere. We were pretty much the same until a brash young kid with thick glasses came to me one day—that was Michael McCarty—and picked on my tortellini, picked on my sauce. I'm like, 'Who the hell are you?' But when he opened his own restaurant, I had to say, 'Wow.'" In response to Michael's criticisms, Piero went back to Italy to see what he was missing. In the 1990s, he revamped the approach at Valentino. "The great thing about Italian food," he said, "is it takes only three or four ingredients to make a sublime dish. Very easy to put together as long as you use the best material, the best products. When we flew in the first Treviso radicchio, the ladies were saying, 'What is this? It's nothing but glorified cabbage.

Why should I pay $10 for a side dish?' And you cannot tell a customer it's because the crate cost me $25 but the air freight cost me $140! When we started having local mozzarella, *burrata,* ricotta, and the smoked cheeses, it was spectacular, because it replaced the tremendous cost of freight. Certain products have to be Italian. Truffles have to be Italian. The great prosciutto has to be Italian. The great olive oils have to be Italian. But then, compromise and make it—that is my belief."

Michael Chiarello also underwent a culinary conversion. He began his career cooking the classic French cuisine that he had studied at the Culinary Institute of America, but his mother wisely advised him to stick to his Italian roots. In 1986, he was the opening chef at Tra Vigne in the Napa Valley, where he offered rustic Calabrese food. He made fresh mozzarella in-house, grew Calabrese tomatoes and basil, pressed his own olive oil, and made his own vinegar. The quality of his ingredients made an impression. That is when Michael attained recognition.

Chef Paul Bertolli apprenticed to a restaurant in Florence and became an expert in the art of making *salumi,* Italian-style cured meats. He introduced Italian flavors to Chez Panisse during his ten years as chef and continued to explore Italian cooking while the executive chef at Oliveto in Oakland.

PAUL BERTOLLI

Chez Panisse, Berkeley; Oliveto, Oakland

Paul Bertolli has *salumi* in his genes. His grandfather was a pork butcher who had come from the Veneto region in Italy and opened a butcher shop in Chicago. At the age of fourteen, Paul went to work for the Petrini market chain in San Francisco. He started as a cleanup boy and progressed to journeyman butcher. He also worked in the delicatessen, where he became familiar with the old San Francisco sausage companies that were still making specialty meat products such as headcheese, *gallantina,* and *zampino,* which aren't often seen anymore.

Paul tried twice unsuccessfully to get a job at Chez Panisse before Alice recognized his talent and hired him as the downstairs chef in 1982. "I was in college in 1972, the year Chez Panisse opened," said Paul. "Bob Waks was cooking steak and Zinfandel dinners for $6. I always felt that something fantastic was going on—I could smell it. I didn't get a job the first time, and when I came back, I spent my last $400 cooking for Jean-Pierre Moullé, Mark Miller, and Alice Waters. But Alice wasn't ready to hire anybody, and she certainly wasn't ready to hire me."

Instead, Paul went to work for Mark Miller at the Fourth Street Grill, where it was "all about the grill. It was an incredibly heavy schedule with lots of different fish. That's when we still had local rockfish. We'd bring in eighty, ninety pounds a night, fillet it out, and go like mad. We had chops and steaks and everything going."

After his stint at Fourth Street Grill, Paul left to explore his heritage. "I decided I wanted to ground myself in Italy and Italian cooking, so I finagled a job in Florence. I got married, moved there, and spent a year working in four different restaurants and one private house. I was working day and night. They don't have shifts there, so you show up early in the morning, finish at 4:30, come back at 6:00, prep, and then clean the kitchen at the end of the night, and do that six days a week. It was an apprenticeship from hell, but I learned a lot about Italian food and Italian kitchens."

Paul's time in Italy introduced him to the traditional art of curing meat. "I always loved this food category. When I lived in Italy, one of the waiters in the restaurant took me home one weekend, and there was this *norcino* who was going to butcher a hog the next day. I asked if I could watch. It was a primitive event. The guy had a big axe, a couple of knives, and a little gun to put the hog down and bleed it. I was fascinated. I thought, 'My god, all these things can be made with this one animal.' I spent a lot of time working with this guy, following the products through the seasons."

After Paul returned to California, he got his shot at Chez Panisse. "When I came back, Susie Nelson, Mark Miller's partner at the Fourth Street Grill, was doing a dinner for some wine importers, and she asked me if I would cook. I made a really nice menu, and Alice Waters was invited to that meal, and she called me afterward and said, 'Your meal was fantastic. I just loved it. Would you come and work for us?'"

In the eighties, high-quality cured meats from Europe were not readily available in the United States, and good prosciutto was hard to find. The American and Canadian products were insipid versions of those from Parma and San Daniele. This inspired Paul to try to cure his own at Chez Panisse. At first the prosciutto was too salty, but over time, through trial and error, he came to understand the proper ratio of salt to meat and the product improved. It was a costly experiment because the legs took ten to twelve months to cure, and by the time they could be tasted it was too late to fix anything that was wrong. But Paul persevered.

He left Chez Panisse in 1992, took a year off to clear his head, and then came back to work for Bob and Maggie Klein at Oliveto, first as a consultant and then as chef-partner in 1995. In addition to curing prosciutti, *salsicce,* and other *salumi,* Paul made pasta with a variety of flours, such as spelt, farro, buckwheat, and semolina; ground his own polenta; and made his own condiments and balsamic vinegar.

To complement his work at the restaurant, Paul built a *salumi* cellar under his house. "I always used a natural cellar. If I needed a little humidity, I'd splash water on the floor. If I needed heat, I'd turn the lights on. If I needed air, I'd open the door. I liked the idea of putting something away, watching it, nurturing it, and also allowing it to do its own thing, because it's a natural product."

Oliveto offered special promotional menus to keep customers engaged. Remembering his experience in Italy, Paul suggested doing a whole hog dinner in January 2000. He put up prosciutti, sausages, mortadella, and pancetta, and also served the whole animal, head to tail. It was one of Oliveto's most popular dinners, and many customers asked if they could buy the cured-meat products they had eaten.

Paul started thinking about making *salumi* on a larger scale. "I was getting older, and I'd been doing the restaurant business for about thirty years. I thought, 'I'm tired of staying up at night. I got family, I got kids. I want to go home to be with them.'" He knew that confined feedlots, the production of leaner pigs, and the use of artificial casings had altered the meat industry. "It was the loss of Old World values as far as that food category was concerned. I thought maybe we had a chance. I started to build a business plan, got informed about what it would take to operate a plant, what I would need." He founded Fra' Mani and started production in 2006 with equipment from Italy, sausage casings from Germany, and meat from the Midwest.

"I had to learn all these machines. I had to learn how to manage the air, the humidity, the movements so that my salami didn't crust on the outside, so they would dry. Things kept breaking, and I didn't know how to fix them. I'd be on calls to Italy at two in the morning. I work harder now than I've ever worked, but we make a great product." Inspired by the *salumi* chapters in Paul's book *Cooking by Hand,* a generation of young chefs have taken up this traditional art.

Regional French and Italian cuisines were being reinvigorated not only in the United States but also in their native lands. The media kept the airwaves alive, reporting new developments in food and agriculture, while chefs traveled and shared ideas about techniques, tools, ingredients, trends, and traditions. Restaurateur Michael McCarty described how the "regional American revolution, starting in 1985, prompted the second generation of French [chefs] to stop trying to emulate their Escoffier and nouvelle cuisine mentors, but to go back to their regions and revitalize what came from each and every one. And in 1985, Lidia Bastianich, Tony May, Mauro Vincenti, Piero Selvaggio, and a group of Italian chefs with restaurants in the States [called the Gruppo Ristoratori Italiani] traveled from region to region in Italy and convinced the *ristorante* owners and the Italian government to teach Italian regional food in their *écoles hôtelières*. In those days, you could still only count on four or five regions where the traditional recipes had been written down and codified. Now everybody cooks a different Italian food everywhere you go." The efforts of the Gruppo Ristoratori Italiani also contributed to the proliferation of Italian regional cooking in America.

Not only were Californians exposed to greater regional and stylistic variations of cuisines from France and Italy, but our omnivorous palates soon delighted in new foods from across the Pacific. Migrations from Southeast Asia in the 1960s and 1970s led to an increase in the number of small ethnic restaurants, especially in Los Angeles, and the emergence of recently arrived chefs cooking high-end Southeast Asian cuisine. Charles Phan and Mai Pham both emigrated to the United States from Vietnam after the Vietnam War. At the Slanted Door in San Francisco, Charles Phan made his family's Vietnamese recipes using top-of-the-line meat and produce, some of it cultivated for him by Asian farmers in California. Mai Pham brought Vietnamese and Thai cuisine to Sacramento diners and sought out farmers who would grow special Asian herbs for her.

MAI PHAM

Lemon Grass Restaurant, Sacramento

Born in Saigon and raised in Vietnam and Thailand, Mai Pham arrived in Sacramento as a political refugee in 1975. "It was a shameful thing. My family and I came here with the clothes on our backs. When you lose your identity, it's very hard to recuperate in a climate where people don't want to talk about where you came from. The only solace you could get was to talk about your heritage, your parents, your roots, but it was not possible."

Mai sought to reclaim her identity by sharing her country's food, and in 1989 she opened Lemon Grass Restaurant. In those days Vietnamese food wasn't well known, especially in Sacramento. Having lived in Thailand, Mai also had grown up with Thai food, but "customers didn't really know the difference," she said. They were unaccustomed to eating at Asian restaurants, and when they did, they expected the dishes they had become acquainted with at Americanized Chinese places. "They were coming into the restaurant and asking, 'Do you have the red sweet-and-sour sauce?' They all asked for bread."

To introduce her customers to authentic Thai and Vietnamese food, Mai had to find the right ingredients. She located fresh tofu at Sacramento Tofu and tracked down a fish supplier, but finding produce turned out to be harder. At the farmers' market she introduced herself to one of the regulars, a woman who brought a little basket of herbs from a community garden. Mai would buy everything the woman had, but it wasn't enough for the sixty covers she was serving daily. When Mai asked if she would grow several kinds of mint or a greater selection of herbs for the restaurant, the grower hesitated, until Mai promised to buy whatever she could provide. Their unofficial contract benefited both of them: the grower and her family now own twenty premium acres in the Sacramento area, and they still supply Mai's restaurant.

Mai found that she could get the produce she needed almost year-round. When herbs weren't available from her supplier in the winter, she would import them from Mexico or Hawaii. The farmers' market in Sacramento drew in a wide variety of Asian growers, including Thai, Hmong, and even Mien people—many of whom came from Laos, like the Hmong, but cultivated slightly different vegetables. Sacramento also had a thriving Koreatown, as well as large Filipino, Indian, and Vietnamese communities. Mai said that being exposed to this ethnic and cultural diversity led her to branch out in the ingredients she uses in her cooking.

For the first ten years, Lemon Grass offered mostly popular dishes and served larger portions than would be typical in Vietnam. Mai wanted to present authentic small plates, but her friends said that they wouldn't fly. Today, however, now that diners are better acquainted with tapas restaurants and Vietnamese cuisine, Mai can sell the small plates she always wanted to. "In recent years," she says, "my knowledge has definitely deepened. I'm reaching out to more traditional recipes, recipes that I would have been afraid of trying years ago. We do them as specials, and the customers always seem to order everything that we put on the menu. At the same time, I've broadened. I love Indian and am intrigued by Persian food. I'm recently into Korean food. The barbecue style of Korean food, the *panchan*—the small things and the pickled kimchi—are so good. So I will do some Korean dishes as specials, whereas years ago I would have worried about the customers' response. But they love it."

Other culinary professionals gained expertise in Asian cuisine by immersing themselves in it over the course of many years. Bruce Cost, at the short-lived Monsoon in San Francisco and later at Ginger Island, cooked traditional pan-Asian food with local produce. At China Moon in San Francisco, Barbara Tropp faithfully reproduced classic Chinese recipes using fresh California ingredients. Unlike most of the Chinese restaurants in San Francisco, China Moon did not use canned bamboo shoots or water chestnuts, or any of the mediocre produce that could be purchased in discount markets in Chinatown. It was criticized for being more expensive than the average Chinatown restaurant, but Barbara used ingredients from the same quality purveyors as Stars, Chez Panisse, Zuni, and Square One. In the introduction to Amy Nathan's book *Salad*, published in 1985, Barbara wrote about her use of California produce: "Red radicchio leaves cradle Cantonese minced squab; tiny gourdlike yellow tomatoes enliven Peking cold noodles, or a shower of lavender chive blossoms lend their pretty bitterness to a festive bowl of shrimp and pine nut fried rice."

Replicating authentic flavors and honoring recipe traditions was important. Chefs would often bring back seeds from their travels abroad and give them to farmers to cultivate so they would have the proper ingredients to capture a country's defining flavors. Soy sauce, lemongrass, cilantro, and tortillas were all considered exotic at first, but after appearing in restaurants, they made their way into supermarkets and then into home kitchens.

The Eclectic Menu

While some chefs were content to probe the cuisine of a single country, others were more culinarily restless and wanted to cook food from more than one part of the world. Often their travels provided inspiration. Judy Rodgers learned to love French cuisine when she was living with the Troisgros family, but later she wholeheartedly embraced Italian cuisine after spending time in Italy; inevitably, she wanted to cook both. Chez Panisse and Wolfgang Puck's Spago were built on French foundations, but pasta and pizza eventually found their way onto their menus. Patricia Unterman at Hayes Street Grill offered Sichuan peanut sauce and tomato-poblano salsa along with tartar sauce and lemon-caper butter to spoon over fish. Jeremiah Tower was a hard-core Francophile, but he was so well traveled that Russian *coulibiac* (salmon, mushrooms, and rice in a pastry crust), Latin black bean cakes with *crema*, and Indian-spiced lamb infiltrated the Stars menu, along with New Orleans–inspired gumbo. At Square One there would not have been enough days in this lifetime for me to cook all the foods that captured my fancy after I had lived in Italy and traveled in France, Spain, Morocco, Egypt, Greece, and Turkey.

Anne Gingrass was a chef at Spago for about six years before she and her then husband David Gingrass moved up to San Francisco to open Postrio for Wolfgang Puck in 1989. The Postrio menu provided a snapshot of the eclectic Bay Area food scene at the time. "In San Francisco we decided to make the menu more multi-cultural," said Anne. "Food was going that way at the time. Wolfgang wanted to have some things from Chinatown, some things from North Beach, and some of the old San Francisco staples like sand dabs and cracked crab. It was acceptable to have tomato basil angel-hair pasta and pot stickers on the same menu."

Mary Sue Milliken and Susan Feniger at City Restaurant offered an eclectic array of items on their menu, influenced by their travels in India and Thailand. They didn't hesitate to add dishes from these countries to their originally all-French repertoire. A trip to Mexico led to their opening Border Grill, which celebrated the foods of Latin America.

They called their cooking "City cuisine," but the press mislabeled it as fusion. Culinary Institute of America chef-instructor Bill Briwa noted that the food press had trouble distinguishing eclectic California menus from fusion, which involved merging diverse cultures in a single dish. At an eclectic restaurant, "you might have an Italian dish on your menu; you might have something French; you might have something Asian," said Bill. "They could all live happily side by side on a menu. But that wasn't fusion." Far-out fusion experiments gave eclectic cuisine a bad rap during the 1980s, and Mary Sue said, "We hated fusion. It was never something we were interested in." City Restaurant's style was more accurately described by restaurant reviewer Sherry Virbila, who said that "each dish was as authentic as they could make it, and in some cases probably more authentic than the ethnic restaurants at that time, which were always trying to please too many people."

MARY SUE MILLIKEN AND SUSAN FENIGER

City Café and City Restaurant, Los Angeles; Border Grill, Santa Monica

Mary Sue Milliken grew up in the Midwest and moved to Chicago when she was seventeen to attend Washburne Culinary Institute. After graduating, she was hired by nouvelle cuisine chef Jovan Trboyevic at Le Perroquet, where she was the first female chef. There she met her future business partner, Susan Feniger, who would go on to work at Ma Maison in Los Angeles and L'Oasis in France. In 1981, the two women—later known by the nickname "Too Hot Tamales," after their Food Network show—joined forces to open City Café.

City Café was originally a small espresso shop without a kitchen. Mary Sue and Susan brought in a couple of hot plates, put two hibachi grills in the back parking lot, and began making such items as lobster soup, duck confit, brisket sandwiches, and pickled tongue with pears. The makeshift kitchen, according to Susan, had "no dishwasher, and the bathroom for the restaurant was in the kitchen, which was pretty fun at that point because we had celebrities coming in even though it was a tiny little café. We had received our first write-up in *Gourmet*, so we were getting some notoriety. The first time Julia Child came, we were freaking out. She came into the kitchen to go to the bathroom, sort of leaned over, and bumped her head on the pots."

After four years, they had outgrown City Café and needed "a real kitchen and a real restaurant," said Mary Sue. They opened City Restaurant in 1985. "We started cooking the foods we'd eaten and cooked in all the restaurants where we'd worked. We were attracted to rustic, country French things." But then Susan took a trip to India, and Mary Sue took a trip to Thailand. Both of them arranged for apprenticeships in kitchens while they traveled. When they came back, they put Indian and Thai dishes on the menu alongside the country French.

"Every product was available in LA because of the different ethnic areas," said Susan. "Even then you could go to Indian markets and get chickpea flour, tamarind, curry leaves, and black mustard seeds. The menu would be country pâté, pork rillettes, chickpea vegetable *pakoras* with chutneys, a vegetarian plate with mung bean dal, escalope of salmon with *brunoise* of cucumber, and a Chinese sausage salad. It was totally all over the place geographically—a very eclectic menu for sure."

While City Restaurant was under construction, Mary Sue and Susan pondered what to do with City Café. They thought they might turn it into a taco place, and they closed City Café for three weeks while they took an exploratory trip to Mexico. "When we got to Mexico City," said Mary Sue, "we were blown away by the food. We went to the main central produce market and bought chiles and achiote and all these ingredients we had no idea how to use, and asked the family [we were staying with], 'How do you make tortillas? How do you make a salsa? How do you make mole?' And they taught us. Every day we'd go to a different market, and every day we'd come back to the house and cook. No matter what country we're in, we're always drawn to the street food. The tiny *fondas* that are outside of markets where the vendors go to eat at 7 A.M. because they've been up since 3 A.M. are the kinds of places we get the most inspiration. It was a life-changing trip. When we came back, we opened Border Grill. We wrote the menu in the car!"

"Sourcing ingredients in LA was an adventure," Mary Sue continued. "There are so many authentic ethnic populations. We would do a lot of sourcing in little markets, and once we found something, we would get our produce company or somebody to get it for us, because you can't afford to go out and forage unless you're Alice Waters. You couldn't go to every one of these markets every day, so you had to have a company or a person collect everything that you needed."

"We went to Chino Farms for probably a year or so," said Susan, "but we were very cost-conscious, and they weren't accommodating in the way that we needed. Then we met a woman who was starting a horticulture therapy program at the VA hospital in Los Angeles. She started planting anything we wanted— black mustard seed sprouts, mizuna, chrysanthemum greens, sweet potato greens. The vets were planting, learning how to garden, picking, and delivering. It was fantastic."

"I think as far as City Restaurant's look and feel and menu and price point, we were pretty rebellious," said Mary Sue. "We could've probably gone another direction and made a lot more money, but we kept our price point far below the Spagos and Trumps. We wanted our friends to be able to afford to come and eat our food. We didn't want a parking lot full of Rolls Royces and Mercedes. We specifically talked about that, and we would be so proud when we'd look out in the dining room and see a table of businessmen in three-piece suits next to Attila the hairdresser with the twelve-inch-tall Mohawk next to a couple celebrating their fiftieth wedding anniversary with their kid. Our goal was to throw people together and push them a bit. Not playing to their comfort zone, but creating an atmosphere that was edgy and interesting. We had so many good times there."

Restaurant diners in California were as exhilarated about sampling from this innovative menu as chefs were about creating it. According to Mary Sue Milliken, "It was a great time in the early 1980s because the customers were excited about everything we cooked, and they wanted to try new things. They were like, 'What've you got next? What else can you do?'"

In New York, which was considered the benchmark for restaurant sophistication, diners expected their upscale restaurants to be French, Italian, or Continental,

A P P E T I Z E R S

Soup - roast eggplant & lentil with lemon cream	5.00
- Italian mushroom with parmesan	5.00
Poona pancake - crispy rice pancake with tomatoes, chilies & yogurt	7.50
Potato bhujia with mint chutney & yogurt	7.75
Country pate & duck liver terrine with assorted garnishes & toast points	9.00
Roast sweet pepper with feta, basil & extra virgin olive oil	8.25
Gnocchi with parmesan & cream	9.25
Stuffed rigatoni with chicken fennel mousse & parmesan cream	10.00
Tandoori skirt steak with horseradish mustard sauce=	9.00
Beef carpaccio with parmesan, chives & capers	8.25
Panfried cornmeal catfish with bourbon, bacon, lemon & scallions	9.75
Marinated rock shrimp with cucumber, cilantro & chilies	10.75

S A L A D S

Caesar	9.25
CITY	8.75
Arugula & radicchio with stilton cheese, pear & walnut croutons	9.00

P L A T T E R S

City vegetarian plate with daal, potato khorma & basmati rice	18.25
Spaghetti with feta, garlic beans, tomato & calamata olives	16.75
Tandoori specials with sesame seed naan	
chicken with indian yogurt marinade, raita & pickled tomatoes	19.75
marinated skirt steak with red cabbage & fried onions	20.25
Grilled loin lamb chops with roasted winter vegetables, braised lentils & garlic cream	24.00
Roast pork tenderloin with horseradish frisee slaw & red vermouth sauce	19.00
Grilled turkey paillard with san bai su & mum greens	18.00
Thai red duck curry with basmati rice, cilantro & lime	19.75
Grilled baseball steak with madeira sauce, stilton cheese & crispy potatoes	22.00
Tripe stew en croute with tomatoes & herbs	18.50
Moqueca- Brazilian fish stew with shrimp, scallops, mussels, plantains & mango	20.25
Roast sturgeon with morrocan charmoula & cous cous	19.75
Grilled salmon with salsa basquesa	19.75
Naan breads sesame seed, garlic & parsley or potato	3.00

April 08, 1991

CITY
DINNER

City Restaurant dinner menu, April 8, 1991, where India,
Morocco, Brazil, Thailand, and Italy join France and the United States
on one great California menu.

with familiar menus. So it stopped them and some critics in their tracks when the first eclectic menu appeared in New York. Danny Meyer opened Union Square Cafe in 1985. He was told that Union Square Cafe would fail because New Yorkers would not know how to categorize the food. But it was popular from day one, and beginning in 1997, the Union Square Cafe was rated Favorite NYC Restaurant by the Zagat guide for five years in a row.

Danny was looking for "something rustic, not refined," rather than the usual sophisticated but stodgy Continental cuisine. Union Square Cafe offered a relaxed sensibility, friendly service, and a menu that represented an amalgam of Danny's favorite dishes: traditional Italian pastas, Asian-inflected tuna with soy and ginger, black bean soup with Spanish sherry, and country French confit of duck with garlic potatoes. This was very American (omnivorous, we love it all) and very Californian (a multicultural menu). In place of the then-ubiquitous long menu, Danny offered a limited number of menu items, so that the food was always fresh and carefully selected.

Raymond Sokolov, one of New York's most sophisticated restaurant critics, wrote in a 2010 *Wall Street Journal* article that Union Square Cafe was "far more original and ultimately influential than the naïve California sieving of France so overpraised at Chez Panisse in Berkeley." Union Square's eclectic menu approach was indeed revolutionary for New York at the time, but Sokolov failed to look beyond the well-known and highly praised Chez Panisse to the other innovative restaurants in California that were the first to revolutionize the menu. Danny revealed that he had drawn ideas from an exploratory restaurant tour he had taken to San Francisco and Los Angeles and readily acknowledged his debt to the Golden State: "California was enormously inspirational to me—my early experiences at Square One and Stars and Spago. There was the permission to stylistically present the food and wine in a way that was accessible to people. In New York City in 1985, the prevailing wisdom was that if you wanted to eat well, a restaurant pretty much had to start with 'Le' or 'La.' And if you wanted to have fun, the restaurant was probably not going to be taken seriously. What California gave me was the permission that didn't exist at that time in New York: to try to do it all."

Fusion and Innovation

While Bay Area chefs focused primarily on mastering traditional styles of cooking, much of LA's cooking was trying to be fresh, hip, and multiethnic. The trendy places were concerned with style and originality. Searching for ideas, chefs delved into the ethnic enclaves of Los Angeles to unearth unexplored flavors and new ingredients that they could absorb into their cooking.

Los Angeles had and still has a diversified and vibrant ethnic dining scene. There were innumerable Mexican restaurants in East Los Angeles, an amazing number of Chinese places in the San Gabriel Valley, and scores of restaurants in the large Cambodian, Vietnamese, Thai, and Persian food communities. Areas of the city were called Little India, Little Tokyo, Little Central America, and Koreatown, not because a few token restaurants offered that cuisine, but because there were so many that each area was like a small village. For new California chefs, dining at these places was part of their culinary education and palate development.

Starting in the 1980s, Asian and Latino ingredients began to be assimilated into the European kitchen. Ingredients such as ginger, cilantro, and chiles appeared on formerly mainstream French restaurant menus. This crossover, practiced by many creative chefs, was not considered fusion. For example, Michel Richard opened Citrus in LA as a classic fine-dining French restaurant, but after getting complaints from diet-conscious diners that his cuisine had too much butter and cream, he replaced the dairy with miso to enrich his sauces. He would never have said that Citrus was serving fusion food—he was simply giving his cooking a creative twist. But the kitchen door had been cracked open far enough to let in greater innovation, and fusion cooking arrived on the scene.

Chefs of a more experimental bent started to cook the food of their fantasies. They took trademark components from one cuisine and combined or incorporated them into dishes from another. Familiar ingredients were matched up in unexpected ways: Indian cucumber raita was served with Moroccan couscous; grated ginger migrated into French sauces. The youthful, still-developing California cuisine had no restrictions—only freedom of expression. This was not always successful, of course. In the late 1980s and early 1990s, when fusion was most widespread and egregious, inexperienced chefs borrowed ingredients or flavor combinations in the forms of sauces and condiments from three or four countries and blended them in ways that showed no understanding of their original cuisines. Mark Miller called it "cultural strip mining." It was time to run when a chef decided to cook *ossobuco* but threw in a little wasabi *gremolata* for fun and finished the dish with *tobiko*, or served Moroccan lamb and prune *tagine* with raita on a bed of wok-fried noodles topped with goat cheese and cilantro salsa. Such combinations produced only fusion confusion. In the wrong kitchen, the food of dreams could become the food of nightmare. But in skillful hands, tempered by an experienced palate and careful curating of ingredients, it could be illuminating and delightful. Witness the success of Wolfgang Puck in seducing the Los Angeles food community.

Food writer and editor Colman Andrews credited Wolfgang Puck with "virtually inventing what we understand as Asian-fusion cooking." Wolfgang's California career began at Ma Maison, where his nouvelle cuisine–inspired food was a great success with the dining public and the restaurant was jammed with Hollywood celebrities. But his culinary curiosity did not allow him to stay in the French bubble. In France there had been few opportunities for him to investigate Asian cuisine, but in Los Angeles he quickly found himself won over by new flavors and ingredients as he sampled dishes in Chinatown, Little Tokyo, and Koreatown. Wolfgang wanted to break new ground and broaden his repertoire, and he was excited and inspired by these different cuisines and their cooking techniques. He started to experiment. "I like to cook what I don't know well yet, but not exactly the way people made it before. If I do Chinese food, I don't do it like real Chinese food. And when I do Italian food, whether pasta or pizza, I make up my own style." This is a perfect description of food of dreams.

Spago had an eclectic menu, with European classics such as Dover sole, served alongside grilled lamb and grilled salmon, and fusion dishes such as squab with Chinese five-spice powder, corn soup with jalapeño cream, grilled swordfish with tomatillo vinaigrette, and smoked salmon hash topped with guacamole. Wolfgang's menu at Chinois on Main, executed by Richard Krause and Kazuto Matsusaka, was pure Asian fusion. His daily menus included *satays* and stir-fries, duck with plum sauce, rare tuna tempura, and Chinese roasted squab on a bed of fried noodles with spicy mushrooms. Reading the names of the dishes can be misleading: the titles are Asian, but the sauces, techniques, and presentations were French. Chinois and Spago were both pioneering restaurants, and the food was received with acclaim and enthusiasm. Wolfgang's cooking is ever evolving, and his interests are even wider today. His boldness, combined with his culinary skill, has helped make him one of the most successful chefs in the world.

Other early fusion chefs also worked with French and Asian flavors. As Asian cuisines became increasingly common, pairing their flavors with those of traditional French cuisine became a trend. At Chaya Brasserie in LA, Shigefumi Tachibe often combined Japanese, French, and sometimes Italian ingredients in one dish. Shiitake mushrooms and prosciutto topped pasta, fried Japanese eggplant was stuffed with Camembert, and ginger lobster was served on radicchio.

APPETIZERS

Fish soup with garlic toasts	8.50
Grilled rare beef salad with spicy mandarin orange vinaigrette	12.50
Sauteed American foie gras with sweet and sour plum sauce	13.50
Sauteed Pacific oysters with tomato cilantro salsa	9.50
Grilled Louisiana shrimps with cucumber salad	12.50
Smoked salmon with dill sour cream on country bread	12.50
Cold asparagus with lemon mustard sauce	9.50
Chopped vegetable salad, Philippe's recipe	9.50
Garden salad with fresh goat cheese sauteed in olive oil	10.50
Sauteed shrimp cakes with lime herb butter and rocket salad	12.50
Marinated fresh tuna with avocado, kaiware and sweet onion	11.50
Andrea's salad with Parmesan croutons	9.50

PASTAS

Grilled baby chicken on mushroom raviolis	12.50
Spicy fettucine with sauteed lobster in a lobster basil sauce	13.50
Roasted black pepper pistachio sausage with tortelli and wilted arugula	9.50
Angel hair noodles with goat cheese, broccoli and thyme	9.50
Duck filled herb raviolis with cognac duck sauce	11.50

PIZZAS

Calzone with smoked ham, goat cheese and bell peppers	11.00
Pizza with duck sausage, tomatoes, basil and shiitake mushrooms	12.50
Pizza with prosciutto, goat cheese, thyme and red onions	11.50
Pizza with artichokes, shiitake mushrooms, eggplant and caramelized garlic	11.00
Pizza with lamb sausage, eggplant, fresh Maui onions and cilantro	11.50
Pizza with spicy Louisiana shrimps, sun dried tomatoes and leeks	12.50

ENTREES

Roasted Chinese duck with spicy kumquat ginger sauce	19.50
Grilled striped bass with Maui onion herb vinaigrette	18.50
Grilled veal loin with crispy potato pancake and grilled eggplant relish	22.00
Grilled tuna with tomato basil vinaigrette	18.50
Farm raised chicken with Italian parsley and double blanched garlic	18.50
Grilled calf's liver with onion marmalade and port wine sauce	19.50
Grilled squab with a parsnip pancake and mulberry sauce	19.00
Sauteed sweetbreads with arugula salad and sherry wine vinegar butter sauce	19.00
Roasted Sonoma lamb with artichoke mousse and rosemary sauce	22.00
Roasted Alaskan salmon with ginger, black pepper and cabernet butter	19.50
Whole fish roasted in our wood burning oven	
Special fish of the day	

Our breads are made fresh every day and include olive sour dough and six grain

Split 2.00

DESSERTS

Deep dish summer pie with creme fraiche ice cream	5.75
Marjolaine with raspberry sauce	5.75
Apple pie with caramel ice cream	5.75
Creme brulee	5.75
Exotic fruit sorbets in a brandy snap tuille	5.75
Chocolate bread pudding with espresso ice cream	5.75

BEVERAGES

Coffee, Espresso, Tea, Fresh mint tea	2.50

BARBARA LAZAROFF—INTERIOR DESIGN

The art in the restaurant is on consignment and is available for purchase

At Wolfgang Puck's Spago in 1984, the eclectic California-inspired menu
was created by co-chefs Hiro Sone and Anne Breuer (later Gingrass).

RICHARD KRAUSE - Chef

FIRST FLAVORS

Shanghai fish soup with fresh lemon grass and salmon	4.50
Egg drop sizzling duck soup with shitakes, tofu and sesame oil	4.50
Warm sweet curried oysters with cucumber sauce and salmon pearls	7.50
Shredded chicken salad with papaya tossed in sesame oil and rice vinegar	6.50
Twice cooked clams and mussels in their shells with minced garlic and onion	9.00
Spanish Mackerel in fish net, sashimi style	7.00
Stir-fried salad of scallops and sweet spinach leaves with five color vegetables	8.00
Himalayan chicken fry in ginger sake batter and two-flavor sauce	7.00
Tender young pork ribs, charcoal grilled and honey-glazed	6.50
Five style assortment, Dim Sum	7.50

ENTREES

"Phoenix and Dragon" Pigeon and lobster with cabbage rolls and red wine sauce		16.50
Bird's nest quail, stuffed with roasted shallots		13.50

Peking Duck "served for two" in four courses
   Egg drop soup with wonton
   Thinly sliced breast with pancakes and plum wine
   Stir-fried dark meat with vegetables and soy sauce
   Salad of fresh greens with duck liver
	(per person)	24.00

Cantonese roast duck with fresh plum sauce and mustard greens		15.00
Stuffed chicken, grilled with five willow sauce		11.50
Grilled Mongolian Lamb with spring onions and tofu		13.50
Thinly sliced roast veal kidney with mustard sauce and stir-fried mushrooms		9.50
Saddle of rabbit on crisp fried noodles with tomatoes and Chinese parsley		11.50
Ginger stuffed whole sizzling fish, cloud-ear mushrooms and sweet pepper sauce		14.50
Swordfish, grilled with ginger, zest of orange and fresh mint		14.50
Steamed Grey Sole "served for two" in soy, sake, ginger and scallion sauce (per person)		9.50
Fresh crab in twice spicy black bean sauce		14.50
Fresh fish, steamed or grilled, changing by season availability and inspiration of the day		

VEGETABLES, RICE, NOODLES

Stir-fried vegetables	5.50
Steamed vegetables	5.50
Vegetables, deep-fried in ginger sake batter	6.50
Steamed rice	3.00
Fried rice	3.50
Cold Szechuan noodles with chili oil and spring onions	4.50
Crisp fried noodles	4.50

DESSERTS

Various cookies of good fortune	4.75
Three styles of glazed cream - ginger, mint and Mandarin orange	4.75
Fresh melon in plum wine with mint tea sherbert	4.75
Almond cake with lemon butter sauce	4.75
Rice tart flavored with lychee wine	4.75
Orange coup with ginger ice cream and candied citrus	4.75
Assorted sherberts and fresh fruit	4.75

BARBARA LAZAROFF - Architectural detailing, decor, kitchen and lighting design, logo concept

The "on consignment" art at Chinois is available for purchase.
The work, (primarily California artists) is rotated every few months;
therefore, I am interested in viewing art for possible placement.

Menu from Chinois on Main, 1982, featuring Wolfgang Puck's fusion
interpretation of Asian cuisine prepared with French culinary technique.

Roy Yamaguchi opened 385 North in LA in 1985. Born and raised in Japan, and a graduate of the CIA in Hyde Park, Roy had worked at L'Ermitage with Jean Bertranou and at Michael's with Michael McCarty. His training and recipe repertoire were classical French, but at his new restaurant, he combined these with his Asian heritage. "At 385 North, some of the menu ideas were fusion. I wrapped a sea urchin in Napa cabbage. Then I made a Chardonnay cream sauce, but instead of a straight Chardonnay cream sauce like I had learned at Michael's, I took seaweed—wakame—and had a sauce that was totally different. And I said, 'Wow, this is the way I should be cooking.'" He continued to experiment: "I made a salad with duck teriyaki. I took the skin off, marinated the duck in teriyaki, and then grilled and sliced it. Then I made a vinaigrette with raspberry vinegar, shallots, garlic, and extra virgin olive oil. I put in ingredients like fresh raspberries, very California." Pot stickers added a Chinese note to the finished salad. Roy continued to branch out, combining French, Chinese, Japanese, and conventional California ingredients to create his signature cuisine.

The Asian fusion trend continued into the 1990s and made its way north. Elka Gilmore and Traci Des Jardins moved to the Bay Area from LA and cooked together at Elka's namesake restaurant in San Francisco's Japantown, opened in 1992. "The food was a collaboration between the two of us," said Traci. "I was purely French, 500 percent, and she had the knowledge of Asian ingredients. We meshed together, and it was very exciting. We were making really, really good food." Elka and Traci dished up foie gras with caramel sauce, seared scallops with sweet pea flan, avocado soup with crabmeat, and coriander-encrusted ahi tuna.

Bruce Hill was a master melder of cultures and flavors. He cooked at Stars and Aqua in their early days, and then in 1993 was tapped to become chef at Oritalia in San Francisco, which served a fusion of Italian and Asian food. "Mr. [Nori] Yoshida made me an offer, and I said, 'Gosh, my first full restaurant. I'll be executive chef, and I'll be in control of my destiny. But, boy, I'd better figure out what all this Asian cuisine's about.'" He embarked on an intense course of learning about Asian food and ingredients, shopping and eating his way up and down Clement Street. He fell in love with new ingredients. He substituted Chinese celery leaves for dill in his gravlax and used crunchy Asian pears instead of Comice in his salads. He was one of the first, along with Chaya's Shigefumi Tachibe, to offer tuna tartare, which is ubiquitous today but in 1993 became a topic of conversation for chefs and diners alike. He had wise words of advice for would-be fusion cooks: "I learned that if you're going to bring two things together, you can only draw from one Asian culture. If you're going to have something Chinese with something

Menu

Small Plates

Tuna Tartare, Asian Pear, Scallions, Sticky Rice Cakes	8.50
Grilled Portobello Mushrooms, Plum Wine Jus	5.75
Beer Steamed Gulf Prawns, Chinese Black Bean Tomato Sauce	8.95
Fried Monterey Calamari, Oritalia Cocktail Sauce	7.25
Creamy Asparagus and Lemon Risotto	6.75
Crispy Fried Shrimp And Pork Dumplings, Cilantro-Mint Sauce	6.95
Grilled Crostini Sampler—Tomato Basil, Caponata, Roast Garlic	7.50
Chicken Satay, Five Spice Glaze, Spicy Shredded Vegetable Salad	7.95
Shrimp, Scallop, & Calamari Mu-Shu, Whole Wheat Mandarin Pancakes	8.75
Satsuma Potatoes, Creme Fraiche, Tobiko Caviar	8.25
Sweet Maine Crab Cakes, Red Pepper Curry Cream	8.95
Korean Barbecue Beef, Served In Romaine Leaves	7.75

Salads

Arugula, Sweet Peppers, Roast Onions, Toasted Garlic Vinaigrette	6.95
Hearts of Romaine, Caesar Dressing, Fried Ginger	6.50
Grilled Vegetables, Field Greens, Soy Ginger Marinade	6.75

Pastas

Bruce's Seafood Extravaganza, Linguine, Basil Tomato Sauce	13.50
Potato Gnocchi, Rock Shrimp, Cilantro, Ginger Cream, Tobiko Caviar	9.25
Spinach & Tomato Raviolinis, Braised Lamb, Parmesan Broth	8.75

Large Plates

Miso Poached Salmon, Celery Root Puree, Baby Leeks & Onions	14.75
Peppered Ahi Tuna, Creamy Potato Gratin, Red Wine Black Bean Sauce	14.75
Sauteed Chicken Breast, Herbed Polenta, Truffled Spring Vegetables	13.75
Grilled Fillet of Beef, Crisp Potato Tart, Sweet Onion Confit, Asparagus	17.75

Bruce Hill carefully melded Italy and Asia on Oritalia's menu, 1994.

Italian, you can make that work. But if you go Chinese, Thai, and Italian, that's not going to work. So that was my rule, *fusion with discipline*. I tried to be as careful and as sensitive as I could be about it."

Despite its excesses in early years and the derision heaped on it, fusion cooking survived, and then, along with eclectic and authentic cooking, it unfurled in increasingly interesting ways. Trained and self-taught cooks drew influences from the East and West, from elite and humble kitchens, and gave them new life and new forms in California. But not only the food evolved—menus morphed too, growing longer, then shrinking, then expanding again in response to trends within California cuisine.

6

New Menus

The Daily Menu and the Story behind the Food

The arugula salad served at lunch is picked at 9:00, brought into the restaurant at 10:00, and typed on the menu at 11:00. There are no daily specials, as everything is a daily special. A dish might not be there tomorrow given the whims of Mother Nature, the produce supplier, or the chef.
—Chef Michael Chiarello, Tra Vigne

For twelve years I ran a 130-seat restaurant with an à la carte menu that I rewrote from top to bottom every day. That was hard work! I took on this demanding task because by 1984 California diners—and I—had developed a taste for adventure. We were turned on by the concept of fresh daily fare and boundless variety. Smaller restaurants such as Chez Panisse and Sally Schmitt's French Laundry also created new menus each day, but they were not à la carte. They made the daily format work by serving a single menu, comprising four or five courses, to a fixed number of guests. This enabled them to estimate fairly accurately how much food to order and how many staff to have on hand on any given night. Chez Panisse had a staff of four or five to cook for eighty to one hundred guests over the course of an evening, usually with two seatings. The original French Laundry served between forty and fifty guests with one person to assist Sally in the kitchen during service.

Restaurants like Square One, Chez Panisse Café, Stars, and Spago, which catered to hundreds of patrons every day, including walk-ins, faced a much greater challenge. Every night we prepped for a war. We ordered large quantities of items we thought would be big sellers, and we always had another dish in the walk-in marinated or prepped for the next day's lunch that could be offered if too many items sold out during service. Any leftovers were added to the following day's lunch menu or repurposed as a salad or pasta. This model required resiliency, creativity, and a highly adrenalized and passionate staff.

In the 1950s, the average restaurant patron was reassured by unchanging, predictable menus. Dishes were familiar and recognizable, and diners found that comforting. When they ordered something, they knew exactly what they were going to get.

In those days *piccata* was reliably veal *piccata*, not pounded swordfish with capers and Moroccan preserved lemon; *canard à l'orange* was always roasted duck with an orange *gastrique* sauce, not rare duck breast fanned around orange slices topped by a confit of duck leg and orange foam. To today's diners, who are accustomed to constant innovation and taste titillation, a set menu serving the same dishes all year long may seem boring. But in the 1950s and early 1960s, people ate out less often and thus did not tire of menus that never varied. They were what the restaurant trade calls event diners, those who go to restaurants to celebrate special occasions such as birthdays and anniversaries.

By the late 1960s and early 1970s, as more people traveled abroad and cooking shows began to appear on television, the predictable menu started to seem less appealing. In 1963, Julia Child's program, *The French Chef*, attracted a legion of devoted fans, and viewers also loved the antics of Graham Kerr, who appeared as the "Galloping Gourmet" from 1969 to 1971. Chefs and food trends received increasing coverage on television and in food magazines. *Gourmet*, founded in 1941, and *Bon Appétit*, first published in 1956, were joined in 1978 by *Food & Wine* magazine. These monthly publications enticed home cooks with recipes and glossy photos and kept them current by running restaurant reviews and chef interviews.

Food became a topic of interest and conversation, and diners began to want more from their dining experiences. Restaurants started adding new dishes, and menus grew longer. Items were prepared in advance and then languished in walk-ins for days, or were even frozen and reheated, a common practice at the time. Chef Mark Franz said that when he worked at Ernie's in San Francisco, of the eighty items on the menu, 90 percent were kept in the freezer. "Everything was frozen. The menu hadn't changed in years. There were maybe a few new things, but that was it."

The omnibus menu gradually fell out of favor with the introduction of California cuisine. The formerly impressive long menus began to appear overwhelming and led customers to wonder if the staff could actually make so many items consistently and well. A smaller offering of dishes that could be prepared quickly implied freshness, one of the hallmarks of California cuisine.

A New Menu Every Season—or Every Day

The seasonal menu made its storied debut at the opening of the Four Seasons Restaurant in New York in 1959. Joe Baum, of the hospitality management firm Restaurant Associates, and cookbook author and caterer James Beard were behind this highly touted and prestigious American restaurant that was patronized by the rich and famous. The menus were completely revamped four times a year according to the availability of ingredients. The extravagant décor followed suit, from the staff uniforms and the table decorations to the trees in the Pool Room. It was show business. But despite the new format, the chefs at the Four Seasons were mostly cooking traditional Continental cuisine, albeit with better ingredients.

California took the metamorphosis of the menu a step further. In 1971, both Sally Schmitt at the original French Laundry and Alice Waters at the newly opened Chez Panisse decided to offer menus that would change daily. Neither was a trained chef, and they were uncertain how to prepare an à la carte menu. A single daily bill of fare made sense to them, because it was like a dinner for company, only served in a restaurant setting. Longtime restaurateurs such as Modesto Lanzone thought they were destined to fail. When winemaker Paul Draper was courting his wife, Maureen, they often ate at Modesto's restaurant in San Francisco. "It had a fixed menu with a couple of interesting dishes and these standard dishes that his old customers demanded," said Paul. "When Modesto first went to Chez Panisse, he was astounded. He said, 'Alice is out of her mind to make a different menu every night. You can't do that—you'll lose your old customers.' He could not comprehend the transition into something that focused on quality, interesting food, and fine raw materials, fresh each day."

Judy Rodgers observed that corporate entities and restaurant developers could more easily manage a seasonally changing menu by standardizing the proteins and then, four times a year, swapping out a few sides, sauces, salads, and fruit desserts to feature the season's bounty, running an occasional daily special for a week or two. What made Chez Panisse different was that the entire menu changed each day. "I think Chez Panisse without the changing menu wouldn't have caused the changes that it did," Judy said. "The kind of person who was attracted to work there wasn't your typical corporate line cook. But the most interesting thing, cul-

THE FRENCH LAUNDRY MENU

JUNE 30, 1982

APPETIZERS

BASIL EGGS

SMOKED TROUT FROM OREGON

WARM SALAD OF SWEETBREADS AND MUSHROOMS

TONIGHT'S DINNER

GARLIC CHIVE SOUP

NORMANDY PORK

SALAD OF RED LETTUCE

WITH CHEESES

DESSERTS & COFFEE

FRESH PICKED RASPBERRIES

CHOCOLATE CHINCHILLA

PEACH SHORTCAKE WITH HOT CREAM SAUCE

PRICE $24.00   SERVICE 15%

The June 30, 1982, daily menu for Sally Schmitt's French Laundry,
where less was more.

turally, was there we had the beginnings of a common agreement about what was a sensible, affordable, nourishing, delicious thing to cook here, today, at this time of year." The daily seasonal menu got its critical mass in a restaurant.

In other words, the movement back to seasonal cooking was first championed by California chefs, rather than by home cooks. Home cooks still expected supermarkets to stock strawberries and tomatoes 365 days a year. (And sadly, some restaurants serve them all year long as well.)

Food writer Colman Andrews said that although the dishes served at Chez Panisse in the 1970s were themselves conservative and traditional, "the most revolutionary thing Alice did was as simple as saying, 'We will write the menu based on what food we can buy that's good.' Which nobody did, period! Previously, you sat down and you wrote the menu, and you might have a special or a few specials from time to time, but you served escargot however many days you were open. If you didn't buy it fresh, you bought it canned, frozen, or dried. People don't believe me today when I say that. Being aware of the seasons and using things when they were at their best was absolutely not done."

Jeff Jackson, chef at the Lodge at Torrey Pines in San Diego, said he "took a 180-degree turn" from his training in traditional French restaurants, where the recipes and menus are set and the cooks prepare the same dishes day in and day out. "I removed myself from that classical French frame of mind and became more of an Italian. We don't fuss with stuff. We get this great product, and we try to take our hands off and leave it alone and let it speak for itself. I find 75 percent of what I do is to pull my cooks' and chefs' hands out of the plate and tell them to remove ingredients." He cooks a daily menu based on the produce he receives twice weekly from the Santa Monica farmers' market.

JEFF JACKSON

Shutters on the Beach, Santa Monica; The Lodge at Torrey Pines, La Jolla

Born in Oklahoma, Jeff Jackson was raised in a family of engineers. He was groomed to follow suit but preferred working in restaurants. He started as a dishwasher and a busboy at the age of thirteen. His story was typical, he said: "You begin by washing dishes, peeling potatoes and carrots, and pretty soon, they show you how to cook the potatoes and the carrots, and then you're doing salads, and you're on your way up. I always worked in two or three restaurants at a time in high school." After he graduated, he found out about the Culinary Institute in Hyde Park and told his parents he wanted to be a chef. "At first, they thought I was nuts, but I had the greatest parents in the world. They asked my two older brothers to find out if I was for real, and my brothers reported back, 'This is what he wants to do.' I went to the Culinary Institute and was fortunate enough to get into some really good kitchens and learn about craftsmanship and passion."

In the 1980s, Jeff worked for two years for chef Jean Banchet at Le Français in suburban Chicago and for five years at Le Tour restaurant at the Park Hyatt in Chicago, first as executive *sous chef,* then as chef. In 1988, Jeff won the American Bocuse d'Or, a competition organized by renowned French chef Paul Bocuse, which advanced him to the international event held in Lyon, France, where he competed against winners from twenty-five other countries and placed fifth. When he returned to the United States, he was contacted by hotelier Sam Stein, who was preparing to open a restaurant called Shutters on the Beach in Santa Monica in a new hotel that would be operated by Park Hyatt. Jeff said, "At that time, in the Midwest, everybody looked at California cuisine as this weird thing. It was like nouvelle cuisine sprayed with Miracle-Gro. A lot of people were doing some really crazy stuff, especially in Southern California." He wanted to be a part of it, so he packed his bags and got on a plane.

Unfortunately, the Shutters project ran out of money before it even opened. While waiting for a second wave of financing to come through, Sam sent Jeff to open up new hotels for Hyatt. "I found myself in Maui for four months and then in Asia. Sam felt that it would benefit me to experience Asia, so I spent a month traveling, cooking, and working in kitchens, which was fantastic. I came back and opened up the Hotel Nikko in Beverly Hills and was there for about a year and a half." In 1990, new owners bought Shutters on the Beach and brought him in as chef.

Jeff stayed at Shutters for almost eleven years. He rejoiced daily in Southern California's good weather and fine produce. The Santa Monica farmers' market blew him away. "That's where I started to understand what California cuisine is. California cooking is based on those ingredients. It sounds cliché, but it's the farm, the produce, the foodstuffs that you work with." He began to cultivate relationships with farmers, which he maintained after moving in 2001 to the Lodge at Torrey Pines in San Diego.

Jeff connected immediately with Bill Evans, the owner of the Lodge. "Bill basically said, 'Do what you think should be done.' I had relationships with a lot of the farmers at the farmers' market in Santa Monica, and Tracey Webber has become, for lack of a better term, my forager there. She calls me every

Wednesday and Saturday from Santa Monica. She lets me know what the farmers have got, collects it, and sends it down here to me the next morning."

"I don't know how I ever cooked differently than this," said Jeff. "It's amazing, inspiring. These guys walk in the door and set their box down, and here are beautiful leeks and greens and everything. It helps you create a menu. My *sous chef, chef de cuisine*, and half my staff have been with me since the beginning. We all sit around together and ask, 'Okay, what are we going to do?'"

Recalling the overly complicated cooking of the 1990s, he said, "In those days I was this 'creative genius,' and looking back on it, some of the food was really good. Some of it was frightening. But then I came to California, and gradually I completed the circle to where I'm back to less is more. I find myself working with my chefs and my cooks to teach them about simplicity." He believes in offering the kinds of foods that people don't take the time to cook at home anymore, like meat that has been slow-braised for twenty-four hours, or house-made pickles and sauerkraut.

The year that he came to the Lodge, Jeff started a festival called Celebrate the Craft, which has become an annual event. "I invite every farmer that I've used from as far up north as Carpinteria and Paso Robles. A dozen farmers come, and I match them with a chef in the San Diego area a month beforehand. We build a huge farmers' market out on the lawn, and each chef prepares what the farmer brought. We connect a winery with it, too. It's become this family affair. The same people come all the time, and it's so much fun. It's like Christmas for me."

The festival is Jeff's way of demonstrating California cuisine in practice. To him, California cuisine "has to do with the partnership between the purveyors and the chefs. That is key, because without it, our cooking wouldn't be what it is. The word *spirit* comes to mind. When I think about the early days, it was a very free-spirited time. That spirit has translated into an open-armed camaraderie between the sources of the food and those who prepare it."

By the mid-1980s, fresh produce and meat could be delivered to restaurants almost daily, and with the advent of desktop publishing, chefs were able to design and print their menus in-house. If a vegetable or fish didn't come in as ordered, or if a dish ran out during the course of a busy evening, a new menu could be printed on the spot. That way the waiter would not be embarrassed to report that an item was sold out and the diner would not be disappointed if the dish he or she was set on turned out not to be available ("It was the *one* thing I wanted!").

The changing menu required a daily briefing of the waitstaff. No longer could they get by with rote recitation. They needed to be able to describe what the chef chose to cook from the market that day, where the fish was caught, what farm the greens came from, and which new wines by the glass the sommelier had selected. There were food and wine tastings for the staff so that they could confidently share this knowledge with guests. This new way of working with staff, introduced in California in the early 1980s, became known as the daily "line-up." My sommelier son, Evan Goldstein, noted that we at Square One were among the first to do such a briefing: "The wines by the glass changed daily to reflect the food changing daily. If servers didn't do their homework or were going on what they had remembered from the day before, they would be wrong. The exercise helped them build their understanding of wine and food." This model is now embraced nationwide.

More than the Sum of Its Parts: Listing Ingredients

In the 1950s and 1960s, most restaurants wrote their menus in English, unless they were serving the food of another country. If the restaurant was French, the menu was written in French, often without any translation. The Continental menu was customarily written in English with French culinary terms. Dishes such as Dover sole *meunière* and veal chop *bordelaise* were given a touch of prestige and pizzazz through the use of foreign culinary terms. Italian restaurant menus were written mostly in English with a few familiar designations. *Alta cucina* and regional cuisine had not yet entered the dining scene, so Italian menus generally stuck to widely known dishes like antipasto, spaghetti, pizza, and veal scaloppine.

Chez Panisse's early menus were written in French because the restaurant's recipes were based on country French classics. One day in 1976, Jeremiah Tower, Chez Panisse's chef at the time, had an epiphany while leafing through a cookbook by Charles Ranhofer, the famed French chef at Delmonico's. In the book he found a recipe for *crème de maïs à la Mendocino,* or cream of corn soup from Mendocino. The proverbial light went on. If a French chef could be so impressed with California ingredients that he mentioned them by name, why wasn't Chez Panisse doing the same? Why couldn't Northern California be conceived of as a region? Why weren't they writing their menus in English? They were not in France! They were a fine-dining restaurant in California using California ingredients to cook recipes derived from French classics. Chez Panisse began to highlight California sources on the menu, although it took a while to make the full transition from French into English, and titles of dishes remained bilingual on and off well into 1979.

Diners asked so many questions about the unfamiliar dishes that were showing up in new California restaurants that some restaurants began to write every ingredient on the menu. Chef David Kinch described this as "comma cuisine." A single fettuccine dish might include eggplant, basil, tomato, olives, garlic, and Parmesan—a list that would not have been necessary if every diner had known what went into *pasta alla Norma*. Enumerating the ingredients was part of the guest's culinary education.

At Square One, we tried to teach our customers about food traditions in the Mediterranean. We didn't offer lemon peel with the espresso, cheese with the seafood pasta, or a spoon with the spaghetti—the *gente per bene*, or well-bred Italians, would not use any of these things. We had been in Italy, and we knew how it was done. But at a certain point, if guests asked for a spoon, you gave them a spoon. And if they asked for cheese, you gave them cheese. The only thing we didn't give them was lemon peel to put in our excellent Italian espresso. There I drew the line.

Many of the ingredients themselves seemed exotic, and restaurants listed them on the menu to avoid bewilderment when a dish came. It was the waiter's job to explain to diners what these new items were. These were the days of iceberg lettuce, and few people had encountered arugula, radicchio, mâche, cilantro, and lemongrass. "They threw frisée off the plate," said chef Jesse Cool. "I would name the produce, like Lollo Rosso lettuce. People would jokingly say, 'What is this, and would you please talk my language?' So I would have to tone it down a bit."

JESSE COOL

Late for the Train and Flea Street Café, Menlo Park

Jesse Ziff Cool was a hippie child of the 1960s and a pioneering advocate of natural foods. She grew up in a coal-mining town in western Pennsylvania, outside of Pittsburgh, where her whole family was involved in food. "I'm Jewish and Italian. My dad grew food organically. He owned a grocery store, and my Orthodox grandfather lived above the store. My uncle owned the local meat-processing plant, aka slaughterhouse. I did everything I could to get away from food because I saw both the joy and the dysfunction of it. But I ended up realizing that every time I got near a community or needed to nurture myself, it was always through food."

In the mid-1970s, Jesse was a single parent newly graduated from college. She met a computer programmer from Palo Alto who convinced her that California would be a perfect fit for her. "I packed my kid, his bicycle, and everything I owned, and took three months cooking my way across the southern United States." When she arrived in Palo Alto in 1975, the first thing Jesse did was to join the community food co-op.

To earn a living she became a waitress at the Good Earth, the only natural food restaurant in Palo Alto. There she met Bob Cool, who planned to open a steak place with a friend. Jesse told him, "'I cook, I belong to the food co-op, I'm using organics and whole foods, and I would love to join you and do this.' And then we fell in love." The steak house concept went by the wayside. At Late for the Train, which opened in 1976, Jesse and Bob used exclusively organic ingredients, and all the food was made from scratch. They bought their equipment at Goodwill and had no clue what it meant to be in the restaurant business, but because of their flavorful ingredients and appealing preparations of familiar recipes, the restaurant was an immediate success.

Jesse was one of the early chefs to shop the Palo Alto farmers' market. "I drove my old '67 truck to the market, and Paul Muller and Dru Rivers from Full Belly Farm would let me in before 8:00. I would haul the food out, and we'd go back and cook whatever we got. I remember being on the back of Paul and Dru's truck as they peeled back an ear of Silver Queen corn and said, 'You can eat this raw. Just taste this.' Oh my god. They taught me from the beginning, and they still teach me."

The Peninsula was a culinary desert at that time. Food delivery trucks wouldn't come down to Palo Alto, so Jesse had to pick everything up herself. "It was very hard to get everything organic. We bought from a produce company called 3:30 A.M. Produce, [run by] a lesbian couple who bought from Veritable Vegetable. We got beautiful organic produce."

Asked about the public's reaction to Late for the Train and later Flea Street Café, which she and Bob opened in 1982, Jesse replied, "No one comes back to the table unless it tastes good. But it was definitely challenging to use the word *organic*." In the 1970s and early 1980s, most people thought organic meant odd, expensive hippie food, and diners assumed Jesse's food would be crunchy granola and nut loaves. So she set out to seduce them with fluffy biscuits and down-home American cooking. "I cook from my heart and my soul and use some of my family recipes. The food was rich and delicious, but people used to make jokes and hold up a napkin and ask, 'Is this organic too?'

"I remember going to Chez Panisse and Alice asking me if I wanted a vegetarian meal. I looked up and said, 'No, I eat meat, and I love gin.' Because I promoted organics they thought I was vegetarian. From the beginning, I had Diestel turkey. We roasted chickens if we could find them. I couldn't find any local beef until Niman Ranch came along. Local pork wasn't available.

"It's changed now. My clientele is much more sophisticated, but I'm [still] in this bedroom community. I remember once sitting with Joan Baez, and saying, 'I wish I didn't live here for so many reasons.' She said, 'You need to be here because this is where you'll make a difference.' People would go to Europe and eat small plates of vegetable-driven food with local wines, but they'd come back home and want mac 'n' cheese, meat 'n' potatoes. But we had a very loyal clientele, and they still eat with us."

Over the years Jesse's food has gotten lighter. "The restaurant's more contemporary. Though the simplicity of the food is the same, it's gotten a little more delicate, but not to the point where it's precious. You get plenty to eat in my place."

Identifying the Producers

Once chefs began to serve out-of-the-mainstream ingredients, including unusual lettuces and greens, organic chicken, and sustainably raised pork or beef, they felt they had to credit their suppliers, who were now partners in the California cuisine revolution. Stating the provenance of your menu items "may go back even further than the Four Seasons," according to *Wine Spectator* editor-at-large Harvey Steiman. "I have menus from California restaurants in the 1940s with farms identified. In the Nero Wolfe novels [mysteries written about a food-loving detective in the 1930s through the 1970s], ingredients that the main character cooks are constantly identified by source. But," he added, "no one made more of a fuss over their sources than the Four Seasons." These sources were anything but local. Importing foods was considered prestigious, and the Four Seasons featured foie gras from Strasbourg, smoked salmon and fresh grouse from Scotland, Dutch herrings, Milanese truffles, lamb and trout from Colorado, geese from Wisconsin, and blue crabs from Virginia. The menus did, however, emphasize seasonally available fruits and vegetables. Produce was raised to order on Long Island truck farms, and edible flowers, such as nasturtiums, were used as salad ingredients. Cookbook author and restaurant consultant Barbara Kafka told me that lettuces were picked daily and wheeled through the dining room on a salad cart, and herbs were grown on the roof of the Seagram Building, fifty-two stories up!

Yet the Four Seasons' "farm-to-table" program did not bring about a produce revolution in other restaurants. In 1959, garden lettuces and fresh herbs did not make headlines, because the country was not yet food crazy. What captured attention when the restaurant first opened were the design of the Seagram Building and the restaurant's interior, created by Philip Johnson and Mies van der Rohe. Today, when a restaurant grows vegetables or herbs on the roof, it gets full coverage in the press, and if a restaurant has its own farm, it is lionized.

When Michael McCarty started listing sources on his menu in the 1980s, the public's response was cynical and bemused. *Los Angeles Times* food columnist Russ Parsons said, "Michael McCarty was one of the first people who did line-by-line attribution of ingredients. He got a lot of heat, because it seemed ostentatious. He would say, 'This pork comes from such and such a farm,' or 'The vegetables come from such and such a farm,' and people gave him a hard time. The line was, 'Do I have to know who grew all my vegetables?' That was the majority opinion."

Listing farmers' names on the menu was an important step in helping people understand that some ingredients were superior to others and that they were selected because they tasted better or were grown more sustainably or raised more humanely. In California, chefs identified their sources and suppliers on the menu as a sign of respect. This led to some products—such as Warren Weber's organic produce, Laura Chenel's goat cheese, Bill Niman's beef, and Bud Hoffman's chickens—gaining widespread recognition.

Whereas these entrepreneurs set up new businesses, Jim Reichardt's accomplishment was to take an established business and make something new out of it. Branching off from his family's hundred-year-old duck farm, Jim bred a duck that became the favorite of California chefs.

JIM REICHARDT

Sonoma County Poultry–Liberty Ducks, Petaluma

Until twenty years ago, there were only two duck farms west of the Mississippi—one in Los Angeles and the other, Reichardt Duck Farm, in Petaluma. Reichardt Duck Farm was founded by Jim Reichardt's great-grandfather in 1901. "I grew up on the farm," said Jim, "and since I was eight years old I had worked every weekend picking eggs, putting out straw, checking water." Jim left the farm to pursue a degree in architecture, and after graduating he took up architectural photography. But the economy was in recession, and Jim returned to the ranch in 1982. He told his father that he didn't want to run a slaughterhouse, but he did want to take on the promotional end of the business. He was also interested in raising ducks on a smaller scale and without antibiotics or hormones.

For over eighty years, Reichardt Duck Farm had sold only to Chinatown markets. In turn, Asian poultry shops were the main suppliers to restaurants and the general public. Jim entered the family business during a transitional period. Although the first-ever dinner at Chez Panisse had featured duck with olives, made with poultry from Jim's family's ranch, by the 1980s, many restaurants had stopped serving Chinatown ducks. The ducks simply did not have enough meat on them—one breast was not enough for a serving, and two breasts were too much. "Alice Waters had enough exposure to European duck that she wasn't happy with the Chinese ducks, my family's ducks, anymore," said Jim.

Through caterer Hallie Donnelly, Jim met Bruce Aidells, and through Bruce he met China Moon chef Barbara Tropp. Like Alice, Barbara tried to impress on Jim the need for a larger, meatier duck similar to those sold in Europe. "I was trying to convince her that I couldn't sell it in Chinese markets," said Jim. "The Chinese were mostly going for skin. A little bit of meat underneath was an excuse to eat the skin. They wanted a 4¾-pound duck with the head and feet on. If you got up to more than 5 pounds they started complaining. But what Barbara was saying really planted it in my brain." Jim began to breed a duck that he could sell to California cuisine chefs.

He broke through when he switched to a strain of Pekin duck developed in Denmark, which he christened the Liberty duck. "The Liberty duck is actually the same breed, just a different strain, bred to be meatier." In 1992, he founded Sonoma County Poultry, aka Liberty Ducks. The name "Liberty Ducks" was in part a poke at the fact that in those days the USDA would not accept the label "free range," as standards were not yet in place.

Sonoma County's temperate climate allowed Jim to raise the ducks in the open, in a low-stress environment. Under these conditions, he didn't need to use antibiotics. He could bring the ducks to market at the age of nine weeks, a couple of weeks later than ducks destined for Chinatown. The result was a larger, more tender, more flavorful bird prized by California cuisine chefs. And he was able to stay small, processing about five hundred ducks a day, as opposed to the six thousand a day processed by his family's business.

Today Chez Panisse buys from him, and Bay Wolf's Michael Wild has Liberty ducks on the menu every day. Jim's clientele includes Betelnut, a pan-Asian restaurant, as well as Jardinière, La Folie, Zuni, Bistro Jeanty, Domaine Chandon, and the French Laundry in Northern California, and Michael's, Spago, Lucques, Mélisse, and Bouchon Beverly Hills in Southern California.

"It would be tough to do what I do in any other market," said Jim. "But the Bay Area puts names on menus. It's amazing how many people come up to me at events and say, 'You know, if I see Liberty duck on the menu, I order it because I figure it's going to be good.'"

Chefs wrote the names of these and other suppliers on menus. "There was a conversation or competition going on between the East and West coasts," said chef Loretta Keller, "and I think certain chefs in California felt that to have a national platform, they had to list everything." As in movie credits, each participant got a mention.

When I was chef at Chez Panisse Café, I used to write the menu, and Niman Ranch, Star Route Farms, Green Gulch Farm, Hudspeth Farm, Laura Chenel cheese, and Pigeon Point oysters were named almost every day. My son Evan and his roommate once grew some tarragon for a dish I made, and on the menu I noted, "Tarragon from the Goldstein Ranch."

Eventually there were casts of hundreds, and the concise daily California menu ballooned and became ripe for parody. Some menus became so verbose that after a while chefs began to list the farms and purveyors they supported in one condensed paragraph at the bottom or back of the menu. (Today they refer guests to their websites to find out more about the suppliers.) Doing this made for easier reading, and the waitstaff could talk about the products directly to engage guests. Aziza's Mourad Lahlou joked, "When I first started out, my menu used to be long because every single item had five farms. It took forty-five minutes for people to order. They would have a seven o'clock reservation, and it would be eight o'clock, and I still wouldn't have their ticket!"

"The first thing I think of when we talk about the difference between Northern California and Southern California is the wording on the menus," said chef Suzanne Tracht of Jar in Los Angeles. "There are a lot more words on a menu in a Northern California restaurant, like the name of the farmer, maybe his driver's license number." In a more serious vein she added, "A big difference is that your customers know about those farmers, and about the foragers. In LA, they don't ask, 'Where does this come from? Who's your farmer?' Sometimes I will put where something is from on the menu, but it won't be wordy. Sometimes people feel it's a little pretentious."

Amelia Saltsman, author of the *Santa Monica Farmers' Market Cookbook*, applauded Michael McCarty for "listing farms on his menus from the get-go," but she added that Nancy Silverton and Mark Peel were also doing so at Campanile in 1989. "There was Weiser potato this, and Schaner farm that. The first thing that was noticeable was a celebration of provenance, crediting the farmer. Years later there was a little tagline talking about supporting local growers."

Farmers and other purveyors profited from the attention. For Andy Griffin of Mariquita Farm near Watsonville, listing farmers' names on the menu "was an especially big step. For example, baby lettuces were a tremendous crop early on. There were a lot of farmers who thought that was just the stupidest thing in the world. And it took farms a while to realize that what was going on with these restaurants could possibly be the very best promotion that any farm could ever get, because restaurants, by nature, have to be in the publicity business—otherwise they're not going to be around. Very few farms had marketing campaigns. Farms really benefited from this exposure, and still do."

On rare occasions, some restaurants wrote the names of prestigious farms on their menus even if they did not buy those farms' produce. "I was dismayed when somebody said that we were the basil provider for a pesto menu in, like, March," said Andy. "We didn't even have the basil in the ground yet. But that doesn't happen very often." Lynn Brown of Forni-Brown Gardens in Calistoga told a similar story. "We had one restaurant owner and he says, 'Don't give me stuff. I'll leave your name on the menu anyway.' I said, "Why do you want to do that?" and he says, 'If I have your name on it, I can charge an extra dollar.'" Lynn admitted there are restaurants that have listed Forni-Brown on the menu and never bought a single leaf. "I think of it as free advertising. If we grew as much as our names are on the menu, we'd probably have to be three or four times bigger."

Many chefs explained that when they put a name on the menu, they were giving customers a "story." The story behind the food is an important part of our awareness of what we're eating, reminding us that it comes from people, that somebody raised or grew it and brought it to us.

In his keynote address at a conference of the National Association for the

Specialty Food Trade in 2010, chef Dan Barber of New York's Blue Hill discussed the importance of linking consumers with their food. "Pleasure is affected by more than the food's taste," he said. "When you connect people with where their food comes from, it tastes better. People who love food care about the story of the people who are producing it." It is these narratives that have made the California food movement so important. Bill Niman believes that over the years Americans have lost touch with where our food comes from. "I think the story is a way of reconnecting, because one hundred years ago, everybody knew where everything they ate came from. People wanted to put a face on their food."

Every Menu Tells a Story

When I was interviewing chefs and purveyors for this book, the phrase "the story" came up in almost every interview. There was always a story behind the menu. In Spago's early days, Anne Gingrass's responsibility was to hunt down the finest ingredients for the restaurant. "Wolfgang was always inspired by the products that came in," she said, "so we spent a lot of time seeking the best. You spent half your day talking to people. You'd get the whole background. We called people in Alaska and we'd be talking to somebody who's on the pier and we could hear the wind blowing in the background. It was much more personal, the connection with the food." That story was told to the staff during the daily briefing, and they in turn passed it on to the guests.

Chef Nancy Oakes of Boulevard in San Francisco has a garden of her own in Healdsburg. There she grows radishes, which she brings into the restaurant. "We do them here as an *amuse-bouche* or something else. The staff tells the guests, 'These are Nancy's radishes. They came from her garden.' And I can't believe how touched people are. The radishes, I have to admit, are really delicious, and the story speaks to people's desire to be connected."

The story offered a humanizing counterbalance to the corporate forces of agribusiness and the industrial food chain. "Telling a story is in direct response to fighting off or holding at bay the industrialization of food," said CIA chef Bill Briwa. "If you can find a way to help people reconnect with where their food comes from, that's huge, because we've lost that in this country. And if California is pushing that agenda, more power to us." Although this preoccupation with origins made California chefs the butt of East Coast jokes, it also raised culinary awareness nationwide, created respect for the joint endeavors of chefs, farmers, ranchers, and artisans, and helped make converts to the crusade for local foods and environmental justice.

The story can be about the artisan, the farmer, or the origin or inspiration for a recipe. For years fish tacos have been a big seller at Border Grill. Chef Susan Feniger tells her staff how the dish got on the menu, and they tell the guests. "It was the first time we ever tasted fish tacos," Susan recalled of a trip to Mexico with her partner, Mary Sue Milliken. "We were in Mérida, standing in front of this tiny storefront that was probably 10 feet by 12 feet. In the window is this huge guy, and in front of him is all this lobster and salmon and crab and radishes and peas and olive oil and baby limes and these tiny warm corn tortillas. He's putting them in his hand, taking the salmon, drizzling it with olive oil, putting on a cabbage slaw, and then radishes and peas. Mary Sue and I are standing out front [watching] for probably an hour. Then he comes out with two mini beers and two plates of tacos and invites us in. We end up spending the whole day there with him. We designed Border Grill Santa Monica with a front station to do fish tacos, totally taken from that guy."

When Alex Ong at Betelnut listed his special Vietnamese fish dish *cha ca la vong* on the menu, guests would ask about it. He would wheel a cart around the dining room, showing them how he assembled the dish and explaining where it came from. He had encountered it at Old World Hanoi restaurant, which has been around since 1871. "It was a life-changing experience for me to be in that old part of Hanoi, climbing up these rickety stairs, and having this dish. They bring the whole charcoal brazier with a pan of fish, a form of catfish, which they cook in turmeric oil with a little bit of fish sauce. They bring a bowl of rice noodles, and fresh herbs, including dill—who would've thought dill in Vietnamese cooking? Also tiny little leaves of cilantro, and scallions. They fold in all the herbs and spoon it onto your rice noodles. You add fish sauce, chili, whatever you want. The dish haunts me to this day." After finishing that meal, he said, "I closed my eyes and thought, 'We could never duplicate this in California.'" But once back in California, he figured out how to recreate the dish with local sea bass, and people loved it.

ALEX ONG

Stars, Le Colonial, and Betelnut, San Francisco

Alex Ong was born and raised in Malaysia. His family was ethnic Chinese and their *nonya* cuisine combined Chinese techniques with Malaysian flavors. Food was of supreme importance in his home. "At 6 P.M., everybody's at the table. If you were late one minute, that door was locked, and you're watching the family eat from outside." Alex started working at age seventeen in the kitchen of the Shangri-La Hotel in Kuala Lumpur. During his three-year apprenticeship he concentrated on French cooking. "At that point, young and naïve, I thought that Chinese cooking—Asian cooking for that matter—was not fancy enough."

Alex then cooked in Bermuda at the Southampton Princess Resort, where he was recruited by the Ritz-Carlton Buckhead in Atlanta, followed by the Ritz in Florida. Living in Florida, he craved Asian flavors and once a month would travel forty-five minutes just to eat at Panda Express, the closest Chinese restaurant. Finally, after six years, he moved to California, where at the old Straits Café on Geary in San Francisco he rediscovered the amazing and familiar flavors of home. The chefs there were cooking all of the *nonya* dishes that he had grown up eating. "What a joyful feeling it was to have a bowl of wonton soup, simple, nothing fancy."

Alex eventually started working as a *sous chef* at Stars with Jeremiah Tower. At that time, Jeremiah's interest in Asian food was growing. In the early 1990s he had opened Stars Peak Cafés in Hong Kong and Singapore and then started incorporating more Asian flavors into the Stars menu back in San Francisco. Alex was a perfect fit because he had an intuitive understanding of the ingredients. Jeremiah would tell Alex what he had in mind, and Alex and the team would go back to the kitchen and produce it.

After about three years, Alex left to open Le Colonial, where he cooked traditional Vietnamese food with French colonial influences. In 2001, he became the chef at Betelnut. There he offers interpretations of Southeast Asian street foods made with California ingredients. He uses the customary Asian spices but also likes to experiment with new flavor combinations, as in the case of his goat belly. "The goat belly is the most misunderstood dish on our menu. People are like, 'Ewww! I don't want to hear about it.' In Malaysia it's traditionally stewed, chopped up, and eaten like a beef stew. We enhance it so Americans are more willing to try it. We braise it nice and tender, take everything out and cool it, then put the meat back in the braising liquid all night. During service we pan sear it until it's crispy on the outside, then add a little bit of jalapeño vinegar, which is not Asian whatsoever; it's more Mexican.

"Part of the California experience is eating out, tasting other things, and then asking, 'Does this work for my food?' Sometimes you might say no, it's perfect the way it is, like the Vietnamese fish. Other times you think, 'You know, I want to sex up this goat belly. I think that jalapeño vinegar will lift it off the plate.' No one's gonna come in and say, 'Hey Alex, that's not authentic,' because it's my dish. It's personal."

He said that over the years, his cooking has become simpler. "I've tried to source better products and let the product be the highlight. After all my years of experience, I know there's no point in trying to add twenty items to a dish to make it taste good. I buy the best product, cut it the best way, and let the flavors speak for themselves. My ego has also gone a lot softer. When I was young and dumb, I was yelling and screaming at everybody in the kitchen. Now I just look at them. My wife says, just one look from you says, 'You fucked up. Shut up, don't say anything.'"

Alex educates his largely American staff about the differences between Vietnamese, Malaysian, and Chinese cuisine. "With any new employees, after their training shift, at the end of the day, they sit down with me and a server, and we tell them the difference between, say, something as mundane as Japanese curry versus Singapore curry, and the history behind it. We educate them with notes, videos, demos, and a lot of eating. People's palates generally change completely after working here a couple of years. We want to craft that little experience for them where they will feel as if one foot is in Vietnam and one foot is in China."

"For me," said chef Hoss Zaré, "food is love. When we eat, we share memories, stories, laughter. I have this amazing, rich memory of childhood, my parents' food. Why not bring that to the table? When I see people eating Persian meatballs, it reminds me of kids running around, and my mom's cooking, and I share this story. People come for the shared stories."

The Menu Manifesto

In the 1950s and 1960s, when chefs constructed a menu, they were not expected to create dishes for vegetarians or vegans or diners with allergies. They weren't pressured to tell you where their ingredients came from. They didn't have to deal with citizen reviewers on Yelp or animal rights crusaders at PETA. They wrote the menu and cooked their food the way they wanted to. In the 1980s, the following phrase began to appear on the menu in many California restaurants: "We serve local, organic, and sustainably raised food whenever possible." It is one thing to offer the best, freshest food and to credit all the participating farms and ranches and artisans. It is another thing to feel compelled to state your ethical position about organics and sustainability.

Farmer Andy Griffin believes that California cuisine is not so much about the food on the plate as it is about "bringing an environmental consciousness to the party, a political, environmental consciousness that came from Berkeley. And it came from there for very clear reasons: that's where you had this environmental awareness that got married to notions of good living. So in the 1980s, when you put that statement on your menu, it was taking a stance against what corporate America and big agriculture had done to our food." Chefs and restaurateurs were engaged in political action when they avoided mass-produced food, found people to grow or raise products for them in a healthy and sustainable way, and then made the public aware of their actions and the importance of supporting these practices.

Backing local farmers comes at a cost. Their "items are delicious but cost more and are going to be more labor-intensive or more hassle to incorporate on the menu," said Judy Rodgers. "I'm not doing it only because it's delicious. [I'm doing it] to support a smaller farmer—you want to keep these people in business. It's the mass of people making that decision, which is just a matter of a penny a pound, or maybe a dollar a pound, that adds up to something. It's making your world as much as you can, with your choices. As a chef, you vote with your dollars."

Chef Charles Phan is a strong supporter of local farmers and ranchers who live by their convictions. "We're at an impasse right now," he said, "like with chicken. Chicken was so cheap all these years. Some of these small farms come out now with chicken that is four bucks a pound, and it *should* be four bucks a pound. We're getting to the place where we have to educate the customer and say, sorry, you need to pay more for this stuff. Maybe you should eat a little less. You shouldn't have chicken every day. In Vietnam, you only do chicken when there's a party, birthday, or something special. You have to slaughter it, pluck it—that's a big deal. It's expensive.

"It's not good enough just talking about organic anymore. You have to talk about how it's raised, how it's housed, what kind of breed you're using. When we're talking about pork, it's not enough to say 'all natural.' Our demand for quality and consistency has gone beyond that, so we'll pay a lot more for a pig if we know the breed and how it's being raised. I think that people continue to push on the quality level."

CHARLES PHAN

Slanted Door, San Francisco

Charles Phan moved with his family from Vietnam to San Francisco's Chinatown in 1977. Today he is the chef-owner of the immensely popular and successful Slanted Door at the Ferry Building, and Out the Door in Pacific Heights. He is also the chef-operator of a Chinese restaurant called Heaven's Dog and creates the menu for the restaurants in the California Academy of Sciences in Golden Gate Park and the SFJazz Center.

In high school, Charles pursued design and architecture. His pottery work led to a national art award and invitations to go to art school, but because his parents objected, he went to college instead. He had always been interested in food and often made Vietnamese dishes at home with his mother. He started his restaurant life as a busboy at Café Royale in the 1980s. Though he had never cooked professionally, in 1994, he boldly opened a restaurant offering Vietnamese food. He saw a niche for Asian food with a "modern, hip sensibility but the Chez Panisse attitude. It was going to be simple, with few things on the menu." He financed the restaurant with $140,000 from savings, credit cards, and donations from relatives.

"I didn't like the stereotype of Asian restaurants with Asian motifs, so design was really important. We called it Slanted Door because we didn't want to have an Asian name. The pastry was European because I grew up with cream puffs and baguettes and French desserts. In fact, the Vietnamese don't eat dessert; they eat fruit." Charles also offered a diverse selection of quality wines instead of the few generics on the menus of most Asian restaurants at the time. Charles knew in his heart what the food had to be. He was going to bring a little piece of Vietnam to San Francisco. "It was grounding for me to say that I'm giving you Vietnamese food. Whether you like it or not, or whether I'm a good cook, could be argued, but you couldn't really argue a shrimp and pork spring roll."

Charles started with a short menu and used all fresh produce and locally sourced ingredients. Initially he was willing to give up a bit of authenticity to please his American diners. One of his compromises was deboning the chicken. "Personally I would not debone chicken. But I was praying I would sell two hundred bucks' worth a day. So I was doing some dishes, like clay-pot chicken, for the American palate. They want it boneless. Also, those first couple of years, we were serving whole fish, only five a night, and three of them would get returned.

Amazingly enough, fifteen years later, we serve fifteen to twenty whole fish a day and not a single fish has been returned in the last three or four years."

Though his cooking naturally melded Vietnamese and French influences, Charles found the fusion trend of the late 1980s "off-putting." He didn't understand the rationale behind it and was terrified that his food might be considered fusion. On his honeymoon in Maui he was turned off by a dish of *opakapaka* (a type of snapper) with black bean sauce and cream. He understood that chefs like to play with food, but he preferred the food of a particular culture—regional cuisine that brings back memories. "I remember eating Ethiopian food in Berkeley at the Blue Nile. It was so exciting. You just immerse yourself in it. You learn how to eat it and try to imagine their culture. You almost have to learn their taste."

He's not hesitant to hybridize cultures, if it's done thoughtfully. "I'll use an Italian bread oven to speed up my fish cooking. Or I use olive oil to diversify my oil intake, and it tastes better, even though it's not made in [my] country. I'll adapt things like searing a scallop, not frying it, and getting the skin crispy and the inside medium rare. But I have this rule, if looks too much like Mediterranean food, then you gotta stop."

Charles wants to maintain his principles while his palate evolves. "As long as I don't get into blue cheese, and stick to a tight and concise mission statement, then for the customer it is much easier to understand what I'm trying to do. Subconsciously they're taking it in." A couple of years ago, he would not have allowed any deviation from his roster of Vietnamese recipes. Today he lets his chefs add other influences—Chinese, even a bit of Mediterranean—as long as they don't overdo it. "I've got to let the cooks have space to grow. We borrow techniques to get the product more consistent, or we do classic short ribs braised with tomato paste but put lemongrass and ginger in. As I get older and spend longer in this business, I feel a little bit more freedom." When he was young, he was nervous about trying certain things because he was afraid that they would be perceived as "not Asian enough."

"I try not to think about what people want, but what I want to do, where I want to be ten years from now. I might run out of the traditional dishes of Vietnam if I do it long enough. I travel back, and I try to copy different things. Funny enough, people don't think of me as Vietnamese. Sometimes I hear diners say, 'Well, do you feel like Thai, or Italian, or do you feel like Slanted Door?' Somehow, it's a different category."

The menu manifesto had some detractors, especially in Southern California, where chefs often preferred not to announce their political correctness in print. Evan Kleiman hosted a radio show called *Good Food* on KCRW, which is still on the air today, and was an adamant supporter of the Santa Monica farmers' market, but she didn't proclaim her values on her Angeli restaurant menus or list the farmers whose produce she used. "I think because of my persona through the show, people just assumed that I would be doing the right thing." Her staff was briefed to give information about the ingredients' provenance to anyone who asked.

Suzanne Goin had worked at Chez Panisse before opening Lucques, but she resisted putting a statement on her menu for a long time. "Alice Waters actually hounded me. Every time she'd come in, she'd say, 'You need to write that on the menu.' So I finally did."

Even in politically correct Northern California, some chefs and restaurateurs resisted publicizing their ethical principles. They offered different reasons for this. "Part of me says I should," said Marsha McBride of Café Rouge in Berkeley, "but my husband thinks people can ask. I am still on the fence about it. This is the food, and I stand behind it. Berkeley people, when they ask questions, it's different than San Francisco. It's not because they're interested in the food for what it is. It's more like a challenge. Michael Pollan came in not too long ago and was grilling our best waiter on where our chickens came from and what they are fed. I do put Hoffman chickens on the menu. I give credit, but not for everything."

Elizabeth Falkner, when she was chef-owner of Citizen Cake and Orson, also rebelled—at least initially. "I hated the same language on everybody's menu: 'We support local, and we're holier than everybody.' I'm not part of that church. At first I refused to write that on the menu. Of course, I succumbed." Inquiries from guests prompted her to add the following, slightly unorthodox, manifesto: "We buy from great farms and people passionate about cuisine, keeping it local, organic and sustainable when possible and exotic given the opportunity." On the dessert menu, she was even more direct: "Local and exotic ingredients, because it's dessert, for heaven's sake."

Manresa's David Kinch has steadfastly refused to participate in the name game (although his relationship with Love Apple Farms is well known, making it unnecessary for him to advertise his pro-organic stance). "That's not because I don't care. I just don't want a mission statement on my menu. I don't want to preach to people. I want to subtly educate them through my cooking. What I try to do here is a hedonistic experience."

Chef Mourad Lahlou, who assiduously puts flavor and quality first, believes that "it's the responsibility of the chef or the restaurateur to provide the customer with the best-quality product. Just because something is local doesn't mean it is better. I think we need to use local stuff as long as it makes sense, but if the fish from Japan is better than what we have here, I'll use it. It's my responsibility to do that."

Thomas Keller agrees, because he feels he's sustaining more than California businesses. "When I started thinking about local, my definition changed. It wasn't about geography; it was about quality and freshness. It's a balancing act, because if I stop buying my lamb from Keith Martin in Waynesburg, Pennsylvania, for example, he would lose his business. He has revolutionized the way modern animals are raised and he's done such a tremendous job in creating a protocol and actually having it patented that I want to support him to make sure that he is able to continue to influence and impact farmers. Hopefully one day his protocol will become something that is consistent throughout the livestock industry. It's a really interesting tightrope that we walk today as chefs, and our responsibility to our guests has to be primary. The guest is the end of the line, and we can't lose sight of that."

Whether or not their restaurant posted a menu manifesto or listed every purveyor by name, California cuisine chefs tried to source the best products for their particular cuisine. Some believed that sustainability, quality, or authenticity trumped buying locally. But all held their relationships with their customers and purveyors in high esteem.

7

Restaurants Reimagined

Transformations in the Kitchen and Dining Room

The design for my restaurant, Square One, was the work of Charles Pfister, a well-regarded architectural interior designer. The space was large and airy with a few supporting columns. Other than one wall near the entry that separated our venue from other ground-floor units, the restaurant was a single expansive, open room. Charles understood that I wanted the restaurant to resemble a modern Mediterranean trattoria, with rustic Italian chairs, white tablecloths, and china. Color would come from the food and the guests, echoing the design ethos behind Angeli Caffe and City Restaurant in Los Angeles. Charles was attentive to every detail, from determining how the wood floor abutted the tile to hiding three layers of sound insulation material under the wooden ceiling grid. Although the trend today is to create a loud and energetic dining area with piped-in music to give people the impression that they're in a hot, happening place, I wanted my guests to converse with ease.

I designed the front and back kitchens. Our prep kitchen had windows facing onto Front Street, giving us the luxury of natural light in our work area. We had an open cooking line, which needed to look good at all times because it was in full view of the guests. I dressed it up with a pair of terra cotta geese and a ceramic still life of lemons that I had bought in Venice.

Los Angeles would have embraced Square One's look immediately. As a young city not burdened with a strong architectural tradition, it was more tolerant of modernity. San Franciscans, on the other hand, were fairly conservative in their architectural tastes—more comfortable with enclosed spaces and dark wood paneling and furniture—so at first many were taken aback by the spacious dining room. One Bay Area reviewer called it a "corporate cafeteria." It took a few years for the locals to become comfortable with the clean and understated style.

•

Most of the Bay Area's formal Continental restaurants had faded away by the late 1980s, and by the early 1990s they had largely disappeared from Los Angeles as well, done in by the competition from the new California restaurants. Tired of receiving condescending and pompous treatment in the bastions of haute cuisine, diners wanted a more relaxed environment with friendly service. They gravitated to restaurants like Square One, Stars, Chez Panisse Café, and Spago, which were designed to recreate the energetic and convivial atmosphere of European trattorias, bistros, and brasseries. The new restaurants served up both good food and fun.

Chefs and restaurateurs understood that they needed to keep pace with changing expectations and were intent on providing a new style of service: informed but informal. They listened to their customers and accepted feedback gratefully, as they learned how to create the kinds of restaurant experiences people were hungry for. Innovations such as open kitchens, giant grills, and wood-burning ovens, which permeated the rooms with wonderful aromas, were introduced to please this new generation of diners.

The New Restaurant Design

In the 1960s, upscale restaurants such as Ernie's, the Blue Fox, L'Etoile, Perino's, Scandia, and Chasen's were decorated to the max with deep, cushioned booths, brocade walls, lush carpets, low lighting from sconces and chandeliers, and floor-length tablecloths. Steak houses were outfitted with old-fashioned red leather banquettes. Seafood houses were ornamented in the Barbary Coast style, with wooden wainscoting and even private booths with curtains where backstairs deals or clandestine liaisons could be arranged.

Restaurant designer Pat Kuleto described classic Continental restaurants as "dark, stuffy, and intimidating." They were so gloomy, in fact, that "you couldn't read the menu, you didn't know what the hell was happening." "Dreary" was chef Michel Richard's judgment. He recalled that the first thing owners would do at a new location was to cover the windows. "It was very dark. You'd go inside the restaurant, and it took ten minutes to be able to see anything." But by the time Michel opened Citrus in Los Angeles in 1987, the scene had changed.

While the San Francisco Bay Area pioneered the California ingredient revolution, Southern California led the way in restaurant design. In the vanguard was restaurateur Patrick Terrail with his campy Ma Maison, which he opened in 1973 with $35,000 borrowed from friends. Susan Feniger had worked there in the early days and laughed as she described it. "The building was a piece of crap. [Patrick] couldn't have spent one cent to open that restaurant. It had a very indoor-outdoor feeling." One of its more endearing features was the Astroturf on the patio floor. Yet despite the ramshackle decor, or maybe because of it, the place was packed every night with celebrities enjoying Wolfgang Puck's high-priced nouvelle cuisine.

Michael McCarty went in a different, but equally innovative, direction when he opened his first restaurant, Michael's, in 1979. He gutted a Santa Monica bungalow, painted the walls a cream color, hung up millions of dollars' worth of modern art, planted umbrellas in the backyard garden, and put the food on oversized white plates. There was a new design sheriff in town.

Michael's was followed in 1980 by Trumps, where Michael Roberts served his adventurous French-California food in a remodeled gas station, topping the tables with exotic succulents and lining the walls with art. Next came Wolfgang Puck's Spago, with its Malibu beach-house-without-the-beach vibe and indoor use of outdoor patio furniture. The dramatic and stripped-down City Restaurant opened in a former carpet warehouse. Relaxed dining was now in, but with fine-dining prices.

Bruce Marder took over Casa Blanca Restaurant des Artistes in Venice and turned it into the West Beach Café, a slightly run-down place with casual furnishings but an upscale menu. The building looked like a rickety white shoebox. Rather than remodel, Bruce simply put up a new sign, added some tables and chairs, and started cooking. Venice was an artists' community, so Bruce borrowed artwork for the walls from those he considered up and coming, changing the exhibits every week. "It was a community place, and it became really popular. I never wore a chef's jacket when I didn't have to. I didn't want to play by the rules." After a time Bruce started adding Mexican entrées to his menu on Monday nights, and his "Mexican breakfasts" became famous. In a 1988 restaurant review, Ruth Reichl wrote, "Bruce Marder had duck tacos on his menu before the term 'Southwestern cuisine' was coined. Before there was a City Café to build a tandoori oven, Marder was playing around with Indian food. He streamlined French cooking and reinterpreted American food."

Bruce next decided to open a Mexican restaurant called Rebecca's. The space was designed by architect Frank Gehry, who had an office in Venice and was a regular customer at West Beach Café. Bruce described Rebecca's as an "outlandish architectural phenomenon using materials in a different fashion than you would

WEST BEACH CAFÉ

June 11 – June 17

APPETIZERS

LIVE MAINE LOBSTER LASAGNE with pesto, Fontina cheese, pinenuts
    and Italian parsley in a yellow tomato coulis   12.00

CHARRED EASTERN OYSTERS on a confit of Maui onions, scallions,
    smoked salmon, Japanese red chili and baby dill on a
    bed of Kentucky limestone lettuce and creme fraiche,
    finished with French butter and salmon caviar   10.00

DINNER
(includes soup or salad)

VERMICELLI AND CHARRED MEXICAN SHRIMP with julienne of tortillas,
    Italian plum tomatoes, garlic, cilantro and mint in a
    light olive oil, finished with dry Mexican cheese   18.00

GRILLED BREAST OF CHICKEN (thinly sliced) on a bed of lightly saute'
    spinach leaves with fresh sage in a cream reduction with
    Califronia virgin olive oil and cracked white peppercorns,
    finished with pancetta strips   18.00

CHARRED SWORDFISH AND HAWAIIAN TUNA in a seafood sauce finished with
    fresh rosemary, served with baby vegetables   20.00

GRILLED JOHN DORY in a champagne vinegar butter with fresh basil and
    baby chives, served on puff pastry strips, sun dried
    tomatoes and sliced courgette   20.00

GRILLED PROVIMI VEAL LOIN (thinly sliced) on shitake mushrooms
    in a light veal reduction with fresh thyme, finished
    with lemon sections   22.00

GRILLED RACK OF LAMB with wild rice, julienne of celery and fennel
    seeds in a lamb glaze with fine herbs   24.00

CHARRED PRIME NEW YORK STEAK in a 3 mustard sauce with roasted
    white rose potatoes   24.00

ASSORTED CHEESE   5.00

SELECTION FROM OUR PASTRY TABLE   4.00

SPECIAL DESSERTS MADE TO ORDER   6.00

PIZZA IS MADE TO ORDER AFTER ELEVEN AT NIGHT

Bruce Marder's West Beach Café menu for the week of June 11, 1980,
explaining to diners how each dish was prepared.

see in Mexico." He made creative use of traditional tiles and onyx. There were animal motifs and the latest tuck 'n' roll seats. "It was pretty incredible. Honestly, the only problem was that it cost twice as much as I had wanted to spend."

The design aesthetic in many of the LA restaurants that opened in the late seventies and early eighties was minimalist, because the chefs and architects wanted the focus to be on the food and the guests rather than the surroundings. City Restaurant, Angeli Caffe, and Trattoria Angeli, for example, were carefully designed to look spare and unfinished until people walked in, making dining there a more relaxing and interactive experience. These new restaurants were the beginning of the end of the oppressively dark, hushed French model that had reigned over fine dining for so many years.

Josh Schweitzer, who is married to chef Mary Sue Milliken of Border Grill, was the architect for City Restaurant and Border Grill, as well as for Campanile and Röckenwagner. He declared that in Southern California there was a union of architecture and restaurant design early on. "Compared to San Francisco, there wasn't any kind of architectural vernacular to play off, only warehouses and funky buildings. People like Frank Gehry paved the way for us kids to be able to do what we wanted. And other architects, early modernists like Thom Mayne and Michele Saee at Morphosis, did some great things here. I credit Frank for the fact that, at that point, Southern California was the star of the world architecturally, and it gave all of us that opportunity to follow in his wake."

JOSH SCHWEITZER

Schweitzer BIM, Los Angeles

Josh Schweitzer was only thirty-one years old when he received his first restaurant commission. Susan Feniger, a childhood friend, asked him to design City Restaurant for her and Mary Sue Milliken in 1985. This led to a flurry of commissions through mutual connections. Hans Röckenwagner knew Mary Sue and Susan, so when he came to LA from Chicago in 1985, he hired Josh to design his eponymous restaurant. After seeing his work for City, Nancy Silverton and Mark Peel hired him to do Campanile. All these young, ambitious chef-owners were interested in making a statement with their restaurants—not only with their food, but with the design of their spaces as well. Because these were start-ups, the chefs were looking for someone who could be creative under the constraints of a tight budget.

"It was both fun and a challenge to make sure the restaurants were as efficient and as cheap as possible but still looked good," said Josh. "Those who came into the restaurant business later had more money. They had better sources of income to design restaurants, and I moved into a designer realm and away from an architectural realm. But I think that for myself as an architect, the great thing was the belief that young people could do amazing things and that Southern California [seemed] to be the place everybody looked to as a youth culture with a lot of ideas."

Josh designed kitchen equipment and had the pieces fabricated for less than what they would have cost commercially. "Frank Lloyd Wright said that if you could design everything and keep it all together, it would be more interesting. So that's how I approached it. Whether it was tableware design or the general layout and chairs, if I could design those and have them made, then that's what I would do."

Since City Restaurant was built from an old warehouse of no architectural value, Josh was able to start from scratch and create something from the ground up. Former *Bon Appétit* food editor Kristine Kidd recalled that "one of the astonishing things about City was the stark setting. You sat down to this plain white table, and then they started decorating the table with the dishes, [all in] different shapes and unusual colors, so a painting evolved in front of you."

Josh designed Campanile in 1989. "Campanile was in an interesting, really old structure for LA. I loved its heritage and wanted to respond to that in a way that would allow me to keep a modern tone, because I am a modernist, but to play with it and warm it up with some wood. There were aspects of the building that were really beautiful, and I didn't want to screw them up, just enhance what was there. In essence it's a concrete brick box with a few design accents that I preserved and highlighted, keeping the lines really clean."

He's grateful that "the movie and music industry allowed people like me, with no experience other than working for other architects, to come into this environment and take on projects. People would give half a million or a million bucks to a thirty-year-old guy because he's done something interesting and let him go with it."

The Bay Area preferred nostalgia. San Franciscans embraced the traditional style of long-standing restaurants such as Tadich Grill, Sam's, and Jack's. When Patricia Unterman created the Hayes Street Grill in 1979, she patterned it after Tadich, with high wooden wainscoting, white tablecloths, and dark wood furniture. Jeremiah Tower's multileveled brasserie Stars also harked back to the past with its grandiose elegance and dramatic antique bar. The Bay Area accommodated design diversity if it was not too extreme, like the Arts and Crafts style of Chez Panisse and Bay Wolf, the clubby upholstered interiors of Masa's and Campton Place, the country inn aura of Lark Creek, and even the Polynesian shtick of Trader Vic's. People also appreciated the retro look of the Fog City Diner and the Southwestern vibe of Zuni Café. Because everyone loved a view of the San Francisco Bay, people took to the Trident in Sausalito, with its wall-to-wall windows, and to the minimalism with hippie touches at Greens in Fort Mason. Modernism, however, was not yet part of the Bay Area aesthetic. Jordan Moser's avant-garde design of the Cypress Club, with its breast-shaped light fixtures, wood panels, and burgundy drapes, was a curiosity at best. It took LuLu to blow up the paradigm in Bay Area restaurant design.

In 1992, Cass Calder Smith was in his final semester of architecture school at UC Berkeley when the opportunity to create LuLu came his way. He described it as "a fluke." Cass owned a house on Potrero Hill in San Francisco where chef Reed Hearon rented a room. One day Reed told Cass that he'd met someone who wanted to create a restaurant in a building that she owned. Cass took a look at the space—a 1910 warehouse in the South of Market area—and was so excited that he prepared a formal presentation for the owner, Rowena Wu. Reed and Louise Clement (his girlfriend at the time) cooked, and Cass did a number of drawings and assembled them into a slideshow.

Cass was a modernist and liked the looks of few Bay Area restaurants. Warehouses can be overwhelming to work with, and he knew that this building presented a huge challenge, but as an architect he recognized that Rowena's building was spacious in the right way. He ignored the nagging voice in the back of his head that told him to "be safe and break it down," because he didn't want it to be a series of small spaces. That summer he had traveled in Europe, where he had spent his leisure time hanging out in the piazzas. That gave him his big idea. He would keep the design generous and open and make the restaurant feel like a lively public space—just like a piazza. He used the Campidoglio on Capitoline Hill, designed by Michelangelo, as his architectural model. He loved what Michelangelo had done spatially, placing the Palazzo Senatorio at one end, with a monumental building flanking each side, and he said, "I'm doing that for LuLu."

Cass described the design: "The bar and the raised dining areas are splayed apart, and the kitchen became my Senatorio. From the entry level you go down to the main dining area, which is shaped as a gigantic ellipse. Soon I was drawing fireplaces all over the building. Reed said, 'Let's cook with them.' I think I had six. I just went for it. I was thinking, 'I'm going to have fun with this.'"

Rowena Wu called back a day or two after Cass and Reed presented their plans and said, "Let's do it!" They were shocked. When it opened in 1993, LuLu captured everyone's imagination and attention and brought the drama of the open kitchen and grand open dining room to the fore of San Francisco's consciousness.

Breaking Down the Wall: The Open Kitchen

Sometimes a new idea is an old one that has been hiding in plain sight. This was the case with the open kitchen. In the early 1980s, when the press enumerated the distinguishing characteristics of California cuisine, the open kitchen had a prominent spot on the list. It has played an important part in the democratization of the dining experience and is a major factor in the stylistic evolution from the unimaginative and uptight establishments of the sixties to the bustling and easy-going places we frequent today.

The open kitchen format dates back to the 1930s. Back then, at diners and five-and-dime stores you could sit at the counter and watch as the chef slapped your grilled cheese sandwich on the griddle and smothered your ice cream sundae in hot fudge. You couldn't miss the open kitchen in Musso and Frank Grill in LA, or those in such classic San Francisco restaurants as Tadich Grill, the Swan Oyster Depot, and Original Joe's. At a sliver of a place called Little Joe's, patrons stood in line to get a seat at the tiny counter. At the late, lamented Vanessi's, you could watch line cooks grill your veal chop and then whip up a frothy zabaglione right before your eyes. California cuisine didn't invent the open kitchen, but it gets credit for popularizing it.

A large part of what brought open kitchens into vogue was the spotlight on the celebrity chef. These new culinary icons could be viewed onstage, and during a break they might come out to mingle with the guests. Soon chefs were known by name and linked with their restaurants.

The proximity of the open kitchen also changed the relationship between diners and those who cooked their food. Now the chef, cooks, waitstaff, and guests all interacted, creating a more personal connection to the restaurant, one that went deeper than the perfunctory "Good evening, nice to see you." Diners bonded with establishments where they were recognized and felt at home.

Chef Michael Chiarello explained the premise. "We understand and enjoy the theater of the restaurant. The open kitchen sets a pace and a tone for the room and brings up the energy. You can see the seriousness or the fun or the bustle of it. We Americans are a voyeuristic community. We love to [observe]. We love to see behind the scene. The best table in the house now is next to the kitchen."

The cooking line became the center of activity at Fourth Street Grill, Hayes Street Grill, and Zuni Café in 1979. All three of these preceded the press magnets Chez Panisse Café in 1980 and Spago in 1981, which received most of the recognition for creating the concept. After seeing the open kitchen at Chez Panisse Café in 1980, Wolfgang Puck put one in at Spago. "I thought, I'm going to be the chef and manager, and it would be great for the customers to see the kitchen, how everything is working," he said. "The guests loved it. It was different, it was fun, they could see, and I could see everybody. When somebody came in I could make them a pizza or send them a little appetizer, so it was a great way to run the business."

When Barbara Lazaroff, Wolfgang's wife and partner at the time, started designing Spago in 1981, she knew she wanted the kitchen to be the first thing guests saw when they entered the room. To enable that they took out the weight-bearing walls and put in structural I-beams. She said, "It was cutting edge, having the exhibition cooking hoods, the actual exhaust hoods, exposed like that. I got this negative critique about how it was too industrial. [But] Spago Hollywood was hardly industrial. With all of that bleached wood, it was a Malibu beach house kind of look."

After a fire almost destroyed Chez Panisse in 1982, Alice Waters had to make a major decision about reconstructing her flagship downstairs restaurant. Should she rebuild the wall between the kitchen and the dining room or remove it completely? She decided on the latter, largely because the popular upstairs Café with its open kitchen and lively energy was a huge success, and also because she had noticed the public's growing interest in cooking. Alice also put in a rustic wooden table, on which she set up a still life of ingredients from the day's menu. Chez Panisse chef Jean-Pierre Moullé returned from a trip to France to find the downstairs kitchen exposed to the dining room. "It was a big transition, but it worked out fine," he said. "At the beginning, it was a little strange for us, but it opened us up not only physically but in other ways, meaning that we couldn't hide anything. We had to be real. We had to be honest to our clients. It [was about] being transparent."

After Chez Panisse and Spago opened up their kitchens, the trend caught on like wildfire. Kitchens were given a prominent place at Chinois, Stars, and Square

One in 1984, and at China Moon in 1986. In 1987, Michel Richard's Citrus opened with a central glassed-in kitchen that echoed the style of kitchens built by the great chefs of France. The open kitchen was a feature in 1989 at Campanile, and blockbuster open kitchens appeared in 1993 with the debuts of LuLu and One Market. Within ten years, the open kitchen had become the norm for California restaurants, north and south.

Yet some chefs still preferred to keep the curtain drawn. In 1987, Thomas Keller had an open kitchen at Rakel in New York, but for the sake of his highly choreographed style of upscale dining at the French Laundry, he decided to close the kitchen from view. "I realized that here the dining room and the kitchen should be separate. Everybody looks at the kitchen as entertainment, but I think it needs to be a mystery. What happens behind the door is magic, and I don't think that the guests need to see that magic." He added that he tries to set an example with the design, organization, and cleanliness of his restaurants' kitchens. "We want to have people come back into our kitchens, but when they're eating, we don't want them to be part of our lives or us to be part of their experience. We want to have the experiences be separate. And then you draw back the curtain when they come back and say, 'This is where it all happens.' There's so much more excitement about that, like visiting backstage."

Mark Franz also found advantages in having a closed kitchen. The menu at Santa Fe Bar and Grill featured *truite au bleu*, a dish that involved disemboweling a live trout. There was "blood everywhere," he said, "but it didn't matter. That was a closed kitchen."

MARK FRANZ

Stars and Farallon, San Francisco

Mark Franz was a member of the first class at the California Culinary Academy in San Francisco. There he met Jeremiah Tower, who was teaching a tasting class one day a week. The two hit it off right away.

After Mark graduated in 1981, he took a job at Ernie's, which his father's friend Roland Gotti owned with his brother, Victor. "At Ernie's I worked with chef Jacky Robert, a great guy," recalled Mark. "I was his prep cook for about eight months. At the time, he wasn't doing any pasta. I said, 'Why don't we have a fresh pasta on the menu?' He said, 'If you can do all the prep, and make twenty-five pounds of pasta a day, you're on.'" So Mark did it, on a little hand-cranked pasta machine.

After leaving Ernie's, Mark reconnected with Jeremiah Tower, who hired him to cook at the Santa Fe Bar and Grill, which Jeremiah had taken over from Mark Miller and Susie Nelson. "Me and Steven Vranian did it for three years," said Mark. "Bruce Aidells would show up at the back door with a big bag of spectacular andouille; chef Ken Hom lived right around the corner. It was cool. The clients in Berkeley were the best. Adventurous eaters. They were vociferous about praise. Because let's face it, that's all we do it for. At the end of the day, if on your drive home, you think about somebody who came up to you and said, 'That was just fabulous,' it makes your day."

When Jeremiah opened Stars, he brought Mark in as executive chef. "From day one, I cooked. I never left sauté. I was on the line five, six nights a week, ran the kitchen, did lunch, but I ran it cooking. I had the energy to do it, so I did it. And I loved it."

At Stars Mark essentially wrote the daily menu. "The epiphany was when I woke up one day and said to my wife, 'Do you realize that there is nothing that intimidates me in cooking? I'll face anything.' The way I wrote a menu, I was fearless. We all were. We were too stupid to know better. Every week, there was something new. Jeremiah would come with an idea, and I would be the one who would make it happen. He was a genius with the 1–2–3, the simple flavors that were marriages in your mouth. He trained me to think like him."

Mark's first experience with an open kitchen came with Stars, and he didn't like it. "From then on, I've been in a fishbowl. As a client, it's wonderful. As a chef, I hate it. The open kitchen changed cooking. It made it a bit more sterile. You can't do some of the things that you would do behind [a door]. I can't be rippin' guts out of a trout in front of people. So that takes away the spontaneity, because you have to be way more planned. I worked a closed kitchen in the Mandarin Oriental in Hong Kong, and it was fabulous because everything that you cooked, you killed. You would order, the first thing the guy would do, he'd get the ticket, he'd say, 'Four lobsters!' and they'd kill the lobsters. It was heaven on earth. I still do it, obviously, but it has to be more orchestrated." But open kitchens were in fashion and the public loved them, so Mark reconciled himself to working in the open.

After leaving Stars, Mark was approached by restaurant designer Pat Kuleto. "I had won some chef award, and I was coming down from the podium and walking through the crowd. Pat came up to me and said, 'Congratulations. If you ever want to do something, let me know.' About six months later, I called him. He said, 'I'm thinking of doing a place, do you want to be partners?' I said I'd commit for a year, because you never know what you're gonna get.

"We found a place off the square in Sonoma. Great spot, great location. We had it all ready to go, we went to the town council, and they said, 'There's no parking, so you can't do it.' We spent six months putting this together, and a lot of money, and I'll never forget that night. We walked out, it was over, they pulled the plug. I looked at Pat, and he said, 'Does this mean we're done?' And I said, 'Oh no, I'm your partner, we'll figure this out.' We've been tight ever since."

In 1997, Mark and Pat opened Farallon in San Francisco, with an underwater theme. "It had been empty for four years, and they were really trying to find somebody to get it. It's a weird shape, and the bar has always been problematic. We just did it, hook, line, and sinker. In the first six months, we went from doing five or six million bucks a year to twelve million dollars a year. That's big.

"I still like flying by the seat of my pants. That's not the only way I like to cook, but I like to come in to an excited staff, and people who are willing to catch my excitement."

After years at Stars, Loretta Keller of Bizou (now Coco500) also favored a closed kitchen. She found it "hard to work in an open kitchen all the time. It takes you away from cooking to some extent, in terms of managing staff and constantly saying, 'You've got to change your apron, don't touch yourself.'" These were the tradeoffs.

The open kitchen had more adherents than detractors, though. Kitchen specialist Mark Stech-Novak has designed hundreds of places with open kitchens, including the Iron Chef kitchen for the Food Network, and he sees no sign of the trend abating. Some restaurants have added partial glass walls to enclose the kitchen and cut back on noise, but they've left an unobstructed view of the workspace. Chefs seeking to bring more formality back into the dining experience have kept the kitchen partly or completely out of sight to heighten the drama of their culinary presentation. But they are in the minority, and the concept has not lost its excitement, even after thirty years.

When the wall between the bustling industrial kitchen and the formal dining room goes away, the first thing to change is the dynamic in the room. Spago designer Barbara Lazaroff said, "The idea was to have something *beyond* theater. I used to refer to it as participatory theater. You have your guests participating in the process of having their food created and delivered to the table, not unlike being in your own home, where people often gather around the kitchen. You've got the energy level, the chefs moving about, the aromas wafting across the room—the sounds, the noise. All of your senses are enriched and excited before the food even arrives at the table."

A kitchen is not a quiet place, however. You can hear the steady hum of the ventilation fans in the stove hoods. Pots bang, tongs get slapped on pans. In a closed kitchen, cooks are free to shout, scream, and curse. With an open kitchen, they have to develop a mellower demeanor—not easy when a huge rush is on. Kathy King, general manager at Boulevard, explained, "If an expediter is getting frantic, it trickles down. I'll have to go 'uh uh' because they're clanking the pans and I'm hearing it over by the windows. You have to keep monitoring it."

During service cooks often comment to one another on the orders. A demand for a well-done steak may elicit a groan. A request to vary an entrée in a way that a cook thinks won't taste good may provoke a few "ughs" and some X-rated remarks. In these moments of kitchen camaraderie, cooks in open kitchens sometimes forget that nearby guests can hear them. At Spago Beverly Hills, said Barbara Lazaroff, "I was pleased to put the chefs behind these beautiful glass doors I created, because every night at Spago Hollywood I would have to lean over the counter and say, 'Would you stop that?!' The cooks wouldn't be aware of what they were saying, and the tables were literally a couple of feet away."

With all the activity in the room, guests no longer needed to talk in hushed tones. They could relax. Some diners asked to be seated near the kitchen, where they could watch the cooks at work. The removal of the physical and psychological wall eventually gave rise to the phenomenon of setting up a chef's table in the kitchen, where people paid a premium to watch the action up close. In some instances this evolved into participatory cooking classes. The open kitchen restaurant trend also influenced private residences. Homeowners undertook costly renovations, tearing down walls between the kitchen and the dining room so that guests could sip wine at a counter and watch while the host made dinner.

The cooks felt appreciated because they were seen as hardworking professionals instead of invisible food preparers. Guests talked to them. They were thanked for fixing the meal. They could see the smiles on people's faces when they tasted the dish that had just been sent to the table. Chef Bill Briwa said, "When you put the cooks in front of the customers, and you shorten the distance between the food and the customer, you have a group of cooks that stand taller, stay cleaner."

The open kitchen helped professionalize kitchen behavior and led to better all-around hygiene. No longer could the cooks be seen wiping their faces, fixing their hair, or sticking their fingers in pots. Everything was visible to the diner, so the work space had to be kept spotless. City health departments loved the open kitchen. Never had restaurant kitchens been cleaner. There was a constant commitment to scrubbing the counters and keeping the floors swept and free of debris. And with everything in full view, guests were assured not only that the kitchen was clean but also that fresh food, not canned or frozen, was being prepared to order.

Now that cooks were onstage, they wanted to look good. Existing uniform companies failed to pick up on this and kept producing the outdated designs of the 1960s and 1970s—the classic checked pants, tall white toques, and starched white chefs' coats. But one working cook in Los Angeles realized the possibilities. Rochelle Huppin started the pioneering company Chefwear in her guesthouse in Santa Monica, and soon baseball caps and berets appeared on the line, followed by colored chefs' jackets and chili pepper pants. The company has thrived ever since and celebrated its twenty-sixth anniversary in 2012.

ROCHELLE HUPPIN

Chefwear, Santa Monica and Venice

Rochelle Huppin trained as a pastry chef. At her first job, she was handed a pair of polyester pants made for men. She had to get them sized large to fit her hips, but that meant that the waist was far too big. The fiber felt terrible on her skin, so she got a note from a doctor saying that she was allergic to synthetics and made her first set of custom cotton pants. After working at the Hotel Bel-Air and then at Citrus with Michel Richard, Rochelle moved to Marin County in 1988 to open the Lark Creek Inn with Bradley Ogden. There she created the prototype baggy unisex chef pants. They had a three-inch-wide elastic waistband for comfort and tapered legs so dirt would not collect on the hems as she walked through the kitchen.

When Wolfgang Puck hired her to work at Spago, the pastry department uniform was white pants and a white jacket, both made out of polyester. Rochelle designed a pair of striped black-and-white cotton pants and started her clothing business by strategically handing out six pairs to big-name chefs. "I gave Wolfgang a pair, because I was working for him. I gave a pair to Bobby Flay, who was a friend back then, a pair to Jonathan Waxman, and then three other chefs who were working for Wolfgang at the time. When I was in New York with Wolfgang at Rockefeller Center doing a Meals on Wheels event, Linda Zimmerman wrote a little article for the *LA Times,* and there's a picture of the pants and a blurb about how the pastry chef didn't like the [old] pants and now makes them herself. There were 175 phone calls the first day."

Rochelle was surprised to find that she had hit a nerve and that she wasn't the only one who hated the traditional chef's uniform. Two conditions helped her new business, Chefwear, grow. First, the open kitchen put cooks on display, and they wanted to look cool. Second, more women were becoming chefs, and they needed pants and jackets that were made to fit their bodies. Rochelle's chef pants production was an underground business at first. "I had a little white Pontiac Fiero, and after working a twelve-hour shift at Spago, I would drive around in my little car with a very small trunk. I would go to Campanile and to all these places, wherever people had called me. I had five hundred pairs of pants made and sold them very, very quickly."

In food magazines at the time, uniforms were publicized in tiny eighth-of-a-page black-and-white ads showing a tall paper hat on a chef—noticeable only if you were looking for them. In marketing her Chefwear line, Rochelle wanted to do something different. "I grew up in an entrepreneurial family, and my dad always said, 'Don't be afraid to spend money on advertising.' So I took thirteen chefs, put them in front of Chinois on Main with [my] first line of clothing, everyone barefoot, and did a full-color, full-page ad in *Food Arts*. And boom, it got attention right out of the box because there wasn't anything like that."

The business grew rapidly. At first, people called them "clown pants," but that soon changed. Rochelle believes that her brand of stylish and unconventional clothes helped lift chefs out of blue-collar jobs to become celebrities.

Inside the New California Kitchen

Historically the kitchen and the dining room were two different worlds. The former was a space filled with industrial stainless steel, tile, and clean washable surfaces. It was the domain of kitchen design specialists—with their traffic flow charts and equipment spec sheets—and refrigeration, plumbing, electrical, and ventilation experts, all with up-to-date information on health department regulations. For the dining room, restaurant owners hired interior designers to select tables and chairs, drapes, carpets, upholstery, artwork, light fixtures, and the overall color scheme. Rarely did kitchen and dining room designers meet.

As more restaurants were owned and operated by chefs, the design dynamic changed. Chef-owners wanted to plan the layout of their work areas according to their personal culinary vision, cooking technique, and menu concept. One size no longer fit all, especially when dealing with chefs who wanted giant grills, rotisseries, and wood-burning or tandoori ovens. Building an open kitchen in the middle of the dining area affected the entire design scheme of the restaurant. Kitchen specialists had technical expertise, but now they were stepping into the realm of visual design. They had to take appearance, sound, and lighting into consideration in a new way. And they had to coordinate with the designer who was doing the dining room décor.

For architect Josh Schweitzer, the design was determined by the budget. "Mark Peel and Nancy Silverton wanted an open kitchen at Campanile. I told them, 'Unless you spend some money in that kitchen, you won't want to look into it.' A standard utilitarian kitchen is not that great to look into, with its plastic sheathed walls and institutional stainless steel. For somebody like Mark, who wants to stay in that front spot at his grill station, it's important to make that a keynote place. I made it so that everything was clean and tiled and looked attractive, and then there was Mark, standing at his station, with his people around him."

Cass Calder Smith has created many restaurants since his dramatic debut and trial by fire at LuLu. He has glassed in a few kitchens to reduce the noise factor, but he prefers fully exposed ones. Due to his lack of experience at the time, Cass ran into problems with LuLu's open kitchen. He created an impressive space that the public adored, but the kitchen was a line cook's nightmare. The stations were so far apart that it was impossible for the cooks to coordinate the orders. The salad guy could not see or hear the grill guy. The sauté team could not communicate with the wood-burning-oven team. The solution was for the cooks to wear headsets, which the press and public thought was really cool. The same problem occurred at One Market, where there were parallel cooking lines; the front line cooks could not see or hear the cooks on the back line to coordinate orders. Again, headsets saved the day.

The open kitchen at Postrio, Wolfgang Puck's signature San Francisco restaurant, presented a different complication. As guests descended the grand stairway leading from the bar down into the dining area, the sweeping vista of the kitchen was going to be seen from above—a difficult angle from a design perspective. A kitchen in front of you can look dramatic. A kitchen viewed from above usually looks like a war zone because you can see all the debris that accumulates on the floor. Fortunately, Pat Kuleto, one of the nation's most experienced restaurant designers, was up to the task.

Pat's design solution was to use the pastry station, which was neat and pretty, as an interim buffer area to partially conceal the cooking line. "You could keep it cleaner, and you didn't have tons of shit all over the floor." His goal was to make the kitchen "gorgeous. We did tile on the walls and the whole area was really

APPETIZERS

Sauteed scallops with soy ginger vinaigrette and potato chips	11.50
Giant blini with smoked salmon, sour cream and salmon caviar	13.00
Smokey Szechuan duck sausage with warm bok choy salad	9.50
David's homemade charcuterie plate with marinated artichoke salad	9.50
Sauteed crab cakes with smoked red pepper sauce and chinese parsley	12.00
Marinated tuna with avocado, sweet onions and a lime ginger vinaigrette	10.50
Foie gras terrine and smoked duck carpaccio on young arugula leaves	14.00
Crispy fried gulf shrimp with spicy peanut sauce	13.00
Mixed Sonoma field greens with Parmesan croutons	7.50
Smoked sturgeon with a trio of horseradishes and brioche	12.50
Sauteed Tomales Bay oysters with cucumber daikon vinaigrette	12.00
Stir fried garlic lamb with fresh chili and mint	10.00

PASTAS

Wild and exotic mushroom risotto	12.50
Grilled quail with spinach and soft egg raviolis	10.50
Steamed half Maine lobster with angel hair and roasted tomato eggplant fondue	15.00
Veal tortellinis with smoked tomato rosemary sauce	11.00

MAIN COURSES

Tuna steak grilled rare with spicy curry sauce and crispy fried ginger	19.50
Roasted Sonoma lamb with garlic potato puree and caramelized garlic	21.00
Chinese style duck with spicy mango sauce on arugula leaves and onions	19.50
Roasted salmon with an almond black pepper crust on warm spinach salad	21.00
Grilled baby lamb chops with wilted green salad and cilantro honey vinaigrette	24.00
Roasted dungeness crab with herb linguine and black bean green onion sauce	20.50
Grilled squab with ginger plum sauce and parsnip hash browns	19.50
Crisply sauteed sweetbreads with warm radicchio salad and mustard fruits	19.50
Grilled farm raised chicken with red onion goat cheese tart and garlic butter	18.00
Roast rack of veal with caramelized onion butter and arugula salad	24.00
Grilled quail on fresh corn pancakes with tomato green bean salad	19.00
Oven roasted whole fish with marinated summer vegetables	22.00

Split 2.00

Our lower level is a designated non-smoking area

James Rosenquist "Bird of Paradise Approaches the Hot Water Planet" on generous loan from
Erika Meyerovich Gallery, 231 Grant Ave., San Francisco, CA

7/1/91

Wolfgang Puck's Postrio, July 1, 1991, where chefs Anne and David Gingrass
and designer Pat Kuleto brought LA style to San Francisco.

good looking. We shoved the prep and dishwashing to the back, out of the way. Everything had to be ornamental. The hood was a big part of the design. We had to use better product, and I had the idea of making it look like furniture, movable pieces of cabinetry as opposed to kitchen equipment."

PAT KULETO

Pat Kuleto Restaurant Development and Management, San Francisco

Pat Kuleto likes to joke that he was born with a building permit instead of a birth certificate. He got his start in the restaurant business in the 1960s by designing steak houses in Hawaii. Ever since those early days he has been a convert to open kitchens, which he has installed in Kuleto's, Splendido, Postrio, Boulevard, Farallon, Water Bar, and Epic Roasthouse. Chef Mark Franz said that when he was negotiating with Pat about their partnership at Farallon, he asked Pat how attached he was to an open kitchen and what would happen if Mark said no to the concept. Pat said he would find another partner.

Speaking about the evolution of the open kitchen, Pat said, "In the bad old days, you worried about the quality of food and how much was coming out of frozen boxes. With these steak houses we didn't have the great chef, but the open kitchen was so people could see the quality of the food, they could see the steaks being cut out of a strip. They weren't coming out of a plastic package. You could see the kitchen was clean. It was all part of this honesty thing. We had nothing to hide."

In 1989, Pat was hired to design Postrio, where he stylistically combined Northern and Southern California sensibilities. "We had different levels, to watch people going up and down. It was like a show. The bar was LA, which was glitzy. It was shiny and copper, and the pizza oven was the energy source and focal point. Wolfgang's pizza from Spago did well; it was perfect bar food, and they did other cool [dishes] up there, too. I kept the downstairs pretty traditional. The one modern LA touch downstairs was the giant Robert Rauschenberg painting. Rauschenberg was a friend of Wolfgang's, and he donated a $2 million painting, or so the story goes.

"So I had this LA thing going on upstairs and this traditional San Francisco thing going on downstairs. During the development process, we were under construction and I had one of my 3 A.M. screamers where I sat up and said to myself, 'Whoa! It's too disjointed. I have to come up with something that can weave these things together.' I came up with the ribbon motif. I decided to put big ribbons in, starting in the floor, and then going down through the carpet pattern and down the stairs. They ended up going up into the light fixtures as confetti and then down the hand railings." Bay Area foodies were dazzled by his visual melding of LA glitz and San Francisco tradition.

Pat said he does not have one magic formula for kitchen design because each kitchen works differently. "It depends on the style of cooking. Do you want an expediter? Do you want to pull from both sides or do you want a linear line? I spent time talking with chefs about the mechanics and I was always a proponent of doing a much smaller kitchen than the chefs wanted. If you have a big kitchen like Epic Roasthouse, you have to put people in all those little spots to make it work, and it's scattered all over." He thinks Boulevard has one of the best ratios of kitchen to square footage, and "Fog City Diner is even better. It's the teeniest kitchen in the world, like a ship's galley. I've had a lot of boating background, and I always think of kitchens like a ship. Every time I look at a space, I look at every little thing."

Whether working in California or abroad, he designs with the community in mind. "As a restaurant designer who works around the world, the first thing I do is spend some time in that city trying to go to as many restaurants as I possibly can. I look at the menu, the bar, and the people. What are the price points, the cuisine, and the level of service and design? You need to figure out the cumulative palate for that given community and where they are in terms of their culinary evolution. Creating a restaurant is like building a spider web: what are you trying to catch? You've got to figure out what's missing in the market. The bigger the city, the smaller the gap is that you have to slip into."

Michael Brennan has been designing restaurants for twenty-five years, but his love affair with open kitchens goes back to his childhood. "When I was a kid, we used to go to Marin Joe's. I sat there every Sunday with my parents and watched them cook my hamburger. I thought that was pretty exciting, knowing that that was my hamburger and I could watch these guys cook it. Next I saw them plate it, and then the waiter picked it up, brought it over to me, and I was in heaven."

Over the years Michael has learned that the two things he needs to know before putting pencil to paper are the menu and the number of seats. With this information he calculates how many burners are needed to get the food out. What can happen if this isn't taken into account is demonstrated by what occurred at the original kitchen at the Wine Spectator Restaurant at the Culinary Institute of America in St. Helena.

Adam Tihany designed the tile- and wood-trimmed circular kitchen, guided by Ferdinand Metz, the CIA's director at the time. The open kitchen was the restaurant's focal point, and everyone coming into the dining room would stop and stare. The original concept was for every customer to have ready access and the opportunity to talk to the cooks. The idea was even floated to allow guests to harvest something from the garden and give it to the cooks to prepare, but this was eventually rejected as wildly impractical. While the kitchen was pretty, the unfortunate reality was that there were only twelve burners, a small electric grill, and a huge but inefficient rotisserie to tend to a restaurant with almost two hundred seats. The cold station, which had the largest menu, also had the least amount of counter and storage space. The circular layout prevented one cook from stepping over to help another when he was in the weeds. Due to the insufficient number of burners, the average time it took to get the food to the table after the waiter asked for it was well over fifteen minutes, twice as long as required for timely service. Since opening, the restaurant kitchen has been remodeled, and there are now more burners on the line.

As California cuisine developed, so too did the configuration of equipment and the size of stations for both open and closed kitchens. The French culinary model included ovens for roasting and braising, a sauté line, one or more flat-top stoves, possibly a fryer, and a few low stock stoves. There were no grills. Steak and seafood houses had gas-fired broilers.

The traditional pantry, or cold station, was small and multipurpose because only a few basic salads were offered. Desserts and prepared appetizers might also come from the pantry. It was often set away from the hot line, with no access to burners. This setup implied that no last-minute culinary finishes were required. All that was expected of the pantry cook, or *garde manger,* was to toss some salad greens with a house dressing, put a slab of pâté on a chilled plate, arrange shrimp in a cocktail coupe, or serve a wedge of apple tart with ice cream. Thus, by default, pantry became the standard entry-level position. The cooks who worked this station were trained by rote to turn out formulaic salads (drizzle, toss, mound, and serve) and desserts (slice, scoop, arrange, garnish, and serve) without having to make any flavor decisions. Presentation usually triumphed over concept and content.

By the early 1980s, the typical pantry station had expanded because restaurants were offering many more salads. California had always been known for its salads. The green goddess salad was created at the Palace Hotel in San Francisco in 1923, and the Cobb salad was invented at the Brown Derby in Los Angeles in

1930. But California cuisine greatly expanded the salad repertoire. Along with the basic mixed greens and the classic Caesar, there were salads with warm dressings; salads garnished with avocado, citrus, and cold crab; and salads topped with myriad cooked elements, including baked goat cheese, poached eggs, sautéed wild mushrooms or chicken livers, seafood, and grilled game birds. As salads became more varied and complicated, access to burners was needed to prepare them. Mediterranean dishes also made inroads into California cooking, and *salumi* and appetizer assortments such as antipasti, hors d'oeuvres, tapas, and *mezze* became popular. All of this helped make the pantry one of the busiest stations in the restaurant, and the cook in charge became far more than a humble salad tosser.

In some places desserts still came from the expanded pantry station, but upscale restaurants gave pastry its own dedicated area, with stoves and ovens. At last garlic croutons were no long being baked in the same oven as cookies and cakes.

Focus on Fire: Grills and Wood-Burning Ovens

Dedicated readers of *Sunset* magazine know that Californians have always delighted in outdoor cooking and grilling. As far back as 1911, *Sunset* reported on an outdoor rancho party in Pasadena featuring suckling pig with all the trimmings. There were articles about backyard wood-burning terra cotta ovens in the 1920s. Jerry Di Vecchio, the food editor at *Sunset* for over forty years, said, "We were doing outdoor kitchens in 1929, for crying out loud—with built-in refrigeration. About that time, Weber came along with the kettle, and Mike Kempster [brought us] the very first one. They were giving them away to get us to try them. And, I have to say, it was a tool that worked."

Michele Anna Jordan, the author of numerous cookbooks on California cuisine and host of a radio show about California food and kitchens, said that from the earliest days, the grill was considered essential in California. "Before hotels, we had the rancheros, and people traveled by horse from ranchero to ranchero. The food was cooked outside. You could show up, if you were a traveler, and eat. Cooking outside, cooking over wood has always been a part of California." So it's not surprising that one of the signature aspects of California cuisine was live-fire cooking, whether it was done on a grill or in a fireplace or wood-burning oven. It reflected the California lifestyle and the casual outdoor environment that people are able to enjoy all year long.

Grilling was never a trademark of the Continental kitchen, so when it appeared in California restaurants, often in full view, it seemed new. This rustic style of cooking started with gas broilers, mainly in steak houses and seafood restaurants, and it was quite distinct from Texas barbecue, although many Californians refer to outdoor grilling as barbecuing. Barbecue is a method of long, slow cooking in an enclosed space using the indirect heat of a low fire, often mesquite. The food is flavored by the smoke and sometimes a spice rub, and it is usually basted during cooking and sauced toward the end, with additional sauce spooned on after cooking. Grilling is a method of cooking quickly atop an open wood, charcoal, or gas flame. The meat or fish may be marinated, but it is not sauced until it's put on the plate. In the California kitchen, with the new wood-fired or mesquite grills, the protein would be bathed in a marinade, cooked, and then maybe topped with a compound butter, additional marinade, or salsa, preparations that were novel at the time.

When guests walked into a live-fire restaurant, they were hit with the smell of smoke, followed by the fragrance of hot food, straight off the grill, being carried through the dining room. People would stand and watch the cooks, transfixed, as if they had never seen a grill before. Their small backyard grills were dwarfed by the five-foot monsters in restaurants. At Santa Fe Bar and Grill, Mark Franz oversaw a mammoth seven-foot grill, which he would fire up with an entire forty-pound bag of mesquite charcoal. At Michael's, Jonathan Waxman, a veteran of the grill station, said, "I was five years in front of the grill. My tushie is still hot."

JONATHAN WAXMAN

Michael's, Santa Monica

In 1976, with his music career as a trombonist not advancing, Jonathan Waxman returned to an earlier pursuit—cooking. Borrowing money from his parents, he arrived in Paris on his twenty-sixth birthday and struck out for Anne Willan's cooking school, La Varenne.

Upon returning to the United States in the fall of 1977, he found a job at the Domaine Chandon restaurant. The following year he got a call from Alice Waters asking if he could come to Chez Panisse to fill in while Mark Miller was on hiatus. "I did a test, which was a complete disaster. When I was at La Varenne, I had worked at the Troisgros restaurant. Blown away by their [menu], I tried to emulate it—really bad idea!" Alice Waters hired him anyway, ostensibly on the basis of his interesting handwriting ("that was her little excuse for hiring me"). Jonathan joined Jean-Pierre Moullé, Lindsey Shere, and Judy Rodgers in the kitchen.

He was green, but Jean-Pierre tolerated him. Jonathan remembered, "The first day, Jean-Pierre said, 'Make vegetables à la grecque,' and I said, 'What the hell is he talking about?' I had to look in my *Larousse Gastronomique*. But they were all nice to me."

When Mark Miller returned, Jonathan paid another visit to France to gain more experience. When he came back, he found a job with Michael McCarty. "I was hired as the *sous chef* to Ken Frank. Mark Peel was another *sous chef*, Jimmy Brinkley was the pastry chef, and Kazuto Matsusaka was another line cook. Michael and I got into each other's heads. I knew what he wanted, and he knew what I was capable of. When we opened we had tumultuous fights, but he knew that I was seasoned enough. I had made my mistakes in all the different places, and I was ready for the challenge."

The menu at Michael's "snitched a little bit from restaurants that Michael liked in Paris, like Pierre Vedel, the Bistro de Paris, and La Seine, and Jean Bertranou's menu," said Jonathan. "I did that menu, and then over the years, I basically transformed it into my menu. My philosophy was to take our French culinary background, which we both had, and apply it with a California sense. The grill, rather than the sauté station, became the focal point.

"Michael's idea was that the steaks should come from the grill. And I was like, let's do everything from the grill. It was an integral part of the menu planning. When we first started getting whole baby lambs, I would break them down, and I would take the legs, and I didn't roast them, I put them on the grill. That was my comfort zone."

Like many of his peers, he was inspired by his travels. "I started going to other places—Venice, Florence, Spain—and that helped me become more confident about how I could evolve my style. But it took a long time; it did not happen overnight. It was not easy for me to do 250 covers every night. But it was doing that, six days a week, that worked. People came back, and they were happy.

"Being a musician, it was easy for me to improvise. You had to do scales hours a day before you could improvise, because otherwise it sounded like crap. With California cuisine, you had on-the-job training. If you made a mistake, you tried a different way."

In 1981, Jonathan was invited to do a dinner in Lake Tahoe and left Mark Peel in charge of the kitchen. He got a call from the wife of Gordon Naccarato, who was assistant pastry chef. She told him Mark had gone crazy. He had put twenty-five specials on that night. He had his whole menu ready; he was ready to try out all his dishes. "That's the essence of what was happening," said Jonathan.

"People were percolating ideas and watching over their shoulder what other people were doing. We were collaborative, but we were also a little bit competitive. We all went through this odyssey together. We kept turning each other on."

Chez Panisse opened in 1971 with a small lava-rock grill that investor Paul Aratow had donated to the kitchen. It couldn't handle big dinners. When Mark Miller was hired, he started setting up grills in the alley alongside the restaurant. In 1978, a proper open fireplace grill with a spit was finally added to the kitchen. Jean-Pierre Moullé recalled, "The grill, for me, it's your Wild West. In France you go to a three-star place, you don't see anything grilled. For them, it's not refined."

The grill eventually became one of the symbols of California cuisine. It got its first burst of press in 1978, when Jeremiah Tower grilled an entire lunch outdoors over mesquite for one hundred food editors from around the country. It was at an event called Innovations in Food, held at Beechwood, the famed Astor mansion in Newport, Rhode Island. French superstar chef Guy Savoy was given access to the tiny kitchen, and Jeremiah and his Santa Fe Bar and Grill crew were asked to leave, because Savoy's dinner took precedence over their lunch. Undeterred, they gathered their food and moved outside, where they lined up four five-foot grills, determined to cook a fabulous lunch that would blow the press away. Jeremiah claimed that this luncheon thrust the grill into the national spotlight and may have been the moment when the term "California cuisine" was coined. "The full-page color spreads in the food editions of the newspapers had huge headlines, 'California Cuisine.' It was completely different. It wasn't just the grill. It was the directness and simplicity of the things coming off the grill. Traditionally, something off the grill always had sauces on the side, never sauces poured on [top]. That fosters a certain trueness in flavor."

People who work the grill station are a special breed. They have to be able to withstand incredible heat and need amazing stamina because this is often the busiest station in the restaurant. Steve Vranian was one of the early grill cooks at Fourth Street Grill, Santa Fe Bar and Grill, and Stars. He first worked the grill at Norman's in Berkeley in 1979. The chef, Charles Miles, started doing dinners he called "new California cuisine." He set up oil-drum grills in the back parking lot and cooked over mesquite charcoal. Not shy, Charles invited people like Alice Waters and Jeremiah Tower to attend. Steve said, "I don't know that we knew what we were doing, but we were full of passion. Looking back at it, it was pretty simple, marinating and grilling, but these were all new to me."

STEVE VRANIAN

Fourth Street Grill and Santa Fe Bar and Grill, Berkeley; Stars, San Francisco

In 1978, Steve Vranian had completed hotel restaurant management classes at Michigan State University and was madly in love. His girlfriend said, "Let's go to San Francisco," and he said yes. The relationship lasted about nine months. They broke up, but he decided to stay. After a stint on the grill at Norman's, Steve worked at Fourth Street Grill for Mark Miller and then at Santa Fe Bar and Grill and Stars for Jeremiah Tower. He was the consummate grill warrior.

When Steve was in his teens, his father, who worked for Ford, was transferred to Argentina. They went from a middle-class lifestyle to one that involved chauffeurs, live-in maids, swimming pools, and travel. "That's what exposed me to hospitality, hotels, and restaurants," said Steve. "Also, my mother was a very good cook. My heritage is Armenian and we always had big Armenian cookouts."

In San Francisco, he pursued a career in food. "Waiter, busboy, dishwasher—I always went back to the kitchen." He bounced around a couple of jobs until he ran into chef Charles Miles at an English pub–themed restaurant called the Ben Jonson at Ghirardelli Square. "Charles introduced me to fresh herbs and taught me that you didn't have to open a can to get beans."

When Charles Miles left Ben Jonson, Steve followed him to Norman's in Berkeley. Shortly thereafter, when Charles and Steve could not raise the money to open their own place, Steve took a job as a line cook at Fourth Street Grill with Mark Miller.

Fourth Street was "just insane," said Steve. "There was no refrigeration, and we had hotel pans full of ice and fish and steaks. We'd throw a bag of mesquite on the grill and just keep on going. The dishes were overcomposed, with way too many ingredients, but the place was packed and people loved it. The style—Mediterranean-Southwestern—was a mix of everything. I remember a lot of roasted peppers and salsa verde, Mexican pastas. Everything had shoestring potatoes. We banged out food in a cramped teeny kitchen night after night."

One day Lawrence DeVries, who owned a wine store in San Francisco, called Steve and told him to get over to the Santa Fe Bar and Grill and meet with Jeremiah Tower. "Jeremiah had a table set up on the front lawn. I walked over and did an interview. I remember him saying, 'We're going to be cleaning the kitchens tomorrow. If you want to come by, that would be great.' That was it. I went to Fourth Street the next day and did my daytime shift, and then I went over to the Santa Fe. I strolled into the kitchen, and there's Mark Franz on a ladder washing the ceiling and the walls. I grabbed a bucket and started washing the baseboards. Jeremiah walked by and said, 'Oh, I didn't expect to see you here.'"

Steve was hired, and he and Mark Franz became a team. "Jeremiah had brought a core handful of people from the Balboa Cafe—Noreen Lam, Brad Barker, and a few more. We all hit it off."

The original menu at Santa Fe drew several dishes from the Coach House restaurant in New York, which was frequented by James Beard. "We had the James Beard burger, we had the black bean soup. We had various things that were all from that era in New York." Steve was also inspired by what he was reading. "I would bring in Elizabeth David's books. Paula Wolfert was huge. Jeremiah made copies of her book and one of Richard Olney's books and said, 'You have to read these.'

"Jeremiah wrote an outline of the menu. It was just a list of ingredients, not even measurements. He was fortunate to have a group of people that, after the first three or four months, figured it out. The weaker ones left because you didn't stand a chance in that kitchen. Mark had a big background in cooking, and Noreen was major. Some of the old-timers from Chez Panisse also drifted in and out."

Santa Fe Bar and Grill was all about the grill. Mark Miller had had it custom-made, and it was beautiful. It was seven or eight feet long. I remember everyone looking around asking, 'How do we work this?'" They also had to figure out a way to get the servers back to pick up orders, since it was a closed kitchen. They decided on ringing a bell. Steve remembers things being smoky, noisy, and crazy. "I used to paint my face with charcoal at Santa Fe because I was just a screaming lunatic on the grill. No one could see you back there.

"Santa Fe was so much fun. We were really tight, and when we were closed we all hung out at each other's houses. I met my wife, Julie, there. When I look back, that was probably the most fun I ever had. It was hard work, and stressful too, but when I look back, the memories are just the good ones."

The atmosphere was much different at Stars. "Jeremiah's stamp was cleaner and simpler," said Steve. "We had a much bigger kitchen and prep area. We had stations, so everybody was doing just a couple of dishes. Sauté one was always Mark, and it had two dishes. Sauté two was usually a newer person; that had two dishes. The grill was me; there were three dishes. Dessert at that time was my wife. When our first child was born, my wife left Stars, and then Emily Luchetti, who my wife had taught, said, 'I want to do desserts.' Dessert had its own station. The cold salad had its own station. The warm salad had its own station. That put a lot of emphasis on quality, and everything was fresh.

"The menu changed every day. At the end of the shift, we would sit around, usually Mark and I and Noreen Lam and the cooks. We would have a couple of beers, or three or four, and write the next day's menu. We'd leave a big long note, and the daytime guys would come in and do the prep. We would know for sure the vegetable and the garnish, or the basic idea of it, but we might leave the protein empty so that when I came in at 5:00 or 6:00 in the morning, if the fish wasn't up to snuff, I could change it, and sometimes even change the whole dish. Mark would come in at night, and we would talk about it, and then we would just do it. We were very good at guessing how much to prep.

"Jeremiah painted the lines around the edges in terms of style. He had— and I assume he still has—an incredible talent. But I think personality is what drives a restaurant. Whatever twist of fate brought that core group together, it was magical."

In Southern California, Tony Gulisano left his job at Chinois on Main because he wanted to learn how to cook on a wood grill. He went to the "busiest wood grill in town," which at the time was at Prego in Beverly Hills. "This is 1983 or 1984. Everything was wood-grilled. I was there as a line cook, and I felt like a construction worker. My hands were swollen, my hair was all frizzy, I was getting slaughtered night after night. But I still love wood grills and wood ovens, which are so intimidating to so many cooks. I love the unpredictability and live aspect of each thing."

The grill became the most popular station in many California restaurants. Whoever worked it usually got slammed with orders, and coworkers had to be able to slide over and help plate or do whatever was needed to get the food out on time and looking good. At Stars and Square One there were only three people cooking entrées, and if you did four hundred covers, there'd be nights where the grill did well over two hundred of those dinners. Chef Bruce Hill worked the grill at Stars early on. "I had my training wheels taken off on that thing, and I had some very difficult days, and an overwhelming amount of food being ordered. I remember cutting swordfish for Saturday night—swordfish back then was very common—and I remember cutting like a hundred and fifty pieces. We sold it all, too. One time I was on vacation in New York, and I went down to the Bowery, where all the knife stores were. I was looking for a knife that was big enough to cut through these swordfish. I [found] this fourteen-inch straight fish knife—it needed to be that long just to get halfway through."

APPETIZERS

WHOLE AVOCADO AND LIME 1.75   WATERCRESS AND ORANGE SALAD 1.75
MIXED GREEN SALAD WITH FRESH HERBS AND HOUSE DRESSING   1.75
SPINACH SALAD WITH MUSHROOMS, BACON, MUSTARD DRESSING & SIEVED EGG   3.75
CAESAR SALAD WITH PARMESAN CHEESE & GARLIC CROUTONS (FOR TWO)   4.50
GRILLED BROCHETTES OF CHICKEN WITH MANGO CHUTNEY SAUCE   3.50

SEAFOOD

GRILLED FRESH PACIFIC ROCKFISH WITH LIME AND FRIED POTATOES   6.95
SMOKED TROUT WITH HERB MAYONNAISE AND CORNICHONS. SERVED WITH A
                                              HOUSE SALAD 6.25

CHARCOAL GRILLED MEATS

NEW YORK STEAK CUT FROM AGED MIDWESTERN BEEF 10.75
TOP SIRLOIN STEAK SERVED WITH CHILI-ONIONS 7.75
CHICKEN BREASTS MARINATED IN ORANGE & SERVED WITH A CHILI-CITRUS SAUCE 5.95
WHITE SAUSAGE SPICED WITH FRESH CORIANDER & GREEN CHILES   5.95
HOT SPANISH SAUSAGE SERVED WITH BLACK BEANS & FRIED POTATOES   5.95
CURED PORK LOIN SERVED WITH GINGER-ORANGE SAUCE & BLACK BEANS 5.95

SANDWICHES

GRILLED CURED PROK LOIN SERVED WITH MARINATED SWEET PEPPERS ON A
  BAGUETTE. SERVED WITH FRIED POTATOES 4.25
THINLY SLICED BREAST OF CHICKEN SERVED ON A BAGUETTE SPREAD WITH
  CHUTNEY. INCLUDES FRIED POTATOES   4.25
SANTA FE BURGER SEASONED WITH CHILIS AND COOKED ONIONS. SERVED ON A
  BAGUETTE WITH FRIED POTATOES   3.95 WITH CHEESE   4.25

SPECIALS OF THE DAY

POZOLE: A SPECIAL SOUP FROM NEW MEXICO MADE WITH CORN, PORK, CABBAGE,
  FRESH RADISHES & CHILI   CUP 1.25   BOWL 2.25
RED BEANS AND RICE MADE WITH SPICY HOT SAUSAGE   4.50
GRILLED PORK RIBS SERVED WITH BLACK BEANS AND POTATOES   5.25

DESSERTS

CHOCOLATE TRIPLE-SEC SUNDAE   2.00   CARAMEL CUSTARD WITH RUM SAUCE 1.75
CHOCOLATE-KAHLUA MOUSSE PIE   2.25   PECAN PIE 2.00   LIME TART 2.00

****

THERE IS A MINIMUM CHARGE OF FOUR DOLLARS PER PERSON IN THE DINING ROOM,
EXCLUDING BEVERAGES.

The February 13, 1982, menu at Mark Miller's Santa Fe Bar and Grill,
where Latin American flavors make their chili-fueled debut
in American classics.

The wood-burning oven became another focal point in the typical California cuisine kitchen. Although there are revisionist stories that Alice Waters was inspired to put in an oven after a trip to Italy, according to most accounts, Chez Panisse Café's pizza oven was inspired by the oven at Tommaso's Restaurant, which opened in North Beach in 1935. Both Jeremiah Tower and Jean-Pierre Moullé remember going there with Alice. Jeremiah said, "We used to go to Tommaso's all the time and Alice said, 'One of these days, I'm going to have one of those,' because of the quality of the crust."

I have known Tommaso's owner, Agostino Crotti, for over forty years, since he emigrated from Rome as a seventeen-year-old and made my espressos at Caffe Trieste in the 1960s. He told me with pride that both Alice Waters and Wolfgang Puck sent their bricklayers to copy the dimensions of his oven for Chez Panisse Café and Spago. When the Café opened, Agostino and his family were even invited to celebrate. The Chez Panisse oven was built for cooking pizzas and calzone, and these dishes became so popular that the oven was full all the time. Over the years the Café had to cut back on pizzas so other dishes could be cooked in the oven.

Wolfgang Puck explained the impetus behind his wood-burning oven at Spago. "When I was in Provence, we went to a place called Chez Gus, and they used to make great pizzas. We cooks didn't make a lot of money, so that was probably the only restaurant where we could afford to have a salad and then a pizza. When I came to America I could not find good pizza anywhere. When I was still at Ma Maison I said, 'We're going to open a restaurant and do some pizzas,' and they said, 'Well, you can't have the wood-burning pizza oven because of the fire department.'" Finally somebody told him that Alice Waters had a wood-burning oven at the new café. "Naturally I went up to see and said, 'That's crazy. How come they told me I can't have that?'" Wolfgang sat in booth number one of Chez Panisse Café, drawing up plans for Spago. He asked Alice who built her oven, and she recommended "this crazy German guy," said Wolfgang. "I wanted to build it really complicated because I wanted to roast a baby lamb in there. So I didn't build it perfectly for a pizza because it was deep inside, so it needed a lot of wood."

To try to lure Judy Rodgers to take the job as head chef at Zuni Café, partners Billy West and Vince Calcagno promised her a wood-burning oven. The original plan was for Zuni, which opened in 1979 with a Southwest-themed menu, to have a brick oven to do barbecue, but Judy told them she wasn't going to do barbecue. She was going to cook Italian with some French traditional. "I didn't want to be a pizza restaurant. I certainly was alert to Chez Panisse's woes with the brick oven, where all they could do was pizza." When she started designing her oven in 1987, Judy told the builder, "I want an oven where I can do pizzas because I need that fallback, but I want to be able to do other things." She wanted to cook dishes "à la the village bread oven, where you do your *gigot à sept heures* [seven-hour lamb]. I needed two decks. Everything short of temperature controls." Today Judy's roast chicken, cooked to order in the wood oven, is world renowned and worth waiting for.

Bradley Ogden wanted both a wood grill and a wood oven at Lark Creek Inn and One Market. He said these features added a romantic element to the menu and offered him a greater variety of cooking techniques. The wood also enhanced the food's flavors. At Lark Creek they used the fireplace oven in the dining room to cook suckling pig and cassoulet, as well as to smoke sausages and to roast meat and fish. At One Market they also cooked seafood, leg of lamb, and suckling pig in the oven, as well as a little stew of black-eyed peas topped with tiny California lamb chops.

The wood-burning oven has been responsible for many restaurants' signature dishes: Chez Panisse's pizza, Zuni's roast chicken, Bizou's flatbreads, LuLu's mussels, roasted in an iron skillet, and Spago's smoked salmon pizza. The romance of live fire infused California cuisine.

Dining Casually in the New High-End Restaurant

The open kitchen had service implications in the dining room. The energy in the room was higher and the buzz louder. Often, although the environment was casual, the price point was at fine-dining level and the quality was at three or four stars. Guests expected professional service.

Restaurant clientele was changing along with the dining environment. As restaurants became more approachable, customers dined out more often. They began to see a restaurant dinner as a replacement for a home-cooked meal and often went back to their favorite places on a regular basis. While some guests made reservations, there were now more walk-ins and regulars who had to be seated. The casualization of the dining experience meant that a customer could come in without a tie or dress and still relax, be acknowledged, and enjoy a delectable meal, smoothly and courteously served. Danny Meyer, co-owner of New York's Union Square Cafe and many other restaurants, is revered as a paragon of hospitality and service. What California restaurants did that was so appealing, in his opinion, was "to try to prepare things really well; have a wonderful wine list; warm, engaging, knowledgeable service but such that people didn't have to dress up if they didn't choose to; and food that wasn't gussied up beyond what was delicious."

The press coverage on California cuisine and celebrity chefs attracted tourists, who appeared at restaurant doors clutching old reviews. Some were dressed in shorts and flip-flops, while others wore business clothes. Attire no longer advertised the status of a client. During the dot-com era, it was not unusual for a man in a suit to order a fifty-dollar bottle of wine, while a guy in shorts with Birkenstocks ordered a four-hundred-dollar bottle.

The early days of Spago were "a phenomenon," according to Barbara Lazaroff. "People had been used to getting all dressed up. Now we had Johnny Carson in a sweater sitting with Linda Evans in a jumpsuit. We had our mailman sitting near them, and a mélange of people of every walk of life and every profession. Since we were in Hollywood, there were a lot of stars. It was casual, kick-back, fun. The tables were close to each other, the kitchen was right there, people could get up, look at the food, talk to the chefs, and say, 'No, no, I want this.' It was a culinary playground."

To put guests at ease, service personnel needed to strike the proper balance between formality and informality, attentiveness and unobtrusiveness, friendliness and professionalism. The staff knew many of their regular guests, and the daily changing menu required even greater interaction. It was not enough for the waitstaff to know proper table service; they now had to be able to talk knowledgeably about the food and the wines, which could vary every day. They tasted and learned, and so did the guests.

Some of the best front-of-house people emerged out of the California cuisine restaurant scene of the late 1970s and early 1980s. In Southern California, notable hosts included Michael McCarty at Michael's, Piero Selvaggio at Valentino, and Manfred Krankl at Campanile. In Northern California, those providing exceptional hospitality included Doug Washington at Square One, Postrio, and Jardinière; Kathy King at Square One and Boulevard; and Nick Peyton at Masa's and Gary Danko. They adapted to the more relaxed environment while still delivering outstanding service, remembering everybody's names, and making guests feel at home.

Michael McCarty created an atmosphere of what he called "civilized dining" by paying attention to every detail. "We're not a formal, stuffy restaurant, but the professionalism was beyond reproach, whether it was the execution of the food, the way the plates looked, the service, the music, the attitude, or the art on the walls." He also created a new concept of service; instead of having a captain take the order and then have a back waiter bring the food, he had only one person serve each table.

Doug Washington has worked the front of the house for many celebrated restaurants. He came to the Bay Area after serving in a restaurant in Vancouver that he characterized as "stiff and very pretentiously French." So when he started working at Square One in 1987, there were some things he wasn't used to. "You'd have the pastry cooks putting food out front in the dessert station, and everyone would be oohing and aahing. I had never worked an open kitchen, and I remember thinking, 'This is really odd, and off, and wrong,' and then a week into it, thinking, 'This is exciting! This is very much what people want.' They loved seeing what was going on. They interacted with the person plating the pastries. I was excited by seeing the walls starting to break down."

Doug was new at the business and very inexperienced when he started at Square One. When he went on to Postrio, he could afford only inexpensive suits although he was serving the most luxurious of foods. "At Postrio, we were tasting LaTache and DRC wine, and first-growth Bordeaux. They were bringing out caviar in tin sizes that I probably haven't seen since then. It felt like you were in the middle of something really big, you could feel it in the air. All of a sudden it wasn't French restaurant up here, neighborhood restaurant down here, fast food down there. There was something forming in the middle, and I was most interested in that."

The service at Postrio was great, said Doug, though the restaurant didn't have a sommelier and left wine service to the waitstaff. "The food was spectacular. They were using lots of local and organic ingredients, everything the most expensive and remote they could find.

"Guests walked in and the energy hit them over the head. There were famous people. Beautiful women with very little clothing on. Men wearing $2,000 worth of 'casual' clothing. They loved what they ate, but there were times in the very beginning, I felt like it didn't matter that much. People were just so excited."

When Kathy King was promoted from seasoned waiter to general manager at Square One, she held the servers to strict professional standards. Plates were put down and cleared properly, tables were marked with new silverware after clearing a course, glasses were polished, and waiters knew who got the steak and who got the fish without asking. After Square One she took her management skills to Postrio and then to Boulevard, where she became general manager. "Boulevard was a little more casual than Postrio. The staff talks about how much I elevated and changed the service style, which I had no direct intention to do. I just kept doing what I do, and I got a training manual together, and a cycle of service written, because for me, service is really important. The open kitchen makes the restaurant comfortable, and it's casual, but it still has to be perfect service." Boulevard chef Nancy Oakes reinforced this. "We have developed a very professional style of service. I think that that has spread, and I see it in New York. I know it doesn't come from New York; I know it comes from here. It's that great combination that I adore—and almost every French person I've ever met adores it also—serious food in a competent, well-informed, and well-run environment, but more casual. I think it is a real contribution from California."

8

A New World of Fresh Produce

Reviving the Farm-to-Table Connection

It's so exciting to have somebody who is passionate about the produce. You give chefs information, they give you information back, and it's this incredible synergy. This is where some of the best food is created.

—Master gardener Jeff Dawson

You can't ever have it quickly enough. The first hot day, chefs want the basil. It doesn't matter that this may be the first day that it's appropriate to plant the basil. That's the day they want it. They are married to the notion of seasonality without actually understanding the nuts and bolts of seasonality.

—Andy Griffin, Mariquita Farm

A lot of the farmers came out of the academic world, not just the chefs. Farmers were experimenting in the field the way chefs were experimenting in the kitchen. We were all learning together.

—Georgeanne Brennan, Le Marché Seeds

After I opened Square One in 1984, on those rare times when I could get away to Europe I would come back with spices, dried legumes, and seed packets stashed in my luggage. I carried pits from Italian white nectarines and seeds for unusual beans and greens and scimitar-shaped Turkish peppers with a sneaky heat component. I would give the seeds to Andy Powning at GreenLeaf Produce and ask him to find farmers to grow them out for me. Although not all of them could be successfully cultivated, to my delight, the seeds for *puntarelle*—a chicory native to the countryside around Rome—grew well in California. At last I had a local source for the bitter green needed to recreate the salad of Catalogna chicory with anchovy-garlic vinaigrette that I used to eat in my favorite trattoria in the Eternal City.

In the 1980s, thanks to the enthusiasm of California cuisine chefs for new varieties of fruits and vegetables, farmers began to grow these previously unavailable selections locally and, increasingly, organically. I was able to find tiny green beans, new potatoes, and fresh basil to recreate the classic Ligurian pasta with green beans, potatoes, and pesto. I combined Chioggia beets and radicchio to make a multicolored salad with warm pancetta vinaigrette. I rejoiced every time something of quality came in: tender young fava beans, zucchini blossoms, fragrant herbs, ripe figs, and tiny strawberries—even *fraises des bois* on rare occasions. Whenever Connie Green came to our back door with chanterelles or porcini she had just foraged, I would call some of my most loyal customers to let them know these treats would be on the menu that evening.

·

America during the mid-twentieth century underwent major changes in food production and consumption. Before World War II, American food was, by necessity, farm to table. In the 1950s, small farms, short supply chains, and fresh produce began to give way to agribusiness, long supply chains, and processed, packaged, frozen, and canned food. Supermarkets replaced small grocery stores, neighborhood produce stands, and independent butcher shops.

The modern distribution system required farmers to harvest their produce, pack it into standardized containers, and load it onto trucks for delivery to wholesalers in terminal markets in San Francisco, Los Angeles, and other large metropolitan centers. The wholesalers would sell the produce on the spot to distributors, restaurants, hotels, and grocery stores, or reload it into refrigerated trucks to be shipped to new destinations. Fruits and vegetables were picked before they were fully ripe so that they would be less likely to spoil or be damaged in transport. Growers selected the varieties of crops they planted based on pest resistance, cosmetic appearance, ease of harvesting, and familiarity—not flavor.

Chefs were disappointed in the poor quality and limited variety of produce in the marketplace, but there weren't a lot of options. Unlike today, when chefs have one-on-one relationships with farmers, in the 1970s and early 1980s, they usually delegated the ordering to others. In larger restaurants, especially hotel restaurants, in-house purchasing agents were responsible for obtaining products. They would call a distributor, find out what was available, and place an order. A few high-end restaurants imported specialty items such as haricots verts and mâche from Europe, even if they arrived in less than pristine condition. Established chefs resigned themselves to these conditions, but the new California chefs sought to break the stranglehold of the commercial supply chains. In the 1960s, chefs had begun to travel abroad, particularly to Europe, and to discover a world of specialty fruits and vegetables. To bring these to their tables back home, they needed to find seeds for the new plants, farmers to grow them, and new ways to transport them from the farms to the restaurants. California chefs became energized, and the result was a revival of farm-to-table cooking.

Alice Waters was the first to agitate for change. Although Chez Panisse served French country fare, the restaurant never imported products from Europe. Instead, Chez Panisse chefs shopped locally, even when the pickings were slim. They bought staples at the Berkeley Co-op, right across the street from Chez Panisse, and purchased ducks and seafood in Oakland's Chinatown.

For produce, the Monterey Market in Berkeley was the first stop for all East Bay chefs, including Michael Wild at Bay Wolf in Oakland; Judy Rodgers, then at the Union Hotel in Benicia; and Patty Unterman, then at Beggar's Banquet in Berkeley. Bill Fujimoto, the manager, offered the best fruits and vegetables at the best prices. In the back room, Bill offered wholesale prices on special items that he had put aside for restaurant professionals. Judy Rodgers, a longtime Monterey Market shopper, said that "Bill Fujimoto made a market for farmers' miracles and let chefs come in the back door to shop and taste."

BILL FUJIMOTO

Monterey Market, Berkeley

The Monterey Market opened in 1961, when Bill Fujimoto was in elementary school. His parents were running it as a full-line grocery store, but his father's heart was in produce. When Bill graduated from college, his dad said, "No more college tuitions!" and turned the grocery into an all-produce market. Bill took a job in Sunnyvale in rocket engineering, but he missed the store, where he had worked on Saturdays starting in the third grade. He came back to Berkeley to partner with his father in 1978, and his brother Ken joined them in 1979.

In the 1960s, Bill's dad, Tom, purchased almost all his merchandise at the wholesale market in Oakland. There he made connections with the farmers who delivered to the market on a regular basis. "He was always looking for something different, something new, or something old," said Bill. "My father would gamble on certain farms, give them a shot, and support that shot [by giving their produce a space in the store]. It took me a while to realize how many years some of these projects would take. What my father always understood and I learned was that once you started those communications with the farmer, you could see what they're capable of, what they excel at."

Bill helped his mother, father, and brother run the Monterey Market until his mother had a stroke in the early 1980s. His father stepped away from the business to take care of her, and Bill and Ken managed it together until Ken opened a store in Palo Alto, leaving Bill in charge. "The store continued to grow," said Bill, "primarily because of Berkeley and food."

As part of Bill's education, his father made him taste everything in the store raw. He remembers one notable lesson with eggplant. His father said, "Taste this one and this one. This one's bitter and hot, and this one's sweet. That's why you shouldn't buy those purple ones." The taste of a pie pumpkin might linger with Bill all day. Late in the garlic season, he observed how the bulbs had gone from being sweet and mild to hot and fierce. The constant sampling helped Bill develop his palate and become a discriminating buyer.

It also led him to prioritize flavor over cosmetic beauty. He explained that in the 1980s, "there were things that were available that had great flavor that you never saw coming through the supermarket. You would be explaining to farmers to be less worried about size and color and blemishes and go for flavor, pick for maturity." Bill's stance was validated by both local residents and chefs. "In Berkeley, people would appreciate those things. The chefs could make everything taste better once they found the desired ingredients. If there is something that came out of the revolution, it was flavor first."

For chefs, the Monterey Market was an ad hoc center of taste education. If a customer asked about a product, Bill could turn around and ask someone else in the store what he or she did with it. He was always learning. "The chefs instructed us on what was good. It was about taste. And the people who taught us taste were the chefs."

In 2009, Bill was pushed out of Monterey Market as a result of a messy family conflict. The chef community was outraged, but he is philosophical. He now consults and attends conferences. He is also the subject of a 2007 documentary, *Eat at Bill's*.

Bill cultivated relationships with farmers in the area for over thirty years, quietly championing heirloom and specialty produce. His buying practices encouraged small growers within a one- to two-hundred-mile radius. Mas Masumoto in Fresno County was one of the farmers who benefited from his support.

DAVID "MAS" MASUMOTO

Masumoto Family Farm, Del Rey

Mas Masumoto is the poet of peach farmers. He is a third-generation farmer on his family's eighty-acre organic property just south of Fresno. He and his wife, Marcy, and their children, Nikiko and Korio, grow mostly peaches, along with some nectarines and grapes that they dry into raisins. Mas also is the author of five impassioned and influential books that reflect on his life on the farm and the meaning he derives from his work and community.

"I've always thought that we were lucky to farm in California, where there was some tradition, but it didn't go back eighteen generations. Because it's hard to break those traditions when your father or grandfather is saying, 'My great-grandfather did it this way and it worked for him.' I learned farming by osmosis, and by doing it over and over. You teach yourself how to farm, and then accept change over the years."

Mas moved away to go to college. "As a student, I didn't plan on coming back to the farm," he said. "I studied sociology, ethnic studies, and community development, which gave me the eyes to see the world differently. So when I did come back, I started seeing farming, and our farm, in a broader context."

Mas was growing Sun Crest heirloom peaches that had delicious flavor, but he couldn't sell them because they bruised easily. But he trusted himself, and he trusted his palate. He knew he had a fabulous peach, and he wasn't going to give it up. He credits Bill Fujimoto at Monterey Market and Glenn Yasuda at Berkeley Bowl for the survival of this and other heirloom varieties. "I was struggling to find a home for our peaches. Even though Bill and Glenn could handle only 10 percent of our crop, that 10 percent was enough to justify what I was doing. They had institutional memories. They remembered what these old heirloom varieties tasted like. So when I'd say, 'Hey, I have this Sun Crest peach,' or 'I have this Le Grand nectarine,' they'd go, 'Oh, I remember that. It was great.' That memory is critical to the work that we do. Because if you don't have that memory of flavor, how do you know if what you're eating is good or bad?"

Mas thrived on his interactions with customers. Even when business as a whole was slow, the public's praise and enthusiasm for his produce would lift his spirits. "As a grower, that's very important, because we work in isolation so much. If we don't hear those conversations, we begin to doubt ourselves. The marketplace is telling you that your smaller, off-color fruit that does not have shelf life isn't good, and you say, 'I guess I'm doing it wrong.' Then, hearing those conversations, you realize, 'No, I am doing something right.'

"California cuisine revived and elevated memory to a position that rewarded flavor and those of us on the farming side who were trying to grow flavor, before it was too late. People are paying attention to memories more, and understanding the value of them. This whole movement came at a time when people still remembered spending a few weeks on somebody's farm or an uncle's ranch where they tasted this heirloom tomato or peach, and when they taste it now, it catapults them back."

Today Mas tries to get away occasionally during the busy harvest season to visit restaurants and see what they're doing with his fruit. "Sending peaches to a restaurant for the first time is sort of like dating. The first date, we just send them something, and we talk in general about it. They explore it and give us feedback, and we tell them what we think. By the second and third date, which is like the second and third year, we're forming a relationship. For over twenty years, we've been finding others that share our passion, be it a restaurant, a chef, a food distributor, or an outlet. It sounds almost goofy, but we're constantly falling in love every year. And sometimes farmers, when they hear me give a talk, stop and say, 'You know, I had forgotten how passionate I was when I started farming.' And they want to rekindle that.

"This notion of personal and passionate goes beyond economics. I always fear that we're going to lose the cultural part of agriculture, because it's becoming dominated by the business of agriculture. If you approach this as a personal endeavor, your personal baggage is going to be part of what you do, and you *want* it to be that way, whether it's the way you handle things, raise things, or educate people."

In the seventies and eighties, providing good, healthy meals was viewed as a political enterprise, and the community often pitched in. Friends, neighbors, and family members pressed small baskets of lettuces, herbs, or radishes on chefs. In Mendocino, locals stopped by Café Beaujolais with berries or other tidbits they had grown in their gardens. In one case, chef-owner Margaret Fox received "a very, very small bag of green beans." She remembers thinking, "Okay, that's not going to last long, but it's going to be the salad of the day as long as it does."

When an ingredient wasn't available, cooks improvised, sometimes growing their own herbs and greens or trying to persuade others to plant them. At Chez Panisse, opening chef Victoria Wise recalled running down the block to clip rosemary off a nearby hedge to season a leg of lamb because there were no fresh herbs at the market. Pastry chef Lindsey Shere brought seeds for arugula and other greens back from Europe and had her father grow them for the restaurant in his garden in Healdsburg.

Joseph Broulard, chef at La Grange in LA, grew mâche in his backyard and would bring bags of it to L'Ermitage chef Jean Bertranou. Wendy Krupnick, who had volunteered in the Alan Chadwick Garden as a student at UC Santa Cruz and later worked with Warren Weber at Star Route Farms, tended a little restaurant garden where she grew produce for Jesse Cool's two restaurants in Menlo Park— Flea Street Café and Late for the Train.

When he opened his eponymous Santa Rosa restaurant in 1980, John Ash would invite the purveyors to come for dinner. "Small growers would come, and maybe ask, 'What else can I grow for you?' We used to say, 'We'd love to try this. We'll front the seed, and we'll buy everything you've got, whether we can use it all or not. Even if it doesn't work, we'll make sure that you won't go in the hole for doing this.' It was a little like micro loans. Half the time it would turn out, and the other half it would fail—we grew the wrong thing in the wrong place."

Other restaurateurs, influenced by the back-to-the-land movement, aspired to be totally self-sufficient. Virginia Mudd hired master gardener Jim Fellows in 1978 to plant an organic produce garden on her seven-acre site in San Ramon. She wanted to sell fruits and vegetables to nearby restaurants, but when that effort fizzled, she decided she would use the produce in a restaurant of her own. In 1981, she opened Mudd's. Though the garden never grew enough to satisfy the restaurant's needs, it elevated the farm-fresh cuisine cooked by chef Amaryll Schwertner.

Green Gulch Farm and Greens restaurant, opened in 1979, achieved the most successful symbiotic relationship. Both were owned and run by the San Francisco Zen Center. Green Gulch in Marin enjoyed the advantages of sufficient land to grow a wide range of cold-weather crops and an ample staff, drawn from students at the Zen Center. "From Green Gulch we got beautiful herbs, astounding lettuces, lovely potatoes, all the brassicas—basically, all the cold-weather produce," said Deborah Madison, Greens' first chef. But she quickly determined that Green Gulch could not be the only supplier for the restaurant. "It is in a very foggy clime, and the farm wasn't as fully developed as it is now." To supplement the produce from Green Gulch, she looked for farmers in the Central Valley with the sun power to grow tomatoes, zucchini, eggplant, and other hot-weather produce. Deborah enlisted Dorothy Coil, a farmer from

Lodi, to drive down twice a week. In addition, said Deborah, "my *sous chef,* Jim Phelan, and I found a you-pick farm up in Suisun, so on Saturday mornings, Jim and I would drive up there, pick produce, drive it back, and plan the dinner menu while we were driving."

After visiting Green Gulch, Alice Waters dreamed of having a farm to supply produce for her restaurant. The first attempt at a Chez Panisse organic garden was the Hudspeth Farm, owned by gastronome John Hudspeth. John had attended the James Beard Cooking School in Seaside, Oregon, in 1971, where he had met Marion Cunningham. "We both loved food and restaurants," he said. "And she said, 'You must go to Chez Panisse.' So I went, and I fell in love with it and with Alice and Jeremiah."

In 1978, John moved to Berkeley and rented an apartment in Alice's building on Cedar Street. He proceeded to eat at Chez Panisse almost every night for months. At the end of that time he asked if he could work in the kitchen as a volunteer *commis,* or prep cook. For the brief period he was in the kitchen he observed how "Alice wanted every vegetable to be perfect. I remember watching stuff go into the garbage because it didn't meet the standards, and it was very frustrating." He thought he could do better.

He asked his father, a businessman, for the use of his family's horse ranch in Sacramento, which was on river-bottom soil that was lying fallow. John knew little about farming and hired Karen Montrose, who had been overseeing the organic garden at the Golden Door Spa in Escondido, to grow vegetables for Chez Panisse. A self-professed dilettante, John did little work on the farm himself. "I didn't get my hands dirty. I bought a fancy new tractor and ran it around a couple of times, and then put it in the garage." His father and his company paid the bills.

Andy Griffin of Mariquita Farm worked at the Hudspeth property and described it as "a two-acre biodynamic French intensive garden. They had a galaxy of tiny French lettuces. Arugula at that time was virtually unknown, and so of course they had that. They probably grew eighty or ninety different kinds of things." Unfortunately, according to Andy, that included "many things that really had no value to the restaurant and couldn't be used by the restaurant." Although some items may have made sense from a biodynamic perspective, Chez Panisse couldn't use all of what the farm grew. "Even though we didn't have a lot of okra, they couldn't possibly use the amount of okra that we had." They made many mistakes because their production was unreliable and they weren't running the farm like a business.

In 1982, the lumber company that was supporting the ranch went under, and

John's family went bankrupt. Since the farm was not self-sustaining, "everything came to a screeching halt," said Andy. "It was a short run. Maybe two seasons."

Around this time, Chez Panisse expanded the role of Andrea Crawford, a young waiter at the restaurant who was living on a boat but yearned for a garden. Andrea was enlisted to create a garden for the restaurant, and in 1982, she, Sibella Kraus, and Thérèse Shere, Lindsey Shere's daughter, installed French intensive beds in the backyard of the house Stephen Singer and Alice shared on Monterey Avenue. There they grew lettuces, herbs, and edible flowers, such as nasturtiums, hollyhocks, calendula, and squash blossoms.

This and other urban gardens filled some of the restaurant's needs, but Alice continued to harbor the dream of having one farmer who would grow everything for Chez Panisse. Finally, after Andrea left, Bob Cannard was chosen to be the primary grower for the restaurant. Bob had started farming organically in the 1970s, selling his produce at the Sonoma County farmers' markets when they were first getting under way. The family farming tradition traced back to his father, Bob Cannard Sr., who had begun farming in 1960 in Sonoma. Both Bob and his father taught horticulture at Santa Rosa Junior College.

"In the mid-1980s, Chez Panisse came around and asked if I'd be interested in working with them," said Bob. "Alice was keen on promoting what we were trying to do—freshness and localness." He stopped attending farmers' markets and devoted himself exclusively to supplying the restaurant.

The chefs at Chez Panisse sometimes told him what they wanted him to plant, and sometimes he told them what he thought he did best. "David Tanis and Jean-Pierre Moullé were extremely flexible and open. They'd run into a variety or crop they thought they might like and would bring me a small package of seeds to trial. They suggested, and so did I. It was always a gentle back and forth. If I grew something and it fit, great, and if I grew something and it didn't fit, well, it just didn't fit."

Chez Panisse still supplemented with produce from other farms, including Chino Farms. According to Jean-Pierre Moullé, "We're not dealing with one farm; we're dealing with forty, maybe more, and that's the miracle of California. The farmers were willing to change, and they got rewarded by becoming more visible. They also did a big business. They grew up with us. They understood our needs, and that's beautiful."

While many chefs in Northern California sought out high-quality seasonal produce, in Los Angeles, freshness was not as important as presentation. Chef Octavio Becerra described LA in the 1970s and early 1980s as "a gastronomic desert with little oases here and there. The quality of the food wasn't a focus, so the chefs were kind of shocked at having to put a lot of effort and energy into finding people to grow ingredients. The little mesclun salads, the baby frisée, even the baby vegetables and haricots verts, were uncommon. But nevertheless, the French, Italian, and German chefs pursued it, and they had a great deal of influence."

Jean Bertranou was one of the first chefs in Southern California to challenge the status quo by making his colleagues aware that produce could be better. A classically trained French chef, he opened the elegant L'Ermitage in West Hollywood in 1975. At the time, he famously and disdainfully remarked, "When it comes to ingredients, California has nothing." Like chefs at other deluxe Continental restaurants in Los Angeles, including St. Germain and L'Orangerie, Jean imported a gamut of products that he couldn't find in California, from ducks, fish, and foie gras to herbs and greens such as chervil, sorrel, arugula, and mâche. He was also the first Los Angeles chef to bring in seeds and commission farmers to grow vegetables for his restaurant. Unfortunately, he died in 1980 at the age of fifty and did not live to see LA chefs follow his lead in promoting fresh, local produce.

In the 1980s, Wolfgang Puck began to realize Jean Bertranou's dreams and raise the standards for produce in LA restaurants. In 1985, Wolfgang contacted Andrea Crawford to see if she would come to LA to grow herbs and lettuces for his new restaurant, Spago. He sweetened the deal by offering to pay to plant the first garden, and she moved down to LA with her husband and son. Andrea's Kenter Canyon Farms still supplies Spago and other restaurants and markets with such items as mesclun, frisée, radicchio, and arugula. (Meanwhile, her sister, Heidi, supplied salad greens to Square One and a few other restaurants in Northern California.)

Urban community gardens were another source of organic fruits and vegetables for LA chefs. In 1986, Mary Sue Milliken and Susan Feniger began working with the horticulture therapy program at the Los Angeles VA Hospital, which supplied unusual items for their Border Grill restaurants, including black mustard seed sprouts, mizuna, chrysanthemum greens, and sweet potato greens.

San Diego's premier chefs joined Wolfgang Puck, Michael McCarty, and Alice Waters in buying from Chino Farms in northern San Diego County. Since 1969, Tom Chino and his family have cultivated fifty acres in Rancho Santa Fe. They sell their produce in a farm stand alongside the property. Gaining attention first with Silver Queen corn, introduced in the 1960s, they went on to become one of the early purveyors of multicolored bell peppers and heirloom tomatoes, and their new and heirloom varieties, picked at the peak of ripeness, are considered among the finest in the state. "The Chinos are the best," said San Diego chef Jeff Jackson. "It never ceases to amaze me what Tom Chino can do with any vegetable that he grows." The farm ships only to Chez Panisse and Spago, and other chefs have to drive to the ranch and wait in line to buy produce. "We made the Chino Farm famous because we put the Chino vegetable salad on the menu," said Wolfgang. He visits the farm frequently to touch base and nurture their special and prestigious relationship.

The Farm-Restaurant Project and the Tasting of Summer Produce

In Northern California, farmers and chefs began to move closer together with the Farm-Restaurant Project, under the aegis of Sibella Kraus. Sibella began her culinary career in catering, and in 1981 she was hired as a line cook at Chez Panisse Café. She soon realized that restaurant line work was not for her but that she was interested in sourcing produce for the restaurant. She became the restaurant's first official "forager," tasked with finding the best ingredients available in the Bay Area. Most restaurants looked at the bottom line and assigned this job to *sous chefs* and kitchen managers, but for Alice Waters, the ingredients were paramount.

In 1983, Sibella launched the Farm-Restaurant Project with seed money from seven restaurants—Chez Panisse, Fourth Street Grill, Bay Wolf, Hayes Street Grill, Greens, Mudd's, and Union Hotel. The restaurants agreed to pool their resources to buy produce from local farms. The network of participating farmers developed by word of mouth and was mainly drawn from organic farmers in Sonoma, Yolo, and Santa Cruz counties. Sibella would visit the farmers and, if she liked what she saw, she would ask if they were willing to grow produce for one or more of the participating restaurants, depending on their needs. Sibella arranged for delivery, often picking up the items herself.

Warren Weber at Star Route Farms was in the first group of farmers Sibella contacted. Andy Griffin was working for Star Route at the time. One of the farmers' worries, said Andy, was, "If I grow this crop of *ronde de nice* [an heirloom squash] for you, which I can, and which you say you want, and then somebody else comes in and they have one they'll sell you cheaper, then what do I do? I'll have lost everything because you bought it from him. We farmers are going to be in this everlasting downward spiral." To instill some stability and predictability into the relationship, Sibella tried to get the farms and restaurants to sign contracts, a concept that many farmers initially resisted, but then accepted as mutual trust was established. Warren signed a contract with Chez Panisse and still supplies produce to the restaurant today.

WARREN WEBER

Star Route Farms, Bolinas

Warren Weber's Star Route Farms is the oldest certified organic farm in California. Warren grew the first organic lettuce served in many Northern California restaurants, and he is an icon in the organic farming movement. After earning at PdD in English, he moved to Bolinas in 1974 to join a community land trust where participants were teaching themselves to farm organically.

Because his background was intellectual rather than agricultural, he knew little about farming and sought advice from the farm advisor at the University of California Cooperative Extension. "A guy from UC Davis came down and looked around. He was very nice, and he said, 'You're not going to be able to grow leaf lettuce here because in California you have to have two hundred acres to grow leaf lettuce. Secondly, you say you want to grow it organically. I don't know anybody at Davis who can tell you how to do that.' That ended our conversation. They didn't have the intellectual capital at the land grant universities or any of the state universities to tell you how to do it because they had already been industrialized."

Warren was sure there was a future in the organic movement, and he taught himself what he needed to know about cover cropping, composting, cultivation (initially using a horse-drawn plow), crop rotation, and other organic techniques. He became a specialist in greens, and for the first nine years of his farming career, he sold to small natural food stores. Then, in the early 1980s, Sibella Kraus came to visit Star Route Farms on behalf of the Farm-Restaurant Project. According to Warren, she was not primarily interested in whether his produce was organic or not. At the time, chefs were more concerned with quality. "Alice Waters had connections with Chino Farms, which was not organic. For years Chino was her favorite personal grower, and Chez Panisse still works with them. I had a serious discussion with Alice about this. I said, 'We have organic standards, and we're trying to make them better. It's not just 'I like the taste of this versus that' or 'I like this person versus that person.' She got it right away. When the restaurant started to hook up with smaller specialty farmers who were growing good produce, it turned out that they were all organic farmers. So the organic thing took off."

For a while, the bulk of Warren's business continued to be with natural food stores and wholesale distributors like Veritable Vegetable. In the 1980s, selling to a restaurant was very different from selling to a distributor, explained Warren. "The distributor is buying a lot of product from a lot of people in a seasonal fashion. They know when your season is, so if they liked your butter lettuce last spring, they want it next spring. During the summer and winter, they're buying from other people. But when spring comes around, they'll pick you up again. Restaurants aren't like that. If you have butter lettuce, they want it all year long, not just in the spring."

The restaurants wanted arugula and a mesclun mix, so Warren bought seeds from Le Marché to diversify his offerings. As the demand from restaurants increased, he decided that Star Route should try to grow year-round for the restaurants. In 1989, he installed greenhouses in the Coachella Valley, south of Palm Springs. "In California, we have seasonality in some things almost twelve months a year. Star Route Farms' arugula is seasonal every day of the week. In the wintertime, we're growing it in the desert, and it's actually better quality than it is here up north."

By the late 1990s, organic agriculture had become so successful that it attracted large-scale farmers. "The conventional grower-shippers had been sitting back, watching the [organic] industry expand, pooh-poohing it, trying to stop it, trying to kill legislation, hitting the press, whatever they could do. But seeing that it had a 20 percent growth rate, Grimmway Farms [in the southern San Joaquin Valley] and other companies decided it was time. They jumped in and killed the natural food market for the small growers, a lot of whom went out of business."

Others were saved by the shift toward small and local. "As the organic industry got big, some within the community said, 'Oh, bad, big, global,' and they adjusted their taste and their desires. Restaurants and the farmers' markets were the saving grace. They began to promote local and regional identity."

Warren's high standards are well known in the industry. Chef Traci Des Jardins recalls that, when she moved from Los Angeles to San Francisco in 1991 to become kitchen manager at Aqua, "I was learning the lay of the land, learning who the purveyors were. I'd ordered six cases of lettuce from Star Route Farms. When they got to the restaurant, I knew I'd overordered, so I sent three cases back. I didn't have the good sense to realize that they had cut this lettuce all for me. Oh, was Warren upset. I had never had the experience of being yelled at by a purveyor. That was the turning point for me. I realized how much integrity he had, how much he cared about the quality of his product."

To celebrate the first five months of the Farm-Restaurant Project, Sibella organized an event called the Tasting of Summer Produce, which was held at Greens in 1983. Chefs cooked for the farmers, and it was the first time some of the growers had eaten gourmet food. "Warren brought the whole crew," said Andy Griffin. "Because I spent all my time either in the field or in the truck dropping stuff off, it was the first time I'd ever eaten in a fancy restaurant. I got to see all these people who I had heard about through the grapevine, and it was really fun. And it came at a time when I was not making any money working on these farms and needed something to keep me going. A little bit of enthusiasm goes a long way."

The event was so well received that Sibella organized a second tasting, in 1984, also held at Greens. The third was hosted by Robert Mondavi and Margrit Biever Mondavi at the Robert Mondavi Winery.

The 1986 Tasting of Summer Produce at the Oakland Museum was a touchstone for everybody in the Bay Area food movement. This spectacular event was open to chefs, the press, and the general public. It was held in August, and juicy samples of melons, peppers, grapes, and tomatoes covered the long tables. "It was the best showcase of food I've ever seen," said Dexter Carmichael, who assisted Sibella with logistics and is now the director of the Ferry Plaza farmers' market. "I always look at the tasting as something of the effect I want to achieve with the marketplace." The diversity of the offerings was a revelation, and the farmers who attended were given a boost by the exposure.

The event grew, and in 1987 and 1988, some thirteen hundred restaurant chefs, produce wholesalers, and food aficionados bought tickets to taste the contributions of more than one hundred growers. The last Tasting of Summer Produce was held in 1989. After that, Sibella turned her attention to establishing the Ferry Plaza farmers' market in San Francisco. But by then the Farm-Restaurant Project had made great strides in advancing its aims of fostering community between urban and rural groups, protecting agricultural land, running events like the tastings, and promoting agritourism in the form of rural trekking, farm trails, and you-pick programs. The tastings also succeeded in forming alliances among a number of disparate groups, including People for Open Space (now Greenbelt Alliance), the American Institute of Wine and Food, the San Francisco Professional Food Society, and the UC Small Farm Program.

Similar events sprang up elsewhere in the state, including a Summer Harvest Tasting in the Sacramento area and a Summer Tasting of California Farms at the wholesale produce market in Los Angeles. These tastings were not open to the public and were more akin to trade shows. But they were well attended and their aims were comparable: to help small farmers find new markets and to help chefs at upscale restaurants locate the specialty produce they sought.

Stimulated by the tastings and associated publicity, chefs were eager to get their hands on new specialty varieties. Farmers for their part were ready to branch out and experiment. But first they needed seeds. Seed packets brought from abroad by chefs couldn't meet the demand.

Many farmers became affiliated with Seed Savers Exchange, founded in 1975 by Iowans Kent Whealy and Diane Ott Whealy. The organization was dedicated to preserving rare heirloom plant varieties by collecting seeds and sharing them among its members. Master gardener Jeff Dawson, who curated the gardens at Fetzer Vineyards and Copia, participated in this effort. But Le Marché Seeds, founded by Georgeanne Brennan and Charlotte Glenn in 1982, was the seed supplier most closely tied to specialty produce farmers. By 1986, the company was offering some 280 varieties of European, Asian, Mexican, and American fruits and vegetables.

GEORGEANNE BRENNAN

Le Marché Seeds, Dixon

Georgeanne Brennan grew up in Laguna Beach, California. In 1970, she and her husband moved to a farmhouse in France, where they raised goats and pigs. They had intended for the move to be permanent, but three years later family circumstances forced them to return to California. Georgeanne got a job teaching high school in the Vacaville School District, where she met Charlotte Glenn, the first certified woman agriculture teacher in the state of California.

In 1982, after almost ten years of teaching, Georgeanne was looking for a change. When Charlotte approached her about starting a seed company, Georgeanne embraced the idea. She suggested importing seeds from Europe, and they phoned Vilmorin, a seed company in France, announcing themselves as a small seed vendor in Northern California, even though at the time they had only the germ of an idea. Vilmorin arranged for a representative, Walter de Maat, to meet with them. When asked for their office address, Georgeanne said, "Oh, let's meet someplace where we can have some coffee and something to eat." So they met him at the Nut Tree in Vacaville.

Charlotte told him that they weren't interested in buying patented seeds from hybrids, so de Maat gave them a list of open-pollinated seeds, including haricots verts Fin de Bagnols, romaine Rouge d'Hiver, and mâche Coquille de Louviers.

With their first shipment of seeds from Vilmorin, Georgeanne and Charlotte were intent on changing the mind-set of American gardeners. "Americans were concerned with who could grow the biggest cucumber or the biggest pumpkin, and the notion was that you plant your garden in spring, harvest your produce in fall, and then can it." Georgeanne and Charlotte instead promoted the concept of the year-round garden, "where you plant in different seasons and you are always harvesting." Their catalogue included the stories behind each seed variety, as well as recipes, "because why would you grow these unless you were going to cook?"

When they mailed the first Le Marché catalogue to magazine and newspaper food editors, they got a tremendous response. Calls came in from emerging organic growers, including Warren Weber at Star Route Farms, Dru Rivers and Judith Redmond at Full Belly Farm, Jeff and Annie Main at Good Humus Produce, and Dale and Stuart Dickson at Stone Free Farm.

To build their business, Georgeanne and Charlotte traveled to Europe to obtain new varieties. Whereas American seed growers were not very supportive, brushing them off as housewives, Europeans took them "dead seriously," according to Georgeanne. "They brought us to lunch and led us out in the fields. In one catalogue there's a picture of me with Hans Van der Meer, who was with an Italian seed company outside of Cesena, Italy. He took me out to see the fields of Chioggia beets and lacinato kale. I thought they were fabulous, and we imported those seeds. We were the first company to introduce those."

Georgeanne and Charlotte not only sold seeds but also taught farmers how to grow them. Many of the vegetables Le Marché offered were so new, no one knew what to do with them. One company in Salinas hired the two women to explain how to grow radicchio. The farmers knew it was going to be a hot item but were trying to grow it like lettuce, giving it high nitrogen, which will cause radicchio to go to seed. Georgeanne and Charlotte were happy to share their knowledge. "It was a very collegial time," said Georgeanne.

In addition to running the company, they wrote about cooking and gardening for newspapers, magazines, and books. In 1983, most people either cooked or gardened, but not both. For several years, Georgeanne and Charlotte wrote a column together called "Cooking and Gardening" for the *San Francisco Chronicle*. In 1985, they coauthored *The New American Vegetable Cookbook* with Isaac Cronin, who taught them how to organize and develop a recipe. Over the years, they found new interests, and in 1991, they sold Le Marché Seeds to Renee Shepherd's seed company so they could pursue different careers. Georgeanne became a cookbook writer, and Charlotte (now Charlotte Kimball) became a landscape contractor and revegetation expert.

Renee Shepherd started Shepherd's Garden Seed Company in 1985. She had a large trial garden in Felton, near Santa Cruz, in which she tested and evaluated European vegetables and herbs such as kohlrabi, Rosa Bianca Italian eggplant, Dutch broadleaf cress, French tarragon, and the tiny pickling cucumbers used to make cornichons. Hybrids propagated for kitchen gardens in Europe did well in California's Mediterranean climate. Upon acquiring Le Marché Seeds in 1991, Renee expanded her offerings. She supplied home gardeners as well as farmers with seeds for unusual produce until she sold the business in 1997.

Once new connections with farmers had been forged by the Farm-Restaurant Project, chefs no longer needed to rely on the commodity-oriented wholesale markets. Jean-Pierre Moullé, who cultivated a small garden himself, described how the chefs at Chez Panisse "slowly stopped going to the wholesale produce market in Oakland. We started to have guys delivering special produce to our door, and we worked with them for years, bringing up the quality, bringing up what we had a vision for. I was asking for chervil, mâche, and all those things which did not exist in California yet." One of the more elusive specialty items was Belgian endive, which was grown only in Europe until Rich Collins started his endive farm in Solano County in 1983.

RICH COLLINS

California Vegetable Specialties, Rio Vista

Rich Collins grows only Belgian endive. He cultivates the classic pale white endive, a red variety that is a cross between white endive and Treviso radicchio, and a rosy-red variety called Endigia that is a cross between endive and Verona and Chioggia chicories. He is the only commercial producer of endive in the United States. We used Rich's endive at Square One in many of our favorite salads, and every year for Valentine's Day he sends me a bouquet of the red and white varieties.

Rich's family always had a big garden, and ever since he was a kid growing up in Sacramento, he wanted to be a farmer. In 1978, when he was a senior in high school, he worked as a dishwasher and later a busboy at a French restaurant called Restaurant La Salle. "It was the nicest restaurant in Sacramento—very French, very posh, with a Swiss maître d' and a Ugandan chef. One evening the owner was braising a head of endive for a VIP birthday banquet and he said, 'You ought to grow this. I paid $4 a pound for it.' They were flying it in from Belgium."

That May, Rich announced to his parents that he was going to cultivate endive. To his surprise, he found out his mother had been best friends in grade school with the wife of Stanley Corriea Jr., the owner of Stanley Produce, a specialty produce distributor in San Francisco. She arranged an introduction with Stanley, and Rich, only eighteen years old, drove into San Francisco to meet him. Stanley agreed not only to buy Rich's endive but also to help finance his enterprise. It took five years for Rich to learn how to grow endive successfully. Stanley was patient.

Rich studied agricultural and managerial economics at UC Davis and tried cultivating a few acres of endive, but he couldn't figure out how to do it. He wasn't the first to have problems with the tricky crop. "When I started, there was no domestic production," said Rich. "I quickly found out that's because it's so hard to grow." Endive, a type of chicory, must be kept away from sunlight during cultivation in order to keep its leaves white and tender, so it is usually grown indoors in dark temperature-controlled rooms or outside in lightproof tunnels.

In 1982, Rich went to Europe to find out as much as he could about endive farming. "I worked on farms throughout Belgium, Holland, France, and into Switzerland and Spain," said Rich. "I visited seed companies and research people and got a good working knowledge of endive. Then Stanley financed us to the tune of maybe $15,000 in the early years. We harvested our first box on Thanksgiving Day 1983."

"We started really small, but we seem to have started at the right time." As the company expanded in the late 1980s, Rich began to send endive to Los Angeles, working with LA Specialty Produce. In 1986, Herman Van Den Broeck of Coosemans Specialty Produce offered to buy Stanley's entire crop. "And I thought to myself, 'That's pretty interesting. A Belgian guy wants to buy everything I have. I must be doing something right.'"

Distribution networks were the last piece to fall into place. Few restaurants could afford to send someone to the farms to pick up produce. And few farmers had the time to drive into town every day and make the rounds of all the places using their produce. Nor did most kitchens have loading areas that could accommodate the multitude of trucks and people required to check in so many small deliveries. The issue was how to get the produce from the farmers to the restaurants quickly and efficiently.

Steve Walton and Jameson Patton, who had formed GreenLeaf Produce in 1976, realized that their company was positioned to fill that need. Since it wasn't practical for restaurants to contact all the individual farmers and then wait for each truck to show up, GreenLeaf arranged for farmers to bring the produce to one spot, where GreenLeaf would pick it up for distribution. GreenLeaf provided a great service to both farmers and restaurants by consolidating the gathering and delivery of produce. Up until the early 1980s, they had dealt with just a few restaurants, but by the time Andy Powning joined in 1982, they were ready to expand.

ANDY POWNING AND BILL WILKINSON

GreenLeaf Produce, San Francisco

GreenLeaf was the creation of Jameson Patton and Steve Walton, members of a 1970s hippie commune called the Hunga Dunga Tribe. Jameson and Steve would collect money and food stamps from other members and buy food for the collective at the Alemany farmers' market and the wholesale produce terminal. When the house that the commune was renting went up for sale, Jameson decided he and Steve should get jobs so that they could buy it. They started purchasing produce for local restaurants, including Hamburger Mary's and a sandwich shop called the Havens. By 1976, they were successful enough to establish GreenLeaf as a company. Jameson was a savvy businessman with exacting standards. People at the produce terminal knew that he would return subpar goods, which ingratiated him with customers who wanted high quality and good service.

Andy Powning went to work for GreenLeaf in 1982. Produce had been part of his life since his childhood on the East Coast. "In the back of comic books there were ads where you could mail away for seeds to sell door to door and earn prizes. At the age of eight or nine, instead of being a paperboy, I went door to door and sold vegetable and fruit seeds. Growing up we always had a garden, and when I left Connecticut we had a fourteen-acre tree farm and a huge vegetable garden, so it was always near and dear to me. When I started at GreenLeaf, I was doing warehousing and inventory. Jameson didn't have a lot of patience for the more challenging customers and would say, 'You get the phone.' In a month I had a desk."

In 1984, Sibella Kraus came to GreenLeaf as part of the Farm-Restaurant Project to act as a liaison between GreenLeaf and farmers. She amped up the volume and brought in incredible produce from Coke Farm in San Juan

Bautista, Blue Heron Farms in Watsonville, Webb Ranch in Portola Valley, and other growers.

In 1992, both Jameson and Steve succumbed to AIDS, leaving GreenLeaf adrift. Their loyal customers did not want to see the company go under. Fortunately, the late Bill Wilkinson, a fifty-five-year-old retired hotel manager who had worked at the Waldorf-Astoria, Stanford Court, and Campton Place, was looking for a new project.

In 1993, before buying the company, Bill went down to the warehouse, put on a uniform, and packed produce for a few weeks to get a feel for the business. "I realized that there were twenty-four nice people who were all going to lose their jobs. I thought, 'This isn't right.' So I paid the payroll for them that month to see if we could make it last.

"We began to put it back together again. One of the problems was that the owners had a lot of debts, so when they went to sell the company, it was way too much money, and everybody said, 'Let's go bankrupt.' I decided that if we were going to do this, we were going to do this right. So instead of taking them to bankruptcy, I paid off all the bills—hundreds of thousands of dollars. It was crazy, but I couldn't let the big guys in the industry knock out the little guys."

Slowly Bill brought the company out of debt and into profitability. Today GreenLeaf distributes food from one hundred farms to over five hundred restaurants and ships produce across the country.

Distributors not only collect and transport produce but also play a role in what is grown and how it is presented. Andy, for example, created the "toy box" tomato mix. "There used to be two kinds of tomatoes: little ones and big ones," he explained. "Then the Sweet 100 cherry tomato showed up, and it was the M&M of the vegetable world. Everybody wanted them, and for two or three years there weren't enough to go around. The fourth year everybody planted them and there were too many. Then the Sun Golds came up. Same thing—high demand, not enough, then too many, and then the market reached stasis. Soon there were twelve kinds of cherry tomatoes and chefs were saying, 'I want twelve kinds, but I don't want twelve cases.' So I thought, 'Why don't we start doing mixed packs?' We had the farmers start by mixing cherry tomatoes, and that spread to full-sized tomatoes and then to beets, carrots, and baby lettuce."

GreenLeaf was also involved in education, an essential element in the growth of California cuisine. Each item of produce had a story and a season. At the start of the harvest, if old crops finished early, new crops were pushed to market.

The new crops might be more expensive, and they might not have the optimal sugar content or color or ripeness. Conversely, at the tail end of the season, if the new crops weren't ready yet, the old ones would be promoted, and they'd often show signs of age. Andy would field the calls from chefs who wanted to know what was going on. "'How come the Kennebec potatoes are rotten?' 'How come the onions are so expensive?' 'Every May, the limes go up in price, why is that?' I thought, 'We have to get ahead of this. We have to be a partner to our customers and keep them informed." He created a newsletter that started as a list of items but grew to become a two-page bulletin. "When people called," said Andy, "I would answer their question and then ask, 'By the way, are you getting the newsletter?'" "It turned out to be very successful," said Bill. "And using the business as a learning tool is very much a California cuisine kind of thing. We shared information and made it available so people could grow literally and figuratively."

GreenLeaf supports California farmers, but to meet demand, the company also imports items. "GreenLeaf is the farmer's friend and firmly believes in local, seasonal, and sustainable," said Andy. "But we deal with a broad spectrum of customers, and people want raspberries, blackberries, and asparagus year-round. Me, I eat asparagus for two months out of the year until I'm green, and then I don't touch it because it doesn't taste good after that."

"The more local the better," he continued. "Local keeps the money in the community, keeps agricultural land as agricultural land, and keeps farmers in the business of farming. They take the risk to grow stuff that doesn't yield as much, requires more time to ripen, and needs more careful packing. Because of that, the seed is more expensive, and you have to charge more. People may grouse, but you get what you pay for. You can buy a Yugo or you can buy a BMW. There's something for everyone."

Dexter Carmichael, who knew Sibella Kraus from the Farm-Restaurant Project, was working at a small market in Pacific Heights when he received a delivery from GreenLeaf that included arugula from Star Route Farms. Dexter found it so gorgeous that he was prompted to visit Sibella, who was then at GreenLeaf. She told him that she was looking for somebody to run the specialty organic department, and he took the job, starting in October 1984. "I was a young kid and thought it was sort of counterculture to work in the middle of the night," said Dexter. "Sibella had developed great connections with a tremendous number of small growers, and I would receive that product from the farmers, store it, sort it, and distribute it to the orders. I got to know a lot of the small producers. Chefs would come and give us their take on what they were looking for, and Sibella would call hundreds of farmers trying to find the stuff. It was a dynamic time."

Whereas GreenLeaf provided all manner of fruits and vegetables to its clients, Veritable Vegetable in San Francisco distributed only organic produce. Established in 1974 as a woman-owned trucking company involved with a collective called the People's Food System, the company picked up organic produce from small farms such as Star Route and made it available to neighborhood co-ops and groceries. It is still around today, as are organizations such as Cooks Company and LA Specialty Produce, which continue to build the network between purveyors and chefs. However, GreenLeaf was the prototype, the first organization that brought farmers and chefs together with an effective business model.

Restaurants in Southern California bought from GreenLeaf as well as from distributors in Los Angeles. Michael McCarty sourced some of his produce from Dennis Weiss, who was at Northern Produce until he opened a new company called West Central Wholesale Produce in 1983. "We wanted to use more California greens and vegetables," said Michael. "We had a big focus on salads and vegetables. Dennis Weiss was pioneering in getting farmers down here and in Mexico to move into new stuff." Michael also bought produce from Star Route in Bolinas and Chino Farms in Rancho Santa Fe before he finally began to shop at the Santa Monica Wednesday farmers' market, which was right across the street from his restaurant.

Farmers' Markets

After their initial success selling organic produce at natural food stores in the 1970s, small-scale farmers began to grow produce for an increasingly appreciative public, setting the stage for an enormous expansion of farmers' markets. A crucial stimulus was legislative: the passage of the Direct Marketing Act in 1977, during the administration of Governor Jerry Brown, undercut decades of successful lobbying against farmers' markets by retail grocers and big agricultural groups. Now farmers at designated certified farmers' markets would be exempt from standard produce-packaging requirements, enabling them to sell fresh, unprocessed fruits

A SEASONAL TASTING OF FIVE COURSES

highlighting the flavors & textures
which encompass the entire range of our menu
39 per person

• tasting menu requires the participation of the
entire table & is designed for family-style dining •

· salads ·

star route radicchio & grilled little gems lettuce balsamic vinaigrette, parmigiano reggiano	8
mariquita's cardoon pounded parsley, a dressing of meyer lemons, pecorino, mcevoy olio nuovo	7
marin roots farm wild arugula fuyu persimmons & ram das orchards pomegranates	8
gwen avocado & ruby red grapefruit shallot vinaigrette & curly cress	7
roasted full belly farm beets redwood hill goat cheese pearls, toasted anise seed dressing	8

· starters ·

a vegan soup of organic green lentils lemony tomato broth, cilantro-oil drizzle, medjool date	6
mediterranean spreads aged balsamic eggplant mousse, roasted pepper & pomegranate, yogurt-dill, grilled flat bread	9
seared day boat scallops warm salad of diced vegetables, pine nut-currant vinaigrette	10
giant lima beans covered in french feta & oregano, oven baked in a ras el hanout tomato purée	8
willey farm bloomsdale spinach & feta phyllo rolls fleur de sel sprinkled greens, caper-pine nut swirl	8
prather ranch kefta skewers grilled beef & grapes over cucumber-torpedo onion salad, black sesame vinaigrette	9
wild mushrooms in phyllo napa valley's wine forest shiitake, hen-of-the woods & chanterelles, manouri cheese	9
grilled spicy lamb sausage goat yogurt & fromage blanc dip	9
baked seafood triangles prawns & alaskan halibut tucked into phyllo, parslied couscous, saffron essence	10
sesame crusted goat cheese baked cypress grove chèvre, roasted tomato-argan oil compote, zaatar croutons	8

· basteeya ·

baked phyllo pie with a filling of saffron braised chicken & spiced almonds, draped in powder sugar & cinnamon · for 2 to share · available vegetarian	18

· vegetables & grains ·

a hearty stew of charmoula spiced vegetables citrus-tomato base & a poached organic marin sun farms egg	13
steamed aromatic saffron scented couscous seven seasonal crisp vegetables, raisins, toasted almonds, chickpeas	15
berber tagine squash, yellow crookneck, zucchini, rutabaga, turnip, carrot, saffron-ginger broth, couscous	13

· fish, seafood & shellfish ·

longline-caught yellowfin tuna seared rare with a fennel crust, roasted tahini sauce, tunisian salad	19
grilled gulf prawn brochettes steamed saffron couscous with vegetables	18
black cod claypot baked in spanish saffron sauce, parslied little farms potatoes, green olives	17
moroccan spiced prawn tagine on a bed of fresh herbed vegetables	18

· meat & game birds ·

paine farm squab napa valley's wine forest mushrooms, bitter greens, thyme-ras el hanout reduction	23
devils gulch ranch rabbit hungarian paprika smothered, baby carrots, parsnip purée, dried bing cherries	21
saffron infused hoffman ranch guinea hen capped with house-preserved meyer lemons, purple potato mash	22
stewed lamb crowned with charred eggplant ginger saffron broth, sun-dried point reyes tomatoes, sudaniya oil	19
coriander beef stew warmed with ornaments of root vegetables & an herbal essence	18
grilled thyme chicken brochettes steamed saffron couscous with vegetables	18
kumquat enriched niman ranch lamb shank bergamot infused dried fruits, cranberry couscous, grilled green onion	21
couscous aziza steamed floral couscous, crisp vegetables, grilled chicken & prawns, spicy lamb sausage, stewed lamb	20
grilled cattail creek farm rosemary lamb brochettes steamed saffron couscous with vegetables, warm chicories	19

On this menu from Aziza, all the farms are identified
and Mourad Lahlou's Moroccan basteeya gets special billing.

and vegetables directly to the public." Davis became the first certified farmers' market in California in 1977, and it was followed by markets in Redding, San Jose, Santa Cruz, and Stockton. The Alemany farmers' market in Bernal Heights, founded in 1943, was also certified in 1977. The Heart of the City market at United Nations Plaza in San Francisco was founded jointly by the Quakers and the Greater Market Street Development Association in 1981. In Southern California, the first certified farmers' market opened in Gardena in 1979, followed by the downtown Santa Monica farmers' market in 1981. The markets were a huge success with the public, and later with chefs. New ones continued to sprout all over the state. Today California boasts over five hundred certified farmers' markets.

By allowing small-scale farmers to sell directly to consumers, the markets increased farmers' profit margins and allowed them to prosper. In turn, farmers' markets gave consumers access to fresh, noncommercial produce and expanded restaurants' access to a network of farmers. Restaurants would have had fewer small-scale growers, especially organic growers, to turn to in the mid-1980s if farmers' markets hadn't sustained them economically.

The Ferry Plaza farmers' market had a particularly complicated and interesting history. For years, San Franciscans had been petitioning to have the unattractive Embarcadero Freeway torn down. The effort met with failure at the ballot box, but on October 17, 1989, the 6.9 Loma Prieta earthquake accomplished the task, damaging the freeway to the extent that it had to be demolished. The city was visually reunited with the San Francisco Bay, and ten acres of prime urban space near the waterfront became available. Two developers, Tom Sargent and the late Joe Weiner, wanted to transform one of the waterfront piers into a permanent farmers' market along the lines of Seattle's Pike Place Market. They also wanted to create a market-based center to educate people about the value of locally grown, seasonal food and to provide a forum for important food and agricultural issues, such as the need for sustainable agriculture and national standards for organic food products. Bill Fujimoto of Monterey Market, who was on the market's advisory board, recalled that "when that freeway came down, Tom Sargent realized that it was probably the most expensive piece of open real estate in the city. The plan was to build a public market, and in order to do that you had to create this mandate for food, for California food. Everyone was worried that the farmers' market would not do well because there was no one living in the area. And I said, 'You don't have to worry about that.'"

Following extended public debate, the collective behind the public market movement lost out in the political scramble. When they realized that they would not get the piers, they pitched the idea of putting the market in front of the Ferry Building, a landmark sorely in need of rehabilitation. In early 1992, Sibella Kraus was appointed executive director of the San Francisco Public Market Collaborative, a private organization that was authorized by the city to set up the Ferry Plaza farmers' market. The market debuted on the Embarcadero in September 1992. Over ten thousand people came to buy produce from over one hundred regional organic farmers and to dine on street food made by a dozen of the city's best restaurants. It was such a smash hit that in May 1993 it became a weekly certified farmers' market. In Bill Fujimoto's opinion, it was "a great market. The quality of farmers per square foot, per stall was probably higher at that market than anywhere. In the beginning they didn't make money, but all of them who stayed there eventually did very well."

In 1998, the market relocated to Green Street to make way for construction of the new Embarcadero Boulevard and Plaza in front of the soon-to-be-refurbished Ferry Building. By this time 150 farmers were participating. The Public Market Collaborative had not forgotten its original goal of creating a center for education about sustainable agriculture, however. To become eligible for grant funding, the collective founded a sister nonprofit, CUESA, the Center for Urban Education about Sustainable Agriculture. In 2000, CUESA replaced the Public Market Collaborative as governing entity, with Sibella Kraus as director. The organization added educational programs, such as cooking classes for children, and events where the public could meet producers or shop with chefs. The market has become the culinary heart of San Francisco and an inspiration for home cooks and chefs alike, who plan their menus after seeing what beckons to them from the overflowing stalls.

Whereas in Northern California the chefs educated the farmers, in Southern California the farmers' markets educated the chefs. The Santa Monica farmers' market was the largest grower-only market in the Los Angeles area and the most centrally located for downtown chefs. When it opened in 1981, it was a winner with the public, but chefs didn't begin attending until the 1990s. The first devotee was Nancy Silverton. According to market manager Laura Avery, Nancy would "park her truck in an alley and probably get a parking ticket every week. She'd be at the market for, like, three hours, shopping, tasting, and talking to the farmers, then load up her truck and go back to Campanile with all this great food. Everywhere she went she talked about it. 'I like to go to the farmers' market on Wednesday, so the best time to come to Campanile is on Thursday.' It didn't take long for other chefs to notice and to start coming to the market too."

LAURA AVERY

Santa Monica Farmers' Market, Santa Monica

The Wednesday downtown Santa Monica market was opened in July 1981 as one of the first farmers' markets to be certified under the direct marketing program. Laura Avery was hired as the market's supervisor in September 1982.

When the Direct Marketing Act passed in 1977, Ruth Yanatta-Goldway, the mayor of Santa Monica, campaigned to create a market that would attract more foot traffic and bring healthier food to downtown. She enlisted Vance Corum, a former colleague who was working for the California Department of Food and Agriculture, to select a site and recruit farmers. Most were eager to participate because of the financial benefits. "Vance would talk to them and the farmers would go, 'Wow, instead of making fifty cents a case for my lettuce, I can make fifty cents a head.' This was amazing," said Laura.

The market organizers received assistance from the Southland Farmers' Market Association, a self-regulating, self-funded farmer organization founded in 1983. The association's objective was to support the creation of new markets, and its services included developing budgets and business plans and helping with permits, licenses, insurance, and even design. Southland would set up a market at no charge to the sponsor and then have the farmers take a vote. If a majority of the farmers voted to become members of Southland, Southland would take a percentage of the gross sales for ten years to recoup its investment and to support the development of new farmers' markets.

"Ruth started the Santa Monica farmers' market out of the mayor's office, so there was no street closure fee and the farmers were exempt from having to buy a business license," said Laura. "It was just 'Come on down, set up your trucks, we're having a market.' Opening day, July 15, 1981, there were twenty-three farmers, and the gross sales were ten thousand dollars, which was really good. Some of the farmers made a thousand dollars."

After the first year, the organizers realized they needed a full-time person to manage the market. "I had just had my second kid, and I wanted to get out of the house a little more, so I applied for the job," said Laura. "In September 1982, I started with the one market on Wednesday. By the end of the first year, we probably had thirty-five farmers. Vance did a lot to promote the market. Once he came down and we did a strawberry shortcake promotion. We got some kids from the swimming pool to come over and be volunteers, and we served one thousand strawberry shortcakes in forty-five minutes." Events like this helped attract publicity and customers.

In the early days of farmers' markets, any vendor who had a certified producer certificate had to be admitted. This allowed big agricultural interests to come in and sell, which defeated the goal of supporting small farmers. In the mid-1980s, Laura helped push through an amendment to the Direct Marketing Act that allowed market managers to set their own criteria for admitting vendors. This meant that commercial strawberry farmers, for example, couldn't compete side by side with family farmers, and it allowed market managers to keep the mix of produce more selective and diverse.

"The market increased by almost 85 percent in its second year, and another 85 percent in the third year," said Laura. "It was clearly something that people wanted." With this success, in 1982 the city opened the Pico farmers' market, which offered free cooking classes and supplied greens for the school district's student lunch program in a lower-income community.

In 1991, a Saturday market was started on the site of the Wednesday market. For this one, said Laura, "we wanted to have an all-organic market, but we couldn't find thirty-five organic farmers. So we found seventeen organic farmers, and had regular farmers as well." The last of the four markets was opened in 1995 on Sundays.

The Santa Monica farmers' markets feature many of the farms that are popular among Southern California chefs, including Kenter Canyon Farms, McGrath Family Farm, Weiser Family Farms, and Windrose Farm. One perk for the farmers is being invited to eat in the restaurants where chefs feature their produce. "The farmers are energized," said Laura. "It's exciting and rewarding to go to these restaurants, where they are treated like movie stars. They've been able to make the scene."

The growth of the Wednesday Santa Monica farmers' market paralleled the development of the LA restaurant scene. As quality produce began to receive more attention, chefs became more interested in it, and more of them started to shop at the market. The market has accommodated chefs by providing them with preferred parking, handing out about eighty parking passes a year to chefs and produce companies (as does the Ferry Plaza farmers' market in San Francisco), and hosting chef appreciation days.

Amelia Saltsman, author of two cookbooks based on the Santa Monica farmers' market, said that "innovative chefs such as Bruce Marder, Hans Röckenwagner, Suzanne Tracht, Suzanne Goin, Evan Kleiman, and the Hot Tamales [Mary Sue Milliken and Susan Feniger] were there every single week, developing relationships with growers and inspiring others to jump on the bandwagon. The leader was Nancy Silverton. The Santa Monica farmers' market was a place of communion and a forum for learning and dialogue."

Mesclun Madness

> *Unfortunately, I think maybe what we've done is to try to convince people that little lettuce is California cuisine.*
> —Gourmand and grocer Darrell Corti

If anything is symbolic of California's influence on how the rest of the country now eats, it is the bagged salad revolution. What follows is a case study of the development of the food item that everyone associates with California cuisine— baby lettuce.

Bill Briwa, a chef-instructor at the Culinary Institute of America, believes that as a cook, you learn about a place through its food. Bill was immediately impressed by the variety of produce at the supermarket in St. Helena the day he arrived from New York in 1980. "It's love and salads that make a young man's blood quicken," said Bill. "I had my choice of maybe two or three lettuces in New York, and it floored me that I could have access to ten different lettuces in California. There was frisée, endive, romaine, green leaf, red leaf, and escarole. My response was to go home and make a salad."

Californians have always been salad eaters, both at home and in restaurants. In the late 1970s and early 1980s, restaurants expended a great deal of time and effort in creating a house salad mix. Cooks bought heads of lettuces, pulled them apart, discarded the outer leaves, washed the inner leaves, spun them dry in the "Greens Machine"—a giant commercial salad spinner—mixed them in batches, layered them on towels, and stored them in big bins in the walk-in refrigerator. Today this laborious process is unnecessary. Prewashed baby lettuce, or "spring mix," can be found everywhere, from small groceries to Safeway and Costco. When it first came on the market, however, it was special.

The first time these little lettuces arrived on the plate in California restaurants, guests were either amazed or amused. Russ Parsons of the *Los Angeles Times* recalled the early reaction to the baby lettuce mixes. "Everybody said, 'This looks like lawn clippings.'" Despite this early derision, the tasty baby lettuce salad became a poster child for California cuisine.

Depending on your point of view, we have Alice Waters to thank or blame for the American salad revolution. In Provence, mixtures of different kinds of lettuces, wild greens, and herbs are called *mesclun*. Alice wanted to serve this mix at Chez Panisse and was determined to get people to grow the greens and lettuces to her specifications.

Warren Weber at Star Route Farms was one of the first to provide lettuces to the restaurant. Andy Griffin had taken a job with Warren after the demise of the Hudspeth Farm, and he was full of ideas about how they could link with the expanding restaurant market. Warren was not interested. In his view he already had a program that was working. He was growing certified organic alternatives for mainstream produce—real food for real people.

Star Route didn't grow iceberg because it had little cachet among the organic crowd, but it did grow organic red leaf, green leaf, and butter lettuce, along with broccoli, cauliflower, green cabbage, and potatoes—basic, but all organic. Produce was shipped to Veritable Vegetable except for a tiny amount that was delivered directly to two little health food stores in Fairfax and Bolinas. Warren didn't want to do much direct delivery because that would put him in a competitive stance with Veritable, which was taking everything that he could produce. Andy and Warren would load the product onto an eighteen-wheel bobtail truck, and Andy would drive it into the city every other day. He worked in the fields on the other days.

The organic market was growing, but because Bolinas had a small labor force, the farm couldn't expand and become more profitable. "One of the ways that you can get around that is to have a crop that is worth more," said Andy, and selling to restaurants would fetch a higher price. However, "Warren had already pretty much dismissed the notion of reaching out to the restaurants because, among the hardcore 'food for the people' crowd, restaurants were just a garish, ostentatious display of bourgeois bad taste."

In 1983, Sibella Kraus visited Star Route Farms. Andy and Warren were sitting in the farm office, which overlooked a field that had recently been planted with lettuces. The plants were still very small. Sibella introduced herself and said that she had come to find out if Warren would grow lettuce for Chez Panisse. He politely said he wasn't interested. She offered to buy the red leaf, green leaf, romaine, and butter lettuces that were growing nearby, and he said, "This field of lettuce isn't available. It's not going to be big enough to pick for six weeks."

She replied, "I want it now," and he said, "Well, I'll sell it to you now, but you're going to have to pay me the same for a little head of lettuce as you would for a big one because otherwise, I'm not going to make any money," and she said, "Fine." So they cut the baby lettuces and packed them seventy-two to a case with a little absorbent pad at the bottom so they wouldn't wilt. As Andy said, "We put more value into the back of a little Ford Courier than we had in that great big international bobtail."

Warren was happy because he could now make more money out of the same land by harvesting three crops in the time he would have harvested one. Their lettuces weren't the varieties that Alice wanted for her mesclun mix, but Chez Panisse introduced Star Route to Le Marché and other vendors who could supply the seed for the correct varieties.

Star Route branched out to grow chervil, arugula, and other specialty greens and vegetables. When Sibella Kraus left Chez Panisse to work for GreenLeaf, she brought Star Route Farms to the distributor as a client. Sibella suggested that Star Route sell to Monterey Market, where Andy got to know Bill Fujimoto. "Bill insisted on paying us when we did the delivery," said Andy. "As a farmer you got to love that. If somebody pays me when I make a delivery, they move to the top of the list. After I finished unloading, I would find Bill, and he would invariably be out messing around in the store. If I saw something that I didn't recognize, which was easy to do at Monterey Market, I'd ask him. He was very giving with his time, and I really got to know and appreciate him."

One day Warren and Andy were talking about how the restaurant market was becoming saturated in terms of the mixed baby lettuce packs. The restaurants had heightened people's awareness of salad, and Warren and Andy thought it might be time to take advantage of this by coming out with a retail pack for the general public. There was still no economical way to clean and combine the items after picking, so they thought they would put the tiny clusters of leaves in a little plastic clamshell—rows of lettuces with a tuft of arugula and chervil—and call it a mesclun salad pack. Bill Fujimoto was willing to use the Monterey Market as a beta site to sell them. Andy added, "Warren and I knew that this was going to make a ton of money, and we thought we should ask Alice Waters if she wanted in on it." So they made an appointment, and on their way to meet with Alice they spun marketing campaigns in their head.

Alice listened to their pitch, thanked them, and turned them down. "I think this is a product that can have tremendous appeal to the public," she said. "Don't take it personally, but I don't want to have anything to do with it. I've got a little

kid, I'm overworked, plus, this is a big idea, and I'm all about things being small."
"That interview has always stuck in my mind," said Andy. "I think Alice had an awful lot of self-knowledge. I think it takes a big person to see that there is something in [an idea] and then not go after it."

Alice introduced Warren and Andy to Todd Koons, who was going to put together a marketing campaign. Todd had grown up on farms and also loved to cook. He had met Alice Waters through John Hudspeth, and he had worked as a prep cook at Chez Panisse for about five years. To please Alice, whom he was dating at the time, he worked hard in the restaurant gardens with Sibella and Jean-Pierre, trying to create some unique items. He left in 1983, and while working as a consultant, he developed a triple-washing system to prewash salad greens. He then started Todd Koons Organics, or TKO Farms, where he grew salad greens.

They say that victory has many fathers. Lynn Brown of Forni-Brown Gardens in the Napa Valley town of Calistoga was another farmer who took some credit for inventing the mesclun mix. "A lot of people think we were the first people to use the word *mesclun* and sell it as that," said Lynn. Forni-Brown created custom mesclun mixes for such Napa Valley chefs as Thomas Keller of the French Laundry and Hiro Sone of Terra.

LYNN BROWN

Forni-Brown Gardens, Calistoga

Lynn Brown and his partner Peter Forni have supplied exceptional produce to restaurant chefs in the Napa Valley since 1982. Along with Warren Weber, they pioneered arugula cultivation in California, and they were the first commercial growers to buy seeds from Le Marché. Cindy Pawlcyn of Mustards Grill and Cindy's Backstreet Kitchen swears by the Forni-Brown farm. She once took a plate to Barney Welsh, a partner in the Forni-Brown business, and said, "I want my romaine this size. He went, 'Uh, okay.' And he took the plate out in the field and harvested the ones that matched."

Lynn learned French intensive gardening techniques at the Alan Chadwick Garden, an organic teaching garden at UC Santa Cruz. Later he moved to Calistoga. He and his wife were caretakers of a property with fifty acres of old orange, lemon, and Imperial prune trees, and they were allowed to keep anything they grew. In 1979, he started cultivating vegetables on the land and selling them to grocery stores in Santa Rosa, Seventh-Day Adventists in St. Helena, and a few food co-ops. Typical sales were modest at first—a couple of pounds of produce at a time—until one day in 1981 when a soft-spoken Japanese man approached Lynn in a store and said, "That's beautiful elephant garlic, could I get a hundred-pound bag?" It was Masataka ("Masa") Kobayashi, who had recently started cooking at the Auberge du Soleil resort. After filling Masa's order, Lynn began to think about approaching other restaurants, although there weren't that many in the valley at the time.

The first few years Lynn farmed by himself. Then he started getting requests for zucchini blossoms, which needed to be picked before sunup so that they would stay open, making it easier to stuff them. He needed help and asked Peter Forni, a vineyard manager and neighbor, if he'd like to go in on the venture with him. "I said, 'I think this could really take off, growing these vegetables. There are not a lot of restaurants right now, but I think there are going to be more.'" So Peter Forni took on the project of growing and harvesting the zucchini. By 1982, the two were working together as Forni-Brown Gardens, selling to big-name Napa Valley chefs such as Udo Nechutnys at Miramonte and Philippe Jeanty at Domaine Chandon, in addition to Masa Kobayashi at the Auberge du Soleil.

Bruce LeFavour, who had opened Rose et LeFavour in 1980, mentored Lynn and Peter, steering them toward haricots verts, *fraises des bois,* and other produce considered exotic at the time. "We'd bring him *fraises des bois* in recycled egg cartons with six in each segment. He'd get excited and put a couple out on display. At that time nobody was growing the little haricots verts, and we did those until somebody figured it out in Guatemala. We stopped growing them after that because we could never compete."

In 1982, Masa's former gofer, Frank Messmer, bought a van and started Frank's Fresh Foods. He joined forces with Forni-Brown and would collect their produce and drive it down to restaurant clients in San Francisco. "In our heyday," said Lynn, "we did Campton Place, Square One, Fog City Diner, Postrio, Aqua, and the Cypress Club, and then the second generation of all those." They also supplied Masa, then at his eponymous restaurant in the city.

In 1983, Lynn and Warren Weber of Star Route Farms spoke at the first Tasting of Summer Produce. "We realized we were the only two people in Northern California growing arugula," said Lynn. "The big question was, How do you charge for it? How do you determine that this amount is worth that much, especially when you're the only person growing it?" At Bruce LeFavour's suggestion, they decided to link the price of frisée and arugula to the cost of a pack of cigarettes, because Bruce had noticed that they were roughly equal in some countries. "At that time," said Lynn, "I think cigarettes were a dollar."

After seeing an ad for Le Marché Seeds in a horticulture magazine, Lynn called Georgeanne Brennan and Charlotte Glenn. He worked closely with them until they left the seed business in 1991. When Renee Shepherd took over the business, Forni-Brown sold a custom mesclun mix, Monet's Garden Mesclun, through her seed company, and their greens were pictured on the back of her seed catalogue for many years.

They sold the salad mix across the country. "We were in Dean and Deluca's in New York, the James Beard House, and lots of different places." People who had just opened a restaurant would contact Lynn and say, "We get all our reviews in the first month. Could we just get your stuff for the first month?"

They were shipping overnight, which at the time didn't cost that much. "It went by weight, and our salad stuff is so light it doesn't weigh much, so it was very reasonable," said Lynn. "But then shipping changed and they started to charge by volume instead. Something that would have cost $12 to ship overnight, enough to give a salad for thirty or forty people, became $50 or $60. We hunkered down and started doing it only here.

"Forni-Brown was one of the first to offer Chinese red mustard and the first in Northern California to have tatsoi. We'd been doing heirloom tomatoes all along. Most of the heirlooms you see in grocery stores are still picked underripe. We pick them dead ripe and bring them in that day, and it's a whole different thing."

Lynn's favorite tomato is the Giant Syrian. In 2006, *New York Times* writer Mimi Sheraton visited the farm for a piece she was writing on Napa. She told Lynn, "I don't think there's ever been an heirloom tomato I actually liked." Lynn knew the Giant Syrians were top-notch that week, so he picked one, still warm from the sun, and cut out a chunk for her. She almost wept when she tasted it. She said, "That is the best tomato I've ever tasted in my life." She went on to praise the variety in at least three articles.

"Here is somebody whose life and passion is food and she's never been given a properly picked tomato," lamented Lynn. "Sometimes I'll invite a couple of chefs over to my house and say, 'Here's an eggplant I picked this morning. Now you make something with that eggplant.' Then we'll go out and pick another one from the same plant just as they are ready to cook it. And they'll say, 'My god, what a difference.'"

In all likelihood the first farmer to sell salad mixes on a commercial scale was Dale Coke. Dale started growing strawberries in 1980, partly to challenge a neighbor, a nonorganic strawberry grower, who had said it was impossible to grow strawberries organically. Dale started with a quarter acre of berries. He heard that Chez Panisse was looking for better strawberries and sent samples.

Not long after, Sibella Kraus came by Coke Farm. She looked at some zucchini and said, "We could use this, but don't pick them that big. We want them two inches long with flowers on them, and we'll pay you decent money for them." That visit was instrumental in persuading Dale to expand his selection. He heard that there was interest in different lettuces as well as arugula, tatsoi, frisée, and radicchio. He bought seeds from Le Marché, who had "better offerings than almost any other seed company," said Dale. "We continued to experiment with different varieties."

Sibella realized early on that the difficult part of this baby lettuce venture would be transporting the produce to the restaurant in decent shape. At first, Dale would put it on a Greyhound bus or drive it in, but eventually he and Sibella struck a deal with Jameson Patton of GreenLeaf, who set up a delivery system for them.

It was at GreenLeaf that Dale and Sibella essentially defined what America's commercial version of mesclun would be. They put a great deal of thought into it: "How much of each kind? How do you pack it? Do you wash it first? What size is the standard pack? What kind of box does it go in?"

Dale recalled, "Baby lettuces were our mainstay in the early 1980s. We never could sell much tatsoi or mizuna, and this might have been Sibella's suggestion, but we mixed them together with the lettuces so that people could eat it as a salad. It was springtime, so we called it 'spring mix.' It looked beautiful on the plate and for restaurants it was less work and less waste than cutting it up and mixing it yourself. That really propelled the business."

After making initial restaurant connections in San Francisco, Coke Farm started shipping its spring mix directly to restaurants, and via GreenLeaf to Los Angeles, Seattle, and eventually New York, Atlanta, and the Eastern Seaboard for use in high-end restaurants. By the late 1980s, the mix was going to food-service distributors like Sysco and then Safeway. Other farmers hadn't really caught on to this market, so it was a good opportunity for Dale to build his business. As he said, "You pretty much had it sold if you could grow it, and that's pretty rare."

Even Andy Griffin reentered the lucrative salad mix market. After working in Southern California, Andy returned to Watsonville and joined forces with Greg Beccio at Riverside Farms. "Todd Koons was making salads down the road in

Salinas; Dale Coke was making salads down Highway 129. At that time I knew almost everybody who was making these salads and shipping them and the market was relatively small. When we would take the salads to the trucking terminal in Watsonville where they would be shipped to the markets, you could walk up and down the loading dock in the evening and count the entire output going out. If we were selling 75 boxes to Stanley Produce or GreenLeaf or somebody in LA, I could see that TKO was selling 200. They were well ahead of us."

Soon Andy and Greg were competitive, packaging 250 boxes a day, then 500 boxes a day, then 1,000 boxes a day, then 7,000 boxes a day. They were selling under their own labels as well as growing organic greens for Earthbound Farm and other companies. Riverside had grown to seven hundred acres, with another five hundred acres that they were farming with a company that became Lakeside Organic Gardens, with a workforce of 250 year-round employees.

In the mid-1990s, a big company called Tanimura and Antle (T&A) entered the salad mix market. "When you're competing against someone like T&A," said Andy, "you're essentially dead. We heard through the grapevine that Todd was trying to sell TKO and that he wanted $8 million for it. The business environment was such that all the large companies were interested in this. They had land and money up the wazoo, they could bring these resources to bear, but they didn't have an understanding of the product and they didn't have the relationships with the different major buyers for those categories. More important, because this was to be an organic project by and large, they didn't have an organic land base; they could do everything but they couldn't do it organically."

Andy and Greg realized that the salad boom wasn't going to last for them as independent farmers, because as soon as the big companies got into the game, "it's their job to put your head underwater until the bubbles stop." They thought, "We'd better sell our company quick, before TKO goes down and it's bought at bankruptcy. If T&A or one of these big companies buys him, we're out of luck, because then we've got to compete with the real big boys." So they talked to Stan Pura at Growers Express, which packed conventional salad under the Earthbound label. Andy told them, "If you buy our company, look at what you get: a use permit, 1,200 acres of ground, a trained crew, and half your competition because we've been putting out all these different labels. You get the whole game, but you got to buy the company quick." Growers Express bought Riverside Farms for $3.3 million and an agreement not to compete for five years as of December 31, 1996.

Todd came into the office that day and said, "You know, I think you guys were really smart. Congratulations on a game well played." His company was sold at bankruptcy shortly after that. "That scale of business is completely unforgiving," said Andy. "Once you have a fairly large company, the big money can't come from selling to restaurants or to stores or even chains. You need to have contractual relationships with large food service industry types like Sysco.

"They're run by lawyers; there are no cooks around. If Sysco finds out that their competitors' salad has eight items in it, they say, 'Ours has to have nine.' So then the other guy has to have ten, the other guy has to have eleven, and you have this ridiculous situation where these lawyers are creating the recipe for the salad based on their perceptions of what's going to appeal to the market. The retailer wants a balance of color, which means you've got to put a lot of radicchio in to get that flash. You have to have frisée in there because it's white. You have to put in all this stuff in order to have more items than the other guy, so now you've got a salad that is an unbalanced wreck."

The experience led Andy Griffin to embrace a new business model. "I was thinking about what Alice said about how 'I like things small.' The beauty for me of the mesclun salad as I learned to make it working for John Hudspeth was that the farmer would sow a row of lettuces and you'd pick the small ones to thin out for the big ones. You wouldn't throw anything away. You've got this peasant aesthetic, 'You shall not waste.' You take some wild little chicories, some borage flowers if you want to jazz it up, some arugula, which in the Mediterranean is a weed, and you have created this wonderful salad out of virtually nothing. If you're a subsistence farmer, this is getting you to the next day and it's perfect. Later on, you'll have a big head of lettuce and you can make something out of that too. So I had a lot of cynicism about the whole industry based on my experiences from within and I thought, 'Okay, I want to do something small.'" Today Andy owns Mariquita Farm and sells directly to restaurants, where his produce is in great demand.

Spreading the Word

Education and the sharing of information propelled the development of California cuisine. Farmers' markets helped increase awareness of alternate supply chains, but the produce network only developed as quickly as it did because everyone from consumers to small market owners to the farmers themselves was willing to share contacts and information. Especially passionate and generous were the chefs, particularly in Northern California.

Clark Wolf, a New York–based restaurant consultant who got his start in California, explained the importance of this cooperative ethos in comparative terms. He accused chefs in New York of being "stingy with their resources. They wouldn't tell anybody where their things came from. You California guys used to stand on the street and say, 'Would you like to try a ramp? Here's a fiddlehead, do you want some?'"

The East Coast attitude may have been an outcome of the competitive French model, where keeping your sources secret would help keep you on top in the restaurant game. Northern California's attitude reflected its nurturing hippie heritage. It was communal as opposed to competitive.

"What came out of the 1960s was an open heart for sharing," said chef Michael Chiarello. "If there was an ingredient or an artisan you wanted to support, you reached out to the community and said, 'Hey, I have this goat cheese you really have to see. I have this forager who's not making the living they need—take a look at their mushrooms or the wild greens that they're picking.' Much more than the rest of the world, we shared our resources."

9

Custom Foods

Chefs Partner with Purveyors and Artisans

First the restaurants were the rock stars. Then the chefs became the rock stars.
Now the ingredients are the rock stars.

—Steve Sando, Rancho Gordo

One afternoon while driving to see friends in Napa, I was listening to a replay of a *City Arts and Lectures* program that had aired on April 28, 2010. Writer Daniel Handler (aka Lemony Snicket) was interviewing writer and essayist Sarah Vowell. Vowell had lived in the Bay Area for a time, and Handler asked her why she did not stay in California. She replied, "I like goat cheese, but I do not want to have to talk about it." There were knowing roars of laughter in the audience. We Californians, especially in the north, are obsessed with our ingredients and artisanal products. We talk and write about them so often that we probably annoy those who are not as food crazy as we are, but this cheerleading for our local products has helped the artisanal culture to flourish. The dialogue among chefs, purveyors, and artisans was, and still is, one of the unique features of California cuisine. Today this ongoing conversation is ubiquitous nationwide, but at the time it was revolutionary.

•

In the 1960s and 1970s, local sourcing—like local farming—was not an important issue for chefs and diners in the United States. Established European chefs based in California relied on connections abroad. When Michael McCarty moved to Los Angeles in 1976, he surveyed the lay of the land before opening his restaurant, Michael's. Michael called the food editor at the *Los Angeles Times*, Lois Dwan, to pick her brain for food and wine contacts. She introduced him to Jean Bertranou, owner of L'Ermitage, and they became good friends. Michael and Jean both had reliable connections with purveyors at Rungis, the wholesale market in Paris, and flew in ingredients for their respective restaurants.

"I'd call up my purveyors in Paris on the phone and ask for this and that, very fundamental stuff," said Michael. "They would put it in a Styrofoam box. They put the cheeses in a hidden compartment in the bottom, with the fish on top, because we knew that no customs guy would dig around in the fish. We were bringing over sea bream, Dover sole, rouget [red mullet], and Belon oysters. Later we were bringing in ducks and foie gras. My guys would take it to the airport in Paris, put it on the plane, and we'd run over to LAX to pick it up." In the wintertime, they imported the rouget, along with John Dory and berries, from Australia.

There was no concerted effort to source locally. According to Jonathan Waxman, one of the opening chefs at Michael's, "People started bringing stuff to us. In 1980, Joe Gurrera from Citarella in New York showed up with a box of seafood and said, 'I bet you've never seen these before.' There were soft-shell crabs and scallops and swordfish, and I said, 'No, we don't have that here.' For two years he flew out every week and sold me fish. A pilot from Qantas brought me John Dory." When good local products were offered to them, they were happy to accept. "Some French hippies from Santa Barbara started bringing spot prawns. We got quail from Fairfield and magnificent pigeons from Carpinteria."

Most California chefs did not have suppliers dropping in with cases of soft-shell crabs or Moulard ducks from France. They relied on ducks from Chinatown and seafood from local fish wholesalers, as well as seafood from Fisherman's Wharf in the north and Japantown in the south. Gradually, though, chefs began to expand their options by mining their local resources. They encouraged existing purveyors and helped them thrive, working with long-standing ranching and farming families to revive bygone flavors and practices. They supported entrepreneurs of artisanal products who, like many of the chefs, were self-taught, and they cultivated personal relationships with the people raising their food.

Meat and Poultry

In the 1960s, if you had asked a typical American chef which rancher had raised the pigs for the pork he was serving or which supplier had provided the ducks and chicken on his menu, he would have looked at you blankly. In those days a staff purchasing agent picked up the phone, called a wholesaler, and placed an order.

There was no dialogue between the producer and the kitchen staff. A menu might mention general geographical provenance, such as Long Island duck, Maine lobster, or Dover sole, but the specific providers were anonymous. In California by the late 1970s and early 1980s, anonymity had given way to food raised by people we knew. It was still business, but it had become personal.

After succeeding in developing sources of fresher, more varied local produce, chefs in Northern California began to turn their attention to meat and poultry. For the most part, the existing beef and lamb were acceptable. At least they had flavor. The commodity pork, however, had become increasingly dry and tasteless, almost impossible to cook well and keep moist. The factory-raised chickens were flabby and bland. The ducks from Chinatown were tasty but did not have enough meat on them to make usable serving portions.

Chefs reached out to farmers and ranchers to see if their products could be improved. Bradley Ogden contacted Bart Ehman in Sebastopol and asked him to raise a chicken with flavor. Barbara Tropp turned to Jim Reichardt in Petaluma to find out if he could raise ducks with more meat on them. Word of mouth helped expand the range of contacts. Through sausage maker Bruce Aidells, Michael Wild at Bay Wolf heard about Jim Reichardt's Liberty ducks. Friends of Orville Schell's helped him introduce his Niman-Schell hogs to Chez Panisse. The press promoted further connections. After reading about Niman-Schell Ranch in the *San Francisco Chronicle*, Café Beaujolais called partner Bill Niman to place the first restaurant order. And as was their way, the chefs shared sources and information with each other.

Many chefs were concerned not only with improving flavor but also with reforming how animals were raised. Peter Singer's influential book *Animal Liberation*, published in 1975, documented the suffering of animals on factory farms and in laboratories and argued that it was morally wrong to cause them unnecessary pain. Chefs were among the many whose eyes were opened. They were horrified to discover the cramped cages in which animals could not move or even stand, the forced antibiotics used to prevent disease that could spread rapidly because of overcrowding, and the inhumane feedlot practices. The more they learned, the more determined these chefs became to find and support suppliers who cared for their animals, fed them well, allowed them to roam freely, and harvested them in a humane and dignified manner.

In the mid-1980s, purchasing agents were still active in hotel kitchens and the more traditional Continental restaurants, but *sous chefs* and chefs were now sourcing and ordering the food in the new California restaurants. At Chez Panisse, Catherine Brandel sought out small birds and rabbits, while Chris Lee looked for beef, veal, lamb, and pork. Sustainable practices were important to them. They wanted to visit each ranch to see how the animals were housed, slaughtered, and processed. Were they 100 percent grass fed and pasture raised, or were they fed on grass and finished on grain? Was the rest of their feed, if any, organic? Were the animals free of antibiotics? Once assured that the purveyors met their standards, the chefs often bonded with them. Long-lasting, loyal friendships were established.

Niman Ranch was a preferred source of beef and pork and a prestigious brand coveted by chefs and later by home cooks all over the country. Bill Niman began raising pigs in 1974, sold them off in 1981 to concentrate on beef, and then reentered the pork business in 1995, when he was introduced to Paul Willis of Thornton, Iowa, who was trying to revive sustainable farming in the Midwest. Willis set up a network of farmers to raise hogs for Niman the old-fashioned way, according to Niman Ranch's principles. Their pigs—a cross of Duroc, Chester White, and Berkshire breeds—were fed a high-quality vegetarian diet, and the difference in quality between the Niman pigs and commodity pork was like night and day. Flavor and moisture made a big comeback.

BILL NIMAN

Niman Ranch, Bolinas

Bill Niman moved to Northern California in 1968. He and his then wife, Amy, bought a homestead in Bolinas, where they kept a few animals for food while he worked part-time in construction. Bill fell into ranching by chance. "We were a loose extended family, the Bolinas community, just trying to raise food for ourselves, not having any vision of a commercial enterprise."

In 1974, Bill partnered with journalist and food activist Orville Schell to open a pig ranch, and around the same time he became good friends with Warren and Marian Weber of Star Route Farms. All were members of the Bolinas food community, which extended to Inverness and Point Reyes Station. The people of west Marin were aware of some of the failures of the food system and were seeking more wholesome, healthful food. Bill and Orville saw an opportunity to provide them with premium meat.

In 1977, Bill and Orville expanded Niman-Schell Ranch to include cattle. They worked nonstop, consumed with trying to make enough money to pay the mortgage. To feed the sows, they collected spent barley from the original Anchor Brewing Company and past-the-sell-date containers of Nancy's Yogurt from a local distributor. According to Bill, "Orville would have his son sleeping in a car seat, and he would be emptying little containers of yogurt into a fifty-five-gallon trough." They put the hogs up for sale in 1981 to concentrate on the cattle.

At the end of 1984, they sold part of their land to the National Park Service to be incorporated into the newly formed Point Reyes National Seashore. The sale enabled Bill to stop working construction and to focus his energy on ranching. Whatever money they realized, in addition to paying off the mortgage and their debts, went into the property. Orville's writing career was flourishing, so he left the animal husbandry to Bill.

Bill raised the livestock on a natural diet, grazing them on grass and finishing them briefly with grain. Niman-Schell sold pork and beef to the Mill Valley Market and Fairfax Natural Foods, and quarters or halves of beef, cut and wrapped, to neighbors and friends.

His mission, said Bill, was to "raise great food for this community. There was no connection to restaurants until the 1980s." Then, in 1985, *Parade* magazine, a Sunday supplement to the *San Francisco Chronicle*, wrote a story about growers and other producers. Much to Bill's surprise, the media found him, and he was contacted by Chris Kump and Margaret Fox from Café Beaujolais, which became his first restaurant account. Other restaurants followed, and soon he was supplying Zuni Café, Chez Panisse, Square One, and Stars. All this happened within twelve months. "The thing took on a life of its own. We were fortunate to have some neighbors who mentored me on the livestock side and then these incredible people in the back of the house in restaurants who were teaching me the way it's supposed to be.

"I said yes to everything and probably shouldn't have. I did everything possible because people started naming us on the menu. When they put my name on it, if it wasn't good, it was my fault, and I took that very seriously. It was a very steep learning curve."

When you raise an animal you have to sell all of it, so along with the steaks, Bill had to market brisket, chuck, shanks, cheeks, necks, and shoulders. The prime cuts and middle meats were in great demand for grilling, and there was only so much to go around. Chez Panisse bought filets, along with shanks and neck bones for stock. At Square One, we made *sugo* with the briskets. Chef Loretta Keller recalled, "I met Bill Niman when I was a purchasing agent at Stars. I remember him telling me, 'My prime cuts are basically gone. Marsha McBride has my filets on certain days, and Alice Waters is using them other days. Stars has a great hamburger—I'll sell you chuck.' They were killing only twenty head of cattle a week."

In California, "we're living a century ahead of most of the country," said Bill. "New York was another center of change, but they were still living in the veal culture with sauces. It remains important to me today that when you're eating meat, you should be able to taste the meat."

In 1997, Orville left the partnership to become dean of the School of Journalism at UC Berkeley, and the farm became simply Niman Ranch. The company thrived and became a national brand, with a network of ranchers across the country who agreed to raise meat in an eco-friendly manner according to Bill's humane standards. But goodness is not always rewarded. Due to rapid expansion efforts, the company faced bankruptcy a few times. In 2006, to raise money, Bill sold a controlling stake in the business to Natural Food Holdings, a subsidiary of Hilco Equity Partners based in Northbrook, Illinois. His share in the company fell to 12.5 percent, and he eventually left altogether because he did not agree with some of the changes they were making, such as transporting cattle over great distances. Bill was given stock that became worthless. Sadder but wiser, he gave up the right to use his name on new ventures. Bill now owns BN Ranch in Bolinas, where he raises turkeys, goats, and grass-fed beef on a much smaller and more personal scale.

In the late 1990s, restaurant menus and farmers' markets began to feature grass-fed beef from Marin Sun Farms and Prather Ranch, both ranches with long histories that were moving toward more holistic practices. David Evans at Marin Sun Farms was a fourth-generation cattle rancher who wanted to continue his family's legacy in Marin County while implementing sustainable food practices. Walter Ralphs, former president of the Ralphs supermarket chain, bought Prather Ranch in 1964 and converted the herd to certified organic and humanely raised beef.

Premium lamb was available from Dal Porto Ranch in Amador County, Cindy Callahan in Sonoma County, and Magruder Ranch in Mendocino County, the last of which also provided restaurants with grass-fed beef and pastured pork. Don Watson raised sheep for restaurants under the name Napa Valley Lamb and founded a second business offering his sheep as eco-friendly field mowers.

DON WATSON

Napa Valley Lamb and Wooly Weeders, Napa Valley

Don Watson grew up in Stockton, attended UC Davis, and became an economist and then a certified public accountant, working for Arthur Andersen. But he had a life-changing revelation after watching his best friend die. He realized that his work was not fulfilling and that he had another purpose in life. For some mystical reason, he had always wanted to herd sheep. So he and his wife, Carol, moved to Australia, and then from Australia to New Zealand, where Don learned the ins and outs of sheep husbandry. One day they were standing in the immigration line in Dunedin, New Zealand, getting ready to make a visit home. The immigration official said, "You know, if you want in, we'll fill out the papers today." Don looked at Carol, and her face was ashen. She didn't want to become a New Zealand citizen. So they returned to California and bought an abandoned property in the north end of Napa Valley, near her family.

Gradually they acquired a herd of sheep, which they pasture grazed on their property. "I'm a Scot, so we wouldn't spend money to put animals in a feedlot. That would be foolish. If there was grass out there to eat, we would find a way to make the grass work."

The grazing turned to their advantage in a surprising way when the sheep accidentally got into Robert Mondavi's vineyard. "It was really embarrassing," said Don. "All I could think was that I didn't know how to fix this. I thought, 'I'll donate some lamb.' The morning I took it into the winery, nobody was in the kitchen except for an elderly 'greeter.' He asked, 'What's up?' and I told the story about the sheep getting into the vineyard. As I was walking out, I looked up on the wall, and there was his portrait. It was Robert Mondavi!"

Sometime after that Don got a call from Mike Cybulski, the assistant vineyard manager at Mondavi. "When can the sheep come back?" he asked. Mondavi became the first client to pay to have his vineyards mowed by Don's Wooly Weeders. When Don eventually put up a website advertising his environmentally sensitive mowing service, the phone rang off the hook. The sheepherding part of the business is still going strong.

Don began to sell his lamb wholesale in 1987. His first restaurant client was Cindy Pawlcyn of Mustards, who was always looking for good local ingredients. This gave him entrée into several restaurants, since at that time, Cindy was a partner in the Real Restaurants Group, which owned Mustards and Tra Vigne in the Napa Valley and Bistro Roti in San Francisco. Next he was introduced to Jean-Pierre Moullé at Chez Panisse. One day Jean-Pierre asked Don if he could harvest the lambs when they were smaller, and in response, Don began to produce a milk-fed six-month-old lamb with a dressed weight of 35 to 40 pounds. Word got around in the restaurant community, and soon many chefs were calling Don, wanting that lamb.

According to Cindy Pawlcyn, "It's the most delicious lamb, because it's well cared for. Don knows his animals and will say, 'Roast the legs right now,' or 'Braise the legs now.' At some times of the year the meat is younger and tenderer, and sometimes the lambs have been moving more and are tougher. He'll say, 'Grind the shoulders, these lambs are going to be tough.'"

Don also produces a very young milk-fed lamb, as small as 22 pounds, which in Italy is called *abbacchio*. When David Kinch was chef at Ernie's, he asked Don, "Can you consistently bring that very petite leg in? I can put it on the menu, and we can serve a party of four a beautiful little leg of lamb." Soon after, David's friends from as far down as Santa Monica started to request the *abbacchio* as well. Don sold lamb to chefs in Southern California until the demand in Northern California exceeded his supply. Now, when there's a philanthropic event in LA, he'll drive down like he used to and donate the lamb.

"The joy of producing something is to take it to somebody and see what they do with it," said Don. "It is a kick to go in and see what they're doing at Chez Panisse, Oliveto, Camino, or Quince. It is always fascinating to go down and see David Kinch. I say, 'I carry the paint for Picasso.' That's the joy I get out of it."

Restaurant patrons favored beef, pork, and lamb. Chicken was a sure sale, especially among conservative diners wary of new foods, and duck was popular, although at Square One we reserved it for weekends because it took extra prep time. Squab was favored by the more sophisticated clientele. Gary Carpenter, whose family started raising squab in 1921, supplied many Los Angeles and Santa Barbara restaurants, but at Square One we bought our birds from Philip Paine in Sonoma.

We were allotted three dozen Paine squab every other week, and they were precious. The only time I ever said no to a guest's request was when they would ask to have their squab cooked well-done. I'd go out in the dining room and try to convince them to change their minds and try it medium rare. I'd say, "A well-done bird will be dry and taste like liver. You'll hate it, and I will have wasted one of the thirty-six birds that I'm allowed. I don't want to waste a single bird."

PHILIP PAINE

Paine Farm Squab, Sonoma

Before running a squab farm, Philip Paine held what he now describes as "a glamorous job at the British consulate and Australian foreign service" and then took a position with Hyatt Hotels. He always knew that he wanted to be his own boss, and while still at Hyatt, he bought a farm from friends in Sonoma. He thought, "I've got three acres, and I'm forty miles from San Francisco. There must be something that I can make work here."

To get to Sonoma from his job in the city, he'd take a bus to Petaluma and then a jitney to Sonoma, because there was no direct bus route at the time. "While I was in Petaluma," he said, "I happened to be walking on a side street and noticed some pigeons in a coop in the backyard. Ever since I was young I had enjoyed keeping birds, so I introduced myself to the owner and said that I had never seen birds like this. They were French Mondains, an old-fashioned squab breed of pigeon, very beautiful birds. The man said that he'd save me a pair. We struck up a friendship, and I built a little dovecote in the garden of my house in Sonoma."

While Philip had raised other game birds, he realized that squab were ideal for his plans for an independent business. Thanks to Sonoma's mild climate, the birds could be produced year-round. His first customer was a Swiss chef, Max Schacher, who owned Le Coquelicot restaurant in Ross. "He asked for two dozen birds a week. I said, 'I don't have two dozen birds this week,' and he said, "Well, bring me what you've got." Philip also went to Mason's in the Fairmont Hotel, which was run by an Australian chef whom he knew. "So I started with a very small farm but realized that acting independently was going to work," said Philip.

The French Mondains produced about three offspring a year. The challenge was to get them to produce at a rate that was viable commercially. Fortunately, Philip met an elderly Portuguese man who had raised squab and helped him understand breeding genetics and what he could do in a practical way. "I got birds from probably about ten or fifteen different people and was very methodical in selectively breeding them. I was trying to take these French Mondains, which had a big frame and long keel bone, and breed them with birds that were prolific but tended to be small. You wanted to have that speed of production, but you also wanted that size. Longevity was another factor.

"One of the things I learned from my mentor, Manuel, was not to give any medication to these birds. Traditionally they were fed a low-level antibiotic. I remember him saying to me early on, 'Just go completely clean. You're going to lose birds, but the birds that survive are going to be your strongest producers.' It was really good advice."

In the early 1980s, Philip met Catherine Brandel, who was then working at Mondavi Winery, and she connected him with Chez Panisse. Catherine and

Gary Jenanyan came over and visited, but Philip didn't have the inventory for Chez Panisse, which because of its single nightly menu needed enough squab to serve every diner. By 1986, he had built up his flock to a point where he could supply Chez Panisse, along with Square One, Santa Fe Bar and Grill, and Stars.

By the mid-1990s, Philip had two farms, but he has since gone back to being a small producer, selling about three hundred birds a week. He has a handful of restaurant clients, including Oliveto, Chez Panisse, Café Rouge, Zuni, Masa's, Quince, and Oenotri. "It's a small, stable business," he said, "and I like it that way. I enjoy the customers. I'm probably more connected with the food end of it now that I see that final process more.

"I still really enjoy running the whole farm. I'm meeting much more interesting people in agriculture, people who are clearly into the food movement and the quality of the food, and who want to know where their food comes from. It's really nice to see that there are so many more of them now than there were twenty years ago."

Bud Hoffman, another poultry entrepreneur, founded Hoffman Game Birds in Manteca in 1979 with his wife, Ruth, and his son Joe, after discovering an abandoned pheasant nest with viable eggs. They had a hen sit on the nest until the birds were born. They went on to build a business raising pheasant and chukar partridge for the State of California Department of Fish and Game. The young male birds were sold to the state to be released for hunting season, but the state had no interest in the female birds, which are illegal to shoot. Looking for a buyer, Bud contacted Alice Waters, and from 1985 to 1993, Chez Panisse bought all the female birds. Eventually, Bud raised chickens and quail for restaurants and farmers' markets, selling up to one hundred thousand pasture-raised birds yearly.

Bart Ehman, in response to requests from both Bradley Ogden and Wolfgang Puck for a chicken with more flavor, started raising antibiotic-free chickens in 1985. Ehman had started his ranching career raising baby lamb, but he dropped that aspect of his business to dedicate himself to raising the free-range Rocky chickens, which soon appeared on restaurant menus as well as in supermarkets. Fulton Valley Farms and Pitman Family Farms followed suit and began to supply many California cuisine restaurants. Mary Sue Milliken of Border Grill attested to the difference in flavor. "In the early days, our food was bold and highly seasoned, and part of that was because you couldn't get a decent chicken. It didn't taste like anything, so you had to be more creative with it. Thirty years later, there's some amazing chicken that you want to do as little as possible to."

Because these pioneers were supported by California chefs, other small producers came into the business, leading to many more options for pasture-raised lamb, pork, beef, chicken, and rabbits at farmers markets' and supermarket butcher counters.

Fish and Seafood

In the 1950s and 1960s, Continental restaurants in California imported most of their fish from Europe and then froze it for later use. In Northern California, the new California cuisine restaurants bought from wholesale companies at Fisherman's Wharf or from retail markets in Chinatown, which were supplied by these same wholesalers. In the early 1980s, the Monterey Fish Market opened in Berkeley, becoming one of the most important Bay Area seafood companies providing fresh fish to the more ingredient-savvy new chefs, who were demanding a greater diversity of fish and seafood, both local and from other ports.

PAUL JOHNSON AND TOM WORTHINGTON

Monterey Fish Company, Berkeley

Paul Johnson says he has "fish ESP." "For some reason," he says, "I can see a fish clear across the room and tell what it is and whether it is fresh or not. Many people can't see that. I never realized that until years ago when I'd be standing down at Fisherman's Wharf and people who'd been in the business thirty years would misidentify a fish. I'd been in the business eighteen months and I'd think, 'How can you mistake the species? How can you think that that's Dover sole when it's English sole?'"

Paul was always keen on fish. He grew up in Rhode Island and used to go out on boats with an uncle who was a fisherman. Initially, though, he gravitated toward cooking rather than fishing. When he moved to California in 1973, he became a dishwasher at the Berkeley Marriott. He moved up to be an assistant to the Swiss-trained chef there and four years later was hired to cook at Inn Season restaurant in Berkeley.

In 1977, Dr. Jerry Rosenfield, the eccentric part-time fish purveyor for both Inn Season and Chez Panisse, wanted to stop supplying fish for those restaurants. He prevailed upon Paul to take over his job. Paul continued to cook at Inn Season, but in the mornings he'd go to the docks at Fisherman's Wharf, buy whole fish, and bring them to the restaurants. Soon he was also supplying seafood for Bay Wolf. He'd fillet the fish in the kitchens for them to use that night.

In early 1979, after Paul had settled into a smooth routine, Patricia Unterman asked him if he would supply the fish for her new seafood restaurant, Hayes Street Grill. She needed all of her fish filleted, so once he took on the job, he had to give up cooking. "For about a year, I would go to the wharf at 4:00 A.M., take my fillet knives, and cut fish, rain or shine. I can remember many a day cutting fish for two or three hours in the pouring rain. I was working myself to death."

Later that year, Paul was walking down Hopkins Street in Berkeley when he saw a small appliance store with a "For Rent" sign. Paul took over the lease for $300 a month and opened Monterey Fish Market. Bill Marinelli, who has a B.S. in marine biology and later opened a seafood distribution company of his own, came on as his assistant.

At first they handled only wholesale accounts, but later they opened a retail store in the front. Soon they were busy enough to need help. Tom Worthington, a culinary student fresh out of cooking school, signed on with them in 1980 and eventually became Paul's business partner.

At that time fish was caught locally or trucked down from Oregon and Washington. In the mid-1980s, however, the wholesale fish business expanded when airlines realized that they could load the bottom of their planes with seafood. "It changed the game," said Tom. Because air freight was fairly inexpensive, many types of fish became newly available.

Monterey Fish grew rapidly, picking up the accounts of almost every restaurant that spun out of Hayes Street Grill, Chez Panisse, and Bay Wolf. For a while they even shipped fish to restaurants in Los Angeles. By 1988, they had moved their wholesale business into one of the San Francisco waterfront piers, while keeping their retail store in Berkeley.

According to Tom, it was standard in the mid-1980s and into the 1990s for chefs to call Monterey Fish early every morning and ask, "What's good?" Today Monterey Fish faxes or emails clients a daily seafood sheet. "It lists thirty or so fish and twenty-five or so shellfish. This printout has been educational for the chefs; they see where the stuff is coming from and how it's caught, and they can plan their menu."

Paul and Tom support sustainable fishing practices and hook-and-line fishermen. "We learned a lot from them and saw the difference between traditional trawl fishery guys and hands-on fishery people," said Tom. "People feel close to somebody who is doing it by himself. The fish itself holds something that is fleeting. Something disappears from fish that's handled wrong, and people can taste the difference when it's handled properly.

"We respect chefs who say they want mainly local fish, but there are times when you need to support other communities. For example, Monterey Fish deals with small companies like the Chatham Hook and Line Association, based in Massachusetts. There are not enough people in Chatham to support their business. They need to move their fish outside of that area to survive." Tom considers it part of his job as a fish purveyor to tell his clients about Chatham Hook and Line and get them excited about buying Chatham's fish. In turn, chefs tell that story to their customers, helping Chatham stay in business.

The Chatham story is a microcosm of what's happening in the industry. "Mismanaged regulation favors big companies and industrialized methods of fishing. This century has seen the disappearance of small-boat fishermen as the quotas go to the big fishing fleets," said Tom. He equates the small fisherman with the "canary in the coal mine. They're the first ones to tell you when there's a problem, and they're honest about it because they care deeply about it. These are the guys who take their children fishing and want their grandchildren to be able to fish. Sure, there's a monetary part to it, but it's also about them—their identity and their lives."

California's local catch included Dungeness crab, mussels, squid, coho salmon, petrale sole, white sea bass, sand dabs, skate, halibut, and albacore. Abalone, a regional delicacy, became overfished by commercial and sport divers, and in the mid-1970s abalone hunting was banned in Southern California and regulated in Northern California. Only silver-dollar-sized farmed abalone are available today. Sardines, once plentiful, declined in the late 1940s but are making a comeback. What dominated restaurant menus in the 1980s and 1990s were the big fish: king salmon, swordfish, halibut, and yellowfin, ahi, and bigeye tuna.

Oysters were also a popular Northern California specialty. The Olympia oyster flourished in the San Francisco Bay and was a staple in the days of the forty-niners. Hangtown Fry, a combination of oysters, bacon, and eggs, has reputedly been on the menu at San Francisco's Tadich Grill for over 160 years. Oyster farming in California dates back to the 1850s, and in the 1990s oyster culture was practiced in Tomales Bay and Drake's Bay in Marin County, Carlsbad in San Diego County, Morro Bay in San Luis Obispo County, and Santa Barbara.

The Bay Area still harbors a passion for oysters, and they are featured on the menu at many San Francisco restaurants. The long lines at the restaurant at John

Finger's Hog Island Oyster Company and its stand at the Ferry Building attest to the shellfish's ever-growing fan base.

JOHN FINGER

Hog Island Oyster Company, Marshall

John Finger is a partner with Terry Sawyer at the Hog Island Oyster Company. John grew up on the East End of Long Island in New York, where he worked on potato farms and enjoyed fishing and clamming. "My mom had a green thumb, so we always grew things. I loved to fish, and the funny thing is the only seafood I didn't eat growing up was oysters. Raw, cooked, or otherwise, I never liked them. Back east then it was really about clams, raw clams."

John studied marine biology at Southampton College in New York, where he became friends with Bill Marinelli, who went on to work for Monterey Fish in 1979 and to open a seafood distribution company in 1981. In 1978, after graduating, John moved to Santa Cruz to check out the surfing and aquaculture on the West Coast. His first job was for International Shellfish Enterprises, an oyster company in Moss Landing.

"I worked there two and a half years and wound up quitting twice. I didn't like the way they were running it. That same company bought a company in Tomales Bay and hired me back after I had quit the first time. I hired and trained the crew, and then they hired a guy from, I think, the tomato business to run it. But I got to see Tomales Bay and stay up here a little bit."

John married in 1981 and took his wife on an extended trip to Europe. For four months he worked in Ireland, France, and Spain, learning the oyster business. Around the time he and his wife returned from Europe, Bill had started Marinelli Shellfish and was enlisting people to farm shellfish on the West Coast. John and a friend, Michael Watchorn, took a five-acre lease in Marshall in Marin County at the end of 1982, and in July 1983 they planted their first fifty thousand oysters.

Oysters reflect their *terroir*, which John calls "merroir," varying in flavor depending on the food source, minerals, and level of salinity in the water. He and Michael found that the pure, frigid waters of Tomales Bay offered an ideal environment for oyster farming. They cultivated Pacific, Kumamoto, and Atlantic varieties in mesh bags placed on steel racks that kept the oysters off the bottom of the bay, a method that enabled them to grow quickly.

At first they sold their oysters through Marinelli Shellfish. "It was a great symbiosis," said John, "because Billy was the consummate salesman. Back then, selling West Coast shellfish to restaurants in the Bay Area was an uphill battle. They were familiar with Blue Points but not West Coast oysters. There was a lot of education of customers." Bill created an oyster chart and taught seminars for the restaurant staffs.

"I think a lot of our success, not to take away from the fact that we're passionate and very hardworking, is due to our proximity to San Francisco," said John. "This isn't the easiest bay to grow oysters in. But people here appreciate good food and will try different things. If something has a good reputation, people will seek it out and pay what's necessary for you to be in business, because it's more expensive to be in business here."

Bill helped with the initial branding and was the one who suggested the name Hog Island. "We built our brand from Chez Panisse, Zuni, and Square One having them, and then a food writer mentioning Hog Island. The next thing you know, the phone's ringing." John said he's had dairy farmers at the Marin County agricultural roundtables talk to him about how they can niche market "like the oyster guys." "If you can't niche market in the Bay Area," said John, "you might as well hang it up.

"When I look at our clientele, I see how many young people are into oysters. The only thing I can attribute it to is that in California people want to know where their food comes from. I think oysters almost more than any other food are about place. There's not much I can do as an oyster farmer other than planning; once they're there, I'm relying on Mother Nature to provide. Oysters are elemental that way."

Today Hog Island sells three million oysters annually. The company has two Hog Island Oyster Bars and sells on-site at a picnic area opened in 1990. "I finally have the sort of rustic seafood shack I always wanted," said John. "That's what most people want to write about. There's something about being close to the source, and being able to sit outside in this beautiful place, eating those amazing oysters."

Dover sole and turbot gave upscale places like Spago and Michael's their fine-dining credibility. Both restaurants sourced their fish from Europe in the early 1980s. Anne Gingrass, who did the purchasing for Wolfgang Puck during Spago's early years, said that while the restaurant got lobsters from Maine and salmon from Alaska, most of its fish came from France.

Other Southern California chefs purchased from local suppliers, although to supplement their choices they also ordered from Monterey Fish and Marinelli Shellfish in Northern California. Mary Sue Milliken and Susan Feniger purchased their seafood from Pacific California Fish, a Japanese company located in downtown Los Angeles. When it went out of business, they bought from Ocean Jewels Seafood in Santa Monica, owned by Julee Harmon. Santa Monica Seafood, a family-owned business founded in 1939, was a major player in the LA restaurant scene; owners Jack and Frank Deluca expanded from selling California halibut, shark, sea bass, tuna, and lobsters to tourists on the Santa Monica Pier to working with the top LA chefs, including Evan Kleiman and Piero Selvaggio. P&D Seafood in Los Angeles, which opened in 1985, distributed both locally and nationwide. Michael McCarty tended to be the exception to the rule, continuing to source his seafood from Rungis market in Paris, Joe Gurrera at Citarella in New York, and Andy Arons at Flying Foods, a specialty foods importer who flew in Dover sole in addition to European produce.

As chefs in both the north and south began to capitalize on the new meats, fish, and fowl that were increasingly available, they were also making the most of products that simply hadn't been made in California prior to the 1980s.

The Artisans

In 1982, while working at the Great Chefs cooking school at Mondavi Winery, Gary Jenanyan was asked to produce an event for the State of California, which he called "The Many Faces of California Cuisine." He invited California-based cooks, from Narsai David and Darrell Corti to Barbara Tropp, to do demonstrations at the fourteen-day event. Each chef cooked something different. One day, it was Italian, the next day Mexican, and the next Chinese. During each demo, he also brought in a California artisan whose product he thought would have legs. One of the items was Laura Chenel's goat cheese. "She was hand-wrapping them, and I said, 'Laura, you gotta get a machine to seal these.' She and Cindy Pawlcyn were serving the cheese. It was a very exciting time."

In 1985, Cakebread Cellars instituted its annual American Harvest workshop. Chefs from all over the country were invited to cook two wine-and-food-pairing dinners, prepared with products from selected artisanal purveyors. John Finger of Hog Island Oyster Company, Don Watson of Napa Valley Lamb, Jim Reichardt of Sonoma County Poultry, Bob and Dean Giacomini of Point Reyes Cheese, and Cindy and Liam Callahan of Bellwether Farms brought samples of their food for the guest chefs to taste. According to Cakebread's chef, Brian Streeter, the guest chefs were blown away by what they tried.

It would not have been possible for Gary Jenanyan or the Cakebreads to produce events like these in the 1960s or 1970s. The goods simply didn't exist. Cheese, foie gras and charcuterie, condiments, and olive oils were imported from Europe without a second thought. But by the 1980s, people were starting to dream about the possibilities of local production. Most of the innovators were in Northern California.

Consistent with California's entrepreneurial traditions, most of the food artisans—the charcuterie producers, bread bakers, cheese makers, and olive oil producers—were self-educated. Like many California chefs, they came from the school of try it and see if it works (and then try it again until it does work). Some began their careers in restaurants until, eventually, one aspect of the business absorbed their attention and they set out to master this craft. Nancy Silverton began her career as a pastry chef at Michael's, refined her bread-making skills at Spago, and then opened La Brea Bakery with her then husband Mark Peel. Diane Dexter, a founder of Metropolis Baking Company, worked in pastry at Inn Season, Chez Panisse, and Square One. Olive oil producer Albert Katz was the owner of Broadway Terrace restaurant in the Oakland Hills. Peggy Smith and Sue Conley worked in Berkeley restaurants before starting Cowgirl Creamery. Paul Bertolli was chef at Chez Panisse and Oliveto for years before he opened his Fra' Mani *salumi* company. His summation of how he became a food artisan would probably resonate with most of his peers. "I've always thought of myself as a specialist. I like to concentrate on one thing. And I think I have an entrepreneurial spirit and found something that I thought was missing in the marketplace and realized I could use everything that I've ever learned about food to express it."

Some of the earliest craft food enterprises originated in Berkeley in the so-called Gourmet Ghetto on Shattuck Avenue. Chocolatier Alice Medrich described the area as alive with the cross-pollination of ideas and culinary excitement. "Here was a group of people who were educated, well read, articulate, and able to talk about what they were doing. Rough edges didn't matter; you had a chance to polish things up, and you had a chance to learn. The customers were hungry and excited. They came in because here was something new and delightful, and they wanted to know what it was, and they wanted to taste it. It was just a perfect time." First to open were Peet's Coffee in 1966 and the Cheese Board in 1967. Victoria Wise gave up her job at Chez Panisse to open her charcuterie, Pig-by-the-Tail, in

Spring Dinner
MAY 10, 1997

ANTIPASTI
CHILLED KING SALMON, ASPARAGUS, AND MEYER LEMON 9.50
INSALATA PAESANA WITH DUCK PROSCIUTTO 9.00
TUSCAN STYLE LIVER CROSTINI 6.00
BEET AND ARUGULA SALAD 7.50
VEAL CARPACCIO 8.00
PLATTER OF HOUSE-MADE SALAMIS 9.50
*SALAD OF SPRING LETTUCES, GOAT CHEESE, AND WALNUTS 8.75
SALT COD BAKED IN THE WOOD OVEN 8.50

PASTAS AND SOUP
CHILLED POTATO AND SORREL SOUP 6.50
PAGLIA E FIENO AL LIMONE 12.50
GNOCCHI WITH BROWN BUTTER AND SAGE 13.50
TAGLIATELLE WITH MOREL MUSHROOMS 13.75
TAGLIARINI WITH CLAMS, MUSSELS, AND FENNEL 13.50
RADIATORI *AL RAGU* 13.50
CANNELLONI OF RABBIT 14.00

GRILLS, SAUTES, AND ROTISSERIE
BEEF SHORT RIBS BRAISED IN RED WINE 18.00
VEAL MEATBALLS WITH ARTICHOKES AND OLIVES 16.00
ARISTA 17.00
LAMB TWO WAYS: SPIT-ROASTED LEG AND GRILLED SAUSAGES 18.00
SWORDFISH WITH ARTICHOKE CRUST 17.50
ROTOLO OF CHICKEN WITH MORELS 17.00
STEAMED ATLANTIC COD WITH HERB SAUCE 17.75
GRILLED WHOLE PIGEON WITH FAVA BEANS 18.50.

VEGETABLE SIDE DISHES
SPRING LETTUCES VINAIGRETTE 6.00
HEARTS OF ROMAINE WITH ANCHOVY VINAIGRETTE 7.00
FLAGEOLET BEANS COOKED IN THE WOOD OVEN 3.00
NEW POTATO, SPRING ONION, AND GARLIC GRATIN 4.00
STEAMED SPRING VEGETABLES *AGRUMATO* 5.50
MASHED POTATOES 3.00
BLACK CABBAGE WITH GARLIC 3.00

*While available

Oliveto

AN 18% GRATUITY MAY BE ADDED TO PARTIES OF 8 OR MORE

Paul Bertolli celebrates Italy with California
ingredients, including a platter of house-made salamis,
in this Oliveto spring dinner on May 10, 1997.

1973, which was followed by Alice Medrich's Cocolat bakery in 1976 and Marilyn Rinzler's Poulet restaurant in 1979.

VICTORIA WISE

Pig-by-the-Tail, Berkeley

In the past five years, there's been a spate of well-publicized butchering events where crowds of carnivores come to watch strong chefs—usually male, with tattoo-covered arms—break down an animal and serve *salumi* they had made earlier. For me, it's heartening to know that it was a petite woman who started the artisanal charcuterie movement in the Bay Area. After a year at Chez Panisse's kitchen, opening chef Victoria Wise moved across the street to open her own business, Pig-by-the-Tail, in 1973. While her experience at the restaurant had been gratifying, Victoria didn't like working at night. "It's not when I'm at my best. Also, there wasn't quite enough room in that kitchen for me and Alice. Although our ideas were basically the same, we're both bossy women."

Victoria was stimulated by what was going on in the neighborhood. "I loved the ambience and the excitement and the challenge of what was happening there. The Cheese Board had been open for ages," said Victoria, "and so had Peet's Coffee." There were three butchers in the neighborhood: Lenny's Meats, the Ideal Meat Market, and Mr. Murphy at the North Berkeley Market.

Mr. Murphy taught Victoria much of what she needed to know to do her work. "He was a fabulous old guy, a character. He taught me how to twist sausages into braids, how to cure hams, and how to wrap with a butcher's string. Those skills made what I was doing look more professional."

In the beginning Victoria prepared mostly French charcuterie, but she soon transformed Pig-by-the-Tail into a deli with a charcuterie component. The European tradition of the charcuterie shop was too limited and unfamiliar to American shoppers, who were used to Italian and Jewish delicatessens. Along with hams, pâtés, and sausages, she sold a large number of prepared vegetable dishes. In a classic French charcuterie, the vegetables were basically cornichons and celery *rémoulade*. "We had those too," said Victoria, "but the vegetables almost started crowding out the meat. People wanted to be able to pick out an entire meal." The prepared salads were so enticing and colorful, they seduced people stopping in for pâté or *boudin blanc*. All they needed to do was go next door to the Cheese Board for cheese and bread and they had a delicious handcrafted dinner.

Pig-by-the-Tail developed an enthusiastic clientele but "never made any money," said Victoria. "It was not a business; it was an artist's workshop." During the recession in 1985, with a one-year-old son at home, Victoria decided to close the shop. She asked herself, "Why am I doing this? I have a child to raise, I'm not making any money, and I'm getting older." Closing the business was difficult. "I missed it at first, because that kind of intense, maniacal work can become so ingrained in your being that it's hard to let go. But I never have felt that I didn't make the right decision." Victoria has gone on to write numerous excellent cookbooks about charcuterie, sausages, and her family's Armenian food.

Chefs making California cuisine revered handcrafted foods and cooking from scratch. To them, mass-produced food was bland, uninteresting, and devoid of personality. These chefs were preoccupied with flavor, quality, and individuality. Just as they wanted to know the farmers who grew their produce and the ranchers who raised their meat and poultry, they wanted to promote the local artisans who made their cheese, sausage, bread, and olive oil. They were willing to pay a bit more for distinctive California products, and they listed producers' names on the menu. In turn, home cooks sought out the products they ate in restaurants and asked their neighborhood markets to carry them.

Over a century ago, three major Italian sausage companies sold their wares throughout the Bay Area. Molinari was established in 1896, Gallo Salame in 1910, and Columbus Salame in 1917. All were started by northern Italians who missed the flavors and artisanal products of their homeland. Their successful businesses grew into large commercial enterprises that used commodity meats and mechanized production. The California cuisine movement brought small-scale production back into vogue.

In 1978, Hobbs Shore retired from his career as an economist and moved to Marshall in west Marin. With time on his hands, he built a primitive smoker out of an old refrigerator and started smoking fish, meat, and poultry for friends. After chef Bradley Ogden of Lark Creek Inn sampled some of Hobbs's products at a party, he called to order them for his restaurant, and Hobbs's second career as a charcutier was launched. Eventually his applewood-smoked bacon landed on the menu at Postrio, the French Laundry, Bizou, and Boulevard. He branched out into making Westphalian hams, chorizo, *soppressata*, *coppa*, mortadella, and prosciutto, mining his taste memories from growing up alongside the diverse ethnic groups in the Bensonhurst section of Brooklyn and working in his Norwegian grandfather's smokehouse in upstate New York.

In the East Bay, Bruce Aidells was cooking at Poulet, down the street from Pig-by-the-Tail. Bruce tried his own hand at sausages in the early 1980s, first supplying them to restaurants and eventually branching out to retail sales in markets. He was a constant fixture at food events, making his a household name.

BRUCE AIDELLS

Aidells Sausage, Berkeley

Bruce Aidells went from a biology lab into a Gourmet Ghetto kitchen. He claims his mother was a terrible cook who turned out "perfunctory overcooked meals during the week," but on weekends they dined out, which exposed Bruce to the wealth of inexpensive ethnic restaurants in Los Angeles. "It took me beyond my mother's humble attempts. I learned early on if you want to eat well, you've got to learn how to do it yourself."

Bruce moved up to the Bay Area to attend college, where a roommate left him a battered copy of one of James Beard's cookbooks, which lured him into the kitchen. "I found that the small independent markets in Berkeley had better prices than Lucky and Safeway. So we shopped at Monterey Market, and in those days Monterey Market was an actual market. It had a meat counter. We couldn't afford packaged foods, so we never bought that stuff."

In 1965, Bruce went to Europe, where he encountered foods that he hadn't tasted in Los Angeles or Berkeley. At that time, "dining choices were limited. Your high-end restaurant was Hank Rubin's Pot Luck, where you would go on a special date or a special occasion. If your parents came up, you usually went to the Claremont Hotel, because they had an all-you-can-eat buffet. The opening of Pig-by-the-Tail was major, because it was a real European type of store. And the Cheese Board. It all started there, in my opinion." Bruce was fascinated with Chez Panisse and Narsai David's. "They opened with two different points of view," he said. "Narsai's was a Continental place—fancy, formal, frilly. Chez Panisse was doing home-style French cooking. I was there early on, eating the boeuf bourguignon, coq au vin, and quiches."

By 1972, Bruce was studying for his PhD at UC Santa Cruz. While there, he was given the opportunity to open a tiny restaurant on campus. "I cooked all the ethnic dishes that I had always wanted to make. I learned how to make them from the Time-Life series. These were the most important books for me, and I still refer to them."

After receiving his PhD in 1974, Bruce worked in England, took a tenure-track position at the National Institutes of Health, and then was accepted at a lab in Berkeley to do postdoctoral work in cell biology. In 1979, he heard that funding was going to dry up and the lab was going to close. Fortuitously, at the same time, Bruce met Marilyn Rinzler, a graduate student in social work who was opening a small restaurant serving simple, healthy, gourmet take-out meals. Chicken was the theme of the restaurant, which she called Poulet. Bruce told her he was an experienced chef, though his sole experience was at the campus restaurant, and she hired him. "Marilyn loved chicken. I didn't particularly love chicken, so we slipped in a lot of nonchicken things. That's when I started getting into the sausages, pâtés, and special meats. That was a great three years."

Bruce's sausage breakthrough came in 1980. On a visit to New Orleans, he befriended Steve Armbruster, who cooked at a music venue called Tipitina's. Steve showed Bruce how to make andouille sausage and other New Orleans specialties. "I invited him out to Poulet," said Bruce, "and he brought an alligator tail with him. We did this big Louisiana thing. The Oakland Raiders were going to the Super Bowl in New Orleans, so it was perfect timing." In 1983 Bruce left Poulet and went into the sausage business.

His first two customers were Michael Wild at Bay Wolf and Jeremiah Tower at Santa Fe Bar and Grill. Timing was key, as was hard work. Paul Prudhomme was touring the country with his blackened redfish and Cajun martinis, igniting a Cajun cooking craze. "If you were a hip American restaurant," said Bruce, "you had a lot of Louisiana stuff on your menu. I was the only guy that was making a real andouille sausage, so I had the whole market to myself." He followed up with sweet and hot Italian sausages, fresh herb French sausage, chorizo, and a duck sausage with sun-dried cherries.

The business took off. "It didn't take off on its own, trust me," said Bruce. "We never waited around for the telephone to ring. I was hitting the street, making cold calls, and following leads.

"I couldn't figure out what to call the company, so I just called it after myself. That was good, because every activity I did helped to build a brand. I was part of the food community and did a lot of food events and wrote cookbooks, which all helped." But then Bruce experienced the downside of using his own name for a successful business. In 1993, he sold 60 percent of his business to Ernie Gabiati, the owner of Gallo Salame, and in 2002, he sold Gabiati the remaining 40 percent. "I sold the brand and then all of a sudden, somebody else controlled my name and face. But when you think about it, there wasn't anything to sell without the brand; it succeeded partially because all these other activities added credibility and authenticity to the brand."

Cheese making, like sausage making, had a long history in Northern California. Cheese has been produced in the Bay Area since 1865, when Marin French Cheese Company was established. By 1900, the business was producing soft-ripened cheeses like Camembert and a little round disk called a "breakfast cheese." Tom Vella started his cheese company in Sonoma in 1931 selling Monterey Jack. Later his son, Ig, perfected the aging of dry Jack cheese for the Italian community to use as a substitute for Parmesan, which was unobtainable during World War II. These were marketed as everyday cheeses, not gourmet items.

In 1967, Elizabeth and Sahag Avedisian opened the Cheese Board in a tiny closet of a shop on Cedar Street in Berkeley's Gourmet Ghetto. There they sold mostly imported cheeses. They changed the ownership structure to a workers' collective in 1971 and moved to a larger store on Shattuck Avenue in 1975. The shop's selection of local cheeses expanded with the California cuisine movement.

To Laura Werlin, the author of books on the American artisanal cheese movement, no cheese maker had a greater impact on California cuisine than Laura Chenel, who introduced her goat cheese in Sonoma County in 1979. Alice Waters "took that cheese, put it on the plate and into the mouths of people who, at that point, were open to trying new things." The goat cheese salad is the only salad that has remained on the Chez Panisse menu for over thirty years.

After Laura Chenel's goat cheese landed on the menu at Chez Panisse, it brought attention and prestige to the cheeses from Marin French Cheese Company and Vella Cheese Company. Eventually these companies' products found their way onto high-end menus. By the 1990s, Vella dry Jack was being shaved on restaurant salads in place of Italian pecorino.

In the 1980s, Ellen Straus, co-owner of the Straus Family dairy farm and creamery with her husband, Bill, began to mobilize her neighbors to protect agricultural land and revitalize the dairy industry in Marin. An ardent environmentalist, Ellen had founded the Marin Agricultural Land Trust in 1980 with her friend Phyllis Faber, a wetlands biologist, to prevent the encroachment of urban development. In the 1990s, Sue Conley and Peggy Smith, who used milk from the Straus's Holstein cows to make their Cowgirl Creamery cheeses, picked up the torch and began to educate chefs and the public about the story of cheese, from land to plate. Sue and Peggy "have been instrumental in educating people by way of their brand and by their consistent message about using organic milk and taking care of the land," said Laura Werlin. "Their message about Marin and saving the dairy lands was very important. Sue and Peggy paved the way for people like Cindy Callahan."

California's artisanal cheese movement grew from a few cheese makers—all men—to many cheese makers—mostly women. Some went to Europe to learn how to make the cheese they aspired to produce. Laura Chenel went to France, as did Peggy Smith and Sue Conley. Cindy and Liam Callahan went to Italy. They did not have formal apprenticeships, but by careful observation they could see how others made cheese and could learn what they were doing wrong or differently. In the process they discovered their own *terroir*. Our California climate affected the flavor of the milk, and our environment harbored different molds. The cheese would not be the same as those that inspired its creation, but it would be uniquely Californian.

Cindy Callahan at Bellwether Farms said that Sonoma has evolved to become a haven for cheese makers. "When we started in the early 1990s, Laura Chenel and Ig Vella were the only cheese makers in this area. Patty Sammons [now Patty Karlin], at Bodega Artisan Cheese, and Jennifer Bice and her husband, Steven Schnack, of Redwood Hill Farm, made their first batches of cheese here. They would come on the weekends when we weren't using our cheese room and make their cheese. Cowgirl hadn't arrived yet. And now there are people all around us, and cows, goats, and sheep, which is amazing."

Bellwether Farms is known for its superb sheep's milk cheese and ricotta as well as a few cow's milk cheeses and yogurts. Cindy Callahan and her son, Liam, introduced Bellwether's cheeses at farmers' markets and through Tomales Bay Foods, a small retail operation started by Sue Conley and Peggy Smith that brought west Marin and Sonoma dairy products to market.

CINDY AND LIAM CALLAHAN

Bellwether Farms, Petaluma

Cindy Callahan, a nurse, moved from Manhattan to San Francisco in 1967, when her husband, Ed, a physician, received a fellowship at UCSF Medical Center. In 1986, they purchased a thirty-four-acre ranch in Sonoma County. They bought sheep to keep the grasses and weeds under control and then bought a ram and started raising lambs. After a couple of years, they had more lamb than their friends and family could eat, so Cindy "picked up the phone, called Chez Panisse, and told them, 'We have some wonderful lamb.' Chris Lee, their forager, interviewed us, and Chez Panisse became our first commercial customer. At that time we were doing a full-size market lamb. Now our specialty is a baby milk-fed lamb because we wean these lambs at a very young age so we can bring the ewes up to the dairy." Today their principal restaurant customer is the French Laundry, but they sell to about ten restaurants when the milk-fed baby lamb is in season. "I call when I know the lambs are getting close to three weeks old in the spring," said Cindy, "so the restaurants have time to change their menus."

In 1989, a friend of a friend came to the farm and said, "There's nothing like sheep's milk yogurt." It had never dawned on the Callahans to milk the sheep. But they looked into it and decided they would learn to make not yogurt, but cheese. Theirs became the first sheep dairy farm in California.

Their friends Carol Field, a food writer, and Carlo Middione, a chef, advised Ed and Cindy to go to Italy to learn how to make classic sheep's milk pecorino. In the spring of 1992, the Callahans spent nearly a month, mostly in Tuscany, traveling from sheep farm to sheep farm and watching the process of milking and making cheese.

When they got home, their son, Liam, had just graduated from UC Berkeley with a degree in political economy. His friends were going to business school, but he decided to stay on the farm. Before long, he had become the cheese maker. Cindy had been making fresh *fromage blanc* and simple cheeses modeled on chèvre, which they sold at farmers' markets. But after the trip to Italy, Cindy and Liam began making aged cheeses. Their first effort, modeled after pecorino toscano, was called Toscano.

In 1994, it was Liam's turn to go to Italy to pick up techniques for improving his family's cheeses. "The great thing about cheese making is we all use the same techniques," said Liam. "We change the timing, temperature, milk, and equipment, but the principles are the same: fermenting, coagulating, cutting, putting the cheeses in the forms. By changing those, you come up with different cheeses. A cheese maker can see a cheese being made that's very different from the one they're making at home and still learn a great deal."

When Liam returned from Italy, he began to make cow's milk cheeses with milk from the Straus Family Creamery in Marshall. His fledgling effort with cow's milk was a *fromage blanc,* which he made for the next two years, in addition to improving Bellwether's sheep's milk cheeses. "I gained perspective while visiting Pienza in Tuscany, which is well known for its sheep's milk cheeses," said Liam. "Maybe a dozen manufacturers surround that town, marketing cheese under the name pecorino toscano, yet all the cheeses were different from one another. The light went on in my head. Modeling our cheese after one six thousand miles away, and using that name, didn't make much sense. We were never going to be able to accomplish what we were holding in our mind as the original ideal when these people who were two miles apart couldn't do it. We needed to decide what we liked about the cheese and then change our recipe and our methods to highlight those elements."

Liam was determined to capture the flavor of Sonoma's unique *terroir*. He understood that there was no way that his cheese could taste like Tuscan cheese, nor should it. The milk from Marin County has a very clean flavor because the animals are outside more. Italian ewes spend more time in the barn sheltering from the heat or snow, and their milk has a gamier flavor, which produces a sharper cheese. Liam wanted to make cheeses that reflected where they were from—the essence of California cuisine.

Bellwether phased out its pecorino toscano in favor of a cheese named San Andreas, after the local earthquake fault. Liam and Cindy took this sheep's milk cheese in a different direction, deemphasizing the saltiness and tanginess and creating a smoother body, with subtle flavors that emerge more on the finish than up front, the opposite of most of the Tuscan cheeses.

Feeling that he had more to learn from travel, tasting, and observation, Liam went back to Italy in 1996 to witness the production of cow's milk cheeses in Piedmont. The two cheeses that resulted from that trip—Carmody and Crescenza—are two of Bellwether's best sellers.

The buttery Carmody was inspired by young table cheeses made in Italy for local consumption. Liam used milk from the Jersey cows at the nearby Bianchi Dairy, which had a more interesting flavor and a higher butterfat content than milk from the Straus's Holsteins. "For a small cheese maker, higher solids meant more milk per vat, an important consideration. Jersey has a beautiful large fat globule that gives a richer texture and flavor at a younger age. So the cheese is ready to eat at five or six weeks." Carmody is named for the road that runs by the farm.

The second cheese Liam mastered was Crescenza. Carlo Middione had specifically instructed Liam to find this soft-ripened, runny cheese, traditionally eaten on focaccia and flatbreads in Italy but unknown in California at that time. Today, along with the cow's milk Carmody and Crescenza, Bellwether Farms makes two sheep's milk cheeses—San Andreas and a raw semi-soft sheep cheese called Pepato—crème fraîche, *fromage blanc,* and ricotta. In 2007, they came full circle and began to make a sheep's milk yogurt—the idea that had started it all off.

"The great thing about California," said Liam, "is the excitement people have for foods that are made traditionally and nearby. We certainly sell beyond what you would call 'nearby' at this point, but the excitement for traditional hand-made food is still growing."

Bellwether Farms cheeses can be found at the Cowgirl Creamery, twenty-five miles down a country road in the bucolic town of Point Reyes Station. Peggy Smith and Sue Conley—the cowgirls—are partners in the Creamery. They started their company as distributors for local cheese makers and ended up in the cheese business themselves. "We're the second or maybe the third wave of the artisanal cheese movement," said Peggy. "California is a place where a person can follow a dream, have a good idea, and get support to see it through," added Sue. "I don't think that Peggy and I could have done what we did anywhere else, except maybe Vermont or Wisconsin. Having an educated clientele in the Bay Area, with food being one of the major industries, gave us a good leg up. Then the farmers' markets provided promotion and education, which filtered into the shops."

"When we went to our first American Cheese Society meeting in Rohnert Park in around 1995," said Peggy, "Ari Weinzweig of Zingerman's was putting the competition cheeses out and the table was as big as your dining room table. Now there are two thousand cheeses in the competition."

SUE CONLEY AND PEGGY SMITH

Cowgirl Creamery, Point Reyes Station

Peggy Smith and Sue Conley both began their careers in Berkeley restaurant kitchens, Peggy at Chez Panisse and Sue at Bette's Oceanview Diner. In 1995, ready for new challenges, Sue and Peggy formed a group called Tomales Bay Foods in Marin County. It included the Straus Family Creamery, Bellwether Farms, Redwood Hill Farm, and the Vella Cheese Company. They sold cheese in a little store on Green Street in San Francisco.

After meeting Albert and Ellen Straus, Peggy and Sue were attracted to becoming part of the dairy community in west Marin. In 1996, they applied for a Small Business Administration loan to renovate a barn in Point Reyes Station, where they hoped to open a market. The week before they were to break ground, the lender pulled out, deciding that it was too risky. The loan manager whom they had been working with had left and the new loan manager said, "Are you kidding? There are only three hundred people in this town. Who's going to come here to shop?" So they turned to friends and family to put together a construction loan.

At their new store, Peggy and Sue continued to sell cheeses made by other manufacturers, but in 1997, they also began to produce their own cheeses under the Cowgirl Creamery label. Sue said, "We used a model that we learned in Europe at Fromagerie Jean d'Alos in Bordeaux and Neal's Yard Dairy in London and made fresh cheese that could be seen through the window. We built an open kitchen in our creamery, so there's integrity to the process and education, and people start to understand how cheese is made." Sue took cheese-making courses, and for the first few years, they sold the very simplest cheeses—cottage cheese, *fromage blanc,* and crème fraîche—made from organic Straus milk.

Then in 1999, a dairy scientist from the Netherlands named Fonts Smith came to intern at the creamery. Fonts knew how to make only Gouda. Peggy and Sue wanted to make "a cheese that everybody would want to put out at a party, one of those soft, ripe, gooey cheeses like a Saint André, only more delicious," said Sue. To accommodate their wishes, Fonts said, "I know how to make it softer. We have something like this in the Netherlands." He started with a cheese a little smaller than a hockey puck with a white mold. They worked with it, lightening up on the cooking, adding more cream, and aging it at a slightly warmer temperature. "That's how we developed the Mt. Tam, which continues to be our most popular cheese," said Sue. "It was in the Saint André style and has a cooked curd, unlike Brie." Another aged cheese, Red Hawk, is similar, "but has a washed rind, so it's unctuous and a little funky. That's the one the French people go for."

Sue thinks that the dairy area's location on a peninsula in west Marin has helped it maintain its integrity and sense of community. Dairies have been passed down from generation to generation in the same families. She observed that what's going on currently in agriculture is similar to what went on in the restaurant business in the 1980s. The new farmers are college-educated, well-traveled people, some changing careers, filled with passion in a profession that is now becoming respected. "In the past being a farmer wasn't a high-status position. People used to joke about Petaluma and the chicken farmers," she said. "Now Petaluma is renowned for its fantastic food, the duck farms, the oyster farms, the great dairies. There is an appreciation of *terroir.*"

They do not sense a similar appreciation in Southern California. "Food is one of our main industries in the Bay Area," said Peggy. "In Los Angeles, that's not so. The service industry in LA is a sideline of the film industry, which makes a big difference in people's attitudes toward food and the way they approach it." "We distribute to Los Angeles," said Sue, "driving down there every other week because we can't find a distributor who handles cheese like ours. Yet with all of our connections and recognition, it's a struggle to make sales in that market."

Most Bay Area cheese lovers bought cheese at specialty shops where they could taste the cheese first. The Cowgirls were cautious about putting their cheeses into grocery stores, where they could not be sure it would be properly handled or stored. "How you move your product," said Sue, "is as important as how you make your product. Otherwise you're going to end up places you shouldn't be and that's only going to speak poorly of your product." Today 90 percent of the cheese they make is distributed through their own trucks and shops. They also bring in and care for hundreds of cheeses in their store at the Ferry Building. And they deliver to five hundred customers in the Bay Area, to restaurant chefs and specialty shops, and to selected markets.

In the Bay Area, bread has an even older history than cheese, having been a San Francisco specialty for over two hundred years. San Francisco has long been known for its sourdough, a product of its unique humidity and temperate climate, which nourish the yeast in the special wild-fermented starter. Today most of the original sourdough bakeries are gone except for Boudin, which was founded in 1849. After World War II, Bay Area bread declined in quality, and most of what was available was baked in large factories. California cuisine inspired the return to craft baking, and the Bay Area was at the forefront. Around 1978, the Cheese Board in Berkeley started baking baguettes to accompany its cheeses, and Narsai's Market in Kensington soon followed its example. The East Bay saw a proliferation of artisanal bakeries in the 1980s, including the Acme Bread Company (started by Steve Sullivan), Semifreddi's (Michael Rose and Barbara and Tom Franier), Grace Baking Company (Glenn Mitchell), and Metropolis Baking Company (Diane and Perry Dexter). In San Francisco, the Zen Center ran Tassajara Bakery in Cole Valley from 1976 until 1992. Karen Mitchell's Model Bakery opened in St. Helena in 1984, spurring a new batch of bakeries in the North Bay over the subsequent decade. These included Craig Ponsford's Artisan Bakers in Sonoma, Ruben Barrera's Panorama Baking Company and Kathleen Weber's Della Fattoria in Petaluma, and Chad Robertson's Bay Village Breads in Point Reyes, which he opened in 1997 and then transplanted to the Mission District in 2002 as Tartine Bakery.

Of all of these, Steve Sullivan's Acme was the benchmark. Steve revolutionized bread making in California by introducing hand-formed bread made with organic flour, which eventually sparked a nationwide revival of artisanal bread baking.

STEVE SULLIVAN

Acme Bread Company, Berkeley

Steve Sullivan started working at Chez Panisse as a busboy when he was still a teenager. He taught himself how to bake and eventually began making bread for the restaurant. "I loved working at Chez Panisse," said Steve. "My father told me, 'You may not make as much money working there as you would at another restaurant, but there's something special going on, and you want to be there while it's happening.'" Chez Panisse opened in the midst of the political activism of the 1970s. Steve remembers working there as being "important in a positive and nourishing way, not in a destructively revolutionary way. People were being brought in and made happy. What more could you want than to be upending things and helping usher in something new?"

After Steve read Elizabeth David's *English Bread and Yeast Cookery*, he started baking bread for friends in his college dorm room. "My roommate was horrified at the amount of mess relative to the exceedingly small amount of anything edible that this process was producing, so he called in his mother. She had been raised on a farm and could stuff a turkey with one hand and roll out a pie crust with the other." She gave Steve some basic pointers, and he kept experimenting. Though he was no longer working at Chez Panisse at this point, he brought his bread to the restaurant for critique.

While Steve was perfecting his technique, the Venetian bakery that had been supplying Chez Panisse with brick-oven baguettes went out of business. After that, a succession of little bakeries opened that would initially offer interesting bread, but as soon as they had some success the owners would buy new equipment, automate their process, and start producing inferior product. Steve's bread was getting better while the bread that the restaurant could purchase was getting worse. "Alice, in her inimitable fashion, spotted the point when those lines crossed and asked if I would make the bread for the restaurant." Steve agreed and was brought in to team up with Patty Curtan and Lindsey Shere, both of whom had professional bread-baking experience. Each day he and Lindsey would make whichever breads they wanted. Once the Café opened in 1980, Steve also began making pizza dough and pasta.

As the Café got busier, more bread was needed. The demands of the Café, coupled with those of the downstairs restaurant, made it almost impossible to keep pace with production. When oven space maxed out, Steve decided it was time for him to find his own place. In 1983, he opened Acme Bread Company on San Pablo Avenue, next to Kermit Lynch's wine shop.

Acme became a success, said Steve, because "there wasn't any good bread broadly available on a wholesale basis anymore. It had become more of an industrial product. After the San Francisco bakeries consolidated in the mid-1980s, professional bakers came to Acme to apply for work. They would try out and say, 'I can't do this. I've never formed bread by hand. I run machines.' The bread-baking system in this country had produced a bunch of people who didn't know how to make real bread."

Apart from Peter Overton from the Zen Center, Acme's first bakers were "skate punks who used to work for Narsai David, and for whatever reason hadn't been able to show up regularly enough, had offended him in some way, or had gone off in a huff. They knew how to roll baguettes, though, and that was a lot of help."

Steve's first four breads were sourdough *pain au levain*, sweet baguette, challah, and "upstairs bread," so named because it was served up in the Chez Panisse Café. He used whole-grain organic flours, and beginning in the 1990s, incorporated more organic and locally sourced ingredients, including olive oils, nuts and seeds, and butter.

At first restaurateurs believed that nobody would pay extra for better bread. Bay Wolf's Michael Wild said to Steve, "I love your bread, and I'll write you a letter to help you get a bank loan, but we're not going to buy bread from you." Steve was shocked and asked why. Michael told him, "In a French bistro, you buy the cheapest bread you can, because you're giving it away. Your bread won't be the cheapest. I'll buy it for myself, but I can't buy it for the restaurant." Within six months, Michael's customers had started to demand Acme. "It should've been a no-brainer," said Steve. "For one dollar instead of 75 cents, you could get the best bread available versus industrial bread. Good bread is actually one of the ways that people can get the best of something without having to be a millionaire."

Today Acme supplies Bay Area restaurants with *levain,* baguettes, Italian sweet and sour *bâtards,* olive and walnut loaves, and custom rolls. It is a selling point for restaurants and markets to say, "We have Acme bread."

Bread making appealed to California's women entrepreneurs as well. Model Bakery owner Karen Mitchell grew up in Oregon in a food-centric family. Her father was a fisherman and a hunter, and her grandmothers and mother were homemakers who had gardens and baked from scratch. One great-aunt owned a pie shop in eastern Oregon, and another owned a restaurant in Portland, so Karen was brought up around fresh homemade food. In the mid-1970s, Karen and her husband settled in the Napa Valley, where she and a couple of friends started a catering business.

Karen discovered that there wasn't any good bread in the area and decided that was where she might make her mark. She leased an old bakery called the Sugar House in St. Helena and opened the Model Bakery in 1984. The bakery's gas-fired ovens had been built by Italian masons in the 1920s with bottoms made of bricks set in sand, two air vents in back, and steam lines running down the sides to distribute the heat. Karen had to figure out how to light the ovens herself, since the owner of the Sugar House, who had been evicted following a dispute with the landlord, wouldn't show her how to do it. There weren't any baking programs at the time, so Karen taught herself. "There was a learning curve. We built it up slowly, doing catering for three or four years until we could afford to do just the bakery." The Model Bakery grew successfully over the years and remains the only bakery in St. Helena.

Mutual education was a distinctive feature of California cuisine, and Karen became a charter member of the Baker's Dozen, a community of professional and home bakers brought together by cookbook author and teacher Marion Cunningham and bakery owner Amy Pressman. From a first meeting of forty bakers in 1989, the group grew to over three hundred members, including Bay Area experts Lindsey Shere, Carol Field, Fran Gage, Peter Reinhart, and Flo Braker. In regular meetings, participants explained what they knew, listened to what others had to offer, and tasted one another's products. Whether self-taught or professionally trained, everyone in the group shared a commitment to learning by doing.

Kathleen Weber began baking as a hobby using a wood-burning oven on the grounds of her Petaluma ranch in 1995. Her son Aaron was working at the Sonoma Mission Inn at the time, and one day the chef, Mark Vann, asked if she would make bread for an olive oil tasting. According to Kathleen, she dropped off the loaves, and he said, "Great, that's going to be enough for two days," and as soon as she reached home he called and said, "They love your bread, and it's all gone. Can you make some for tomorrow?" "It's thrilling when someone likes what you do," said Kathleen. "To be recognized and appreciated is why we cook. I made some for the next day, and about a month later he asked if I could make bread for the restaurant." That was the start of Della Fattoria—or "of the farm"—a name that honors the bakery's homespun roots.

Michel Suas, founder of the San Francisco Baking Institute, put Kathleen in touch with a young Frenchman who showed her how to scale up her original recipes to create larger batches for the restaurant. Then, through her son's girlfriend at the time, Thomas Keller discovered her bread and invited her to make some for the French Laundry. "He bought our *campagne* to start with," said Kathleen. "Then he wanted a whole-wheat bread with seeds. I kept working on it, and the day that we had it the way he wanted, he said, 'Okay, I want ten of those tomorrow.'"

As her reputation grew, Kathleen and her husband, Edmund, built more wood-burning ovens, but working alone became untenable. "I was a one-man band, mixing, shaping, baking," said Kathleen. "I slept about two hours at a time and fell asleep while I was delivering bread." In 1997, her son came on board full-time. "His chef training and ability to set up a line were hugely important in the way we made our bread. He got us streamlined and then found out he loved it. Then we hired a gal who he ended up marrying. Things work out for the best." Today Kathleen's daughter Elisa also works for the bakery, and they have added pastries and other dishes to the menu.

In Southern California, Nancy Silverton, an accomplished pastry chef, was inspired by Steve Sullivan's bread and bothered that, as she put it, "LA didn't have the bread that San Francisco did. We didn't have Acme." Determined to put LA bread on the map, she opened La Brea Bakery in 1989 as part of her restaurant, Campanile. Within ten years, her bread was sold across the country and La Brea had become the largest artisanal bakery in the nation.

NANCY SILVERTON

La Brea Bakery, Los Angeles

Nancy Silverton started out cooking in her college dormitory. She liked being in the kitchen so much that she decided that cooking was what she wanted to do with her life. Her first serious job was at the restaurant 464 Magnolia in Larkspur, run by Michael Goldstein. The menu changed every night. "I was learning from self-taught, college-educated cooks," said Nancy, "so it was a Chez Panisse-y kind of experience."

When she told her parents that she was dropping out of college in her senior year to cook full-time, her father said, "That's fine, but the one thing you've got to do is to go to the Cordon Bleu." After completing the six-month certificate course, she returned to 464 Magnolia and then moved on to Michael's in Santa Monica. As part of her training at Michael's, she enrolled in the Gaston Lenôtre academy in Paris to obtain an education in pastry.

While in Paris, Nancy visited Lionel Poilâne's bakery. "Poilâne was mind-changing," she said. "I'll never forget the impression that first bite of bread had on me. I had never tasted anything like it. In 1983, when Acme opened, and I tasted Steve Sullivan's bread, I realized how close that bread tasted to what I had eaten at Poilâne. Seeing that some young American was making it in this country, I thought I could do that too one day. It reinforced my drive to make this bread."

Nancy worked as a pastry chef at Michael's, then Spago, followed by Maxwell's Plum in New York. In 1988, she and her then husband, Mark Peel, returned to California to open a restaurant of their own. Wolfgang Puck found a niche for her in the Spago kitchen, where she worked while waiting for Campanile to open. Wolfgang was determined to bake bread in-house and asked her to develop his bread program. That gave Nancy the opportunity to transform her Poilâne taste memories into actual loaves of bread. There were two types of bread that Wolfgang wanted: an olive bread that he remembered from his years in France, and a whole-grain bread that he had discovered at a food show. The latter was very simple, just a mix to which water and yeast were added, but it gave Nancy practice in shaping loaves.

"I thought it'd be terrific to be able to make bread at my restaurant too," said Nancy. "I realized from doing it at Spago that it wasn't profitable, and that it wasn't something that was doable at the back of a restaurant kitchen. So I thought that if we found a space that could also house a small wholesale and retail bakery, then we would bake our bread in-house."

Nancy went back to Lenôtre to take the academy's five-day baking class and returned with a handful of recipes. "When I started to recreate them, they were utter failures. Not only is bread a product of its environment, but the flour has an instrumental effect on the success of the loaf. Because it was such different flour, I couldn't just take these recipes and translate them as I could the recipe for a chocolate éclair. There was so much more in bread baking that I had to teach myself, because in 1989 we didn't have the books we have now. There was Elizabeth David's *English Bread and Yeast Cookery*, *Laurel's Kitchen*, and Bernard Clayton's *Breads of France*. That was it. Today anybody can pick up a handful of great books on sourdough bread baking and work with them and have a fine repertoire."

Nancy decided to begin at the beginning. "I disregarded all the recipes from France and started with a tablespoon of this, a cup of that. For the slowly fermented bread I wanted to do, I had to grow a starter, but then I had to wait a day. It wasn't like brownies, where thirty minutes later I could say, 'OK, they're too sweet, too dry, too whatever.' It was really frustrating. I said to myself, 'I need to come up with six breads to open my bakery, and I'll feel confident if I can get those six breads, the first one being a baguette.' I started from there, again, pretty much with no recipe, and definitely with no clear understanding of anything about fermentation. I learned by using just my senses, and my memories of Poilâne and Acme as my guide."

The bakery opened six months before the restaurant, in January 1989, and its popularity took Nancy by surprise. On weekends and holidays during the first couple of years, they would run out of bread. "Our customers would drive across town to the bakery, where they would find the Closed sign. They weren't an understanding customer base. The response was, obviously, to make more bread." To do this, they moved to a larger production facility a few miles away.

Soon after they relocated, Nancy was approached by a frozen food company to see if she would collaborate with them in making a frozen sourdough bread. "I have to say that I am not as much of a purist as Alice Waters, where a freezer could be the enemy. My feeling is that if the end product is just as good, then growth, expansion, and using freezers is not a bad thing. So I started to work with this company." After a trial period, though, she decided that their product was not going to be successful. "All they did was to take my bread and freeze it," she said. "I could do that too. So I decided that this wasn't going to be a viable relationship."

She thinks it was Manfred Krankl, her partner at that time, who first considered what would happen if they partially baked the bread. All the buyer would have to do was to finish the baking. That turned out to be key. "We grew that into a very successful business, one that I am really proud of. I find it thrilling that the bread reaches a lot of people who don't have a neighborhood bakery."

Baker Jim Dodge praised both her technique and the results. "Nancy is committed to the process and the recipe. Her bread doesn't have all the chemicals and additives that are in supermarket whole-grain bread. When I used to go home to New Hampshire, there was no good bread. I had to go to Vermont or to Hanover, sixty miles away, to get decent bread. Now to go into a supermarket and see La Brea bread, it's a gift."

Chocolate is another product that hasn't been the same since the advent of California cuisine. Back in Berkeley in the 1970s, Alice Medrich was perfecting a recipe for chocolate truffles. The daughter of an inventor, she said that her father's philosophy was that you could always find your way by experimentation. Alice's first taste of chocolate was of a Hershey bar, which she says "imprinted" chocolate on her taste buds. But a chocolate truffle in France and a nearly flourless chocolate torte with ground nuts were the inspiration for the shop she opened. When the truffles she was making tasted like those she had eaten in France, she nervously ventured into Pig-by-the-Tail, where Victoria Wise bought her first batch. They were such a hit that in 1976 Alice was able to open a bakery, Cocolat, in the heart of the Gourmet Ghetto. She started with French desserts, but like many California cuisine cooks, she never felt she had to remain "in that groove." "Yeah, this is a chocolate dessert shop, but I'm going to do anything I want," she told herself. "That meant there was a Linzer torte, and a lemon dessert, and I took my inspiration in whatever direction I wanted."

Alice used chocolate in a new way in her cakes, tortes, and cookies, emphasizing the flavor of the chocolate rather than the sugar. Her intense focus on the character of diverse chocolates inspired John Scharffenberger and Robert Steinberg, who teamed together to open Scharffen Berger Chocolate. Experimenting with different cacao beans, they created a line of artisanal chocolates and kicked off the bean-to-bar movement.

The next transformation came with olive oil. Olive trees have been cultivated in California since the Spanish Franciscan monks opened the first California missions. The first olive oil was pressed at Mission San Diego de Alcala in 1803. In 1834, when Mexico declared its independence from Spain, the Mexican government secularized the missions, taking land away from the church and ceding it to the colony of California. The large farms were abandoned and many of the olive groves fell into disrepair.

The gold rush of 1848 brought Italian immigrants, many from around Lucca, to California. Few of these immigrants had success in the gold fields, but most decided to stay on because the Mediterranean climate felt familiar and the landscape resembled Italy. They settled down as farmers and planted vineyards and olive orchards. By 1870, they were producing olive oil from cuttings from Mission olive trees. Faced with competition from imports and cheaper vegetable oils, however, California olive oil production languished, and many producers turned to selling insipid canned Mission olives instead.

In the late 1930s and following World War II, political turmoil in Europe prevented the importation of olive oil. California growers tried once again to market olive oil despite internal competition from corn oil and cottonseed oil. In 1936, Nicola Sciabica, who had immigrated to the United States in 1911 from Castelvetrano, began limited olive oil production in Modesto. His family still farms the same land today and sells olive oil made by his grandsons.

In 1952, physiologist Ancel Keys published what came to be known as the "Seven Countries Study" on the benefits of a Mediterranean-style diet, which led to renewed attention to heart-healthy olive oil. As imported olive oils began to appear in greater numbers on grocery shelves, California ranchers started producing more and better oil in order to gain a foothold in the market. When Lila Jaeger at Rutherford Hill Winery discovered some old olive trees on her property, she consulted with retailer Darrell Corti, UC Davis fruit scientist George Martin, and Paul Vossen, a farm advisor from Sonoma, to find out how to press the fruit. None of them had much experience with making olive oil, but with growers Ridgely Evers and Nicola Sciabica, olive oil merchant Ken Stutz, and others they formed the Northern California Olive Oil Council to pool their knowledge. As olive growers from all over the state joined their efforts, they dropped the word "Northern," becoming the California Olive Oil Council.

When Nan McEvoy bought her Petaluma ranch in 1990, she learned that she had to keep the land in farm production. She decided to produce olive oil and was the first to import olive trees from Italy. Ridgely Evers, who had owned a ranch since 1982, flew in 2,400 Italian trees. They were held up in customs in LA because of dirt on their roots and weren't released until they had been cleaned and put in pots. Many were lost in a freeze once they finally made their way north, but the surviving trees, planted in 1991, were lovingly tended. Ridgely's Da Vero oil won a blind tasting in Italy in 1997. Whereas Ridgely Evers and Nan McEvoy used Tuscan olive varieties, such as Leccino and Pendolino, other growers planted the Greek Koroneiki, Spanish Arbequina, and French Lucques varieties.

Over the years, the flavor and spirit of Tuscany entered the California olive grove. More Italian olive varieties were imported and planted. New presses were installed. The California extra virgin olive oil revolution had begun. Initially some of the Italian-style oils were overly strong and bitter, but the producers learned how to mellow the flavor. In 1997, the California Olive Oil Council established a taste panel following the guidelines set by the International Olive Oil Council and began to set standards.

Today California extra virgin olive oils compete with the best from Italy and

Spain, often beating out the imports, which do not maintain such stringent standards. Oils from Pasolivo, B. R. Cohn, Katz, Sciabica, California Olive Ranch, and Corto are sold coast to coast. You know California's olive oil has arrived when producers open olive oil tasting rooms on their property and chefs mention it on their menus.

Chefs supported their local suppliers with pride. Olive oils, breads, cheeses, fish, poultry, and meats were being made by people they knew whose standards were as high as their own. Together chefs, farmers, and purveyors brought acclaim to California cuisine.

The growth and refinement of artisanal ingredients paralleled developments with California wine. While the Gallos and Almadens were doing mass production, wine makers such as Robert Mondavi, Joseph Swan, Paul Draper, Richard Graff, Josh Jensen, Joe Heitz, and others were crafting single-variety wines. These specialty winemakers became part of the team, committed to raising the profile of California products, and their wines added notes of distinction to California cuisine menus.

10

Merging the Worlds of Wine and Food

Common Cause

I think of that ongoing wish in California always to learn more. There were always new wineries, new wines, and new ingredients.

—Shirley Sarvis, wine educator

I was driving up to the Culinary Institute of America in St. Helena recently when I glanced over to the side of the highway and realized that what used to be an open field where I had picnicked with my family in the late 1960s was now covered with grapevines. Back then, when you drove up to the Napa Valley, the roads were quiet. Route 29 through the valley was lined with trees, not wall-to-wall wineries. You encountered locals running errands, not long black limos filled with eager tourists, stopping at tasting room after tasting room. If you did go to visit one of the handful of wineries open to guests, you had few options for restaurant dining after the tasting. There was a Kentucky Fried Chicken, an A&W Root Beer stand, the Red Hen, and a few small Italian places serving cannelloni. Today the Napa Valley is renowned for restaurants such as the French Laundry, Bouchon, Terra, Bistro Don Giovanni, and Tra Vigne, as well as newer establishments like Bottega, Oenotri, Redd, La Toque, and Farmstead, many of which serve produce from their gardens and wine from vineyards down the road.

In 1974, wine writer Gerald Asher arrived in California from England and was struck by the divide between people who were concerned with food and people who were concerned with wine: "I didn't feel that the food people were that interested in wine, or that the wine people were that interested in food." Today wine and food are so closely intertwined in California, it is hard to believe that it was not always so.

•

Up until the mid-1960s, wine production throughout the state was being increasingly aggregated in the hands of a score of large industrialized wineries. Only a few wineries were making premium wines, among them Heitz, Stony Hill, and Mayacamas in the Napa Valley, and Ridge and David Bruce in the Santa Cruz Mountains. In 1966, the opening of the Robert Mondavi Winery in the Napa Valley marked the reversal of the trend toward consolidation and inaugurated a period of experimentation, innovation, and rapid growth in California wine that paralleled the evolution of California cuisine. Statewide, there were over 330 wineries in 1975, a number that climbed steadily, to 508 in 1980, 807 in 1990, 1,450 in 2000, and 3,364 in 2010, according to California Wine Institute figures. Napa and Sonoma had the largest concentration of wineries, but new facilities were springing up in every county, notably Santa Clara, Santa Cruz, Mendocino, Monterey, and Santa Barbara, as well as in the Sierra foothills. Today wine grapes are grown in forty-eight of California's fifty-eight counties.

The traditional wineries—Charles Krug, Christian Brothers, Almaden, Beringer, Paul Masson, and Gallo—pumped out a broad but bland repertoire. Josh Jensen, winemaker at Calera in California's Central Coast region, said that when he started in the business in 1975, "each winery made a Johannesburg Riesling, Chenin Blanc, Claret, Burgundy, Chablis, pink Chablis, Zinfandel, and Grignolino. They also made a champagne, port, sherry, and vermouth, and some of them made madeira. It was like a big supermarket." Fortified wines were consumer favorites, and every large winery offered them. Over the next ten years, however, the balance shifted away from dessert wines and toward table wines, and from the industrial giants to small family-run fine-wine producers. Most of these new estate wineries did not aspire to be all things to all people and chose instead to narrow their selections and boost the quality of their wines. That gave rise to the term "boutique winery," which, according to Josh Jensen, "none of us in my line of work liked or embraced. I call us specialist wineries because we specialize in one or two or three things." Focus and specialization were signs that the industry was adapting to suit the tastes of a more well-traveled and sophisticated clientele.

Like the new California cuisine chefs, the new winemakers came from a variety of backgrounds, and many were self-taught. They often had more commitment than capital and worked hard to establish themselves. They wanted to expand the range of wines on the market, improve the quality, and showcase their *terroir*, but they also wanted their products to reflect their individuality. The nascent wineries and recently opened California cuisine restaurants were eager to reach out to one another and partner their passions. They teamed up to promote tourism and to raise the status of California products in the eyes of the world. They connected through winemaker dinners, the creation of proprietary house wines, and the establishment of three influential institutions: the American Institute of Wine and Food in Santa Barbara in 1985, the Culinary Institute of America campus in St. Helena in 1995, and Copia: The American Center for Wine, Food and the Arts in Napa in 2001. Together, the two industries reached out to engage the public through wine and food education and the creation of memorable dining experiences.

California Wines on the Menu

Forty years ago, California wines did not have the cachet of their imported competitors. Upscale California restaurants carried mainly European wines. French restaurants featured French wines; Italian restaurants had Italian wines. Beaulieu, Wente, Inglenook, and Louis Martini were among the few California wines to appear on restaurant lists in the 1970s. But by the late 1980s, restaurants that were complacent in the face of the revolution in California food and wine had become as obsolete as their wine lists.

When Joachim Splichal opened Patina in Hollywood in 1989, he mortgaged his house to buy a $70,000 cellar, which was filled with French wines, because he believed that people preferred them. After customers repeatedly requested California wines, he realized that he had to diversify to keep them happy. Today, 60 percent of the wines served at Patina and at Joachim's chain of Pinot restaurants come from California and the West Coast, including a healthy showing of local wines from Santa Barbara.

Bruce Neyers, a winemaker involved in production, sales, and marketing at Joseph Phelps Vineyards, was one of the first to succeed in convincing resistant French restaurants to buy California wines. He did so with the assistance of Colman Andrews, who had been the editor of *Coast* magazine in the mid-1970s and knew just about everyone in Los Angeles. In 1977, Colman gave Bruce a list of restaurants to approach with his roster of Phelps wines. The French restaurant guide Gault-Millau had recently published an issue on California wines, and Phelps had been recognized for its Gewürztraminer. "I think it got eighteen points out of twenty or something," said Bruce. "I took a couple of sample bottles of that with me to Los Angeles with a copy of the magazine and called on a

French restaurant Colman had suggested. I tasted the wine with the wine buyer, a Frenchman, who was absolutely prepared to close me out. He read the Gault-Millau review, tasted the wine, and bought it. It was the first California wine to go on that wine list. So that became my strategy for a while. Suddenly there was a restaurant breakthrough, and to my knowledge, that occurred first in Southern California."

Colman took Bruce to lunch at Ma Maison, where Bruce met Patrick Terrail and Wolfgang Puck. They did not drink any California wines, because there were none on the list. But when the head waiter, Bernard Erpicum, started holding wine dinners at Ma Maison in 1978, Phelps, again, was one of the first California wineries featured.

BRUCE NEYERS

Joseph Phelps Vineyards and Neyers Vineyards, St. Helena

Bruce Neyers worked at Joseph Phelps Vineyards for over twenty years, starting as Joseph Phelps's assistant in 1975 and working his way up to sales manager and then president and general manager. Today he is the national sales manager for Berkeley-based wine importer Kermit Lynch and runs his own winery, Neyers Vineyards.

Bruce recalled that when he and his wife, Barbara, moved to the Napa Valley in 1971, there were no more than fifteen wineries in the valley. He worked for two years at Mayacamas Vineyards, and then was invited to help with a harvest at Graf von Plettenberg in Germany. When he came back to California in 1975, he worked briefly in San Francisco for Connoisseur Wine Imports, a shop that specialized in European wines. Alice Waters used to come on Saturdays and pick out a couple cases of wine for her restaurant.

Barbara and Bruce started eating at Chez Panisse. "Dinner was around $4.50," said Bruce. "In March of 1975, just after I started at Phelps, I went to dinner one night at Chez Panisse with a group of friends. Alice joined us and mentioned that she was really distraught. She and Jerry Budrick [a business partner and waiter] had had this idea to create a Chez Panisse house wine. They had arranged to buy Zinfandel grapes from Frank Dal Porto in the Sierra foothills, and Mike and Arlene Bernstein at Mount Veeder Winery had agreed to make the wine for them. As it turned out, Mike had a bumper crop of his own, and there wasn't space anywhere, as it was a very small winery. So at the eleventh hour they had to bail out. Alice had already committed to the grapes, so she had to get them and do something with them. A day or two later I explained the situation to Joe Phelps, and he had the idea that we could be involved with this restaurant that seemed to be in the forefront. Joe was very prescient about things like that."

Alice came up to the winery with Jeremiah Tower. "Jeremiah was the negotiator. He was the hammer, and Alice had the concept." A deal was struck, and Jerry Budrick decided, after the grapes were delivered, that they should make not one wine but two, both Zinfandels. Alice thought Zinfandel was well adapted to the food at Chez Panisse, and these first two wines led to the idea of a Zinfandel festival, which started in 1979. "We brought a full barrel of nouveau Zinfandel to the upstairs area," said Bruce, "hooked up a nitrogen device, and served it." At the weeklong festival, the wine, made by Walter Schug at Phelps, sold for $5 a bottle. Tuesday night's menu, labeled "a celebration for Bruce Nyers" (spelled on the menu with only one e), featured marinated wild mushrooms, oysters cooked with muscadet and fennel butter, cassoulet, and salad or cheese, capped off by fruits and nuts.

"At that point Chez Panisse had stopped writing the menu in French, or it was in the days when it was French and English, but having a California wine featured as part of that transition. I think it was a big breakthrough and certainly did a lot to allow for the acceptance of California wines in other French-oriented venues."

Some people felt that Kermit Lynch, who supplied wines to Chez Panisse, pushed a "French agenda," but Bruce saw it differently. "I always looked at having French wines on the list as the proper thing. In thirty years I've heard maybe a couple of people ask, 'How does Alice justify buying local food but not buying local wine?' I say, 'Alice invented buying local wine.' I think that Chez Panisse was all about local wine and the French wines were just part of the theme of the restaurant. The whole time that that was happening, places like L'Ermitage or L'Orangerie in Los Angeles and La Bourgogne in San Francisco had an all-French wine list."

Bruce perceived a sea change in Southern California when Michael McCarty and Wolfgang Puck opened their restaurants. In the early 1980s, Bruce would visit Los Angeles once a month for a sales trip on behalf of Phelps and personally felt a shift in the environment and how he was treated. "I'd walk into restaurants prior to that time and they'd say, 'No thanks, we don't need any. No, we're not interested in tasting the wine.' In the 1980s, restaurants started to say, 'Sure, why don't you sit over there, and let's get some lunch for you. You got anything?' We'd be treated as minor celebrities just when LA was becoming one of the greatest restaurant cities on the planet. I think restaurants cultivated relationships with the wineries because they recognized that rather than buying wine from a middleman, they were now buying it from the person who had made it or overseen the production of it. That was a crucial breakthrough for us in the wine business."

When Wolfgang was preparing to open Spago, he developed the initial wine list himself. Bruce told the story of being in the middle of a tasting at Phelps when Evelyn Dice, who had been Joe's secretary and receptionist for thirty-five years, called down to the lab to tell Bruce he had a phone call. Joe, who had a rule that a tasting was never interrupted, said, "Tell him to call back," and she said, "It's Wolfgang Puck." Bruce took the call. "I talked to Wolfgang for twenty minutes or so, and the restaurant opened with seven or eight Phelps wines on the list."

Michael's was another valued account. "The first time I went to Michael's, I was astonished," said Bruce. "You eat outside in the middle of winter. Michael waited on every table—he had wonderful gifts as a restaurateur—and I love that restaurant to this day. I think it might, at some point, have been the best restaurant in California. By that time I had started Neyers winery in partnership with Joe, and the first check I ever received for a case of Neyers wine was from Michael's. Even though Alice was my first customer, Michael McCarty was my first cash receipt."

Contemplating the future, Bruce continued, "We are at a stage right now where our business is being forced to change. We're looking for new customers, new markets, new ways to sell our wines, new wines to make, and new ways to grow our grapes. We started farming organically in 1999, and we get probably as many inquiries about our farming practices as we do about our wine prices.

"We didn't have that much to do with the food and restaurant revolution that was sweeping California and subsequently the country, but we weren't bystanders either. We were involved with it, and that was always a source of great pride."

When Chez Panisse opened in 1971, it had only two California wines on the list—a Robert Mondavi Fumé Blanc and a Ridge Geyserville Zinfandel. Although the restaurant purchased French wines from Kermit Lynch to accompany its country French cooking, it also gradually came to support California wineries. The house red for many years was from Joseph Phelps, and the restaurant also bought wines from Joseph Swan, Mount Veeder, Navarro, and Green and Red.

Nouveau Zinfandel
Chez Panisse
the first week of December, 1979

1979 Zinfandel from the barrel: made for Chez Panisse by
Walter Schug at Joseph Phelps Vineyards from Napa Valley
grapes ⟡ $5.00 per bottle, a dollar twenty-five the glass

Tuesday $15.00

Beef marrow served with warm toasts
Fresh Dungeness crab sautéed with scallions
Poached chicken with bacon dumplings and wild mushrooms
Salad or cheese
Fruits and nuts

Wednesday $18.50

a Celebration for Bruce Nyers

Marinated wild mushrooms
Oysters cooked with Muscadet and fennel butter
Cassoulet
Salad or cheese
Fruits and nuts

Thursday $16.50

Charcoal-grilled leeks, mustard vinaigrette
Alpine cheese soufflé
Daube of lamb shanks marinated in Zinfandel and provençal herbs
Green salad or cheese
Fruit and nuts

Friday $18.50

Terrine of rabbit with hazelnuts and Chartreuse
Warm spinach salad with bacon and garlic
Filet of beef marinated to taste like venison
Cheese

Chez Panisse holds its first Zinfandel festival in 1979
with wine from Joseph Phelps.

As California chefs began cooking more innovative food, they began seeking more innovative wines, according to Josh Jensen. Restaurants serving California cuisine were enthusiastic about pairing their food with California wines, even if they also included European wines on their list. "There was a sense of local pride," said Josh. "Restaurant chefs and winemakers in California all thought they were the start of a new world."

Winemaker dinners were one way restaurants and wineries connected. The typical format was to invite a winemaker to present three to four offerings over the course of a dinner, and the menu was designed to complement the wine. The winemaker would be present during the dinner to talk about the wines as the diners sampled them. Square One, Stars, John Ash & Co., Fournou's Ovens, Zuni Café, Greens, Ma Maison, and Spago were among the early restaurants to team up with Paul Draper at Ridge, Dick Graff at Chalone, Josh Jensen at Calera, and Randall Grahm of Bonny Doon, as well as Joseph Phelps, Bob Long, Joseph Swan, Robert Pecota, Dan Duckhorn, and Robert Mondavi at their eponymous wineries.

Many of the young wineries in Northern California, however, were garnering reputations but not selling to restaurants. They made most of their sales via mailing lists, through select retail outlets, and by welcoming customers who would trek to the wineries and pick up the wine themselves. In the 1980s, restaurant wine representatives had started to come knocking, interested in tasting and buying California wines. In turn, wineries began to reach out to restaurants.

Until the early 1980s, the person in charge of buying wine at most high-end and mid-range restaurants was often a manager, head bartender, or waiter who was interested in wine. Other than in hotels and upscale French restaurants, few places had someone on staff who was solely dedicated to the wine list and who went out into the dining room and talked with guests. Phil Reich at Michael's, Fred Dame at the Sardine Factory in Monterey, and Evan Goldstein at Square One were the first sommeliers to work the floor in the new California restaurants. These early sommeliers helped establish the concept of the wine director and took charge of buying wines, writing the wine list, and educating and informing diners about wine. They often coordinated wine events with the chef. Most people who dine out regularly today have learned what a sommelier does, but at the time, people wondered, "Who is this guy bringing my wine? He's not my waiter. And why does he want to talk with me?"

EVAN GOLDSTEIN

Square One, San Francisco

My son, Evan Goldstein, created an innovative wine list for Square One at the precocious age of twenty-three. His efforts earned us the first James Beard wine list award in 1991, leading Square One to become one of the first wine destination restaurants in San Francisco. Wine producers, critics, and writers such as Robert Parker, Hugh Johnson, and Gerald Asher came to the Square One dining room.

Evan initially trained as a chef. He cooked in Paris at Le Saintongeais and the Hôtel Lancaster, in Napa with Masa Kobayashi at Auberge du Soleil, and in Berkeley at Chez Panisse Café. But when I decided to open Square One, he opted out of the kitchen and said he wanted to run the wine program. I knew he was passionate and knowledgeable about wine, but I hadn't recognized how gifted he was and what an extraordinary taste memory he had. (It couldn't have hurt that he'd been tasting wine since he was twelve.) At twenty-six, he became the youngest person at the time to pass the Master Sommelier exam.

In 1984, when Square One opened, most people were accustomed to paying $4 to $6 for a glass of wine, with a ceiling of $7 or $8. They were intrigued by California wines but were reluctant to spend a lot of money. Evan searched for superior wines that would allow the restaurant to make a reasonable profit while remaining affordable for diners.

Offering quality wines by the glass was revolutionary. Up until the 1980s, most restaurants bought the cheapest stuff to serve as their house wine by the glass. Square One offered tastes and half glasses, which were relatively new back then. "Our whopping eight choices were also considered radical," said Evan; most restaurants offered no more than four. (Today, new wine-dispensing machines enable diners to order a glass from between twenty and fifty different options.)

Evan endeavored to bring an expansive and unique point of view to Square One's wine list, to match that of the eclectic Mediterranean menu. If the restaurant was showcasing Italian or Portuguese regional food, he made an effort to provide wines from the corresponding areas, but he also championed California wines. "Wine lists throughout the country had been dominated primarily by French wine," said Evan, "but we did not cater to the holy trinity of Pouilly-Fuissé and estate-bottled Bordeaux and Vouvray or offer the basic Inglenook or Louis Martini. There was a growing movement toward smaller, vineyard-driven wineries, primarily in Napa but also in Sonoma and Amador counties. We supported the winemakers who were just starting to cut their teeth in California and took a chance on them before other people did."

Evan helped promote California wines by offering them as Square One's house wines. "Our first house wines were high-quality bulk wines from the D'Agostini Winery in Amador, and they were very good. They were bulk in the sense that they were larger production, but they were delicious for the money. But we realized quickly that diners aspired to something of higher quality and would pay for more. We created a Square One label, designed by Gerald Reis, and Josh Jensen [of Calera] bottled some of his Central Coast Chardonnay as Square One Chardonnay, and his La Cienega Zinfandel became our house red."

While some of the new wineries, like Joseph Phelps and Ridge, actively courted restaurants, other wineries had not yet recognized that restaurants were one of the best ways to put their wines in front of consumers. Evan called on established family-owned California wineries whose products had never been on restaurant wine lists, including Stony Hill, Spottswoode, and Rafanelli. He also targeted newer wineries, such as Long, Duckhorn, Sonoma-Cutrer, and Saintsbury. "Now they are veterans, but at the time they were emerging," he said.

In 1986, Evan started teaching wine and food pairing classes at the restaurant, which would produce dishes to harmonize with the theme. The evening might feature a survey of Chardonnays from around the United States or a deep dive into Chianti or a broad exploration of a single variety or country. Some guests chose to stay and eat at the restaurant afterward.

According to Evan, sommeliers have far more wines to pick from now than they did in the mid-1980s. "When Square One opened, the Argentinean and Chilean wine industries were in political disarray; Australia then meant Rosemount, Lindeman's, and a little bit of Penfolds; South African wine was illegal; New Zealand's first efforts flopped; Portuguese wine selections were limited; and most Italian wines were either Piedmontese or Tuscan. Today's sommelier has much more range available from overseas as well as domestically and can draw from up and down the entire Pacific Coast, from Baja to British Columbia."

In California alone, the number of available varieties has exploded. "You can get California-produced Arneis, Albariño, Vermentino, Nebbiolo—whatever you want. Nobody was doing those back then. Today California wine is ubiquitous and is as important on the East Coast as it is on the West Coast."

The wine-by-the-glass program was an effective way to introduce new varieties to the dining public. No longer were diners offered anonymous options: "We have three wines by the glass: a red, a white, and a rosé." Instead, the white wine was Chardonnay, the red wine was Cabernet, and the pink wine was white Zinfandel. Then, as people became comfortable with those varieties, the scope of selections expanded, and consumers' knowledge broadened further.

Food and Wine Education

As the wine and cooking cultures began to blossom in their separate spheres, people wanted to learn how to combine them. "We weren't a wine-drinking culture at this point," said food writer Janet Fletcher. "People asked, 'How do you use these wines? What goes with them? How do you serve wine with a meal?' It sounds primitive now, but a lot of people were at a loss."

Proximity was important for the initial drawing together of the wine and food communities. With the Napa Valley about an hour's drive from both San Francisco and the East Bay, many residents made regular excursions to wine country for day trips or weekends away. Former restaurateur Narsai David described his initiation to wine culture. "All through my college days, I would visit wineries, and that's how I learned. There were no classes in wine. I'd taste wine at different places, starting out at Louis Martini. Half bottles were common in those days, and I'd buy a half dozen. At dinner with a date, I would open two half bottles, and we'd compare them. It didn't take long for me to realize that Cabernet was my favorite. So then I started getting half bottles of Cabernet from different wineries, and we'd taste a Martini against a Beaulieu or an Inglenook, and that was the learning process."

Like Narsai David, Shirley Sarvis taught herself about wine. She arrived in the Bay Area in 1957 to work at *Sunset* as a home economist and food writer and soon developed an interest in how wine could complement food. She first visited Heitz, Stony Hill, Louis Martini, Beringer, Beaulieu, and Wente. "I would taste the wine and then say to the winemaker, 'Lovely Zinfandel, but what do I serve it with?'" In the early years, vintners concentrated on wine and not on what went with it. Receiving only rudimentary advice, such as that certain Rieslings might go well with corn, Shirley learned to rely on her palate. "I tasted in order to find out what would be right," she said.

In the early 1970s, Shirley joined the Berkeley Wine and Food Society, a group that had been established in 1965 as an affiliate of the London Wine and Food Society. She participated in the group's wine tastings but was perplexed that they didn't have events centered on food *and* wine. She nudged the members until they started hosting food and wine pairing dinners. "Some of the old ideas were useful in getting us started," she said. "Lamb with Bordeaux was fairly well understood by people who were paying attention, but there wasn't much guidance for California wine."

To fill this gap, Shirley started teaching classes in the late 1970s at the Wine and Cheese Center on Jackson Street in San Francisco. She laid out a selection of foods along with several wines for the attendees to sample, and they would then discuss what they liked best. One attendee, Bill Wilkinson, the general manager at the Stanford Court Hotel and later the owner of GreenLeaf Produce, offered Shirley a bigger and better venue for her classes, along with this counsel: "Shirley, you don't have to taste all the foods at once." She took this advice and collaborated with the Stanford Court chefs to design a seasonal menu to show off wines from France, Italy, and California. She offered a choice of several wines with several courses in a luncheon and let people decide which wines to drink with them. They could taste all of the wines with all of the foods—a new format at the time. "You might discover that you liked Cabernet with your fish," said Shirley. "We were not putting a first course with a white wine and then switching to the main course with a red wine; we were having maybe four or five reds, whites, and rosé wines with every course so that it was up to the person to find his or her own taste and not be dictated to by what was expected."

Shirley's food and wine pairing classes at the Stanford Court were the only ones open to the Bay Area dining public until 1986, when Evan Goldstein started teaching at Square One. "Today we take for granted the idea of doing tasting and education with food," said Evan, "but it was novel at the time."

Entrepreneurial winery owners eventually realized that promoting California cooking with their wine would attract more business. They discovered that on-site culinary programs were a means for getting their wines into both restaurants and homes. One of the splashiest wine country educational institutions was the Mondavi Great Chefs program.

In 1974, two enterprising caterers, Michael James and Billy Cross, rented a house in the Napa Valley and invited Simone Beck, coauthor with Julia Child of *Mastering the Art of French Cooking*, to teach a series of cooking classes. Spurred on by the success of these classes, they brought in French celebrity chefs Jean Troisgros, Roger Vergé, and Gaston Lenôtre. They named the program the Great

Chefs of France. It became a major event in the Napa Valley, and guests came from all over the world to attend. The wine flowed freely.

Michael and Billy were dedicated foodies but poor businessmen, and despite the program's success they ended up broke. In 1976, the estate where they held the classes was sold and they lost the lease. Margrit Biever, Mondavi Winery's director of public relations (and later Robert Mondavi's second wife), persuaded Robert to let Michael and Billy hold classes at the winery. This entailed building a large demonstration kitchen. It also took $120,000 to get the two of them out of debt and to move the school to the winery.

In 1980, Michael and Billy found themselves in a financial bind once more and asked Mondavi to buy them out. Axel Fabre and chefs Gary Jenanyan and Catherine Brandel were given responsibility for the program and continued to run it in the same grand style. From 1976 until the late 1980s, two- or three-star French chefs taught at Mondavi, including culinary rock stars Michel Guérard and Roger Vergé.

"It was an amazing time," said Margrit. "They would transform the vineyard room from one meal to the next, and it was always magic." The classes were not participatory because "the chefs felt that if somebody had to be taught how to chop an onion for twenty minutes, forget it. So they went straight to cooking. I did most of the translating and never learned so much about cooking as during those years." One major benefit to the winery was foreign exposure. "For us the symbiotic thing was that all these chefs, every one of them, took our wines to France and put them on their restaurant lists. We were the last item on the last page, but it was the beginning."

The superstar French chefs eventually priced themselves out of the market. The program, however, was such a hit that Mondavi continued it by adding American chefs and famous cookbook authors like Julia Child to the roster. They renamed it the Great Chefs. "We were very proud," Margrit said. "We had stars too." Many of the chefs were from California, including Jeremiah Tower, Wolfgang Puck, Judy Rodgers, and Bradley Ogden, and their food paired especially well with California wine.

Asked about the transition from the Great Chefs of France to the Great Chefs, Gary Jenanyan and volunteer *sous chef* Alan Tangren agreed that the food of the American cookbook authors and guest chefs didn't always have "that refinement or that little tiny edge of exquisiteness that the French chefs brought." Alan noted that in the United States, chefs could be anonymous one day and be in charge of a kitchen the next, whereas in France, chefs put in decades of training before they could advance. "There were people who came to the Great Chefs who might have had good palates and some good ideas, but they weren't great chefs. The most egregious was Martha Stewart. She walked into the kitchen and said, 'I don't cook, you know, so I brought my friend so and so. She's a good Connecticut housewife and knows how to cook, so she's going to make everything.' But she was a huge draw."

Michael Mondavi, son of Robert Mondavi, appreciated California's diversity of culinary viewpoints. "The way Julia Child commanded attention and taught and prepared the foods was totally different from Paul Bocuse or the others. California cuisine created the opportunity to see the great classic chefs and then someone like Julia and then other wonderful American chefs as well. When you go to France, the chefs are all classically trained the same; you go to different restaurants around America, and they're nine hundred ways different."

Other wineries followed suit and created their own programs. Phelps, Fetzer, Trefethen, and Cakebread were among those who built kitchens, hosted guest chefs, and offered cooking classes and special wine dinners on their premises. In the late 1960s, Joseph Phelps, then head of one of the largest construction companies in the country, landed a contract to build the Souverain winery (now Rutherford Hill). He fell in love with the Napa Valley and, in 1973, bought a six-hundred-acre ranch and began planting vineyards. By 1974, the first grapes had been crushed, the first Syrah had been harvested, and the first of his award-winning Phelps Insignia wines had been produced. In 1976, he added a kitchen for demonstration cooking classes and started to invite chefs to cook special dinners at the winery and create menus to go with Phelps wines.

Cooking classes also took place in a light-filled kitchen pavilion at Fetzer Valley Oaks Food and Wine Center in Mendocino County. What made these classes memorable was the organic garden, designed by Michael Maltus, that covered over five acres and contained more than a thousand varieties of vegetables, fruits, herbs, and edible flowers. Chef John Ash was the culinary director of an education program whose goal was to teach hotel and restaurant personnel about pairing food and wine. Started in 1983, this program came to a close when the Fetzer family sold the winery to Brown-Forman, a wine and spirits conglomerate, in 1992.

JOHN ASH

John Ash & Co., Santa Rosa

John Ash grew up on a cattle ranch with his grandparents in Colorado. "It sounds almost apocryphal, but my grandmother cooked on a wood stove. It was a bit like *Little House on the Prairie.* Everything was recycled. Because we were at about 8,000 feet, the growing season was very brief, so even as a little kid, my chores were to help my grandmother cook, to feed the hens, and, during the summer, to can, dry, and preserve like crazy, because that was what we survived on through the winter. It was magical, because my grandmother never used a recipe; it was just intuitive on her part."

John loved to cook but entered the food business in a circuitous way. He graduated from college with a degree in fine arts but at some point realized he wasn't going to make it as a painter. He worked in advertising in New York for a couple of years, and one of the agency's clients was Del Monte Foods. Del Monte lured him to San Francisco to create new products. "I learned about big food, how it gets produced and sold, which later gave me some insights into what's happening with the food systems in America today. I was there for five or six years developing new food products. My first great success was to put basil in the stewed tomatoes. That was the late 1960s, and it was a completely exotic herb to most of America. It took months of debate among management to get that leaf of basil into the can."

In 1970, John quit Del Monte and went to Europe. "I went to cooking schools, never with the intention of cooking professionally, but I thought it would be a way of grounding myself, and also getting involved in local culture, and of course a chance to eat. I went to school in London and Paris. I was lucky enough to hook on with a French family who had a little inn in the north of Burgundy where I was a *commis,* a slave in the kitchen, for about a year. At that time, French cooking was the very best of Western cooking."

In 1975, when John returned to the Bay Area, a winemaker friend took him to what was then considered the finest restaurant in Santa Rosa, the Topaz Room in Courthouse Square. "This was summertime, and the place was filled with lawyers in suits, all smoking. We had lunch, and they served canned vegetables on the plate. And it hit me—I could be a big fish in a small pond here. There were all these amazing producers, and no one was utilizing them." He thought Sonoma County's gentle climate and abundant produce might allow him to cook as he had in France.

He opened a restaurant, John Ash & Co., in Santa Rosa in late 1979. In those days, Sonoma had a bounty of farms and dairies and a burgeoning wine industry, but few restaurants were taking advantage of it. "I remember Laura Chenel with her first goat cheese. She walked in the back door and asked, 'Do you like goat cheese?' And I said, 'Yeah!' She said, 'Well, I've been showing this to people, and they think it's too funny tasting.' And my god, it was the most delicious stuff."

At John Ash & Co., John focused on wine as an integral part of the meal. "It was another flavor to be enjoyed with the other flavors on the plate," said John. "This is a part of California cuisine, this consciousness about the importance of food and wine coming together. We were really committed to wine and regularly did special tastings, dinners, and other educational events around wine." This may be why, many years ago, someone gave him the title "father of wine country cuisine."

John's namesake restaurant is still open, but he is not actively involved anymore except for special events. Through his restaurant he came to know the Fetzer family, who in 1990 offered him the opportunity to be the culinary director at the newly established Valley Oaks Food and Wine Center. John admired Jim Fetzer, who was the winery's president. "He was and still is a visionary. He made the commitment to do everything organically." One of the center's missions was to show people how to be good stewards of the land and to nurture farms that used organic methods. After the center closed, John traveled around the country to talk about organics and sustainability. He remembers that people would call what he was preaching "airy fairy." Now there is far greater receptivity for the idea of knowing where your food comes from and how it's produced and packaged. Today John teaches cooking at culinary schools all over the country and offers taste seminars at the CIA in St. Helena.

For Jack Cakebread, "it's always been wine *and* food." He and his wife, Dolores, opened their Napa Valley winery in 1973 and later offered cooking classes, many run by their in-house chef, Brian Streeter, who has been at Cakebread for over twenty years. In 1986, Cakebread held the first annual American Harvest Workshop, which celebrated its twenty-fifth anniversary in 2011. Five or six chefs would be invited to cook during several days of food and wine pairing. Jack tried to persuade the chefs to steer away from powerfully sweet and spicy components and concentrate on dishes that would complement the wine. His goal was "to make sure that they understand that you open a bottle of wine and taste it and then cook to it. You can't cook something and then try and go down and find a bottle of wine—it's a needle in a haystack. The chef can change the recipe a little, but the winemaker can't change the wine."

The Birth of Wine Country Cuisine

As more quality restaurants sprouted up in the Napa Valley, a distinctive wine country cuisine was born. Wine country cuisine recognizes the importance of cooking food with wine in mind, not as an afterthought. One of the first fine-dining destinations in the Napa Valley was the restaurant in the Domaine Chandon winery owned by the luxury wine company Moët and Chandon. It opened in 1977 with Udo Nechutnys serving up classic French and nouvelle cuisine. About $1.75 would buy a champagne tasting with hors d'oeuvres. In 1979, Phillipe Jeanty took over the kitchen and Udo left to open Miramonte in St. Helena.

Udo had trained in France and taught at the famed École Hôtelière Tsuji in Osaka, Japan. At Miramonte, he felt free to combine elements of East and West, balancing flavors, texture, and visual appeal. While he certainly would not call his cooking fusion, he did not hesitate to use some Japanese flavors and cooking techniques to execute his French food. He felt lucky to be in California, with its varied ethnic cuisines and ingredients, although initially he could not find what he wanted in wine country. "I had to go to San Francisco twice a week because nobody would deliver at that time. My wife drove the truck because I was so exhausted; I tried it twice by myself and almost drove off the bridge." Eventually he made connections with Lynn Brown and Peter Forni, who agreed to grow specialty items for him. He gathered herbs from the Trefethens at the Trefethen Family Vineyards and bought ducks from Mark Leinwand in Sonoma, mushrooms from Connie Green, and good California olive oil from a company operating in back of Tra Vigne. His network of nearby suppliers slowly expanded.

With the success of Miramonte and Sally Schmitt's French Laundry, fine dining made inroads in the Napa Valley. Rose et LeFavour opened in 1980, and Auberge du Soleil followed in 1981. But this was wine country, and some residents didn't want to have to dress up every time they went out for a good meal. With the opening in 1983 of Mustards Grill, where Cindy Pawlcyn headed up the kitchen, wine country cuisine became more casual.

Cindy is the doyenne of Napa Valley restaurateurs. She and Sally Schmitt were the first women chefs to run major restaurants in the valley. Respected and beloved by the wine and food community, Cindy has attracted local diners along with throngs of tourists to her popular restaurants—Mustards Grill, Cindy's Backstreet Kitchen (on the site of the former Miramonte), and, more recently, Cindy Pawlcyn's Wood Grill and Wine Bar.

CINDY PAWLCYN

Mustards Grill, Napa

Cooking and gardening were twin interests for Cindy Pawlcyn from an early age. In Minneapolis, where she grew up, Cindy hunted and fished with her father and learned to cook whatever she came back with. The family had a large garden, and fresh vegetables were always incorporated into the family meal. At thirteen Cindy began working part-time in a culinary school, creating the *mise en place* and providing assistance to visiting teachers, such as Julia Child, James Beard, and Jacques Pépin. While in high school, she also ran a small catering business and attended trade school at night to train as a chef.

To round out her professional education, Cindy earned a degree in hotel and restaurant management from the University of Wisconsin-Stout and then studied in Paris at the Cordon Bleu and La Varenne. When she returned to the United States, her first job was at the Pump Room in Chicago, where she met Bill Upson and Bill Higgins, with whom she would found the Real Restaurants Group.

In 1980, Cindy moved to California, and in 1981 she settled in the Napa Valley. She started off as opening chef at Meadowood Country Club and then became *sous chef* to Bruce LeFavour at Rose et LeFavour. In 1983, in partnership with Bill Higgins and Bill Upson, she had the opportunity to open her own place— Mustards Grill in Yountville, one of the first California restaurants to feature a wood-burning grill and wood-fired oven.

Rather than following the fine-dining model of her predecessors in the Napa Valley, Cindy opted for an easygoing atmosphere at Mustards. "I wanted a place where people working in the vineyards could come in to eat in their work clothes and boots and the servers could wear jeans."

Over the course of seventeen years, Cindy and her ambitious partners at Real Restaurants opened six very successful restaurants—Fog City Diner, Roti, and Bix in San Francisco, Rio Grill in Carmel, Buckeye Road House in Mill Valley, and Tra Vigne in St. Helena. Most of these establishments served a casual eclectic menu. At Tra Vigne, Michael Chiarello prepared a Cal-Italian menu, and Roti offered a few French classics along with the roasts and chickens cooking on the wood-fired rotisserie. The two Bills worked the business side—finding the sites, negotiating the leases, and supervising the buildouts—while Cindy created the menus and trained the kitchen staff. As they opened more restaurants, Cindy found herself constantly driving from venue to venue, introducing new dishes, training new cooks, and troubleshooting. It became exhausting. "I got tired of having to travel all the time. I was spread too thin." She opted out of the partnership in 2000, freeing herself to concentrate on her own Napa Valley restaurants, cultivate relationships with her purveyors, and develop her staff, many of whom have been with her for a long time.

Cindy and I bonded when we found out that each of us has a huge cookbook library and loves to research recipes. She is enamored of rustic foods from around the world. While most of her cooking has a strong California point of view, she offered a globally inspired menu from the beginning and is not afraid to put Mongolian lamb chops, smoked duck spring rolls, or duck burgers with shiitake mushroom ketchup on the same menu as barbecue back ribs with cole slaw, mussels and clams in andouille broth, and blueberry cornmeal upside-down cake.

A longtime advocate of local and sustainable foods, Cindy is a loyal supporter of Forni-Brown Gardens and Napa Valley Lamb, and she was one of the first to buy Laura Chenel's goat cheese. Long before farm-to-table cooking became trendy, Cindy was growing much of the produce for her three restaurants on an acre of land adjacent to Mustards. When she opened Cindy's Backstreet Kitchen, it didn't have room for a large garden, so she put in an acre and a half of fruits, vegetables, and herbs at her own home.

To help her staff understand the farm-to-table connection, she takes them out into the field. "I've introduced them to Mark Haberger, 'the tomato guy,' on Big Ranch Road. He's a classic farmer—tall, strong, doesn't say much. Just cuts his tomatoes in half and starts handing them out, warm from the sun. He has the best-tasting produce in the world. Part of the strength of the culinary movement in California is the partnership between the chef and the purveyors. We couldn't have done it without them, and vice versa."

Mustards's wine list, which draws heavily on local wines, is titled "Way Too Many Wines." In his introduction to Cindy's *Mustards Grill Napa Valley Cookbook*, Bruce Neyers wrote, "The first list included twenty wines, all local. . . . As the area's vintners grew increasingly comfortable with the place, it became a matter of great personal pride to have one's wines represented at Mustards. What better way to secure a spot on the wine list than to offer the restaurant something rare, something sure to impress a visitor. Soon the list was packed with scarce wines, many of them from older vintages long sold out. Without actually meaning to, Mustards had become a sort of a wine geek's paradise."

Domaine Chandon and Souverain were among the earliest wineries to open restaurants on their premises, and in 1981, *New York Times* LA bureau chief

Appetizers, Soups and Salads

Homemade Soup Daily..$2.00
Warm Goat Cheese with herb vinaigrette...................... 3.60
Smoked Trout, fresh horseradish cream and pickled onions... 4.75
Sliced garden Tomatoes and Red Onions with Basil........... 2.50
Chinese Chicken Salad...................................... 6.95
Mixed Greens with Oregon Blue Cheese, Gravenstein Apple
      slices and seasoned Walnuts.......................... 3.25

From the Wood Burning Oven

Half slab Barbequed Baby Back Ribs......................... 8.45
Smoked Herb Chicken.. 7.50
Fresh Sonoma Duck with Onion Jam, papaya, lime and mint....10.75
Smoked Pork Chop with Lemon Applesauce.................... 7.90

From the Mesquite Grill

Fresh Fish (see chalkboard)
Skewered Prawns, home smoked Bacon, smoked garlic sauce.... 9.95
Pounded Chicken breast, orange, chili, cilantro marinade... 7.80
Calf's Liver with home smoked Bacon, Onions and Avocado.... 7.95
Skirt Steak, marinated in soy and ginger.................. 6.90

Sandwiches

Hamburger or Cheeseburger.................................. 4.95
Slow smoked Roast Beef, fresh horseradish, mustard mayo.... 5.80
Grilled home smoked Ham and Jarlsburg cheese
      and tomato chutney................................... 5.50

Sides and Condiments

Onion Rings... 1.95
Grilled Eggplant and Onions with ginger butter............ 2.90
Robinson Bar Potatoes..................................... 2.25
Grilled Illini sweet Corn on the cob...................... 1.25
Roasted Garlic.. 1.00
Tomato Chutney.. .95
Onion Jam... .75

Desserts

Chocolate Pecan Cake...................................... 3.25
Ice Cream and/or Sherbet.................................. 2.95
Tapioca Pudding with bourbon cream........................ 1.95
Peaches and Cream... 2.75

Cindy Pawlcyn's 1983 menu from Mustards highlights the mesquite grill
and wood-burning oven.

Robert Lindsey singled them out as two of the best dining destinations in wine country. In 1986, Wente Vineyards in Livermore, one of the oldest wineries in California, opened the Restaurant at Wente Vineyards. Being in the wine business while California was awakening to its cuisine caused CEO and fourth-generation winemaker Carolyn Wente to reconsider how she obtained ingredients. "I tried to source as many things from our own estate as possible," she said. "I revitalized my grandfather's olive groves under the guidance of Darrell Corti to produce our own estate-certified organic extra virgin olive oil. I also started an organic herb and vegetable garden. In 1986, I started a dry-aged beef program and began to serve our own grass-fed estate-grown beef in the restaurant. This was ahead of its time, as no one really appreciated grass-fed back then; they wanted marbled, corn-fed beef. I was very influenced by what was going on in the California cuisine movement and put into practice many of the things I was seeing and being educated about. I believe the wine industry growth's along with the growth in California cuisine naturally helped each other."

Beringer Vineyards held wine and food pairing events at culinary institutions as an extension of their education and marketing program. They also invited chefs at the Culinary Institute of America, Johnson and Wales, and other schools to work at the winery for a period of time. After winery executive Tor Kenward hosted a book signing for Madeleine Kamman in the early 1980s, Madeleine asked if she could send a chef out from her school in Boston. Beringer said yes, and she sent Gary Danko. Up to that time, Beringer had had a revolving-chef program, but Gary was so outstanding that they hired him full-time in 1985. He became very active in promoting food and wine pairing. "When I moved to Beringer, I got the cover of *Wine Spectator* magazine," Gary recalled. "They were announcing 'wine country cuisine.' What was important historically is that this is the first time that chefs and winemakers actually were presented together." Wine country cuisine, and the partnership between California's cuisine and its wines, had been validated.

In 1987, I was among a dozen chefs invited by Tor to cook at an outdoor dinner at Beringer. The dinner capped off a series of cooking classes and events highlighting women chefs. The roster included Barbara Tropp of China Moon, Alice Waters and Lindsey Shere of Chez Panisse, Cindy Pawlcyn of Mustards, Annie Somerville of Greens, and Margaret Fox of Café Beaujolais. We were excited at the prospect of cooking at this showcase dinner because in those days chef-centered events were still a novelty. Tor revealed, "I was a little shy at first about asking all of you chefs until I found out that it was exciting for the chefs too. That was my selling point to management: by inviting chefs to cook, we're making the wines taste as good as they're ever going to taste. Pairing the wines with really good food can't be beat as far as putting wine in its best light.

"The landscape was far less crowded back in those days," he continued. "When we were doing those events in the 1980s, I don't think there were even one hundred wineries in Napa Valley. There weren't a lot of restaurants doing wine-maker dinners in the late 1970s and 1980s either. We were all working together, chefs and winemakers. It was a renaissance period for California wine. You had people experimenting, sharing, excited, so much stimuli in the air all around. It was the best of times for us.

"Beringer was truly supportive. We had major wine and food events for three or four years." Subsequent events continued on a smaller scale after Julia Child talked Tor into serving on the board of the American Institute of Wine and Food. The AIWF would become instrumental in further connecting the wine community with the food community.

The American Institute of Wine and Food

At a small dinner party in 1981, Julia Child was introduced to Robert Huttenback, the chancellor of UC Santa Barbara. During dinner she complained that there was no place where people who were serious about wine and food could pool their energies and resources. The chancellor thought it might be possible to establish a center for gastronomy on the campus, complete with a library. It happened that at the time a valuable library was for sale, comprising the collections of American cookbook expert Eleanor Lowenstein and French-born food and wine connoisseur André Simon. When combined, they created the largest and most important assembly of books in French, English, and American gastronomy from the sixteenth to the nineteenth century. The library was purchased by Lila Jaeger, co-owner of the Freemark Abbey and Rutherford Hill wineries, who said she would hold the collection in trust until the institute could raise enough money to buy it. In 1982 the nonprofit American Institute of Wine and Food was established at UC Santa Barbara. The AIWF's mission was to enhance quality of life through education about food and drink, with a major experiential component (conference attendees always ate and drank very well). The list of founders and board members was a who's who of food and wine personages, among them Julia Child, Michael McCarty, Jim Nassikas of the Stanford Court Hotel, brewer Fritz

Maytag of Anchor Brewing, food writer Alan Davidson, winery owners Robert Mondavi, Lila Jaeger, Joseph Phelps, Audrey and Barry Sterling, Richard and Thekla Sanford, and Sam Sebastiani, Beringer executive Tor Kenward, and actor and food enthusiast Danny Kaye. Richard Graff of Chalone Vineyards was elected president.

In 1983, the first major fund-raising dinner for the AIWF took place at the Stanford Court Hotel, hosted by owner Jim Nassikas. Top-flight chefs from all over the country participated, setting a precedent for future chef-centered events. The sold-out dinner generated a bonanza of media attention. Larry Forgione served a terrine of three smoked fish, Alice Waters prepared a garden lettuce salad, and Wolfgang Puck and Mark Peel baked Spago pizzas. Mark Miller grilled quail, and Michael McCarty and Jonathan Waxman offered red pepper pasta with scallops. Bradley Ogden and Jimmy Schmidt roasted lamb and made root vegetable gratins, Paul Prudhomme blackened redfish on the balcony so the smoke alarms would not go off in the kitchen, and Jeremiah Tower prepared dessert. To keep the momentum going, in 1984 Michael McCarty held a grand AIWF fundraiser dinner in Los Angeles that featured LA chefs and Hollywood celebrities.

Also in 1984, the AIWF began publishing the quarterly *Journal of Gastronomy*, which featured scholarly articles about wine and food by such writers as Wendell Berry, Ed Behr, Sidney Mintz, Burton Anderson, Gary Nabhan, Frances Moore Lappé, Leslie Land, Barbara Ensrud, and Anne Mendelson. The AIWF produced exceptional educational conferences as well. A tribute to James Beard and Danny Kaye was held in Santa Barbara in 1985, right after Beard passed away. A conference held in the Napa Valley in 1987 spotlighted local chefs and wineries. In 1988, a conference in New York featured speakers from the Mediterranean with an emphasis on Italy. In 1989, long before the words "sustainable" and "locavore" became catchphrases, the AIWF put on a superb conference titled "American Farm, American Food," which examined farmers, consumers, and the food distribution system. Another year, with support from the International Olive Oil Council, chefs from Spain, Turkey, Tunisia, and Morocco came to San Francisco and cooked for AIWF members and local guests at a series of well-attended food and wine dinners.

Greg Drescher, now executive director of strategic initiatives at the Culinary Institute of America, was the original programmer for these early conferences. "Beginning with our first AIWF National Conference on Gastronomy in January 1985, and especially in those first five years, our focus was to break new ground about how culinary professionals, the media, and our society at large thought about food. We were able to create a unique forum where chefs, growers, academics, food writers, health and environmental advocates, and food enthusiasts could build a national conversation about food and share their passions about transforming the role of food in America."

To stay afloat financially, the AIWF established chapters in multiple cities. The board and administration became so busy raising money and building the organization that they began to stray from their original objectives. To keep the local constituencies of each chapter engaged, the AIWF became more of a foodie organization, concentrating on wine and food dinners. This diluted the initial focus on education and gastronomy, and many of the organization's academic and professional members drifted away. "The AIWF never really fused into a coherent vision backed up by a business plan," explained Greg Drescher. "One of the main reasons I left was that the organization was going off in a direction that was pursuing the enthusiasts, but it never came together. A small organization needs to make choices—you can't do everything, and I think Julia's and Bob Mondavi's ambitions overwhelmed the ability of a small young organization to find its footing. There's a negative there, but the positive is that it's reflective of these outsize personalities that transformed American food and wine. In a way, the vision for that organization paralleled the visions of a lot of the people who were involved."

In 1993, Greg Drescher had left and the AIWF board hired Daphne Derven as director of education. The group was trying to transition away from the image of being a fine-dining club, broaden its educational reach, and play a national role in discussions of food policy. It worked with officials at the U.S. Department of Agriculture to ensure that that agency's food pyramid and guidelines were in line with nutritional recommendations. The AIWF also held a series of conferences looking at cultural views of food, wine, and music. It published two volumes titled *Wine, Food and the Arts,* edited by Betty Fussell, which combined essays, photographs, and paintings. The cover of one volume showed Robert Mondavi's hands holding a bunch of grapes; the other displayed Julia Child's hands cracking an egg. Daphne said, "The idea was to get people to look at food as more than ingredients or a meal, to look at it as culturally relevant, as the font of creativity, and not just in the kitchen or on the plate, but in writing, art, drawing, poetry."

Robert Mondavi and Julia Child eventually became frustrated with what they saw as a loss of focus. They felt that the AIWF was all over the place. "The opening of all these different chapters changed the mission," said Daphne, "because you lost control. As soon as it became everybody's party, it changed." Robert and Julia began to discuss how they could create a new organization rooted in

California, which is how Copia: The American Center for Wine, Food and the Arts came into being.

Copia

Robert Mondavi's dream was to establish a center for wine and food in the city of Napa, at the gateway to the valley. In the mid-1990s, he purchased a site near the Napa River and began work to establish a nonprofit organization that eventually articulated its mission as being to "explore, educate and celebrate the pleasures of wine, food and culture." Among its many roles, it was intended to become the headquarters for the AIWF, as well as a venue for exhibits and events revolving around gastronomy, wine, and the arts—part museum and part conference center.

Robert wanted the center to have gravitas. He and the board hoped to partner with UC Davis and the Culinary Institute of America, but when the CIA dropped out, the Cornell School of Hotel Administration was invited to join with them instead. The schools would provide academic relevance, technical advice, programming, and interns.

In the planning stages, the organization was called the Center for Wine and Food and then the American Center for Wine and Food. Because Robert Mondavi's second wife, Margrit Biever Mondavi, was involved in the arts, an arts component was added, and the organization morphed into the Center for Wine, Food and the Arts. Roberta Klugman, a former executive director of AIWF who was on the center's board of directors, said, "I think that became a dividing point. The board lost sight of the idea of American wine and food, period. Then they hired Peggy Loar, who came from an arts background, not a food background."

When Peggy, an experienced museum director, was hired to head the center in 1997, the AIWF started to pull back, worried that they would get lost in the shuffle. Then Daphne Derven, who had a background as an archaeologist and a museum professional, left the AIWF and became the center's director of programs and exhibitions. From 1997 through the opening in 2001, Peggy, Daphne, and the board of directors worked on creating the concept, the architecture, the programmatic focus, and the art content, as well as raising money. They hired architect James Polshek and landscape architect Peter Walker. Then began the negotiations between the board of directors and growing staff to clarify the mission. "We were doing enormous amounts of research," said Daphne, "and having daily discussions. The balance between food, wine, and art would affect how the building was configured. Finally we decided that the food element and the wine element were in conjunction with the arts and were all sort of equal."

In keeping with the museum concept, the title "curator" was given to the various directors of the programs. Daphne Derven was curator of food. Peter Marks was curator of wine. Some of the planners wanted the wine program to be oriented toward the general visitor to the valley—somebody who wanted to have a good time, taste some wine, and learn a little bit about it. But Daphne petitioned the Wine and Spirit Education Trust in England to let the institute offer the programs leading to a Master of Wine certification, and these became among the most successful offerings. "Because what people were really looking to us for was the ability to become more professional, more highly educated, not so much to have fun."

Robert, Julia, and the board thought that the center should have a fine-dining destination, so Julia's Kitchen, as it was named, was configured as a white-tablecloth restaurant. Next to it was a modest café that served coffee and pastries. When the complex opened, it became evident that what museumgoers really wanted was the café. So, while Julia's Kitchen was very good, it struggled to find patrons. It didn't help that initially, in order to eat in the restaurant, you had to pay an admission fee to the museum, a marketing blunder.

The arts components included an outdoor concert space, an indoor theater, and several galleries. There were three classrooms, one with a demonstration kitchen, plus a spectacular organic garden managed by Jeff Dawson.

JEFF DAWSON

Fetzer Vineyards, Hopland; Copia, Napa

Jeff Dawson is a master gardener and farmer who has created custom gardens for wineries including Fetzer, Kendall-Jackson, Staglin, Quintessa, and Round Pond Estate, as well as for the educational institutions Copia and the Culinary Institute of America at Greystone. A fanatic seed saver who is fascinated by new and heirloom vegetables, he has introduced many new produce selections to the marketplace.

When he was in high school, Jeff started a vegetable garden. While attending Santa Rosa Junior College, he began to develop a more serious interest in farming and took horticulture classes from Bob Cannard Sr. (whose son, Bob Cannard Jr., is the principal grower for Chez Panisse). "In 1978, I was at John Balletto's ranch in Santa Rosa, standing in a lettuce field and looking at a beautiful head of butter lettuce. It was a perfect mandala. I had this epiphany that I needed to be growing food. I needed to get my hands dirty, as an occupation."

That year Jeff went to Hawaii to study at the National Tropical Botanical Garden. When he came back to California, he worked in nurseries for a few years before eventually opening one of his own. His transition to farming began in 1986, when he attended the Tasting of Summer Produce at the Oakland Museum and was dazzled by the display of Green Zebra tomatoes grown by Stuart Dickson of Stone Free Farm. Jeff became a member of the Seed Savers Exchange and started a one-acre organic farm. When it did well, Jeff slowly expanded, adding an acre or two each year until he had about twelve acres. Along with many kinds of tomatoes, he grew lettuces, eggplant, peppers, and potatoes. Starting in 1988, he began to deliver produce to San Francisco restaurants such as Stars, Aqua, Postrio, Masa's, Kuleto's, Bix, and Lark Creek Inn.

His paste tomatoes were especially popular. "Postrio did a tomato *concasse,* so they took case after case. Il Fornaio did the same thing for their pasta sauce. There were bread-and-butter items that were simple and easy to grow, and on top of that we did specialty vegetables and varieties." Jeff tried to interest chefs in new specialty produce, although he wouldn't get much response if he only brought in a tomato or two. "If chefs had a whole case of a product, they could do something with it, and they would respond with a high level of excitement."

"A small farm is a treadmill," said Jeff. "You've got to have something in the ground 365 days a year. It's not like you can grow enough things during the summer so that you can take the winter off. It's nonstop." By 1993, after five exhausting years, he was ready for a change. He thought about shutting down the farm, but when his chef clients protested, he downsized from twelve to three acres and took a second job overseeing the five-acre organic fruit and vegetable garden at Fetzer Vineyards, where John Ash was the culinary director. To manage his two commitments, Jeff would get up in the morning and drive over sixty miles from Sebastopol to Fetzer Vineyards in Hopland, put in eight hours of work, and return home, where his crew had picked a truckload of produce. Twice a week he'd jump in the truck after work, drive down to San Francisco, deliver the produce, and come back. "I was still young and ambitious, so I was able to do it. I continued to do that through the time that I was at Fetzer."

Fetzer was an exciting period for Jeff. "There was a beautiful garden and a great culinary program. John Ash was passionate about food and about using fresh products. I was able to do an extensive seed-saving program, and we did seed packets as a marketing conjunction with the wine."

Because Jeff was growing up to 250 varieties a season between his farm and Fetzer, natural hybrids would occur. "In a hundred-foot row of Green Zebra tomatoes, one plant might have a Green Zebra that was kind of orange and yellow. We'd save that seed and grow it out. That seed, the next year, would produce all the potential genetic combinations. In some cases I ended up with eight distinctly different tomatoes. From 1993 to 1996, I ended up producing probably nine tomatoes that we were able to stabilize and get into the marketplace.

"Our farm also ended up introducing heirloom varieties such as the Black Krim, Great White, and Evergreen tomatoes. We would get the seed, grow it out, and after a second year we'd get enough production to begin taking caseloads down to San Francisco. Within a year or two, we'd find pallets of those varieties from other growers in the produce market. It became this game of staying one step ahead."

Fetzer shut down its culinary program in 1995, just as the Culinary Institute of America was opening its Greystone campus in St. Helena. Jeff was asked to design the herb and vegetable garden there. In 1996, Jess Jackson, founder of the Kendall-Jackson winery, hired him to develop a farm at the family ranch in Alexander Valley and then to create a culinary demonstration garden at the Kendall-Jackson Food and Wine Center in Santa Rosa.

The job at the Kendall-Jackson ranch intensified Jeff's interest in biodynamic agriculture. "As a farmer and a gardener, biodynamics was my passion, my life work, and the spiritual connection in nature, so it fed my soul on many levels. Kendall-Jackson was an extension of my work at Fetzer: bringing food and wine together, creating an experience for the visitor, educating. I did cooking demonstrations too, which was really fun because you can't be a farmer and not love to cook."

While creating a biodynamic garden for Apple CEO Steve Jobs, Jeff met Peter Walker, the landscape architect for Copia. When invited to give input on the Copia garden plan, Jeff told them, "When you are ready to do this garden, you're going to need somebody to run it for you. At that point, give me a call." When the center opened, Jeff went to work there as the garden curator. Although Copia closed, the biodynamic demonstration garden was a success, and Napa chefs, including Ken Frank of La Toque, have continued to maintain it.

In 2006, Jeff became curator of the gardens at the Round Pond Estate in Rutherford, where he has developed a new tomato variety, the Round Pond Red. He continues to experiment.

By the time Copia greeted its first visitors in 2001, the budget for the building, originally $12 million, had ballooned to nearly $80 million. Attendance never met expectations. Entry fees were high, at $12, and the center's location, more than a mile off Route 29, meant that tourists just zoomed right by. Finally, the vision for the center confused people. Was it a museum or a culinary center? Many people visited and still didn't quite get it.

The timing was also unfortunate. The center opened one month after September 11, 2001. Silicon Valley had collapsed and the California economy was tanking. "It was very hard to make adjustments," said Daphne. "And one of the adjustments was going to the name Copia [from the Roman goddess of plenty]. The thinking was that it took too long to say 'American Center for Wine, Food and the Arts.' The truth is at least it said what we were. Nobody knew what Copia meant or [who] Copia was." They kept looking for the right focus, constantly trying out different ideas, but the center closed in 2008.

"Copia never happened the way Robert Mondavi had wanted it to happen," said Daphne. "There was an enormous thirst for knowledge about food and wine. It wasn't that people weren't interested; it was that we weren't giving the information to them in the form in which they could take it. They had the best of intentions but they attempted to be too many things." People came to Napa to learn about food and wine, but Copia never engaged them. The CIA did.

The Culinary Institute of America at Greystone

Where Copia failed due to lofty but opaque goals, the Culinary Institute of America, opened in St. Helena in 1995, succeeded because it had a relatively modest initial vision, which it then fulfilled, expanded, fulfilled, and expanded again.

Observing the advance of the California food and wine movements, the CIA's administration and trustees in Hyde Park, New York, decided to open a campus in California. The CIA search team had learned that the Christian Brothers' Greystone property, owned by Heublein Spirits, was on the market for $14 million. This was out of reach for the CIA, because they knew that they'd have to spend a great deal of money to turn it into a culinary school, not to mention to bring it up to seismic code. Greg Drescher, who had left the AIWF and joined the CIA in 1995 as director of education programs, related the story of the acquisition of the Napa Valley property. "Heublein had purchased Christian Brothers mainly to pick up the Burgundy label and a lot of prime Napa Valley vineyard land. They wanted the land and the labels but were less interested in Greystone. It turned out that they wanted to unload the building because it was something of a white elephant." When Heublein heard that the CIA was interested in the building, they negotiated a sale. The final purchase price to the college for the building and thirty acres of Napa Valley land, including fifteen prime vineyard acres next to Markham Vineyards, was $1.7 million. The retrofitting and creation of the culinary school cost well over $14 million. In addition, the town of St. Helena requested numerous accommodations, including low-flow toilets to conserve water.

Meetings with the CIA board and Ferdinand Metz, a former CIA president, assured Greg that the CIA was not intent on creating another campus with a culinary emphasis on Europe and that they would be receptive to a broader teaching perspective. This aligned with his ambition to produce a varied culinary curriculum in keeping with the cultural diversity in California and the expanding American palate. "We developed a curriculum, hired faculty, and worked with adjunct faculty to make it a global focus," said Greg. "And fifteen years later, it turns out that was a good call, because that's how people want to eat today."

The CIA's Greystone campus opened in 1995 with well-defined goals, in part due to restrictions imposed by the city. The school could provide only continuing education, not a degree program. Students would sign up for a class, come in for a few days, and leave. The school wasn't permitted to offer classes or demos for tourists, either. When the town of St. Helena was convinced that the CIA was good business, the parameters were loosened. The school was allowed to offer tours of the teaching kitchen. The gift store—which sold food, cookbooks, and cooking equipment—became a commercial success. The Wine Spectator Restaurant on the building's second floor brought in visitors to the valley. Later the school added a small auditorium for public demos, opened the Rudd Center for Professional Wine Studies to provide an extensive wine immersion program, and created the Williams Center for Flavor Discovery, which offered comparative tasting of ingredients.

In 1997 Greg and the CIA faculty held their first annual Worlds of Flavor conference, which is held each November to this day. Over the years, themes have encompassed the cuisines of the Mediterranean, Asia, and Mexico, and conference titles have ranged from "Global Grilling and Live Fire" to "Global Street Food" and "World Casual." Chefs and food and wine personages from around the world are flown in to teach and cook. These sold-out conferences are influential for chefs and the media as they highlight current or upcoming trends in cuisine and wine. Starting in 2004, the CIA has also teamed with the Harvard School of Public Health to sponsor Worlds of Healthy Flavors, a conference series that brings together leaders in schools, university food service, casual restaurants, and the medical profession to encourage healthy cooking. Recently the CIA added an additional teaching kitchen and a small bakery-café and enlarged its gift store, which now includes an olive oil and chocolate tasting bar. Given the success of these programs, and the continued support from the CIA in Hyde Park, we have not seen the end of this expansion in culinary education.

The Winemaker's Palate

Over time, California cuisine started to affect the state's wine-making style. Winemakers no longer had to match their wines to the old familiar cream- and brown-sauced Continental dishes. Restaurants now featured bigger and more diversified flavors and ingredients. As the accent shifted toward fresh vegetables, salsas, and vinaigrettes and cooking techniques such as grilling and roasting in wood ovens, consumers began to request bolder, more fruit-forward wines to go with the stronger flavors and the char of the grill. According to Evan Goldstein, forward-thinking wineries that were sensitive to wine's place in dining in the 1970s and early 1980s included Acacia, Byron, Duckhorn, Chalone, Fetzer, Iron Horse, Joseph Phelps, Navarro, Sanford, and Spottswoode.

But in an attempt to emulate Europe and make wines that they thought would age well, many winemakers began to make them with overly hard tannins, too much oak, and in time, higher alcohol levels. According to industry magazine *Wine Business Monthly,* the average alcohol level of California wine rose from 12.5 percent in 1971 to 14.8 percent in 2001—and 2002, 2003, and 2004 vintages were hotter still. These wines fought with food.

Paul Draper of Ridge cited 1997 as a tipping point. "The best Cabernets in Napa in the 1990s—1996 would be a beautiful example—can be put up against a fine vintage of Bordeaux in style and quality any day. They're incredible wines. Then, in 1997, the grapes got overripe. The two most important critics validated them, as did the most vocal customers, and newer customers who didn't have a broad base in the world of wine jumped on the bandwagon. Now I would say that well over 90 percent of the Cabernets, not just in Napa but in Sonoma and Paso Robles, are over 15 percent alcohol. They may say 14.9 percent, but they are over 15 percent." The high alcohol "bullies" the food. "What worries me is that those wines don't complement food as well," said Paul. "It's such a dominant beverage at 15 percent that the food becomes secondary." Paul consistently keeps the alcohol levels in his Monte Bello Cabernet between 12.9 and 13.4 percent—an unwavering approach that he has maintained for over forty years of wine making.

PAUL DRAPER

Ridge Vineyards, Santa Cruz Mountains and Sonoma Dry Creek

Paul Draper joined Ridge Vineyards in 1969 after tasting the 1962 and 1964 Cabernets made by Dave Bennion. Dave and three partners had founded Ridge in the early 1960s and were making wines using the simplest approach: natural yeast, and no filtration or fining. "I'd tasted the Inglenooks and the BVs [Beaulieu] from the 1940s and 1950s," said Paul, "and this was deeper, more complex, more interesting. They reminded me of a great year in Bordeaux, and that was the reason I joined. We proceeded to make wines that represented the place, allowing the site to give us the distinctive characteristics."

Paul was another of California cuisine's many autodidacts. Raised on a farm in Illinois, Paul went to the Choate School in Connecticut. During school vacations, when there wasn't time to go home, he stayed in New York with a roommate whose family was Swiss. There he got turned on to wine. At home, Paul's family drank wine only on special occasions, but in his friend's apartment on the Upper East Side, "wine was a part of everyday living. Having grown up on a farm, I fell in love with the idea that something from the earth could transform itself into something so magical, stimulating, mind altering, and delicious as a good glass of wine."

Paul came out west to attend Stanford. "One reason I was happy to come to Stanford was that they grew grapes in California. I started going out once a week to a French restaurant, L'Omelette, the finest restaurant in this part of the Bay Area many years ago. I went through the wine list, buying what I could afford. The finest wines I tasted had been made traditionally, not in the modern Davis style of selected yeast and processes and filtrations and added chemicals. It had been made in a straightforward fashion from very good sites, very good places, and very effectively."

His first experiments in wine making took place in Chile, where he went as a Peace Corps volunteer with his friend Fritz Maytag, who would later found the Anchor Brewing Company. Paul and Fritz planted soybeans in Chile and then tried to figure out how to stay and make money. They realized that Chile had some very good wines but was exporting only 2 percent of its production. "So first we said, 'Let's get the Chileans to export. There are a few things that need to be straightened out—we'll tell them what they have to do to get rid of this taste of raw chili and wood.' The Chileans were very polite, listened to us, and didn't do a thing. We said, 'All right, we'll do it ourselves,' and leased an old bodega. I realized that I had a chance to do what I had always wanted to do but didn't know how to do it."

Paul got his hands on some old books about wine making in the 1800s. "I started making that wine in Chile by nineteenth-century techniques. And when I came to Ridge, though we have stainless-steel tanks and an incredible lab, we make the wine as they made it in the nineteenth century, but with better equipment and better analysis and research on what is happening with the tannins."

When people who want to get into the wine business ask Paul if they should go to school, he tells them to try hands-on work at a winery first, to see if they like it. "At Ridge, when we hire someone, we look for passion. John Olney, who is Richard Olney's nephew, has never been to school. He's worked for Aubert de Villaine at Romanée-Conti, he's worked with Jean-Louis Chave, he sold wine for Kermit Lynch for six years and selected wine in France for Kermit for six years. And what does he have? Passion. If you give me someone who's passionate about fine wine, they don't need a Davis degree. As a matter of fact, I'd prefer they not have it. We will train them, and if they're passionate, they will learn. Nobody in wine making at Ridge has a degree from Fresno or Davis.

"Our head vineyard manager, David Gates, who has been with me for twenty-three years, did get his degree in viniculture from Davis. His assistant, from Cal Poly, is an incredible guy whose father took care of grapes but had no degree. So viniculture is a little different from wine making, but still what is important is that passion."

Paul advocates collaboration. "You're going to do so much better and they're going to be more fulfilled in their jobs if they're able to bring what they have to offer instead of just one person saying, 'This is the way it is.' John Olney at Wilton Springs and Eric Baugher at our Monte Bello Winery have both been with me now between fifteen and sixteen years. I have them sign the labels now. I may make the decisions on the wine with them, but they're the ones who are really doing the work. Everybody has a voice—the vineyard team, as well as everyone in production.

"The greatest compliments are when people say how much the wine has meant to them in their lives, how much pleasure it has given them," said Paul.

A Dinner For

Ridge Winery

———— ৪ ————

Tarte à l'oignon
Onion tart with a puff pastry crust

Homard en choux
Maine lobster steamed in cabbage leaves,
served with black caviar and red peppers in
a butter sauce

Poulet aux truffes
Chicken baked in a sealed crock, with black
truffles under the skin, served with
a leek confit

Fromages suisses
An assortment of Swiss cheeses

Gratin d'orange
Orange gratin à la carte

———— ৪ ————

*Menu inspired by a recent meal at the
Girardet restaurant in Switzerland*

Chez Panisse : Berkeley

13 January 1979

French and English still appeared side by side on the menu
at Chez Panisse's Ridge Winery dinner, January 13, 1979.

"That keeps you going. Satisfaction is doing something that is nurturing. It's giving people something of quality that they recognize and enjoy and gives them a better life." What more could one want as a winemaker or chef than to hear from customers that your wine or food has enriched their entire experience?

Paul's philosophy of wine making—which embraces originality, a willingness to diverge from orthodoxy, and a focus on local character and ingredients—mirrors California cuisine's philosophy of cooking. Northern California wineries and restaurants both took the best local products and, rather than manipulating them, let their quality speak. "I think that California has led the way," said Paul. "We have a climate that provides us with a variety and length of season that is difficult to find in other parts of the country. That has pushed California to the fore. We had the attitude, the creativity, and no stultifying formal structure to overcome."

In wine making, as in cooking, there was a schism between training and instinct. Many of the first wave of winemakers in the late 1970s—a veritable honor role of vintners—came out of the Viticulture and Enology Department at UC Davis. This research and education program was founded in 1880 and became established on the Davis campus in 1935. Following the repeal of Prohibition in 1933, the program concentrated on ways to increase yields, improve quality, and determine the varieties and clones that would do best in the different regions of California; it later moved into wine analysis and methods of crafting fine wines. Fresno State has taught the practical aspects of wine making and grape growing since the 1950s, though it only established its Department of Viticulture and Enology in 2000. It is an important resource for winemakers based in the Central Valley and Southern California. In 2004, Cal Poly San Luis Obispo launched a major in wine and viticulture.

Randall Grahm of Bonny Doon, a graduate of the UC Davis enology program, downplays his own scientific background. "I don't know if winemakers need university training, but I think they do need mentorship. There are some winemakers, amazingly, who just take to it and through travel and observation are natural, intuitive winemakers. I did go to school, but my real training came from traveling in Europe and tasting. California cuisine has come to mean something like extreme dedication to ingredients, to freshness, to lack of artifice, simplicity in preparation—honesty, if you will. Most of our wines are biodynamic, so we work with many restaurants who appreciate natural wines. And with restaurants that serve natural wines, I think their food tends to be less baroque, less ornate, and obviously more natural, working with better ingredients. I'm trying to move from artifice to transparency, and I think that is paralleled in the evolution of California cuisine."

When Doug Fletcher, vice president of wine making for the Terlato Wine Group, entered the wine business, many of the wine makers coming out of Davis were approaching wine from a scientific perspective. "They looked at technique as opposed to what they wanted the wine to taste like." Doug recounted a story describing the learning curve of John Kongsgaard, now the Napa Valley maker of a sought-after Chardonnay. When John graduated from Davis, he had the idea that the grapes had to be 23.5 Brix (percentage of sugar) at harvest. He had picked some that had higher sugar and some that had lower sugar, and before picking the last batch, he calculated the stoichiometric balance between the two and tried to pick the additional number of tons he needed to make the entire lot measure 23.5 Brix. "He now looks back at it and laughs," said Doug, "but I think that was the norm at the time. People would go out and analyze, they would pick the sample and run the Brix on it, and do the titratable acidity and all these things, and I don't think it occurred to them to taste it."

Doug said that successful wine making requires both a scientific background and an excellent palate. "Josh Jensen, Dick Graff of Chalone Vineyards, and the Cakebreads are good examples of winemakers who had tasted a lot of Burgundies and knew what they wanted their wine to taste like, but they had no clue how to get there. Without training in science and viticulture, they arrived by dint of hard work and constant trial and error. The people who have achieved success more often than not understand the science and how they got what they got the last time and how they might try this other thing that might make it more like they want it to taste. That requires a lot of adhering to the scientific method. Winemakers have to be very conservative. How many meals do you make a night in a restaurant? Two hundred? Three hundred? Most winemakers have the chance to cook a meal forty times in their lifetime. If you burn a sauce you can throw it out, but you can't throw out a Cabernet."

Doug is an accomplished cook and bread baker whose wine making has been influenced by the California cuisine movement. "It started with my first tomato-tasting experience, at the Tasting of Summer Produce. The tomatoes were mind expanding. I saw dry-farmed and hydroponically farmed tomatoes, ones from Richmond and ones from Hollister—this incredible diversity of tomatoes." Doug came to the realization that he was making a product out of one ingredient— grapes—and if that ingredient didn't taste good, he couldn't make it into a decent bottle of wine. "I started paying more attention to what we were doing in the vineyard. You can change the character of wine by how you grow the grapes. The ingredients are the most important part."

The California cuisine movement convinced Doug that "wine is not a cocktail. It's something to drink with food." He's tried to instill that sensibility in the public and his fellow winemakers. "It's become a preoccupation of Americans to want to know what the best is. I've tried to get people away from that. With winemakers, it's really difficult. When I get together to do tastings with them, I'll often say, 'Let's not play that game. Let's taste all of these wines and then decide what they would go with."

Winemaker Bob Long of Long Vineyards summed up the ethos and potential of the times. "California cuisine was a gigantic party that blossomed and everyone said, 'Look at all the things we can do.' The positive energy that resulted from partnership created an enormous push to improve the quality of wines and food.

"Very early on, we felt that we needed to go to Europe to find out what we should be doing. We saw the fussiness of the French—'It's got to be exactly this way'—and the exuberance of the Italians—'We can do this *and* that'—and we incorporated it. Then we invited the Europeans over and they were flabbergasted. They could not believe that in a few short years we could create this vibrant food and wine industry.

"Today, Europeans send their kids to California to learn about wine and food. Millions of Americans come as well, because restaurateurs, chefs, and wine people in California awakened a genuine, basic, visceral, cultural need in Americans, introducing a whole generation of Americans to the joys of wine and food."

Afterword

The Continuing Evolution of California Cuisine

Primo restaurant sits on Penobscot Bay in Rockland, Maine. Three thousand miles from the Pacific Coast, the restaurant links East and West by way of California cuisine. Primo serves spring lettuces and herbs grown in its own gardens, dressings made from red wine vinegar that is barrel aged in-house, and pizzas baked in a wood-fired oven topped with grappa-fig sausage made from pigs raised on the restaurant premises. On occasion, the restaurant hosts a whole-hog dinner, which might open with crispy pig tails and finish with bacon-apple quinoa cake. Chef and co-owner Melissa Kelly attended the Culinary Institute of America in Hyde Park and then moved west to work with Reed Hearon of LuLu and Alice Waters of Chez Panisse. "I didn't have a style when I got there," reported Melissa in a CIA alumni profile. "By the time I left, I did: simplicity, seasonality, freshness."

Primo was selected by *Bon Appétit*'s Andrew Knowlton for the magazine's March 2013 roundup of the "20 Most Important Restaurants in America." Like Primo, many of the restaurants on this list could trace their lineage, in one way or another, to the California food revolution. Design trends inaugurated in California have made their way to restaurants nationwide. In the industrial and newly hip Bushwick neighborhood of Brooklyn, Roberta's features a wood-fired oven for pizzas made with vegetables grown on-site, in greenhouses built atop repurposed shipping containers. Chicago's Avec incorporates an open kitchen, which, according to Knowlton, "makes the bustle of the room . . . an integral part of the experience." After working in San Francisco at Campton Place, Daniel Humm at Eleven Madison Park was inspired to forge relationships with local farmers in New York. Sean Brock in Charleston is reviving the cultivation of local southern products such as red corn and golden rice to serve at Husk and McCrady's. Three of the other restaurants in the *Bon Appétit* list—Mission Chinese, Pok Pok, and

Uchiko—offer their chefs' personal interpretations of food from countries whose cuisines they have adopted and adapted.

Five of the twenty restaurants on the list—Swan Oyster Depot, Mission Chinese, Animal, and the Michelin-rated Restaurant at Meadowood and Manresa—are in California. Animal on Fairfax Avenue in Los Angeles's old Jewish neighborhood offers an over-the-top meat-centric menu. Meadowood takes an artful, modern approach to hyperlocal ingredients drawn from its extensive garden, and Manresa partners with Love Apple Farms, which provides the majority of the restaurant's produce. Together, says Knowlton, the twenty restaurants on the list are "the places that define how we eat out" today.

•

As California cuisine matured and spread, the rapid growth of the 1970s, 1980s, and 1990s gave way to a more gradual expansion of the innovations that were already in place. The defining word for the era from 2000 to the present has been "more." Today there are more restaurants of all kinds. More restaurants have specific farm connections. More farmers grow more varied produce and sell it at more farmers' markets. There are more specialty ranchers, thanks in part to the passion for head-to-tail cooking. More artisanal products, especially cheeses, *salumi* and charcuterie, preserves, pickles, and olive oil, line the shelves of more gourmet food shops. There are also more bakers and candy makers. Farmers, producers, chefs, and consumers have more of an interest in and awareness of sustainability, and organic foods can be found at more supermarkets. Chefs have greater access to information via newsletters and printouts from their purveyors, and diners and home cooks are better educated by a tidal wave of food books, magazines, gossip columns, blogs, and television programs. Everyone is more interested in health and nutrition.

The California cuisine revolution broke conventional and accepted patterns of cooking and dining nationwide. It changed how, what, and where we eat—even at home. But growth and transformation have been accompanied by loss and tradeoffs. With abundance comes the paradox of choice. Overstimulated by so many options, we have become accustomed to constant change and instant boredom. Once upon a time the status quo kept us happy, but today diners expect not just to be fed but to be entertained. And chefs want to create their own styles and transcend cultural boundaries. In this final chapter, I offer some observations on recent developments in California cuisine.

The New Professionalism

Today there is less room for amateurs in California's highly professionalized and competitive food business. Moreover, increased press coverage of the restaurant scene continually ups the ante. Restaurants vie for attention on websites like Eater, Chowhound, and Tasting Table; they use social media tools like Twitter and Facebook and have press kits and even professional publicists. The greater prestige and in some cases celebrity accorded to restaurants and chefs have attracted a host of newcomers to the industry. More of them are attending culinary schools or restaurant management programs and coming into restaurants with formal training and cooking experience.

However, many younger cooking students, as opposed to the career-changing iconoclasts of the past, lack maturity and worldliness. They've gone from high school or a few years of college straight to culinary programs. They may not have cooked at home or dined out in the kinds of restaurants they are training to work in, apart from the occasional splurge with their parents. Most have not had the opportunity to travel widely and sample diverse cuisines in their countries of origin, and few have read broadly or deeply in food history. They would be hard-pressed to talk about culinary traditions, much less the nuances of flavor between a date and a fig, or cinnamon and cardamom.

Cooking schools often fail to make up for these deficits. Students are encouraged to master as many basic cooking skills—traditional and modern—as possible, along with the business skills to help them excel in a profession that is obsessed with success. Rather than selecting the highest-quality fresh products, some schools use mass-market produce and specialty food items from their sponsors, so students are not trained in standards of excellence for their ingredients. Although today most cooking schools offer a global curriculum and teach the techniques and ingredients of Asian, Mediterranean, French, and Latin American food, students spend so much time doing and so little time in comparative tasting that they don't develop a true understanding of the cuisines. The well of inspiration can run dry quickly for chefs who rely solely on technique and have limited tasting and dining experiences to draw on.

While they are energetic and jazzed about the fantasy restaurant life as seen on TV, some of these fledgling chefs are entering the field not out of passion for food and culture but because working in restaurants and being on the line looks "cool." As they chop onions and clean squid, or singe their hair in front of the grill, they harbor dreams of fame and glory. The nonstop barrage of television cooking shows raises their hopes and expectations. Exposure on *Top Chef* and *Chopped* may help some gain recognition and potential investors for their restaurants, but most aspiring cooks will not become stars.

Nor will most have a fat 401(k). Those who take out hefty student loans to go to culinary school will not be able to pay them off quickly on the $13-to-$14-an-hour salary of an entry-level line cook. (And this is up from $8 to $9 an hour in the 1980s.) Many hours of work will be needed just for basic survival, with little left over for anything else. Advancement may be slightly more rapid these days because of the increased number of restaurants, but salaries at the next level are still not generous. A *sous chef* earns about $35,000 to $45,000 annually, a pastry chef about $40,000, and a *chef de cuisine* $55,000 to $70,000. Some executive chefs, usually those working in hotel restaurants, corporate venues, or places owned by celebrities or wealthy backers, may net up to $100,000. But salaries for chef, *sous chef,* and pastry chef positions are not based on a forty-hour work week. Double that time and you just about have it.

Of course, there are many young people, as well as older career changers, who are pursuing cooking out of their love for food rather than fame. Some are entering culinary schools, while others are learning on their own and finding more options for education than ever before. As in the past, novices can volunteer and work for free in the hope of being hired for an entry-level job. Those who are truly motivated can learn at home from the many excellent cookbooks on the market that cover specific techniques, the regional cuisines of different cultures, the growing selection of ingredients, and other topics. Television also has the potential for being a learning tool, though given its focus on entertainment and competition, programs tend to offer more in the way of inspiration than education. Cooking magazines, websites, and schools such as the CIA and Cordon Bleu are producing an increasing number of videos featuring experienced chefs, enabling budding cooks to learn everything from beginning knife skills to advanced sugar techniques. Online demonstrations from other countries make it possible to observe the proper methods for preparing traditional recipes. I myself have watched videos of a Turkish chef making *tepsi börek* (a layered pastry filled with cheese and greens) and a vendor at the Campo de' Fiori market in Rome demonstrating the use of a specialized cutter for prepping chicory for the classic *puntarelle* salad. Although these adjuncts to culinary knowledge aren't a substitute for on-the-job training, they do increase a cook's value to a restaurant and give aspiring or novice cooks a leg up on the competition when being considered for hiring or promotion. But in the end, classes, videos, and books are no substitute for cooking and tasting a dish yourself, and then seeing how others may prepare it—in other words, a complete culinary and cultural immersion.

Women Leaving the Restaurant Kitchen

When I opened Square One in 1984, I was buoyed by the presence of a community of similarly entrepreneurial women in the Bay Area. Today many of those women, including Jesse Cool, Traci Des Jardins, Suzette Gresham, Loretta Keller, Nancy Oakes, Cindy Pawlcyn, Judy Rodgers, and Alice Waters, still own their restaurants. But others have left the field, and their shoes have not been filled by new women chefs and chef-owners. The number of women running restaurants does not seem to be increasing or even holding steady from the early days of California cuisine. In Los Angeles, where there were fewer women chefs to begin with, there has been little growth. Susan Feniger, Suzanne Goin, Mary Sue Milliken, Nancy Silverton, and Suzanne Tracht are all accomplished and respected chefs who have been around for a long time, but where are the new women chefs and chef-owners?

One answer may lie in a trend toward "dudefication" in the restaurant industry and a subtle bias in favor of men within the media and business environment. Women and men have been working side by side in California kitchens for over forty years, and there is less overt sexism within the kitchen. But spurred by the success of reality cooking shows, culinary schools and the media are paying more attention to technique, speed, and competition, which has turned off a lot of women culinary students. TV shows feature chefs at war, glorifying backstabbing, ego-driven, abusive behavior that is a turnoff to many women. This has brought back an atmosphere of elevated testosterone in many restaurant kitchens, which deters many young women from wanting to work in them after graduation.

Men also still receive most of the press coverage. This may be because there are simply more of them in the business. In addition, women—having proven they can succeed as chefs and restaurant owners—are no longer a novelty. Everyone is competing for attention, and chefs such as David Chang and Anthony Bourdain attract notice by adopting a "bad boy" persona and hanging out with other male chefs. Witness the success of the food journal *Lucky Peach*, launched in 2011, where, to get attention, smart men took on the style of preteens trying to shock their elders by using as much profanity as possible (although the publication is maturing now that the initial shock value has subsided). The bad boy posse must have struck a chord, because Chang and Bourdain have garnered a large following among male line cooks and both even made an appearance in the HBO series *Treme*, for which Bourdain acted as a writing consultant. The chef struggling to open a restaurant on the show is a woman, but her talent has to be validated by the appearance of these famous guys who come to eat her food.

Some observers worry that the restaurant industry is starting to resemble a boys' club once more. Although a few women chefs, such as Gabrielle Hamilton, flaunt their own particular brand of bravado and raunchiness, most prefer to stay out of the limelight. Women chefs often tell me, apologetically, that they participate in competitive shows only to attract attention for their restaurants, as appearing on television is one of the few ways to keep in the public eye. The failure to gain exposure makes it harder for women to secure financing for restaurants. In 2010, Amanda Cohen, chef-owner of Dirt Candy in New York City, wrote in a blog post, "Odette Fada was called 'one of New York's preeminent female chefs' by [online blog] Eater. Number of times they wrote about her? Twice in three years. In the same time frame, Nate Appleman got tagged on 42 posts, David Chang got tagged on 86, Sam Mason got tagged on 21 and so did Marcus Samuelsson, Zak Pelaccio got 29. . . . Why would an investor back a female chef in a restaurant? He knows that she won't get the hype and attention a male chef will get." In Charlotte Druckman's book *Skirt Steak*, which probes the lives of women chefs, Amanda talked about her own struggle to finance Dirt Candy. She thought her gender was "a deal-breaker." She hypothesized that investors believe that men are better at managing kitchens, multitasking, and handling the financials. In a throwback to the old days, women often have to bring in a male partner in order to raise capital.

With less press coverage, women also garner fewer nominations for food industry prizes, such as the James Beard awards. They're less likely to be listed in food guides and achieve recognition for running long-lived, popular, successful restaurants that consistently deliver great food. The 2012 Zagat Guide honor roll of celebrity chefs in the Bay Area, for example, listed Jesse Cool, Dominique Crenn, Traci Des Jardins, Loretta Keller, Nancy Oakes, Cindy Pawlcyn, and Judy Rodgers while omitting relative newcomer Melissa Perello, chef-owner of Frances, one of San Francisco's most coveted and difficult-to-obtain reservations, as well as respected old-timers such as Suzette Gresham, Gayle Pirie, Donna Scala, Amaryll Schwertner, and Annie Somerville, whose restaurants are busy and well regarded. In the 2012 Zagat Guide for Los Angeles, only three out of the forty-two celebrity chefs listed were women: Susan Feniger, Suzanne Goin, and Nancy Silverton. Though mentioned in the individual reviews of their restaurants, women chefs such as Evan Kleiman at Angeli, Mary Sue Milliken at Border Grill, Suzanne Tracht at Jar, Josie Le Balch at Josie, Pippa Calland at Villetta, and Karen Hatfield at Hatfield's were not deemed worthy of celebrity status, while ten nonresident and rarely present celebrity male chefs with restaurant offshoots in LA were listed. Overall, 80 to 90 percent of the celebrity chefs listed in the Zagat Guides are men. Many women who run restaurants feel slighted and miss out on the boost that awards and recognition would give their business.

If fewer women are going into restaurant kitchens and staying there, it's not because they are less capable. The legions of women chefs leading the food revolution of the 1970s and 1980s have put that issue to rest forever. One contributing factor is the number of hours and amount of energy that the restaurant business consumes. Although working as a chef has always been demanding, today's market makes it more than a full-time job. Between cooking, managing staff, and marketing themselves to stay in the public eye, chefs can find themselves working all the time. And the physical demands are hard on the body.

While both women and men have family obligations, women still do the bulk of the child care. Raising children may be easier for chef-owners than line cooks because they have better control of their hours and can hire help to share responsibilities at work and home. Some are lucky to have a working partner so they are not on call all the time. But the hours and stress of restaurant life can still cause chefs to miss out on a rich family life. As a result, many women chefs elect not to have children. They have a restaurant instead, a baby that never gives up the 2 A.M. feeding.

The gradual exodus of women from restaurant kitchens is not due to lack of passion or failure of will. It is the result of intellectual, emotional, and financial decisions made by women chefs—and potential women chefs. After looking realistically at the costs of being a restaurant professional, many women opt out. They want predictable hours, greater control of their time, and a congenial working environment.

Happily, this does not mean that women have given up on careers in food and wine. Today Barbara Tropp's pioneering organization Women Chefs and Restaurateurs, created in 1993, has over two thousand members and offers a variety of networking, professional, and support services, including a job bank and active website. More than half of the members are neither chefs nor restaurateurs but work in food-related fields. So while there may be fewer women chefs and line cooks, there are still plenty of women working in restaurants in other roles, such as bartender and sommelier. Others have stepped into management positions.

Many are opening food-related businesses. They have become artisans and entre-preneurs, starting bakeries and markets, selling their jams, pickles, and cheese, and making wine. Some are going into research and development for food com-panies, working as chefs for companies like Google or university food service, or becoming private chefs or caterers. Others are teaching, blogging, and writing about food, photographing food, or doing food styling. Many are driving the trend toward better and healthier prepared foods, especially for schoolchildren. Women are leading the food industry in new and exciting ways.

Restaurants Reconfigured

In the 1980s and 1990s, the open kitchen transformed the relationship between the diners and chefs. In the first decade of the 2000s, food trucks and pop-up res-taurants began reshaping the experience of eating out. Writer and critic Jonathan Gold noted that, at fine-dining restaurants, people who would appreciate a chef's food are often priced out of buying it. But street food brings a variety of cooking styles and ingredients within reach of a wide audience, including those without a trust fund. Food trucks allow hardworking amateurs and trained cooks to take a low-risk gamble and try out their cuisine on the public. They can jump into the marketplace relatively quickly and easily, gaining culinary experience, exposure, a loyal following, and maybe even a few investors. These cooks have the freedom to prepare a limited range of food without concerning themselves with service and ambience.

Pop-up restaurants—where a chef cooks at a host restaurant on a night that it's ordinarily closed, or in another venue, such as a bar or even a corner store—have helped advance the careers of chefs who cannot afford to open a brick-and-mortar location or are in between gigs. "There's something about the pop-up that I think is uniquely suited for the moment, and maybe uniquely suited for California," said Jonathan. "It becomes like following a band. There's a band that you like, and you go to a club to see it, and it doesn't matter what the club is, and it doesn't matter who's doing the lighting, and it doesn't matter what the club's called. It matters that your band's playing there."

In Los Angeles, Ludovic Lefebvre has made a career of pop-ups. He has his own television show and recently published a cookbook chronicling his adventur-ous cooking—*LudoBites: Recipes and Stories from the Pop-up Restaurants of Ludo Lefebvre*. After years of nomadic cuisine, he is opening a brick-and-mortar restaurant with Jon Shook and Vinny Dotolo of Animal. Eventually those cooks who develop a dedicated following, like Lefebvre, may have the chance to open a fixed location, where diners can find them on a regular basis and where they enjoy the luxury of a walk-in refrigerator to store leftover food instead of having to throw it out or take it home. Roy Choi, who kicked off the contemporary food-truck fad with his Kogi BBQ-To-Go trucks in LA, now has several permanent restaurants—Chego, A-Frame, Sunny Spot, and Alibi Room. In Northern California, Evan Bloom and Leo Beckerman operated a delicatessen pop-up at the Ferry Plaza farmers' market until they could open Wise Sons in San Francisco's Mission District. Eskender Aseged held pop-up dinners at homes and restaurants and now has a restaurant, Radio Africa & Kitchen, in the Bayview District.

There is a greater diversity of brick-and-mortar eateries today as well, from formal fine-dining establishments to casual diners and cafés, with many mid-range brasseries, restaurants, and bar and grills in between. Price differentials at these venues have less to do with the quality of the ingredients or the skills of the chef—which may be on a par with each other—than with the rent, ambience and décor, location, level of service, size of the staff, extent of the wine list, and quality of the china, glassware, and linens. Restaurants serving California cuisine still depend on fresh, seasonal, and local ingredients, but the more upscale and exclusive the restaurant, the more unusual or costly those ingredients may be.

Responding to the recent recession, which has limited many diners' ability to eat out, some professionally trained chefs with fine-dining experience are opening restaurants that serve moderately priced food made with upscale products. Todd Humphries started his career in ultrafine dining at Campton Place and has since moved to a more relaxed venue, Kitchen Door in Napa. "There will always be a place for the Thomas Kellers and Corey Lees and David Kinches," said Todd, but he thinks there's also room for chefs who want to put out good food "without all the fussiness. No need for tablecloths. The changes that we're going to see are in the style of service—more casual but still serious, well-prepared food at a reasonable price, and quality ingredients." Craig Stoll worked at Campton Place and then Postrio before he and his wife, Anne, opened the cozy Delfina, the first destination restaurant in the Mission when that part of town was dicey. Stuart Brioza and Nicole Krasinsky worked at Rubicon before opening the whimsical State Bird Provisions, and Evan and Sarah Rich of the exciting Rich Table worked at Bouley and Coi.

In LA, diners enjoy the comforting simplicity of David LeFevre's biscuits at M.B. Post. "Here I am, having *staged* at El Bulli and worked at landmarks like Charlie Trotter's and Water Grill, and people just love my *biscuits*," David told

Los Angeles Magazine in March 2013. Josef Centeno worked at such celebrated restaurants as Daniel, La Côte Basque, and Manresa before becoming chef at the wildly popular Bäco Mercat, and Michael Voltaggio left the elegant Langham Hotel in Pasadena to serve casual but cutting-edge cuisine at his restaurant Ink. These highly regarded dining venues invest in ingredients and maintain high-quality service even if the waiters are in informal attire.

Stylistic change is catching. At the CIA in Hyde Park, the old Escoffier Room has undergone a transformation to "reflect the dining revolution in America," said Tim Ryan, the institute's president. It embodies "the shift away from kitchen servitude—and toward creativity and collaboration—that has taken place over the years." The name of the school's restaurant, Bocuse, may honor a French culinary star, but its kitchen reflects the changes introduced in California years before. Instead of the old-fashioned top-down brigade system, the CIA has appropriated the collaborative model pioneered in California restaurants, which allows all cooks to taste collectively and offer input. The rigid separation of classic stations like *saucier* or *legumier* has been done away with, and there is more communication among the cooks. The look is casual and contemporary, and, in a final sign of the times, the haute brasserie food features global accents.

Farm to Table and Beyond

Naming the provenance of every item on the menu is giving way to providing a discreet list of purveyors at the bottom of the menu or detailed information about them on the restaurant website. While local, seasonal, and sustainable is still the mantra of California chefs, some prominent chefs persist in importing ingredients to suit their personal standards of excellence, whereas others simply do what is most convenient. According to former Chez Panisse and Eccolo chef Chris Lee, "Although you hear a lot of talk, you don't always see a lot of walk. It bothers me because I feel that it's an insult to the work that people did in this area to say 'I'm local and sustainable' and then have three things on the menu that are that and the rest purchased from Sysco." Some chefs will serve asparagus in October no matter what fresh-local-seasonal pronouncements they put on the menu. But seasonality will continue to drive the menu in California, both because the state's extraordinary selection of year-round produce makes it possible and because most diners are now as well informed as the chefs cooking for them. They will call you out if you talk the talk but don't walk the walk.

The peerless ingredients at the heart of California cuisine are being produced by a new generation of young people, many of whom are concerned about food safety and environmental issues. By raising the status and visibility of farmers, the California cuisine movement has helped draw many talented and creative newcomers into farming. Michael Ableman, the longtime manager of Fairview Gardens, one of the oldest organic farms in Southern California, said in a 2003 interview with freelance writer Arnie Cooper that today "farming is not a lowly job but an honorable profession. . . . We're not only changing the way people eat; we're shifting the value they place on the land and on the people who grow their food." Chef Jeff Jackson has observed an influx of farmers in the San Diego area who share the fervor and dedication of those who made waves in Northern California a generation earlier. "Today more people going into farming are college grads—academics with intelligence and passion who want to change their way of life." Many have become vocal, active members of the California food community.

The Outstanding in the Field program is a twenty-first-century update of the Farm-Restaurant Project and Tasting of Summer Produce. In 1998, Santa Cruz chef Jim Denevan invited Gabriella Café's suppliers to come to dinner with the restaurant patrons. The farmers and purveyors spoke to the diners about their work, and all enjoyed a great meal. Jim's brother, Bill, one of the farmers who spoke at the dinner, suggested moving the event from the restaurant out to his farm. They did, and the next year the attendees sat at long tables outdoors and ate a five-course meal prepared by Jim and chef Tom King. Guests were greeted by farmer Andy Griffin and addressed by the other farmers in attendance. The idea caught on and was repeated at other farms with other chefs, including David Kinch, Traci Des Jardins, Mourad Lahlou, Craig Stoll, and Charles Phan. Stone Barns Center in New York hosted a dinner in 2003, and now Outstanding in the Field events are held all over the country. Other restaurants engage more informally with the farms that supply them. Dru Rivers of Full Belly Farm described visits from the staff of their restaurant partners, which include Coi, Zuni Café, and Chez Panisse: "They camp out at the creek and we make dinner together and it's so fun. We have a great connection with these restaurants."

Some restaurants distinguish themselves by maintaining their own gardens or liaisons with a few farms or ranches. Dan Barber, chef and co-owner of Blue Hill at Stone Barns in upstate New York and a careful and astute observer of the California cuisine movement, once did a *stage* in Northern California at Chez Panisse. He has also worked in Southern California with Joe Miller. A role model for farm-to-table chefs, Dan sources ingredients for Blue Hill from the surrounding Stone Barns gardens as well as local farms. Dan wants to stimulate active interaction between farmers and cooks. "Chefs need to work with farmers more, give them more feedback, and encourage experimentation. The story of farm to table and of supporting local agriculture has been told. It's a great story. Now it's hit a plateau. To really make a difference in the future of food and to preserve important farmland, we need to take some of the creativity that's being applied in the kitchen out to the fields and to the farm."

Sam Mogannam of San Francisco's Bi-Rite Market, a culinary oasis for home cooks, thinks that more California chefs should follow Dan's lead. "I look at what Dan Barber is doing at Stone Barns, where not only is he working hand in hand with growers and ranchers to produce the ingredients that he wants, but he also has his own hands in the dirt. If it can happen outside of Manhattan in that climate, we should be doing more of that here." Bi-Rite cultivates a few acres in Sonoma to supplement what the store buys from local farmers. Chefs without green thumbs could collaborate or even partner financially with farmers. Manresa takes the connection even further, with some staff members putting in hours at Love Apple Farms as part of their duties.

Another offshoot of the farm-to-table movement is whole-animal or head-to-tail cooking. At restaurants such as LA's Animal and San Francisco's Incanto, the meat-heavy menus feature pork belly, suckling pig, offal, house-cured bacon, sausages, and charcuterie. (Some call this "dude food" because the practitioners are mostly male.) These venues are usually not at the high end of fine dining and can be as informal as a porchetta stand at the farmers' market. Holding head-to-tail dinners such as those pioneered by Paul Bertolli at Oliveto has become popular.

Foraging is also an adjunct to fresh, local, and seasonal. The inspiration for this trend is Danish chef René Redzepi, whose Copenhagen restaurant Noma topped *Restaurant* magazine's World's Fifty Best Restaurants list in 2010, 2011, and 2012. Noma's mission statement eloquently invokes its use of local ingredients: "In an effort to shape our way of cooking, we look to our landscape and delve into our ingredients and culture, hoping to rediscover our history and shape our future." Ingredients are collected from the surrounding countryside and greater Nordic region.

The actions of award-winning chefs such as René Redzepi influence their peers as well as home cooks. Some chefs have turned to foraging to increase the range of ingredients at their disposal while remaining local. "In terms of wild foods in California, the diversity and flavor are unbelievable," said chef Daniel Patterson of Coi, who's working on a catalogue of methods for cooking with native plants. "A lot of the history of our state is written in these flavors." Other chefs have foraging as part of their heritage. Chef Staffan Terje grew up in Sweden, where "spring, summer, and fall, you would go out and pick berries, mushrooms, leaves. My grandfather taught me about a little fern that would grow in the mosses; the root was really sweet and tasted like licorice. So the foraging thing for me has always been there, and now you read about foraging as a big deal." Now he forages regularly with Connie Green for wild mushrooms, which he features on the menu at Perbacco.

Foraging also enables chefs to differentiate themselves from their rivals and gain cachet. They hire foragers to bring in unique and unusual edible plants, including weeds, mosses, pine needles and spruce branches, flowers, berries, nuts, and barks, as well as the more familiar wild mushrooms, all of which they claim have a deeper, more vibrant flavor than farmed ingredients. Some foraged products, including mushrooms, nettles, miner's lettuce, purslane, and chickweed, have begun to appear at farmers' markets to satisfy the demands of savvy home cooks. Whether the aura of foraged foods will be diminished or deepened as more people cook with them at home remains to be seen.

Moving Sustainability Forward

Over the past thirty years, Californians have built a culture around supporting local farmers, ranchers, and artisanal producers, and this movement has spread nationwide. But is that enough to keep our food systems healthy for another thirty years? Whereas in the early years of California cuisine, chefs cooked solely out of love for the deliciousness and sensuality of the food, to feed people and make them happy, today they have multiple responsibilities. Many put their money where their mouth is, choosing to work with farmers and purveyors who share their political views and supporting sustainability and food safety organizations such as Slow Food, Food and Water Watch, Chefs Collaborative, Community Alliance with Family Farmers, and the Monterey Bay Aquarium Seafood Watch.

"We might get very excited about the first corn of the season from Brentwood, the first Blenheim apricots from Winters, without really fully understanding what extreme pressure those lands are under," said Sibella Kraus. "If you say, 'I care where my food comes from,' it's time to start caring about the communities where the food comes from. Do people know what the circumstances are in Aromas, in

Lodi, in cities that they've never heard of? Part of it happens on a personal level with the farmers, but the state and federal policies have much more influence. That's what sets the context."

In 2009, chef Loretta Keller gave a cooking demonstration to the marketing department at the California Academy of Sciences. The average age of the group was about twenty-five, and the audience was largely unaware of the history of California cuisine. She found herself explaining things that were obvious to her but brand new to them. "We need to keep educating the public," she said. "We want everyone to be reminded of where their food comes from. Years ago we didn't have the same environmental challenges that we have now. Today there's more urban sprawl, and more farmland has disappeared. We've got big, big issues. The California cuisine movement has proven to be a very powerful and successful platform for helping make change."

One way California citizens are trying to effect change on food issues is through the initiative process. Proposition 2, which was passed in 2008, mandated better confinement conditions for egg-laying hens, veal calves, and pregnant pigs. In 2012, Proposition 37 proposed obligatory labeling of genetically modified foods, and measures to tax soda were put on the ballot in two California cities—El Monte in the south and Richmond in the north. Although the 2012 measures failed, they initiated public debate and sparked the introduction of similar measures in other states and nationwide, including a GMO-labeling bill brought before Congress in February 2013. You can be sure that Californians will raise these issues again.

Spurred on by the Slow Food movement and events such as the Good Food awards at San Francisco's Ferry Building and the Eat Real Festival in Oakland, more handcrafted, authentic, and responsibly produced goods are appearing in the marketplace. Commercial incubators such as La Cocina in San Francisco help artisans get their projects off the ground, while fund-raising sites such as Kickstarter enable others to raise money. As a result, more people are culturing cheese and churning ice cream, putting up preserves and pickles, curing meats, making oils and vinegars, baking breads and pastries, stuffing tamales, and creating distinctive chocolates and coffee blends. California home cooks have received an education in food politics by dining in restaurants, shopping at farmers' markets, and joining CSAs, where local farm-fresh produce is delivered to them by weekly subscription. All of this has put pressure on supermarkets to expand their selection of organic and sustainably raised foods. Consumers continue to listen and learn.

With the increased interest in head-to-tail cooking, chefs are looking for more locally grown, pasture-raised meat. Unfortunately, onerous federal regulations have led to a scarcity of local slaughterhouses, which makes business more difficult for small producers of sheep, cattle, goats, and pigs. California ranchers often have to drive great distances to high-volume industrial processing plants, where poor butchering can undo the care they've put into raising premium animals. Farmer Andy Griffin would like to see chefs and the public speak up in support of small meat-processing facilities, applying "the same energy that we were able to apply to vegetables and fruits a generation or two ago. Chefs are becoming aware of all these things that they could have, except for the fact that they can't get it done legally because there is no infrastructure to support it. There's a whole world of meat starting and we've got a long, long way to go." Alternatives to large meat-processing plants include mobile abattoirs and small-scale local facilities where ranchers could take their animals for hygienic, humane slaughter and scrupulous butchering.

Wine and Food

The collaboration between winemakers and chefs continues to strengthen. Wineries work with chefs for special events and many have chefs on staff for events and marketing. Master sommelier and wine shop owner Peter Granoff applauded that "finally more chefs are interested [in wine], and they're more knowledgeable as well. We have made progress." He added, "The range of wine that's available is much broader than it was even ten years ago. In the Bay Area, we're blessed or cursed, depending on how you look at it, with one of the most, if not the most, competitive wine markets in the country. We have great wine producers on our doorstep and every major importer wants to be here. So the role of the sommelier or educated wine staff becomes more important, training becomes more important, and the size of the wine list becomes a bigger issue in the training. Even as a professional I can't tell you how many times I go into a restaurant and realize that I don't know half the wines on the list."

Times have changed since Gerald Asher observed that those who were interested in food were not interested in wine and vice versa. The association has become richer, and today there are more certification programs for professionals. The CIA in St. Helena offers classes for aspiring wine directors and sommeliers, along with food and wine pairing classes for chefs and wine classes open to the public. Wine stores routinely provide guided tastings, and an influx of wine bars keeps wine lovers happy and informed.

Melting Pot in the Global Kitchen

As California diners embraced new flavors, ethnic food was viewed more positively, but only recently has it received the critical recognition it deserves. Aziza in San Francisco, which creates modern reinventions of traditional Moroccan dishes, received a Michelin star in 2011. In Los Angeles, Japanese restaurants Sushi Zo, Mori Sushi, and Urasawa were all awarded Michelin stars in 2010. The newer St. Helena campus of the Culinary Institute of America gives global cuisines as much attention as the original Hyde Park campus used to bestow on classic French cuisine.

California's elevation of ethnic food has reverberated all over the country, although the transition from casual to high end took time. When ethnic food went upscale, customers initially resisted the higher prices. Fortunately, this resistance abated, and the dining public became eager for refined interpretations of ethnic classics. Whereas in the late 1980s China Moon was criticized because it was more expensive than typical Chinese restaurants, fifteen years later, nobody complained about the prices at the Vietnamese restaurant Slanted Door when it opened in the Ferry Building, and today it is doing a booming business.

Jonathan Gold, a passionate promoter of LA's ethnic restaurants, has watched as they have come into their own. "Fifteen years ago you would go to a place and they would have Thai noodles on the menu because they thought they should have Thai noodles on the menu. They would get some formula for it from one of those [CIA] folks. And they had never tasted real Thai noodles, even though probably the best place to eat outside Thailand was a mile and a half from the restaurant. There was all this amazing, vital Mexican cooking going on all over LA that nobody, least of all the press, was paying attention to. And I think now they are." Jonathan has mapped ethnic food in greater LA, and both chefs and the public avidly follow his foodie cartography—eating at the restaurants he mentions, and then translating the flavors into their own cooking.

Chef David Kinch observed that California cuisine today is "going deeper into regionalism and wider in its embrace of other cultures." Marc Halperin, culinary director of the think tank Center for Culinary Innovation, agrees. "In California, we have begun to understand that Italian cuisine is regional, and Chinese cuisine is regional, and Vietnamese cuisine and Thai food are regional. Each of those regions has interesting flavor profiles or ingredients that can be incorporated into cooking in California. We have done that over the past twenty years. We're going to continue to do that, but now we're looking at South America and Central America. And it's not Mexican cooking anymore, but regional Mexican cooking." Some chefs are purists, feeling that they could spend a lifetime exploring, interpreting, and recreating foods of memory. Others incorporate new flavors and ingredients to create foods of their imagination that depart from the template of the traditional cuisine. The new ultraregional and melting pot styles of cooking exhibit a more sophisticated use of global concepts, techniques, and ingredients. "There is an increasing acceptance of ethnic cuisines without it being fusion," said David. "There's now an actual melding. That's a big difference. It's not one from column A, one from column B: it's more an actual incorporation of styles." For example, in the past, David might have used a classic fish stock for his dish called "autumn tidal pool"—which presents California abalone, sea urchin, shellfish, and mushrooms in a savory broth. Now, however, he chooses to float the seafood in a dashi-based broth inspired by Japanese cuisine. Susanne Goin at Lucques also carefully composes her dishes. Her grilled fish with black rice, curried cauliflower, and persimmon-pomegranate salsa harmoniously combines the flavors of Asia, the Middle East, and Latin America.

Boundaries between traditional cooking and fusion are shifting. Octavio Becerra is half Mexican and half Chilean. He grew up in a neighborhood near LA's Koreatown but also spent summers in Mexico. When he opened his first restaurant, Palate Food + Wine, he served the upscale Mediterranean cooking he'd learned under Joachim Splichal at Max au Triangle and Patina. "I never ventured into incorporating the Latino flavors or the Korean influences in my commercial cuisine," he said. "I do at home, but I never felt comfortable or needed to be able to do that on a commercial level." However, years of living and dining in multicultural Los Angeles have had an impact on Octavio. At the Napa Valley Wine Auction and at the Beard Awards gala in 2010, he served a Mediterranean sandwich in a Vietnamese *bánh mì* style, an example of a more organic fusion of the food of memory with the food of dreams.

Chef Joe Miller's culinary career path followed a very Californian trajectory. He began with classic CIA French training and cooked at L'Orangerie, Patina, and Cafe Katsu before opening Joe's Restaurant in LA in 1991, which has evolved to assimilate the culinary influences of other cultures. He's still there more than twenty years later, no mean feat in such a fickle town. Like the

California cuisine that he embraces, Joe has been able to change while remaining relevant, responding to a younger demographic that, as he put it, "likes to eat, watches their diet, watches their health, and also likes to have fun with food." His multicultural menu features such varied items as French braised short ribs, Italian lobster risotto, char-grilled octopus with smoked chili and tomato vinaigrette, and Asian-inspired grilled ono with stir-fried vegetables, basmati rice, dashi, and lotus chips. He thinks chefs need to adapt and try new things. Recently he opened Bar Pintxo, a Spanish-inspired tapas bar, expanding his culinary repertoire.

California chefs are now a more ethnically diverse group than they were decades ago. They have also become more connected and comfortable with the flavors of other cultures and integrate those flavors more naturally into their cooking. Awkward fusion has mellowed and given way to a more cohesive culinary style. California cuisine today takes in the influences of chefs' travels and upbringing with greater ease, and the resulting food transcends national borders more fluidly.

Jonathan Gold identified a new breed of chef in LA—Asian Americans who grow up with their family's native cuisine set against the city's multicultural landscape. These chefs approach Western cooking with a novel mind-set, which he called "fusion from the other side." Roy Choi was raised in LA's Koreatown and classically trained at the CIA at Hyde Park. He gained recognition for his food through the Kogi BBQ-To-Go trucks, which combined Korean barbecue and Mexican food in such dishes as spicy *bulgogi* tacos and kimchi quesadillas. Similarly, a Latino chef might take on the Mediterranean. At Bäco Mercat, Josef Centeno cooks *carne picada* with Mediterranean semolina, tahini, pomegranate, and pine nuts. His beef *paleron* with kumquats and cream of wheat made it onto Jonathan Gold's list of things to eat before you die.

The new multicultural melting pot cuisine differs from fusion in that exotic flavors are not merely borrowed and applied as a garnish or enhancement to a dish from another culture. The assimilation of culinary ideas and flavors is more organic. It is the result of a deeper knowledge of how flavors work, how they are used in traditional foods, and how they might be absorbed into a new, unique dish. One might say it's a more evolved or seasoned kind of fusion. With fusion the diner is aware of the seams; with melting pot, the combinations are seamless. This melting pot cooking is not exclusive to California, but it originated and flourished in the multicultural and freewheeling culinary environment here before spreading nationwide.

Technique versus Ingredients Today

In the formative years of California cuisine, Northern California chefs focused on fresh, organic, ingredient-based cooking, creating dishes derived from classic cuisines and presenting them simply and unpretentiously. Chefs in Southern California gravitated toward trend-setting, technique-based cooking and emphasized expensive, high-status ingredients and flashy presentations. Today the two have come together. In recent years, Southern California chefs have become increasingly interested in the provenance and flavor of their ingredients, while some Northern California chefs have adopted more sensational presentations and a greater interest in cooking techniques.

The tension between technique and ingredients persists, however. Given the virtuosity of cooks and chefs today and the scrutiny directed at their creations, there's inevitably more technique and visual drama on the plate. Many contemporary chefs are intrigued by technological innovations such as *sous-vide* cooking or chemical additions like xanthan gum. The practitioners of this modernist style are mainly men, usually in high-end venues. Highlighting technical innovation for its own sake is generally less appealing to women chefs. Although some women may use new techniques such as *sous vide* in their kitchens, they generally do not make them their focus or culinary claim to fame.

All over the country, chefs use squeeze bottles to apply dots of sauce too small to flavor the food or tweezers to place single blossoms or herb sprigs just so, on artfully designed plates. Many have received too much press attention too soon and their plates are pretty but anonymous, lacking the individual signature of a chef or restaurant. In fact, it is starting to look like a rerun of the 1980s and 1990s, with ever more ingredients on the plate and the comma cuisine menu-writing style that inventories all of the ingredients used in a dish.

To compete in the high-end market, a few elite chefs offer seemingly interminable multicourse tasting menus to awe their audience with a display of their skills. Some of these meals inadvertently become an ordeal for the hapless diner who showed up to the table with enthusiasm, only to leave exhausted. I hate to think that after all of the long, hard work of the food revolution to improve and expand the selection of produce and other products, California cooking would wind up a parade of carefully curated ingredients, cunningly arranged, without soul or connection to any food heritage. Rather than leaving the diner with lasting food memories, many a dish is admired, eaten, and soon forgotten.

These overwrought culinary creations are in need of an editor. Jeremiah

Tower longs for the day when chefs "finally have the courage to put something on a plate that's just two or three ingredients—a main ingredient and a couple of supporting ingredients—brilliantly done, very fresh, clean, unadorned, none of these smudges across the plate with the drops and the drizzles and the reduced balsamic vinegar. Why would you reduce balsamic vinegar? Buy the real stuff; it's been reduced for one hundred years."

Tom Worthington, a trained chef and a partner at Monterey Fish, believes that food magazines and television have affected the business. "The chefs think that every plate has to look like it's going to be photographed." Although glossy food magazines have been around since the 1940s, "magazine cooking" is a recent phenomenon, according to Jeremiah. "Everyone's cooking from the photographs in magazines, and the magazines are photographing them. It's a circle of not-so-great talent. You can travel through France, Germany, England and New York, San Francisco, and Chicago and the majority of the food in highly rated restaurants looks exactly the same." Chefs aspire to be creative and original, but with all the immediate reporting of menu items and trendy ingredients made possible by the Internet, there is a lot of copycat cooking going on.

The desire to create photogenic dishes means that flavor increasingly takes a backseat to plate construction. While Paul Johnson of Monterey Fish was pitching his seafood to a famous chef whose mantra is "flavor first," the chef mentioned that he served only Malpeque oysters, a bivalve from eastern Canada. Paul observed that these oysters did not taste very good at that particular time of year and recommended that he serve another kind. But the chef pulled out a specially designed oyster plate and said that other oysters did not fit in the plate. Flavor is not the deciding factor for everyone.

Supporters of the rustic-and-real school see "magazine cooking" and the modernist style as glitzy window dressing and feel that cultural tradition and flavor have been pushed aside in favor of technical wizardry and artistic presentation. They believe that cooking has gone from the passionate and personal to the professional and impersonal. They fear that honest, simple cooking, with its focus on flavor and ingredients, could become a rarity if technique and showbiz take over. It would be the triumph of style for style's sake and a loss of culinary diversity. I agree with Jeremiah Tower, who said, "I think the best chefs now are the ones who have the courage to believe in themselves, cook with the ingredients, and to hell with recognition of the press, with instant recognition. Because the point is, when you cook well, you're going to be recognized."

Redefining California Cuisine

After forty years of California cuisine, some people believe it is time for a changing of the guard. Many of the original chefs and restaurateurs are entering their late fifties and sixties. Restaurant work is hard and physical. It takes its toll after thirty or forty years. There's a new group of cooks behind the stoves and they want to make their mark and not just follow in others' footsteps.

"The longer we go on, the more we define California's style," said David Kinch. "What I would like to see is California's cuisine taking the next logical step and making a generational switch. Daniel Patterson and I want to be true to our California cuisine roots, but we also want to build on them. I think we're both very respectful of the traditions and the history that came before us, which is important because we know about it. But there are a lot of young cooks who don't know about it, and that is a serious mistake. They don't understand what went on in kitchens before. I think a real mark of how this is our time to make a statement is the fact that New York no longer really makes fun of us. In fact, they're taking all of our ideas, and we both know what the next step is, that they're going to claim them as their own."

David was responding to a 2005 piece by chef Daniel Patterson in the *New York Times Magazine* entitled "To the Moon, Alice?" in which Daniel wrote that Bay Area food was delicious but not very original. He expressed frustration with Northern California's adherence to the Chez Panisse style of homey, *bonne femme* cooking, which he described as "the tyranny of California cuisine." In the article, Daniel entreated chefs to use "local ingredients, precise technique and a generous helping of imagination to create a modern, innovative and highly personal style of cooking."

Many young chefs heeded Daniel's call to embrace a more individual approach based on twenty-first-century cooking techniques. Today an active culinary conversation continues between those who follow the real-and-rustic path and those who choose the technical and staged. There is, however, agreement where it counts. The chefs of both schools follow the initial tenets of California cuisine, using local, fresh, seasonal ingredients. As long as the integrity of the ingredients and the connection to place are respected, California cuisine will continue to mature along with the next generation of chefs. Our country's awakening to the power and meaning of real food raised by those who share a commitment to quality and sustainability started in California with a group of passionate iconoclasts.

That passion has been contagious, and we don't want to be inoculated against it. In the introduction, I quoted Wallace Stegner's observation that "like the rest of America, California is unformed, innovative, ahistorical, hedonistic, acquisitive, and energetic—only more so." Stegner's insight into the state's character can help us understand its culinary contributions as well. California cuisine continues to be irreverent, experimental, ambitious, respectful, and rooted. It is American cuisine, only more so.

ACKNOWLEDGMENTS

I'd like to thank the following:

Darra Goldstein for suggesting to UC Press that I write this book

Sheila Levine for acquiring it

Dore Brown for her brilliant and sensitive editing and for dedicating her personal time, above and beyond the call; I am forever grateful

Kate Marshall for leadership and support at UC Press

Eric Engles, developmental editor, for keeping me on target and getting this mass of material in chronological and conceptual order

Elena Goldstein, my amazing granddaughter, for transcribing most of the interviews; she enjoyed getting to know the people behind California cuisine and loved running into them at the farmers' market or in their restaurants

Daisy Chow for excellent and timely transcriptions of some of the interviews

Jean Kim and Deena Fettner for additional transcriptions

Jason Luong for setting up my computer and interview systems

Anne McBride for tracking down old reviews and articles to fill gaps in the history

Barbara Pino for finding the right recording device and showing me how to use it

Evan Goldstein for support and encouragement and for being the go-to wine guy

Marion Nestle for friendship and good advice

Emily Park for dedicated and demonically detailed copyediting

Lia Tjandra for the sexy cover design

Sandy Drooker for the elegant interior design

And everyone I interviewed, for their candor and willingness to share their experiences with me. I wish there had been more space to include all their stories.

Joyce Goldstein

I am indebted to Joyce Goldstein for giving me the opportunity to work on this book. I couldn't have wished for a more patient and generous partner or a shrewder guide to the world of California cuisine.

I'm grateful to the following colleagues and friends for inspiration and valuable contributions: Dennis Cusack, Chalon Emmons, Louise Francis, Darra Goldstein, Frances Harrison, Sheila Levine, Kate Marshall, Scott Norton, Emily Park, Dave Peattie, Thérèse Shere, Tony Shermoen, Karen Stough, Rose Vekony, and Janet Villanueva. Lia Tjandra and Sandy Drooker provided the exquisite cover and interior designs.

Finally, I am beholden to my family: Nick Thurston, who models discipline and creativity for me every day; Genevieve Bjargardóttir, who read and commented perceptively on every chapter; and Gene Thurston, who has literally, figuratively, and lovingly eaten everything I've dished up for thirty-five years—he gives my life its savor.

Dore Brown

INTERVIEWS

Unless otherwise noted, all quotations in the text are taken from the following interviews with the author: Bruce Aidells (April 6, 2010); Toni Allegra (June 2, 2010); Colman Andrews (July 5, 2010); John Ash (March 19, 2010); Gerald Asher (May 17, 2010); Laura Avery (December 16, 2010); Dan Barber (July 14, 2010); Caroline Bates (June 25, 2010); Fedele Bauccio (May 26, 2010); Michael Bauer (April 2, 2010); Octavio Becerra (August 2, 2010); Paul Bertolli (May 19, 2010); Georgeanne Brennan (May 26, 2010); Michael Brennan (July 21, 2010); Bill Briwa (March 18, 2010); Lynn Brown (July 5, 2010); Wendy Brucker (July 13, 2010); Gene Burns (July 6, 2010); Marian Burros (September 28, 2010); Jack and Dolores Cakebread (May 27, 2010); Cindy and Liam Callahan (July 28, 2010); Bob Cannard Jr. (June 28, 2010); Dexter Carmichael (July 21, 2010); Linda Carucci (July 21, 2010); Laura Chenel (June 1, 2010); Michael Chiarello (March 11, 2010); Dale Coke (June 29, 2010); Rich Collins (July 2, 2010); Sue Conley (June 1, 2010); Jesse Cool (April 2, 2010); Darrell Corti (June 30, 2010); Gary Danko (May 28, 2010); Narsai David (March 30, 2010); Hugh Davies (June 2, 2010); Jeff Dawson (March 17, 2010); Michael Dellar (July 12, 2010); Daphne Derven (December 20, 2010); Traci Des Jardins (July 20, 2010); Jerry Di Vecchio (May 14, 2010); Jim Dodge (May 14, 2010); Lissa Doumani (March 23, 2010); Paul Draper (May 15, 2010); Greg Drescher (June 30, 2010; February 4, 2011); Barbara Fairchild (May 4, 2010); Elizabeth Falkner (May 17, 2010); Susan Feniger (June 29, 2010); John Finger (July 1, 2010); Doug Fletcher (May 29, 2010); Janet Fletcher (May 29, 2010); Margaret Fox (June 30, 2010); Ken Frank (May 14, 2010); Mark Franz (June 1, 2010); Andrew Freeman (June 14, 2010); Bill Fujimoto (July 13, 2010); Anne Gingrass (March 11, 2010); David Gingrass (July 2, 2010); Suzanne Goin (June 25, 2010); Jonathan Gold (July 3, 2010); Evan Goldstein (June 18, 2010); Randall Grahm (July 7, 2010); Peter Granoff (July 23, 2010); Connie Green (July 22, 2010); Andy Griffin (July 7, 2010); Tony Gulisano (July 16, 2010); Barbara Haimes (March 26, 2010); Marc Halperin (July 16, 2010); Bruce Hill (April 5, 2010); Gerald Hirigoyen (January 10, 2011); John Hudspeth (July 14, 2010); Todd Humphries (July 19, 2010); Rochelle Huppin

(June 1, 2010); Jeff Jackson (July 28, 2010); Philippe Jeanty (December 17, 2010); Gary Jenanyan (March 18, 2010); Josh Jensen (December 17, 2010); Paul Johnson (August 9, 2010); Michele Anna Jordan (August 24, 2010); Laurence Jossel (July 29, 2010); Barbara Kafka (May 4, 2010); Loretta Keller (June 16, 2010); Thomas Keller (March 9, 2010); Tor Kenward (June 2, 2010); Kelsie Kerr (July 13, 2010); Kristine Kidd (June 24, 2010); David Kinch (May 15, 2010); Kathy King (June 3, 2010); Evan Kleiman (June 24, 2010); Roberta Klugman (April 7, December 14, 2010); Todd Koons (May 20, 2010); Sibella Kraus (May 28, June 18, 2010); Lars Kronmark (September 9, 2010; March 17, 2011); Pat Kuleto (May 27, 2010); Mourad Lahlou (May 20, 2010); Barbara Lazaroff (July 3, 2010); Christopher Lee (October 5, 2010); Bruce LeFavour (July 23, 2010); Bob Long (March 16, 2010); Emily Luchetti (May 25, 2010); Deborah Madison (June 26, 2010); Maggie Mah (July 2, 2010); Bruce Marder (June 24 2010); John Mariani (June 14, 2010); Mas Masumoto (August 25, 2010); Kazuto Matsusaka (July 5, 2010); Marsha McBride (May 19, 2010); Michael McCarty (June 11, 2010); Alice Medrich (June 3, 2010); Danny Meyer (May 3, 2010); Joe Miller (July 29, 2010); Mark Miller (June 17, 2010); Mary Sue Milliken (June 23, 2010); Karen Mitchell (July 20, 2010); Sam Mogannam (July 16, 2010); Margrit Biever Mondavi (July 19, 2010); Michael Mondavi (July 19, 2010); Jean-Pierre Moullé (April 6, 2010); Jim Nassikas (July 14, 2010); Udo Nechutnys (July 28, 2010); Bruce Neyers (July 5, 2010); Drew Nieporent (August 23, 2010); Bill Niman (July 1, 2010); Nancy Oakes (June 15, 2010); Bradley Ogden (July 22, 2010); Alex Ong (July 6, 2010); Philip Paine (July 24, 2010); Catherine Pantsios (June 25, 2010); Russ Parsons (June 28, 2010); Roland Passot (December 15, 2010); Daniel Patterson (May 13, 2010); Cindy Pawlcyn (March 17, 2010); Mark Peel (July 1, 2010); Mai Pham (July 9, 2010); Charles Phan (April 6, 2010); Joseph Phelps (July 23, 2010); Jim Poris (July 12, 2010); Andy Powning (April 7, 2010); Wolfgang Puck (July 27, 2010); René Redzepi (October 4, 2010); Jim Reichardt (July 6, 2010); Ruth Reichl (May 14, 2010); Michel Richard (June 24, 2010); Mary Risley (June 17, 2010); Dru Rivers (July 22, 2010); Judy Rodgers (May 20, 2010); Karola Saekel (April 7, 2010; deceased); Amelia Saltsman (June 29, 2010); Steve Sando (July 19, 2010); Shirley Sarvis (May 26, 2010); Sally Schmitt (July 21, 2010); Josh Schweitzer (July 15, 2010); Amaryll Schwertner (May 19, 2010); John Sedlar (July 30, 2010); Piero Selvaggio (June 25, 2010); Lindsey Shere (July 15, 2010); Nancy Silverton (March 30, 2010); Cass Calder Smith (June 18, 2010); Peggy Smith (June 1, 2010); Annie Somerville (April 1, 2010); Hiro Sone (March 23, 2010); Joachim Splichal (August 27, 2010); Mark Stech-Novak (November 1, 2010); Harvey Steiman (2010); Joy Sterling (July 15, 2010); Brian Streeter (May 27, 2010); Steve Sullivan (April 1, 2010); Alan Tangren (June 4, 2010); David Tanis (June 3, 2010); Staffan Terje (September 15, 2010); Rick Tombari (July 20, 2010); Jeremiah Tower (May 2, 2010); Suzanne Tracht (July 21, 2010); Mike Tuohy (June 16, 2010); Patricia Unterman (June 18, 2010); Sherry Virbila (June 29, 2010); Steve Vranian (June 28, 2010); Doug Washington (June 15, 2010); Alice Waters (May 10, 2010); Don Watson (July 7, 2010); Jonathan Waxman (May 3, 2010); Kathleen Weber (July 28, 2010); Warren Weber (July

1, 2010); Carolyn Wente (2010); Laura Werlin (May 31, 2010); Michael Wild (June 10, 2010); Bill Wilkinson (April 3, 2010; deceased); Denesse Willey (June 29, 2010); Victoria Wise (May 13, 2010); Clark Wolf (April 5, 2010); Diane Worthington (June 4, 2010); Tom Worthington (June 16, 2010); Sherry Yard (July 13, 2010); Hoss Zaré (December 21, 2010).

BOOKS AND ARTICLES

Aidells, Bruce, and Dennis Kelly. *Hot Links and Country Flavors: Sausages in American Regional Cooking.* New York: Alfred A. Knopf, 1990.

———. *Complete Sausage Book: Recipes from America's Premier Sausage Maker.* Berkeley: Ten Speed Press, 2000.

Ash, John. *From the Earth to the Table: John Ash's Wine Country Cuisine.* New York: Dutton, 1995.

Bertolli, Paul. *Cooking by Hand.* New York: Clarkson Potter, 2003.

Bertolli, Paul, with Alice Waters. *Chez Panisse Cooking.* New York: Random House, 1988.

Brennan, Georgeanne, Isaac Cronin, and Charlotte Glenn. *The New American Vegetable Cookbook: The Definitive Guide to America's Exotic and Traditional Vegetables.* Berkeley: Aris Books, 1985.

Brenner, Leslie. *American Appetite: The Coming of Age of a National Cuisine.* New York: Harper Collins, 1999.

Burros, Marian. "California Cuisine: Assessing Its State." *New York Times,* March 3, 1982.

———. "California Cuisine: Fresh and Faddish." *New York Times,* June 20, 1984.

Chenel, Laura, and Linda Siegfried. *Chèvre! The Goat Cheese Cookbook.* Santa Rosa, CA: Pikes Peak Publishing Company, 1983.

Cianciulli, JoAnn. *L.A.'s Original Farmers Market Cookbook.* San Francisco: Chronicle Books, 2009.

Cohen, Amanda. "Girls Can't Cook." *Dirt Candy.* www.dirtcandynyc.com/?p=1888, May 2010.

Cooper, Ann. *"A Woman's Place Is in the Kitchen": The Evolution of Women Chefs.* New York: Van Nostrand, Rhinehold, 1998.

Cooper, Arnie. "Earthly Delights: Cultivating a New Agricultural Revolution. An Interview with Michael Ableman." *Sun Magazine,* June 2003, pp. 4–14.

Cronin, Isaac, Jay Harlow, and Paul Johnson. *The California Seafood Book: A Cook's Guide to the Fish and Shellfish of California, the Pacific Coast and Beyond.* Berkeley: Aris Books, 1983.

David, Elizabeth. *French Country Cooking.* London: Michael Joseph, 1951, 1960.

————. *Italian Food*. London: Macdonald, 1954.

————. *A Book of Mediterranean Food*. London: Penguin, 1955.

————. *French Provincial Cooking*. London: Michael Joseph, 1960.

De Groot, Roy Andries. *Feasts for All Seasons*. New York: Alfred A. Knopf, 1966.

————. *The Auberge of the Flowering Hearth*. New York: Bobbs Merrill, 1973.

Dosti, Rose. *New California Cuisine: Great Recipes from the* Los Angeles Times. Harry N. Abrams, 1986.

Druckman, Charlotte. *Skirt Steak: Women Chefs on Standing the Heat and Staying in the Kitchen*. San Francisco: Chronicle Books, 2012.

Feniger, Susan, and Mary Sue Milliken. *City Cuisine*. New York: William Morrow, 1989.

Fletcher, Janet. *Fresh from the Farmers' Market: Year-Round Recipes for the Pick of the Crop*. San Francisco: Chronicle Books, 1997.

————. "Celebrating the Produce Pioneers." *San Francisco Chronicle*, August 27, 2008.

Fox, Margaret, and John Bear. *Café Beaujolais*. Berkeley: Ten Speed Press, 1984.

Goin, Suzanne. *Sunday Suppers at Lucques*. New York: Alfred A. Knopf, 2005.

Goldstein, Evan. *Perfect Pairings: A Master Sommelier's Practical Advice for Partnering Wine with Food*. Berkeley: University of California Press, 2006.

————. *Daring Pairings: A Master Sommelier Matches Distinctive Wines with Recipes from His Favorite Chefs*. Berkeley: University of California Press, 2010.

Goldstein, Joyce. *The Mediterranean Kitchen*. New York: William Morrow, 1989.

————. *Back to Square One: Old-World Food in a New-World Kitchen*. New York: William Morrow, 1992.

————. *Kitchen Conversations: Robust Recipes and Lessons in Flavor from One of America's Most Innovative Chefs*. New York: William Morrow, 1996.

Green, Connie, and Sarah Scott. *The Wild Table: Seasonal Foraged Food and Recipes*. New York: Viking Studio, 2010.

Harris, L. John. *Foodoodles: From the Museum of Culinary History*. Berkeley: El Leon Literary Arts, 2010.

Hiltzik, Michael. "Growing Pains for a Napa Cultural Center." *Los Angeles Times*, August 9, 2004.

Hirsheimer, Christopher, and Peggy Knickerbocker. *The San Francisco Ferry Plaza Farmers' Market Cookbook: A Comprehensive Guide to Impeccable Produce Plus 130 Seasonal Recipes*. San Francisco: Chronicle Books, 2006.

Jenkins, Kathie. "Toasting the Godfather Who Made L.A. Dining What It Is." *Los Angeles Times*, January 27, 1995.

Johnson, Paul. *Fish Forever: The Definitive Guide to Understanding, Selecting, and Preparing Healthy, Delicious, and Environmentally Sustainable Seafood*. New Jersey: John Wiley and Sons, 2007.

Jordan, Michele Anna. *The New Cook's Tour of Sonoma: 150 Recipes and the Best of the Region's Food and Wine*. Seattle: Sasquatch Books, 2000.

Kamp, David. *The United States of Arugula: How We Became a Gourmet Nation*. New York: Broadway Books, 2006.

Kapitanoff, Nancy. "It Takes 2 Ex-Chicagoans to Give L.A. a Good Mexican Restaurant." *Chicago Tribune*, February 27, 1986.

Keller, Thomas. *The French Laundry Cookbook*. New York: Artisan, 1999.

Knowlton, Andrew. "The 20 Most Important Restaurants in America," *Bon Appetit*. March 2013. www.bonappetit.com/magazine/20-most-important-restaurants-2013.

Kuh, Patric. *The Last Days of Haute Cuisine: America's Culinary Revolution*. New York: Viking Penguin, 2001.

Lahlou, Mourad. *Mourad: New Moroccan*. New York: Artisan Press, 2011.

La Place, Viana, and Evan Kleiman. *Cucina Fresca*. New York: Harper and Row, 1985.

———. *Pasta Fresca*. New York: William Morrow, 1988.

———. *Cucina Rustica*. New York: William Morrow, 1990.

Luchetti, Emily. *Stars Desserts*. New York: Harper Collins, 1991.

———. *Four-Star Desserts*. New York: Harper Collins, 1996.

Lurie, Joshua. "Interview: Chef Jonathan Waxman of Barbuto." *Food GPS*. www.foodgps.com/qa-chef-jonathan-waxman/, March 12, 2012.

Madison, Deborah. *The Greens Cookbook: Extraordinary Vegetarian Cuisine from the Celebrated Restaurant*. New York: Bantam Books, 1987.

———. *The Savory Way*. New York: Bantam Books, 1990.

Mariani, John. *The Four Seasons: A History of America's Premier Restaurant*. New York: Smithmark, 1999.

Masumoto, David Mas. *Epitaph for a Peach: Four Seasons on My Family Farm*. New York: Harper Collins, 1995.

McCarty, Michael. *Michael's Cookbook: The Art of New American Food and Entertaining*. New York: Macmillan, 1989.

McNamee, Thomas. *Alice Waters and Chez Panisse: The Romantic, Impractical, Often Eccentric, Ultimately Brilliant Making of a Food Revolution*. New York: Penguin Books, 2007.

Meyer, Danny. *Setting the Table: The Transforming Power of Hospitality in Business*. New York: Harper Collins, 2006.

Milliken, Mary Sue, and Susan Feniger. *Mesa Mexicana*. New York: William Morrow, 1994.

———. *Cooking with Too Hot Tamales: Recipes and Tips from the Television Food Network's Spiciest Cooking Duo*. New York: William Morrow, 1997.

Mogannam, Sam, and Dabney Gough. *Bi-Rite Market's Eat Good Food: A Grocer's Guide to Shopping, Cooking, and Creating Community through Food*. Berkeley: Ten Speed Press, 2011.

Morse, Kitty. *The California Farm Cookbook*. Gretna, LA: Pelican Publishing Company, 1994.

Muscatine, Doris. *A Cook's Tour of San Francisco: The Best Restaurants and Their Recipes.* New York: Charles Scribners and Sons, 1963.

Nathan, Amy. *Salad.* San Francisco: Chronicle Books, 1985.

Nestle, Marion. "The Slaughterhouse Problem: Is a Resolution in Sight?" *Food Politics* (blog). www.foodpolitics.com/2010/05/the-slaughterhouse-problem-is-a-resolution-in-sight/, May 25, 2010.

Olney, Richard. *The French Menu Cookbook.* Boston: David Godine, 1970.

———. *Simple French Food.* New York: Atheneum, 1974.

Parsons, Russ. "Napa's Copia Closes." *Los Angeles Times*, December 3, 2008.

Patterson, Daniel. "To the Moon, Alice?" *New York Times Magazine*, November 6, 2005.

Pawlcyn, Cindy. *Fog City Diner Cookbook.* Berkeley: Ten Speed Press, 1993.

———. *Mustards Grill Napa Valley Cookbook.* Berkeley: Ten Speed Press, 2001.

Pham, Mai. *The Best of Vietnamese and Thai Cooking: Favorite Recipes from Lemon Grass Restaurant and Cafes.* Rocklin, CA: Prima Publishing, 1995.

———. *The Pleasures of the Vietnamese Table: Recipes and Reminiscences from Vietnam's Best Market Kitchens, Street Cafés, and Home Cooks.* New York: Harper Collins, 2001.

Pinney, Thomas. *A History of Wine in America.* Vol. 2, *From Prohibition to the Present.* Berkeley: University of California Press, 2007.

Puck, Wolfgang. *Modern French Cooking for the American Kitchen: Recipes from the Cuisine of Ma Maison.* New York: Houghton Mifflin, 1981.

———. *The Wolfgang Puck Cookbook: Recipes from Spago, Chinois and Points East and West.* New York: Random House, 1986.

———. *Adventures in the Kitchen: 175 New Recipes from Spago, Chinois on Main, Postrio and Eureka.* New York: Random House, 1991.

Reardon, Joan. *M.F.K. Fisher, Julia Child and Alice Waters: Celebrating the Pleasures of the Table.* New York: Harmony Books, 1994.

Reichl, Ruth. "Gardener with a Greens Thumb." *Los Angeles Times*, January 19, 1986.

———. "How to Build an Empire: L.A.'s Bruce Marder." *Los Angeles Times*, December 4, 1988.

———. "The Legendary Bertranou: Hail to the Chef." *Los Angeles Times*, February 20, 1990.

———. *Tender at the Bone: Growing Up at the Table.* New York: Random House, 1998.

———. *Comfort Me with Apples: More Adventures at the Table.* New York: Random House, 2001.

Reingold, Carmel Berman. *California Cuisine.* New York: Avon Books, 1983.

Richard, Michel. *Home Cooking with a French Accent.* New York: William Morrow, 1993.

Roberts, Michael. *Secret Ingredients.* New York: Bantam Books, 1988.

———. *What's for Dinner?* New York: William Morrow, 1993.

Robertson, Laurel, Carol Flinders, and Bronwen Godfrey. *Laurel's Kitchen: A Handbook for Vegetarian Cookery and Nutrition*. Berkeley: Nilgiri Press, 1976.

Rodgers, Judy. *The Zuni Café Cookbook*. New York: W. W. Norton, 2002.

Saltsman, Amelia. *The Santa Monica Farmers' Market Cookbook: Seasonal Foods, Simple Recipes, and Stories from the Market and Farm*. Santa Monica, CA: Blenheim Press, 2002.

Shere, Lindsey Remolif. *Chez Panisse Desserts*. New York: Random House, 1985.

Silverton, Nancy. *Desserts*. New York: Harper and Row, 1986.

Smith, Andrew F. *Eating History: Thirty Turning Points in the Making of American Cuisine*. New York: Columbia University Press, 2009.

Sokolov, Raymond. "Running a Danny Meyer Marathon." *Wall Street Journal*, January 9, 2010.

Somerville, Annie. *Fields of Greens: New Vegetarian Recipes from the Celebrated Greens Restaurant*. New York: Bantam Books, 1993.

Sone, Hiro, and Lissa Doumani. *Terra: Cooking from the Heart of the Napa Valley*. Berkeley: Ten Speed Press, 2000.

Starr, Kevin. *Coast of Dreams: California on the Edge, 1990–2003*. New York: Vintage Books, 2004.

Steinberger, Michael. *Au Revoir to All That: Food, Wine, and the End of France*. New York: Bloomsbury, 2009.

Suter, Lesley Bargar. "We're Up to Our Biscuits in Biscuits." *Los Angeles Magazine*, March 4, 2013.

Sydney, Russell. *A History of the Farmers' Markets Movement in California*. 2005. [self-published]

Tanis, David. *A Platter of Figs and Other Recipes*. New York: Artisan Books, 2008.

———. *Heart of the Artichoke and Other Kitchen Journeys*. New York: Artisan Books, 2010.

Teller, Betty. "Hog Island Oysters Bring Brine to Wine Country." InsideNapaValley.com, February 16, 2010.

Tower, Jeremiah. *New American Classics*. New York: Harper and Row, 1986.

———. *California Dish: What I Saw (and Cooked) at the American Culinary Revolution*. New York: Free Press, 2003.

Tropp, Barbara. *China Moon Cookbook*. New York: Workman Books, 1992.

Waters, Alice. *The Chez Panisse Menu Cookbook*. New York: Random House, 1982.

———. *Chez Panisse Vegetables*. New York: Harper Collins, 1996.

———. *Chez Panisse Café Cookbook*. New York: Harper Collins, 1999.

———. *Chez Panisse Fruit*. New York: Harper Collins, 2002.

Waters, Alice, Patricia Curtan, and Martine Labro. *Chez Panisse Pasta, Pizza and Calzone*. New York: Random House, 1984.

Waxman, Jonathan. *A Great American Cook: Recipes from the Home Kitchen of One of Our Most Influential Chefs*. New York: Houghton Mifflin Harcourt. 2007.

Werlin, Laura. *The New American Cheese: Profiles of America's Greatest Cheesemakers and Recipes for Cooking with Cheese*. New York: Stewart, Tabori and Chang, 2000.

Wild, Michael. *Bay Wolf Restaurant Cookbook*. Berkeley: Ten Speed Press, 2001.

Wise, Victoria. *American Charcuterie: Recipes from Pig-by-the-Tail*. New York: Viking Penguin, 1986.

Wollman, Cynthia. "At Della Fattoria, Bread Making Is an Art Form." *San Francisco Chronicle*, February 28, 2003.

Worthington, Diane Rossen. *The Cuisine of California*. Los Angeles: Jeremy P. Tarcher, 1983.

———. *The California Cook: Casually Elegant Recipes with Exhilarating Taste*. New York: Bantam Books, 1994.

Ableman, Michael, 309
Académie du Vin (Paris), 51, 71
Acme Bread Company, 252–54, 256, 257
Acquerello, 91
A-Frame, 307
agriculture, 49–50. *See also* produce; *specific farms and farmers*
Aidells, Bruce, 142, 164, 226, 244–46
AIWF (American Institute of Wine and Food), 200, 264, 283–86, 290
Alan Chadwick Garden, 193, 217
Alemany farmers' market, 210
Alexander, Max, 15
Alexis, 18
Alfred's, 18
Alibi Room, 307
Allen, Helen, 7
American Farm, American Food conference, 284
American Harvest workshops, 239–40
American Institute of Wine and Food (AIWF), 200, 264, 283–86, 290
An American Place, 7
Aminifard, Mosen, 35
Andante, 8
Andrews, Colman, 18–19, 124, 134, 264–65
Angeli Caffe, 61, 89, 94–95, 111, 305; design, 154, 158. *See also* Kleiman, Evan
Angeli Mare, 89, 95–96
Animal, 300, 307, 310
Animal Liberation (Singer), 226
Apple Farm, 5
Appleman, Nate, 304
Aqua, 127, 199, 218, 288
Aratow, Paul, 177

Arbulo, Pepette, 99, 100
Arcadia, 89
Armbruster, Steve, 245
Arons, Andy, 239
artisanal foods, 6, 239–40, 312. *See also* producers and purveyors; *specific types of foods*
Artisan Bakers, 252
arugula, 1, 16, 37, 103, 193, 196; pioneering growers, 199, 207, 216, 217, 218–19, 220
Aseged, Eskender, 307
Ash, John, 193, 269, 275–77, 288
Asher, Gerald, 41, 262, 270, 313
Asian foods and flavors, 36, 80, 115–17; Asian fusion, 124, 126–29
Atelier Crenn, 97
Auberge du Soleil, 48–49, 218, 270
Auberge of the Flowering Hearth (De Groot), 16, 92
Auberge of the Flowering Hearth (restaurant), 92
autodidacticism, vii, ix, 47–48, 62; self-taught chefs, 62, 63–69, 76, 301
Avec, 299
Avedisian, Elizabeth and Sahag, 246
Avery, Laura, 211, 212–13
Aziza, 36, 143, *209 fig*, 314. *See also* Lahlou, Mourad

Bäco Mercat, 308
bakeries. *See* bread
Baker's Dozen, 255
Balboa Café, 32, 179
Banchet, Jean, 135
Barber, Dan, 145, 309–10
Barker, Ali, 61

Bar Pintxo, 316

Barrera, Ruben, 252

Bastianich, Lidia, 89, 93, 115

Bates, Caroline, 17–18

Bauer, Michael, 89

Baugher, Eric, 294

Baum, Joe, 109, 132

Bay Village Breads, 252

Bay Wolf, 27, 160, 197, 226, 254; purveyors, 143, 189, 226, 235, 245. *See also* Wild, Michael

Beacon, 80

Beard, James, 65, 92, 132, 179, 244, 279, 284

Beard awards, ix, 42, 270, 304, 315

Beccio, Greg, 220–22

Becerra, Octavio, 67, 195–96, 315

Beck, Simone, 273

Beckerman, Leo, 307

Beggar's Banquet, 189

Bellwether Farms, 6, 8, 229, 239, 247–50

Benihana, 109–10

Bennion, Dave, 293

Benson, James, 35

Bergeron, Vic, 19, 110

Beringer Vineyards, 282–83

Berkeley Bowl, 191

Berkeley Wine and Food Society, 272–73

Bernard's, 21

Bernstein, Arlene and Michael, 265

Bertolli, Paul, 2, 112–14, 240, *241 fig*, 310

Bertranou, Jean, 21, 52, 111, 176, 196, 224–25. *See also* L'Ermitage

Betelnut, 143, 146, 147–48

Bette's Oceanview Diner, 91, 250

Bianchi Dairy, 249

Biba restaurant, 91

Bice, Jennifer Lynn, 8, 247

Biever, Margrit (later Mondavi), 200, 274, 286

Big 4 Restaurant, 91

Bijan, Donia, 91

Bi-Rite Market, 310

Biscuits and Blues, 91

Bistro de Paris, 176

Bistro Don Giovanni, 91

Bistro Jeanty, 143

Bistro Roti, 230, 279

Bix, 107, 279, 288

Bizou, 165, 183, 243. *See also* Keller, Loretta

Blanchet, Michel, 21, 80

Bloom, Evan, 307

Blue Fox, 18, 155

Blue Hill at Stone Barns, 309–10. *See also* Barber, Dan

Blue Nile, 151

BN Ranch, 229

Bocuse, Paul, 20, 21, 23, 81, 135, 275; Restaurant Bocuse, 51

Bocuse d'Or, 135

Bocuse restaurant (CIA), 308

Bodega Artisan Cheese, 247

Bon Appétit, 27, 131, 299–300

Boni, Ada, 16, 92

Bonny Doon, 269, 296–97

Book of Mediterranean Food (David), 16

Boonville Hotel, 4

Border Grill, 110, 118, 120, 146, 158, 196, 233, 305. *See also* Feniger, Susan; Milliken, Mary Sue

Bouchon Beverly Hills, 143

Boudin bakery, 252

Boulevard, 103, 145, 243; design, 166, 171, 172; service and atmosphere, 184, 185–86. *See also* Oakes, Nancy

Bouley, 307

Bourdain, Anthony, 303–4

"boy food," 96, 97

Braker, Flo, 255

Brandel, Catherine, 43, 90, 226, 232–33, 274

Brandt, Norbert, 30

Bras, Michel, 38

bread, 62, 252–58

Breads of France (Clayton), 257

Brennan, Georgeanne, 6, 187. *See also* Le Marché Seeds

Brennan, Michael, 172

Breuer, Anne, *125 fig*. *See also* Gingrass, Anne

Bridges, 91

Brinkley, Jimmy, 52, 176

Brioza, Stuart, 307

Briwa, Bill, 118, 145, 166, 214

Broadway Terrace, 240

Brock, Sean, 299

Broulard, Joseph, 193

Brown, Ed, 19

Brown, Edward Espe, 43

Brown, Jerry, 40, 208

Brown, Lynn, 6, 24, 144, 217–19. *See also* Forni-Brown Gardens

Brown Derby, 18, 173–74

Brucker, Wendy, 57, 71–73, 90

Buchanan, Jacqueline, 90

Buckeye Road House, 279

Budrick, Jerry, 58, 265, 266

Burros, Marian, 21, 23, 28, 30, 54

Buscemi, Paul, 15

Butler's, 90

Café Beaujolais, 65–66, 192, 226, 228. *See also* Fox, Margaret

Cafe Four Oaks, 19

Cafe Katsu, 315

Café Rouge, 152, 233

Café Royale, 150

Caffe Trieste, 182

Caggiano, Biba, 91

Cakebread, Dolores and Jack (Cakebread Cellars), 239–40, 275, 277, 297

Calcagno, Vince, 182

Calera, 263, 269, 271, 297

California Café, 35

The California Cook (Worthington), 30–31

California cuisine, 2–3, 15–38; Alice Waters on, 43; celebrity chefs, 31–32; emergence and naming of, 9–13, 27–32, 177; hallmarks of, 2–3, 5–6, 8–9, 30–31; home cooks and, 3, 30; impact and future of, 319–20; mass-market versions of, 34–36

California Culinary Academy, 32, 71–72, 85–88, 163

California Olive Oil Council, 260–61

California Organic Food Act, 41

California Pizza Kitchen, 35

California Polytechnic University (Pomona), 70

California Street Cooking School, ix

California Vegetable Specialties, 203–4

California wines. *See* wine

Callahan, Cindy, 6, 8, 229, 239, 247–50

Callahan, Liam, 6, 8, 239, 247, 248–50

Calland, Pippa, 305

Camino, 231

Campanile, 89, 256, 257; design, 158, 159, 163, 169; ingredients and purveyors, 144, 211; service and atmosphere, 184. *See also* Peel, Mark; Silverton, Nancy

Campton Place, 49, 160, 206, 299, 307; purveyors, 218

Cannard, Bob, Jr., 6, 195

Cannard, Bob, Sr., 195, 287

Carlisle, Danielle, 86

Carmichael, Dexter, 207–8

Carpenter, Gary, 231

Carson, Rachel, 41

Carucci, Linda, 85–86, 88

casual dining, 183–86

Celebrate the Craft, 136

celebrity chefs, 31–32, 63, 302

Celestino, 89

Centeno, Josef, 308

Center for Culinary Innovation, 314

Center for Urban Education about Sustainable Agriculture (CUESA), 211

Chadwick Garden, 193, 217

Chalone Vineyards, 269, 292, 297. *See also* Graff, Richard

Chang, David, 13, 303–4

Charbonneau, Regina, 91

charcuterie and *salumi*, 112, 114, 174, 242, 300

Charlie Trotter's, 307

Chasen's, 18, 19, 89, 155

Chassereau, Jean-Luc, 86

Chateau Souverain, 91, 280

Chatham Hook and Line Association, 236

Chave, Jean-Louis, 294

Chaya Brasserie, 124, 127

Checkers, 108

cheese and cheesemakers, 6–8, 81, 240, 246–52. *See also* Bellwether Farms; Chenel, Laura

Cheese Board, 41, 240, 242, 244, 246, 252

chefs: as celebrities, 31–32, 63, 302; collaborative working styles, 98, 102–3, 105, 106–8; self-taught, 62, 63–69, 76, 301. *See also* professional training; women chefs; *specific chefs by name*

Chefs Collaborative, 311

Chefwear, 167–68

Chego, 307

Chenel, Laura, 6–8, 81, 141, 239, 247, 276–77; customers, 7–8, 81, 143, 276–77, 280; impact of, 8, 87, 246

Chez Gus, 182

Chez Panisse, 41, 42–43, 57, 140, 197;

Chez Panisse *(continued)*
and "California cuisine" label, 27; design
and equipment, 160, 162, 177, 182–83;
longevity of, 96, 303; wines at, 265–66, 267,
268 fig, 295 fig. See also Waters, Alice
Chez Panisse Café, ix, 28; author at, ix, 35, 42,
62, 143; design, 155, 162; food and menus,
7, *29 fig,* 35, 143, 182, 183, 246; staffers, 270;
wood-burning oven, 182–83
Chez Panisse Desserts (Shere), 91
Chez Panisse food and menus, 31, 111, 246, *268
fig, 295 fig;* bread, 253–54; daily menus, 130,
132, 134; downstairs vs. upstairs, 28; early
years, 19, 27, 244; grilling, 177; ingredients
and purveyors focus, 37, 42–43; Italian
influences, 112, 117; menu writing, 137–38,
143, 152, 266; viewed as conservative, 58–
59, 122, 134. *See also* Chez Panisse Café
Chez Panisse Foundation, 42
Chez Panisse purveyors: bread, 254; cheese,
7, 246; meat and poultry, 142, 143, 226–27,
228, 230, 231, 233, 247–48; produce, 42–43,
189, 192–93, 194–95, 197, 215–16, 220, 298,
309; restaurant gardens and farm, 194, 195,
217; seafood, 234, 238
Chez Panisse staff: ex-staff as artisanal producers, 240, 242–43, 250–54; ex-staff at other
restaurants, 15, 50, 113, 152, 179; self-taught
vs. professionally trained cooks, 62, 66–67,
79, 105–6; women cooks, 85, 90, 91–93,
98, 103, 303; working styles and kitchen
organization, 84, 85, 92–93, 98, 102–3, 106,
108. *See also* Goldstein, Joyce; Miller, Mark;
Moullé, Jean-Pierre; Rodgers, Judy; Shere,
Lindsey; Tower, Jeremiah; Waters, Alice;
other specific individuals
Chiang, Cecilia, 110
Chianti, 89
Chiarello, Michael, 70, 112, 130, 161–62, 223,
279
Child, Julia, 16, 119, 274, 275, 279; and
AIWF, 283, 285–86; and Copia, 287; *The
French Chef,* 131; *Mastering the Art of French
Cooking,* 17; on San Francisco cooking, 54
China Moon, 9, 66, 117, 142, 163, 314
Chino, Tom (Chino Farms), 42–43, 120, 195,
196–97, 198, 208
Chinois on Main, 80, 89, 124, 168, 180; design,

39, 162; food and menus, 23, 31, 39, 54, 124,
126 fig
chocolate, 259
Choi, Roy, 307, 316
Christian, Vance, 52
Christian Brothers, 290–91
CIA. *See* Culinary Institute of America
Ciccarone-Nehls, Gloria, 70, 91
Cindy's Backstreet Kitchen, 217, 278, 280
Citarella, 225, 239
Citizen Cake, 152
Citronelle, 55
Citrus, 55–56, 57, 89, 111, 123, 163, 167. *See also*
Richard, Michel
City Café, 90, 119, 156
City Restaurant, 50, 57, 71; design, 154, 156,
158, 159; food and menus, 9, 72, 118, 119,
121 fig
Claiborne, Craig, 16
Clayton, Bernard, 257
Clement, Louise, 160
Coach House, 179
Coast of Dreams (Starr), 10
Cocolat, 10, 242, 249. *See also* Medrich, Alice
Cohen, Amanda, 304
Coi, 307, 309, 310–11. *See also* Patterson,
Daniel
Coil, Dorothy, 193–94
Coke, Dale (Coke Farm), 205–6, 220, 221
collaborative restaurant kitchens, 98, 102–3,
105, 106–8
Collins, Joan, 23
Collins, Rich, 6, 203–4
Columbus Salame, 243
Community Alliance with Family Farmers, 311
Conley, Sue, 240, 246–47, 250–52
Connoisseur Wine Imports, 265
continental restaurants, 18–20, 82–83, 155
cookbooks, 16–17, 43–44. *See also specific
authors and titles*
Cooking by Hand (Bertolli), 114
cooking classes. *See* education
cooking schools. *See* professional training;
specific schools
Cooks Company, 208
Cool, Bob, 139
Cool, Jesse, 67, 138–40, 303, 304. *See also* Flea
Street Café; Late for the Train

Cooper, Arnie, 309

Coosemans Specialty Produce, 204

Copia, 201, 264, 286–87, 289, 290

Cordon Bleu, 51, 71, 256–57, 279, 302

Cornell School of Hotel Administration, 52, 71, 286

Corso, 73

Corti, Darrell, 18, 214, 239, 260, 282

Corum, Vance, 212

Cost, Bruce, 117

Costa, Filippo, 39

Courtine, Robert, 92

Cowgirl Creamery, 240, 246–47, 250

Coyote Cafe, 61

CPK (California Pizza Kitchen), 35

Crawford, Andrea, 195, 196

Crawford, Heidi, 196

Crenn, Dominique, 97, 304

Cronin, Isaac, 202

Cross, Billy, 273–74

Crotti, Agostino, 182

Cucina Fresca (Kleiman), 94

Cucina Rustica (Kleiman and La Place), 94

CUESA (Center for Urban Education about Sustainable Agriculture), 211

The Cuisine of California (Worthington), 30

Culinary Institute of America, 282, 286, 302

Culinary Institute of America (Hyde Park, New York), 31–32, 70, 85, 112, 134–35, 292, 299, 308

Culinary Institute of America, St. Helena (Greystone), 70, 86, 87, 172–73, 264, 277, 289, 290–92, 313–14

culinary training. *See* professional training

Cunningham, Marion, 65, 99, 194, 255

Curtan, Patricia, 90, 253

Cybulski, Mike, 230

Cypress Club, 218

Cypress Grove, 8

D'Agostini Winery, 271

daily and seasonal foods and menus, 77–78, 79, 102–3, 132–37

Dal Porto, Frank (Dal Porto Ranch), 229, 265

Dame, Fred, 269

Daniel, 308

Danko, Gary, 31–32, 70, 85, 184, 282

Da Vero, 260

David, Elizabeth, 16, 92, 93, 179, 253, 257

David, Narsai, 11, 19, 239, 272. *See also* Narsai's; Pot Luck

David Bruce Winery, 263

Davidson, Alan, 284

Dawson, Jeff, 6, 187, 201, 287–88

De Groot, Roy Andries, 16, 92

Delfina, 97, 307

Della Fattoria, 252, 255–56

Dellar, Michael, 57

Delmonico's, 137

Del Monte Foods, 276

Deluca, Frank, 239

Deluca, Jack, 239

De Maat, Walter, 201

Demolition Desserts (Falkner), 97

Denevan, Bill, 309

Denevan, Jim, 309

Derven, Daphne, 285, 286–87, 290

Des Jardins, Traci, 74, 90, 127, 199, 303, 304, 309

DeVries, Lawrence, 178

Dexter, Diane, 15, 90, 91, 240, 252

Dexter, Perry, 252

Dice, Evelyn, 267

Dickson, Dale, 202

Dickson, Stuart, 202, 288

Diet for a Small Planet (Lappé), 41

Dipti Nivas, 44

Direct Marketing Act, 208, 212, 213

Dirt Candy, 304

Di Vecchio, Jerry, 17, 174

Dodge, Jim, 258

Domaine Chandon, 143, 175, 218, 278, 280, 282

Donnelly, Hallie, 142

Dotolo, Vinny, 307

Doumani, Carl, 81

Doumani, Lissa, 36, 80–82. *See also* Terra

Draper, Paul, 132, 261, 269, 292–96

Drescher, Greg, 284–85, 290

Druckman, Charlotte, 304

Duckhorn, Dan (Duckhorn Vineyards), 269, 271, 292

Dumas Père cooking school, 70

Dwan, Lois, 224

Earthbound Farms, 221

Eater blog, 304

Eccolo, 97

eclectic menus, 9, 117–22, 316
École Hôtelière (Paris), 51, 71
École Hôtelière Tsuji (Osaka), 80–81, 278
École Jean Ferrandi, 71
Eddie Rickenbacker's, 71, 72
Edible Schoolyard Project, 42
education, 222–23; AIWF, 200, 264, 283–86,
290; Chez Panisse Foundation/Edible
Schoolyard, 42; CIA St. Helena programs,
291–93; Copia, 201, 264, 286–87, 289, 290;
food and wine education, 271, 272–77, 282–
83; Great Chefs program, 3, 239, 273–74;
online videos, 302. *See also* professional
training
Ehman, Bart, 226
Eichorn, David, 92
El Bulli, 108, 307
Eleven Madison Park, 299
Elka, 89, 90, 127
English Bread and Yeast Cookery (David), 253,
257
Epic Roasthouse, 171, 172
Ernie's, 18, 19, 25, 71, 72, 131, 155, 163, 231
Escoffier, Georges Auguste, 11, 62
Escoffier Room, 308
ethnic and regional cooking, 8–9, 67–69,
109–12, 114–17, 314–16
Evans, Bill, 135
Evans, David, 229
Evers, Ridgely, 260

Faber, Phyllis, 246
Fabre, Axel, 274
The Fabrication of Farmstead Goat Cheese (Le
Jaouen), 7
Fada, Odette, 304
Fairchild, Barbara, 27, 28
Fairview Gardens, 309
Falkner, Elizabeth, 90, 97, 152
Farallon, 165, 171
farmers' markets, 208, 210–14, 222–23
Farm-Restaurant Project, 197–201, 203, 205,
207
farm-to-table. *See* produce; producers and
purveyors
Felidia, 89
Fellows, Jim, 193
Feniger, Susan, 89, 90, 118–20, 146, 158, 303,

304; on Ma Maison, 156; and purveyors, 196,
214, 239; training, 70. *See also* Border Grill;
City Restaurant
Ferry, Gerard, 21
Ferry, Virginie, 21
Ferry Plaza farmers' market, 45, 200, 210–11,
213, 307
Fetzer, Jim, 277
Fetzer Vineyards, 292; Valley Oaks Food and
Wine Center, 201, 275, 277, 288–89
Field, Carol, 248, 255
Finger, John, 6, 237–38, 239
fish and seafood purveyors, 234–39. *See also*
Monterey Fish Company
Fisher, M. F. K., 16
Flax, Larry, 35
Flay, Bobby, 167
Flea Street Café, 96, 139–40, 193. *See also*
Cool, Jesse
Fletcher, Doug, 297–98
Fletcher, Janet, 67, 272
Flinders, Carol, 44
Flying Foods, 239
Fly Trap, 68
Fog City Diner, 160, 172, 218, 279
Food and Water Watch, 311
Food & Wine, 131
Food Arts, 168
food of dreams, 11, 123–24, 315
food of memory, 11, 94, 109, 111, 315
food television, 131, 301–2
food trucks, 306, 307
food writing, 16–18, 131. *See also* cookbooks;
specific authors, titles, and periodicals
foraging, 48, 311
Forgione, Larry, 7, 284
Forni, Peter, 25, 217, 218
Forni-Brown Gardens, 25, 144, 218–19, 278, 280
Four Seasons, 28, 132, 140
464 Magnolia, 256, 257
Fournou's Ovens, 269
Fourth Street Grill, 59, *60 fig*, 112–13, 162, 177,
178, 197
Fox, Margaret, 64–66, 192, 228, 282
Fra' Mani, 114, 240
Frances, 304
Franier, Barbara, 252
Franier, Tom, 252

Frank, Ken, 52, 67, 176, 289

Frank's Fresh Foods, 218

Franz, Mark, 34, 106–7, 131, 163–64, 171, 175, 178–79

Freeman, Andrew, 39, 40

Freeman, Robert, 35

The French Chef, 131

French cooking: nouvelle cuisine, 20–21, 23, 25, 27; regional, 114–15

French Laundry (Keller), 5, 108, 163; purveyors, 49, 143, 217, 243, 248, 256

French Laundry (Schmitt), 3–5, 278; daily menu, 130, 132, *133 fig*

French Pastry Shop (Santa Fe), 55

French Provincial Cooking (David), 16

Fringale, 79

Fromagerie Jean d'Alos, 251

Fujimoto, Bill, 6, 25, 189–90, 191, 210, 211, 216. *See also* Monterey Market

Fujimoto, Ken, 190

Full Belly Farm, 139, 202, 309

Fulton Valley Farms, 233

fusion cooking, 31, 118, 122–29, 315

Fussell, Betty, 285

Gabiati, Ernie, 245

Gabriella Café, 309

Gage, Fran, 255

Gagnaire, Pierre, 38

The Galloping Gourmet, 131

Gallo Salame, 243, 245

gardens. *See* produce

Gardner, Rachel, 90

Gates, David, 294

Gault-Millau guides, 20, 264

Gehry, Frank, 156, 158

Giacomini, Bob, 239

Giacomini, Dean, 239

Gilmore, Elka, 89, 90, 93, 127

Ginger Island, 117

Gingrass, Anne, 70, 103, 118, *125 fig*, 145, *170 fig*, 238

Gingrass, David, 35, 70, 118, *170 fig*

"girl food," 93–94, 96–97

Glenn, Charlotte, 201–3. *See also* Le Marché Seeds

goat cheese, 6–8, 22, 37, 81, 103. *See also* Chenel, Laura

Godfrey, Bronwen, 44

Goin, Suzanne, 13, 54, 67, 89, 152, 214, 303, 304, 315. *See also* Lucques

Goines, David, 91–92

Gold, Jonathan, 96, 306, 314, 316

Golden Door Spa, 194

Goldstein, Evan, 137, 143, 269, 270–72, 273, 292

Goldstein, Joyce, ix, 16, 38, 64; at Chez Panisse Café, ix, 35, 42, 62; *San Francisco Chronicle* column, 89; and Women Chefs and Restaurateurs, ix, 93. *See also* Square One

Goldstein, Michael, 256

Good Earth, 139

Good Food radio program, 96, 152

Good Humus Produce, 202

Gotti, Roland, 163

Gotti, Victor, 163

Gourmet Ghetto (Berkeley), 41, 240, 242–43, 244–45

Gourmet magazine, 17, 119, 131

Grace Baking Company, 252

Graff, Richard, 261, 269, 284, 297. *See also* Chalone Vineyards

Grahm, Randall, 55, 269, 296–97

Granoff, Peter, 313

Great Chefs program, 3, 239, 273–74

Green, Connie, 48–49, 188, 278, 311

Green and Red Vineyard, 267

Green Gulch Farm, 44, 47, 49, 143, 193

GreenLeaf Produce, 6, 37, 187, 205–8, 216, 220, 221

Greens Restaurant, 44–47, *46 fig*, 91, 96, 193–94, 197, 200, 269

Gresham, Suzette, 71, 91, 303, 304

Griffin, Andy, 144, 149, 187, 222, 309, 313; at Hudspeth Farm, 194, 195, 222; at Riverside Farms, 220–22; at Star Route Farms, 197, 200, 215, 216–17

grilling, 3, 9, 31, 174–80. *See also* Fourth Street Grill; Santa Fe Bar and Grill

Grill Room, 28

Grimmway Farms, 199

Growers Express, 221

Gruppo Ristoratori Italiani, 115

Guérard, Michel, 20, 274

Guernsey, Tom, 58

Gulisano, Tony, 9, 180
Gurrera, Joe, 225, 239

Haberger, Mark, 280
Haimes, Barbara, 15, 40, 64, 66, 90, 97
Halperin, Marc, 314–15
Hamilton, Gabrielle, 304
Harmon, Julee, 239
Harvard School of Public Health, 292
Hatfield, Karen (Hatfield's), 305
Hayes Street Grill, 61, 90, 96, 159, 162, 197;
    food at, 35, 117; and Monterey Fish, 235
Hearon, Reed, 160, 161, 299
Heart of the City farmers' market, 210
Heaven's Dog, 150
Heitz, Joe (Heitz Cellars), 261, 263
Higgins, Bill, 279
Hill, Bruce, 107, 127–29, 180
Hirigoyen, Gerald, 78–80
Hoffman, Bud (Hoffman Game Birds), 37, 141,
    152, 233
Hog Island Oyster Company, 237–38, 239
Hom, Ken, 72, 87, 164
home cooking, 3, 30
Hooker, Alan, 19
Howard, Josefina, 89
Hudspeth, John, 194, 217
Hudspeth Farm, 143, 194–95, 215, 222
Humm, Daniel, 299
Humphries, Todd, 49, 70, 307
Hunga Dunga Tribe, 205
Huppin, Rochelle, 167–68
Husk, 299
Huttenback, Robert, 283

Il Fornaio, 288
Incanto, 310
ingredients, 6–7, 308–11; Alice Waters's influ-
    ence, 43; as California cuisine hallmark, 3,
    30; foraging, 48, 311; listed on restaurant
    menus, 137–38; local sourcing, 3, 187–93,
    224–25; Northern California focus on, 39,
    40, 54, 317. See also produce; producers and
    purveyors
Innovations in Food, 177
Inn Season, 234, 240
International Culinary School, Art Institute of
    California, 85, 88

International Shellfish Enterprises, 237
Iron Chef, 165
Italian Food (David), 16
Italian food and restaurants, 111–12, 115

Jack's, 18, 159
Jackson, Jeff, 57, 70, 134–36, 197, 309
Jackson, Jess, 289
Jacoupy, Bernard, 21
Jaeger, Lila, 260, 283, 284
James, Michael, 273–74
James Beard Foundation awards, ix, 42, 270,
    304, 315
Jar, 143, 305
Jardinière, 143, 184
Jeanty, Philippe, 218, 278
Jenanyan, Gary, 3, 47, 239, 274
Jensen, Josh, 261, 263, 269, 271, 297
Joe's Restaurant, 315–16
John Ash & Co., 193, 269, 276–77. See also
    Ash, John
Johnson, Hugh, 270
Johnson, Paul, 25, 234–36, 318
Johnson & Wales University, 70, 282
Jordan, Michele Anna, 174
Jorin, Robert, 86
Joseph Phelps Vineyards, 264–67
Josie, 305
Journal of Gastronomy, 284
Joy of Cooking (Rombauer), 16
Julia's Kitchen, 287

Kafka, Barbara, 141
Kamman, Madeleine, 282
Kapur, Ravi, 103
Kasbah, 36–37
Katz, Albert, 240, 261
Katzen, Mollie, 44
Kaye, Danny, 284
Keehn, Mary, 8
Keena, Stan, 45
Keller, Hubert, 25, 76, 93
Keller, Loretta, 34, 67, 143, 303, 304, 312; on
    open kitchens, 165; at Stars, 34, 93, 228
Keller, Thomas, 3, 5, 10, 49, 108, 153, 163, 256.
    See also French Laundry (Keller)
Kelly, Melissa, 299
Kempster, Mike, 174

Kendall-Jackson Food and Wine Center, 289

Kenter Canyon Farms, 196, 213

Kenward, Tor, 282–83, 284

Kerr, Graham, 131

Kerr, Kelsie, 102, 103

Kidd, Kristine, 159

Killeen, Johanne, 93

Kimball, Charlotte (formerly Glenn), 201–3

Kinch, David, 38, 70, 138, 152, 231, 309, 314, 319. *See also* Manresa

King, Kathy, 166, 184, 185–86

King, Tom, 309

Kitchen Door, 307

Kleiman, Evan, 67, 89, 94–96, 111, 152, 214, 239, 305. *See also* Angeli Caffe

Klein, Bob and Maggie, 113. *See also* Oliveto

Klugman, Roberta, 286

Knowlton, Andrew, 299–300

Kobayashi, Masataka, 48–49, 76, 218, 270

Kogi BBQ-To-Go, 307, 316

Kongsgaard, John, 297

Koons, Todd, 217, 220–22

Krahling, Heidi, 71, 90

Krankl, Manfred, 184, 258

Krasinsky, Nicole, 307

Kraus, Sibella, 6, 195, 197–98, 200, 215, 217, 220, 311–12; Farm-Restaurant Project, 197–201, 203, 205, 207; and Ferry Plaza farmers' market, 211; at GreenLeaf Produce, 207–8, 216

Krause, Richard, 124

Kroc, Ray, 10

Kroening, Bette, 91

Kronmark, Lars, 86, 87–88

Krupnick, Wendy, 193

Kuhn, Jesse, 37

Kuleto, Pat, 155, 164–65, 169, 171–72

Kuleto's, 171, 288

Kump, Chris, 65–66, 228. *See also* Café Beaujolais

La Bourgogne, 18, 19, 266

La Brea Bakery, 240, 257–58

La Chaumière, 111

La Cocina, 312

Lacombe, Jean-Paul, 76

La Côte Basque, 308

LaDou, Ed, 35

La Folie, 76, 143

La Fonda del Sol, 109

La Grange, 193

Lahlou, Mourad, 2, 36–38, 67, 143, 152–53, 309. *See also* Aziza

Lam, Noreen, 93, 179, 180

Langham Hotel, 308

Lanzone, Modesto, 132

La Place, Viana, 94

Lappé, Frances Moore, 41

Lark Creek Inn, 160, 167, 183, 243, 288. *See also* Ogden, Bradley

La Seine, 176

LA Specialty Produce, 204, 208

Lasserre, René, 51

Late for the Train, 139, 193

La Toque, 289

Laurel's Kitchen (Robertson, Flinders, and Godrey), 43–44, 257

Laurent, 51

La Varenne, 71, 175, 279

L'Avenue, *104 fig. See also* Oakes, Nancy

Lazaroff, Barbara, 93, 162, 165, 166, 184

Le Balch, Josie, 305

Lebovitz, David, 91

Le Castel, 78–79. *See also* Passot, Roland

Le Cirque, 23

Le Colonial, 147

Le Coquelicot, 232

Lee, Chris, 97, 226–27, 247–48, 308

Lee, Corey, 10

LeFavour, Bruce (Rose et LeFavour), 23–25, *26 fig.*, 48, 67, 218–19, 278, 279

Lefebvre, Ludovic, 306–7

LeFevre, David, 307–8

Le Français, 135

Leinwand, Mark, 278

Le Jaouen, Jean-Claude, 7

Le Marché Seeds, 6, 199, 201–3, 216, 217, 219, 220. *See also* Brennan, Georgeanne

Lemon Grass, 115–16

Lenderink, Annabelle, 37

Lenôtre, Gaston, 55, 257, 273

Léon de Lyon, 76

Le Perroquet, 90, 119

L'Ermitage, 21, 52, 76, 80, 111, 193, 196, 224–25, 266

Le Saintongeais, 270

Les Frères Troisgros, 51, 56, 98–99, 102, 175
Le St. Tropez, 79
L'Etoile, 18, 19, 48, 155
Le Vaudeville, 79
Levine, Sarabeth, 89
Liberty ducks, 142–43, 226
Lindsey, Robert, 280, 282
Little Joe's, 161
Loar, Peggy, 286
L'Oasis, 75, 119
Lodge at Torrey Pines, 135–36
L'Omelette, 293
Long, Bob (Long Vineyards), 11, 269, 271, 298
L'Orangerie, 21, 76, 111, 196, 266, 315
Lorda, Jean-Baptiste, 79
Los Angeles. *See* Southern California; *specific chefs and restaurants*
Los Angeles Times, 31, 95, 96, 167, 224. *See also* Parsons, Russ; Virbila, S. Irene
Los Angeles VA Hospital, 196
Louis Martini Winery, 272
Love Apple Farms, 152, 300, 310
Lowenstein, Eleanor, 283
Luchetti, Emily, 34, 63, 70, 93, 179
Lucky Peach, 303
Lucques, 13, 143, 315. *See also* Goin, Suzanne
LudoBites (Lefebvre), 306
LuLu, 160–61, 163, 169, 183, 299
Lynch, Kermit, 265, 266, 267, 294

Madison, Deborah, 44, 91, 193–94
Magnin, Jerry, 52
Magruder Ranch, 229
Main, Jeff and Annie, 202
Maltus, Michael, 275
Ma Maison, 21, 22, 111, 119, 155–56, 265, 269
Mandarin, 110
Mandarin Oriental (Hong Kong), 164
Mangia, 94
Manresa, 152, 300, 308, 310. *See also* Kinch, David
"The Many Faces of California Cuisine," 239
Maple Drive, 89
Marchese, Gualtiero, 39
Marder, Bruce, 64, 70, 156–58, 214
Marin Agricultural Land Trust, 246
Marinelli, Bill, 235, 237–38
Marinelli Shellfish, 237–38, 239

Marin French Cheese Company, 246
Marin Joe's, 172
Marin Roots Farm, 37
Marin Sun Farms, 229
Mariquita Farm, 144, 222. *See also* Griffin, Andy
"The Market Basket," 58
Marks, Peter, 287
Martin, George, 260
Martin, Keith, 153
Martinez, Zarela, 89
Martini Winery, 272
Masa's, 160, 184, 233, 288
Mason, Sam, 304
Mason's, 232
Mastering the Art of French Cooking (Child, Bertholle, and Beck), 17, 273
Masumoto, David "Mas," 190, 191–92
Matsusaka, Kazuto, 80, 124, 176
Max au Triangle, 74, 75, 315
Maximin, Jacques, 75
Maxwell's Plum, 12, 257
May, Tony, 115
Mayacamas Vineyards, 263, 265
Mayne, Thom, 95, 158
Maytag, Fritz, 283–84, 293–94
Mazzola, Pam, 103
M. B. Post, 307–8
McBride, Marsha, 102, 152, 228
McCarty, Michael, 50–52, 103, 111, 114–15, 224; and AIWF, 283, 284; as host, 184–85; professional training, 51–52, 71. *See also* Michael's
McCrady's, 299
McDonald's, 10
McEvoy, Nan, 260
Meadowood, 279, 300
meat and poultry, 312, 313; charcuterie and *salumi,* 112, 114, 174, 242, 300; producers, 112–14, 141–43, 225–34, 240, 242–46
Medrich, Alice, 10, 240, 242, 259
Mélisse, 143
menus. *See* restaurant dishes and menus; *specific restaurants*
mesclun and salad mixes, 1, 199, 214–17, 220–22
Messmer, Frank, 218
Metropolis Baking Company, 240, 252
Metz, Ferdinand, 173, 291

Meyer, Danny, 61, 89, 93, 122, 183–84
Michael's, 50–52, 61, 111, 156, 175, 224; food
    and menus, 23, 52, *53 fig*, 127, 141, 144,
    176, 183; ingredients and purveyors, 143,
    196, 208, 224–25, 238, 239; service and
    atmosphere, 28, 50–51, 52, 184–85; staffers,
    240, 257; wines and wine service, 266, 267,
    269. *See also* McCarty, Michael
Michael's Cookbook (McCarty), 23
Middione, Carlo, 87, 248, 249
Miles, Charles, 177, 178
Millar, Jennifer, 71, 90
Miller, Joe, 70, 309, 315–16
Miller, Mark, 19, 58–61, 64, 67, 93, 100, 284;
    on California cuisine, 12, 54; at Chez
    Panisse, 58, 106, 112, 175, 176, 177; on
    Chez Panisse and its influence, 58–59, 102;
    on fusion cuisine, 31, 123; on Los Angeles
    chefs, 54–55, 57–58, 59. *See also* Fourth
    Street Grill; Santa Fe Bar and Grill
Milliken, Mary Sue, 89, 93, 146, 158, 303, 305;
    background and training, 90, 118–19; and
    purveyors, 196, 214, 239. *See also* Border
    Grill; City Restaurant
Miramonte, 48, 218, 278. *See also* Nechutnys,
    Udo
Mission Chinese, 299–300
Mitchell, Glenn, 252
Mitchell, Karen, 252, 254–55
Model Bakery, 252, 254–55
Modesto Lanzone's, 132
Mogannam, Sam, 310
Molinari, 243
Momofuku, 13
Mondavi, Margrit Biever, 200, 274, 286
Mondavi, Michael, 62, 275
Mondavi, Robert, 200, 230, 261, 269, 274; and
    AIWF, 284, 285–86; and Copia, 286, 287,
    290
Mondavi (Robert) Winery, 230, 232, 263, 267,
    274; Great Chefs program, 3, 239, 273–74;
    Tasting of Summer Produce at, 200
Monsoon, 117
Monterey Bay Aquarium Seafood Watch, 311
Monterey Fish Company, 25, 72, 234–36, 237,
    239, 318
Monterey Market, 6, 25, 92, 189–90, 191, 216,
    244. *See also* Fujimoto, Bill

Montrachet, 89
Montrose, Karen, 194
Moon, Doyle, 32
Moosewood Restaurant, 44
Mori Sushi, 314
Morphosis, 95, 158
Moullé, Jean-Pierre, 182; background and
    training, 76, 105–6; at Chez Panisse, 43, 58,
    79, 102, 105–6, 112, 176; and Chez Panisse
    gardens and purveyors, 195, 203, 217, 230;
    on French and California cooking, 105–6;
    on grilling, 177; on open kitchens, 162
Mount Veeder Winery, 265, 267
Mudd, Virginia, 47, 193
Mudd's, 47, 66, 90, 103, 193, 197
Muller, Paul, 139. *See also* Full Belly Farm
Murphy, Mr. (butcher), 242
Musso and Frank Grill, 161
Mustards Grill, 28, 96, 278; food and
    atmosphere, 278, 279, *281 fig*; purveyors,
    8, 217, 230, 280; wine list, 280. *See also*
    Pawlcyn, Cindy

Napa Valley, 82; CIA St. Helena, 290–92;
    wine country cuisine, 278–83. *See also*
    Copia; wine
Napa Valley Grille, 35
Napa Valley Lamb, 229–31, 239, 280
Narsai's Market, 252, 254
Narsai's Restaurant, 27, 244
Nassikas, Jim, 283, 284
Nathan, Amy, 117
National Conference on Gastronomy, 284
Natural Food Holdings, 229
Navarro Vineyards, 267, 292
Neal's Yard Dairy, 251
Nechutnys, Udo, 48, 76, 80, 218, 278
Negrin, Alison, 91
Nelson, Susie, 59, 113, 164
The New American Vegetable Cookbook
    (Brennan and Glenn), 202
New Haven Restaurant Institute, 70
New Joe's, 18
New West magazine, 65
New York restaurants, 89, 120, 122. *See also*
    specific chefs and restaurants
New York Times, 21, 54, 219, 280, 282, 319. *See
    also* Burros, Marian

New York Times Cookbook, 16

Neyers, Bruce, 264–67, 280

Neyers Winery, 267

Nick and Stef's, 74

Niman, Bill, 145, 226, 227–29

Niman Ranch (Niman-Schell Ranch), 37, 140, 141, 143, 226, 227–29

Noda, Hatsuyo, 42

Noma, 310

Norman's, 177, 178

North Berkeley Market, 242

Northern California Olive Oil Council, 260

Northern California restaurants, 39, 40, 61, 155; conservatism of, 54–55, 57, 59; design, 159–61; food as counterculture, 40–50; ingredients focus, 39, 40, 54, 317; self-taught chefs, 63–69, 76; women chefs in, 90–93. *See also specific chefs and restaurants*

Northern Produce, 208

nouvelle cuisine, 20–21, 23, 25, 27

Oakes, Nancy, 67, 103, 145, 186, 303, 304. *See also* Boulevard; L'Avenue

Oakland Museum Tasting of Summer Produce, 45, 200, 288

Oakville Grocery, 28

Ocean Jewels Seafood, 239

O'Connell, Rick, 91

Oenotri, 233

Ogden, Bradley, 70, 93, 183, 274, 284; and purveyors, 226, 233, 243. *See also* Lark Creek Inn; One Market

Old World Hanoi, 146

Oliveto, 113–14, 231, 233, 240, *241 fig*, 310

Olney, John, 294

Olney, Richard, 92, 179

One Market, 163, 169, 183. *See also* Ogden, Bradley

Ong, Alex, 80, 146–48

open kitchens, 3, 161–63, 165–67

organics, 40, 138, 139, 140, 199

Original Joe's, 161

Oritalia, 107, 127, *128 fig*

Orson, 152

Ott, Diane, 201

Outstanding in the Field program, 309

Out the Door, 150

Overton, Peter, 254

Pacific California Fish, 239

Paine, Philip, 231–33

Paine Farm Squab, 231–33

Palace Hotel, 173

Palate Food + Wine, 315

P&D Seafood, 239

Panorama Baking Company, 252

Pantsios, Catherine, 64, 67, 90. *See also* Zola's

Paragon, 24

Parker, Robert, 270

Parsons, Russ, 31, 41, 57, 141, 214–15

Passot, Roland, 76, 78, 93

Pasta Fresca (Kleiman and La Place), 94

Pasternak, Mark, 37

Patina, 54–55, 74, 75–76, *77 fig*, 89, 264, 315

Patina Restaurant Group, 74

Patterson, Daniel, 67, 108, 310–11, 319. *See also* Coi

Patton, Jameson, 6, 205, 206, 220. *See also* GreenLeaf Produce

Pawlcyn, Cindy, 24, 217, 278, 279–80, 282, 303, 304; background and training, 71, 279; and purveyors, 217, 230–31, 280. *See also* Mustards Grill

Pecota, Robert, 269

Peel, Mark, 12, 74, 91, 169, 240, 284; at Michael's, 52, 176; professional training, 70. *See also* Campanile

Peet's Coffee, 41, 240, 242

Pelaccio, Zak, 304

People's Food System, 208

Pépin, Jacques, 279

Perbacco, 49, 311

Perello, Melissa, 304

Perino's, 19, 155

Perry's, 61

pesticides, 41. *See also* organics

Petaluma Farms, 45

Peyton, Nick, 184

Pfister, Charles, 154

Pflug, Billy, 52

Pham, Mai, 67, 115–16

Phan, Charles, 67, 115, 149, 150–51, 309. *See also* Slanted Door

Phelan, Jim, 194

Phelps, Joseph (Phelps Vineyards), 264–67, 269, 271, 275, 284, 292

Pico farmers' market, 213

Pierre Vedel, 176

Pig-by-the-Tail, 48, 240, 242–43, 244, 259

Pigeon Point oysters, 143

Pinot bistros, 74, 264

Piperade, 80

Pirie, Gayle, 102, 304

Pitman Family Farms, 233

Poilâne, 257

Point Reyes Cheese, 239

Pok Pok, 299–300

politics and political culture, 40; current food politics issues, 312–13; food as counterculture in Northern California, 40–50; menus as manifestos, 148–49, 152–53

Pollan, Michael, 59, 152

Polshek, James, 286

Ponsford, Craig, 252

Ponzek, Debra, 89

pop-up restaurants, 306–7

Postrio, 118, 169, *170 fig*, 171–72, 307; ingredients and purveyors, 218, 243, 288; service and atmosphere, 184, 185, 186. *See also* Gingrass, Anne; Gingrass, David

Post Street Bar and Grill, 61

Pot Luck, 19, 244

Poulet, 244, 245

Powning, Andy, 187, 205, 206, 207. *See also* GreenLeaf Produce

Prather Ranch, 229

Prego, 9, 35, 180

Pressman, Amy, 255

Primi, 61

Primo, 299

produce, 187–223; before the 1970s, 1–2, 5–6, 187–88; early restaurant gardens and farm connections, 47, 192–95; education and information sharing, 222–23; farmers' markets, 208, 210–14, 222–23; Farm-Restaurant Project, 197–201, 203, 205, 207; mesclun and salad mixes, 1, 199, 214–17, 220–22; Monterey Market, 189–90, 191; new distribution networks, 204–8; new varieties and seed sources, 187–88, 199, 201–3, 216, 217, 219, 220; in Southern California, 195–97; Tastings of Summer Produce, 45, 200, 218, 288, 297. *See also* ingredients; producers and purveyors; *specific farms and farmers*

producers and purveyors: bread and bakeries, 252–58; cheesemakers, 6–8, 246–52; chocolate, 259; farms and gardens today, 309–11; fish and seafood, 234–39; identifying on restaurant menus, 140–41, 143–45, 153; meat and poultry, 112–14, 141–43, 225–34, 240, 242–46; new winemakers, 263–64; olive oil, 259–61; rise of artisanship, 6, 239–40, 312. *See also* produce; *specific producers, businesses, and restaurants*

professional training, 62–63, 69–71, 301–3; in Asia, 80–83; European chefs in the U.S., 73–80; sexism in, 85–86, 88–89; winemakers, 292–93; wine training for restaurant staff, 313. *See also specific chefs and schools*

Prudhomme, Paul, 245, 284

Puck, Wolfgang, 21–23, 27, 32, 103, 124, 284; background and training, 21–22, 74; at Ma Maison, 22, 156, 265; Mark Miller on, 54–55, 57–58, 59; and purveyors, 196, 197, 233; as teacher, 72, 274. *See also* Chinois on Main; Ma Maison; Postrio; Spago

Pump Room, 279

Pura, Stan, 221

Quince, 231, 233

Radio Africa & Kitchen, 307

Rakel, 108, 163

Ralphs, Walter, 229

Ranch House, 19

Ranhofer, Charles, 137

Rauschenberg, Robert, 171

Real Restaurants Group, 230, 279

Rebecca's, 156, 158

Redmond, Judith, 202

Redwood Hill Farm, 8, 247, 250

Redzepi, René, 310

Regency Club, 75

Reich, Phil, 52, 269

Reichardt, Jim, 141–43, 226, 239

Reichl, Ruth, 22, 65, 90, 95, 156

Reinhart, Peter, 255

Reis, Gerald, 271

Restaurant Associates, 132

restaurant design, 154–55; grills and wood-burning ovens, 3, 9, 174–75, 180–83; kitchen equipment and layout, 173–74;

restaurant design *(continued)*
open kitchens, 3, 161–63, 165–67, 168–69, 171–72, 183–86; in Southern vs. Northern California, 155–61. *See also specific restaurants*

restaurant dishes and menus: before the 1970s, 131; current trends, 317–18; eclecticism, 9, 117–22, 316; ethnic and regional cooking, 8–9, 67–69, 109–12, 114–17, 314–16; fusion cooking, 31, 118, 122–29, 315; ingredients listed on menus, 137–38; menu as storytelling or manifesto, 145–46, 148–49, 152–53; in Northern vs. Southern California, 57–58, 317; producers identified on menus, 140–41, 143–45, 153; seasonal and daily foods and menus, 77–78, 79, 102–3, 132–37; wine list evolution, 264–69, 270–71. *See also specific restaurants*

Restaurant Gary Danko, 184

Restaurant Le Salle, 203–4

restaurant scene: California cuisine's impact today, 299–300; current trends, 306–8, 317–18; mass-market and lower-priced restaurants, 34–36, 307–8; in the 1960s, 5, 10–11, 18–20, 155. *See also* Northern California; Southern California

restaurant service, 183–86

Rex il Ristorante, 39, 94, 111

Rich, Evan and Sarah (Rich Table), 307

Richard, Michel, 54, 55–56, 74, 155. *See also* Citronelle

Ridge Vineyards, 263, 267, 269, 271, 293, 294–96

Riley, Kathi, 100, 102

Rinzler, Marilyn, 245

Rio Grill, 279

Ritz Old Poodle Dog, 18

Rivers, Dru (Full Belly Farm), 139, 202, 309

Riverside Farms, 220–22

Rivoli, 72–73

Robert, Jacky, 25, 72, 76, 163. *See also* Ernie's

Roberta's, 299

Roberts, Michael, 27, 54, 71. *See also* Trumps

Robertson, Chad, 252

Robertson, Laurel, 44

Robuchon, Joël, 56, 81

Röckenwagner, Hans (Röckenwagner), 158, 214

Rocky chickens, 233

Rodgers, Judy, 38, 90, 98–102, 117, 303, 304; on Bill Fujimoto, 189; on California cuisine, 9, 100, 102; at Chez Panisse, 98, 99, 102, 175; on Chez Panisse and its influence, 98, 99, 102, 103, 132, 134; at Great Chefs, 274; on Lindsey Shere, 91; on supporting producers, 149. *See also* Union Hotel; Zuni Café

Romanée-Conti, 294

Rombauer, Irma, 16

Root, Waverly, 16, 92

Rosalie's, 91

Rosa Mexicana, 89

Rose, Carolyn, 24, 25

Rose, Michael, 252

Rose et LeFavour, 23–25, *26 fig*, 48, 67, 218, 278, 279

Rosenfield, Jerry, 48, 234

Rosenfield, Richard, 35

Rosenzweig, Anne, 89, 93

Round Pond Estate, 289

Rubicon, 307

Rubin, Henry "Hank," 19, 244

Rudd Center for Professional Wine Studies, 291

Rungis market, 51, 225, 239

Rutherford Hill Winery, 260

Ryan, Tim, 308

Saee, Michele, 95, 158

Saint Estèphe, 31

Salad (Nathan), 117

salad mixes, 1, 199, 214–17, 220–22

Saltsman, Amelia, 144, 213–14

salumi and charcuterie, 112, 114, 174, 242, 300

Sammons, Patty, 247

Sam's, 18, 159

Samuelsson, Marcus, 304

Sanford, Richard and Thekla (Sanford Winery), 284, 292

San Francisco Baking Institute, 256

San Francisco Bay Area. *See* Northern California; *specific chefs and restaurants*

San Francisco Chronicle, 89, 202, 226

San Francisco City College Hotel and Restaurant School, 40

San Francisco Express Times, 92

San Francisco Public Market Collaborative, 211

San Francisco Zen Center, 43, 44, 193, 252, 254. *See also* Green Gulch Farm; Greens Restaurant

Santa Fe Bar and Grill, 59, 164, 175, 177, 178–79, *181 fig*, 245; Jeremiah Tower at, 32, 164, 177, 178–79, 245; Mark Miller at, 59, 179, 180

Santa Monica farmers' market, 135–36, 208, 211–14

Santa Monica Seafood, 239

Santana, Deborah, 44

Santa Rosa Junior College, 195, 287

Santo, Joe, 100

Sarabeth's Kitchen, 89

Sardine Factory, 269

Sargent, Tom, 210

Sarvis, Shirley, 272–73

Savoy, Guy, 177

Sawyer, Terry, 237

Scala, Donna, 91, 304

Scandia, 18, 155

Scanlon, SoYoung, 8

Schacher, Max, 232

Scharffenberger, John, 259

Scharffen Berger Chocolate, 259

Schell, Orville, 226, 227–29

Schmidt, Jimmy, 284

Schmitt, Don, 3–5

Schmitt, Sally, 3–5, 67, 132, 278. *See also* French Laundry (Schmitt)

Schnack, Steven, 247

Schug, Walter, 266

Schweitzer, Josh, 158–59, 169

Schwertner, Amaryll, 15, 47, 67, 90, 193, 304

Sciabica, Nicola (Sciabica's), 260, 261

Scott, Alan, 66

seafood purveyors, 234–39. *See also* Monterey Fish Company

seasonal foods and menus, 77–78, 79, 102–3, 132–37

Sebastiani, Sam, 284

Sedlar, John Rivera, 31

Seed Savers Exchange, 201, 288

Selvaggio, Piero, 55, 61, 111–12, 115, 184, 239. *See also* Valentino

Semifreddi's, 252

Senderens, Alain, 20

Señor Pico, 110

Serrano, Julian, 76, 93

Seven Countries Study, 260

Seventh Street Bistro, 75

72 Market, 89

Shandygaff, 44

Shangri-La Hotel, 80, 147

Shepherd, Renee, 203

Shepherd's Garden Seed Company, 202–3, 219

Sheraton, Mimi, 219

Shere, Charles, 91

Shere, Lindsey, 58, 91–93, 175, 193, 253, 255, 282; background and training, 67, 91–92; on Chez Panisse, 85, 92–93, 102

Shere, Thérèse, 195

Sherman House, 91

Shook, Jon, 307

Shore, Hobbs, 243

Shutters on the Beach, 135

Silent Spring (Carson), 41

Silverton, Nancy, 12, 67, 89, 256–58, 303, 304; at Michael's, 240, 257; and Santa Monica farmers' market, 211, 214; at Spago, 81, 240, 257. *See also* Campanile

Simon, André, 283

Singer, Peter, 226

Singer, Stephen, 195

Sinskey, Maria Helm, 71, 91

Skipper, Roscoe, 72–73

Skirt Steak (Druckman), 304

Slanted Door, 115, 150–51, 314. *See also* Phan, Charles

Slow Food, 96, 311, 312

Smith, Cass Calder, 160, 169

Smith, Fonts, 251

Smith, Peggy, 90, 240, 246–47, 250–52

Sokolov, Raymond, 122

Solis, Thomas, 15

Somerville, Annie, 44–47, 91, 282, 304

Sone, Hiro, 36, 80, 125. *See also* Terra

Sonoma County Poultry, 239. *See also* Reichardt, Jim

Sonoma Mission Inn, 255

Southern California restaurants, 39, 40, 54–55, 57; design, 155–59; ethnic influences, 22, 44, 119, 122–23; farmers' markets and, 211–14; food as fashion, 50–58, 61; innovation and experimentation, 54–55, 57, 59, 122–27; professionally trained chefs, 74–76, 78;

Southern California restaurants *(continued)*
women chefs in, 89–90. *See also specific chefs and restaurants*

Southland Farmers' Market Association, 212

Souverain Winery, 275, 280. *See also* Chateau Souverain

Spago, 22–23, 35, 50, 61; daily menus, 130; design, 155, 156, 162, 165, 166; ex-staff at other restaurants, 35, 80–82, 118, 167, 240, 257; food and menus, 22–23, 31, 38, 57–58, 117, 124, *125 fig*, 130; ingredients and purveyors, 143, 145, 196, 197, 238; service and atmosphere, 122, 184; Spago Tokyo, 81; wines and winemaker dinners, 266, 267, 269; women cooks at, 89; wood oven, 182. *See also* Puck, Wolfgang; Silverton, Nancy

Speedo 690, 107

Splichal, Joachim, 54–55, 74–76, 264, 315. *See also* Patina

Spottswoode, 271, 292

Spurrier, Steven, 51

Square One, 61, 122; daily menus, 130; design, 154, 155, 162–63, 185; ethnic and regional dishes at, 83, 109, 110, 118, 138, 188; ingredients and purveyors, 187, 188, 203, 218, 228, 231, 238; kitchen organization and working style, 84, 180; menu, *viii fig*; opening, ix, 15–16, 62; service at, 138, 184; staffers, 57, 66, 71, 72, 103, 240; wine service and education at, 137, 269, 270–71, 272, 273; women cooks at, 90

Stanford Court Hotel, 206, 273, 283, 284

Stanley Produce, 204, 221

Starr, Kevin, 10

Star Route Farms, 193, 197–99, 200, 202, 215–17; customers, 37, 143, 198, 199, 207, 208. *See also* Weber, Warren

Stars, 32–34, 61, 122, 269; Asian branches, 83; design, 155, 159–60, 162–63; ex-staff at other restaurants, 57, 71, 72–73, 127, 147, 164–65; food and menus, 32, *33 fig*, 34, 71, 80, 118, 130, 147, 180; kitchen organization and work styles, 34, 106–7, 179–80; purveyors, 228, 288; self-taught cooks at, 63, 64; women cooks at, 93

Stars Café, 34

State Bird Provisions, 307

Stech-Novak, Mark, 165

Steiman, Harvey, 8, 140

Stein, Sam, 135

Steinberg, Robert, 259

Sterling, Audrey, 284

Stewart, Martha, 275

St. Francis Hotel, 30

St. Germain, 57, 196

Stoll, Anne, 307

Stoll, Craig, 97, 307, 309

Stone Barns Center, 145, 309–10

Stone Free Farm, 202, 288

Stony Hill, 263, 271

Straits Café, 147

Straus, Albert, 250

Straus, Bill, 246

Straus, Ellen, 246, 250

Straus Family Creamery, 246, 248, 249, 250

Streeter, Brian, 240, 277

Strobel, John, 94, 95

Stutz, Ken, 260

Suas, Michel, 256

Sullivan, Steve, 62, 252–54, 256, 257

Sunny Spot, 307

Sunset magazine, 8, 17–18, 27, 65, 174, 272

Sushi Zo, 314

sustainability, 47, 311–13

Sutter, Craig, 15, 91

Sutter 500, 25. *See also* Keller, Hubert

Swan, Joseph, 261, 267, 269

Swan Oyster Depot, 161, 300

Sysco, 220, 222

T&A (Tanimura and Antle), 221

Tachibe, Shigefumi, 124, 127

Tadich Grill, 18, 159, 161, 236

Tangren, Alan, 274–75

Tanis, David, 43, 105, 195

Tartine Bakery, 252

Tassajara Bakery, 252

Tassajara Bread Book (Brown), 43

Tassajara Cooking (Brown), 43

Tasting of Summer Produce, 45, 200, 218, 288, 297

television cooking shows, 131, 301–2

Terje, Staffan, 49, 76, 311

Terlato Wine Group, 297

Terra, 36, 80, 82, 217

Terrail, Patrick, 22, 155, 265

"Thirty Recipes Suitable for Framing," 92

Thomas, Anna, 43

Thoresen, Mary Jo, 91

385 North, 9

Thuilier, Raymond, 22

Tihany, Adam, 173

TKO Farms, 217, 220–22

Tomales Bay Foods, 247, 250

Tommaso's Restaurant, ix, 182

Topaz Room, 276

"To the Moon, Alice?" (Patterson), 319

Tower, Jeremiah, 27, 32–34, 93, 117–18, 177, 284, 317–18; background and training, 32, 63, 64; at CCA, 72, 163; at Chez Panisse, 32, 34, 102, 106, 137–38, 266; at Great Chefs, 274; on Michael's, 50–51; on Tommaso's, 182; work style, 106. See also Santa Fe Bar and Grill; Stars

Tracht, Suzanne, 89, 143–44, 214, 303, 305

Trader Vic's, 19, 160

Trattoria Angeli, 89, 95–96, 158

travel, 17, 301

Tra Vigne, 112, 130, 230, 279. See also Chiarello, Michael

Trboyevic, Jovan, 90, 119

Trefethen Family Vineyards, 275, 278

Treme, 304

Troisgros, Jean, 20, 98, 99, 102, 273

Troisgros, Pierre, 20, 21, 81, 102

Troisgros restaurant, 51, 56, 98–99, 102, 175

Tropp, Barbara, 9, 50, 93, 117, 142, 226, 239, 282. See also China Moon

Trumps, 27, 54, 61, 89, 156. See also Roberts, Michael

Uchiko, 300

Union Hotel, 99–100, 189, 197. See also Rodgers, Judy

Union Square Cafe, 61, 122, 183. See also Meyer, Danny

University of California, Davis, 286, 293, 294, 296, 297

University of California, Santa Barbara, 283

University of California, Santa Cruz, Alan Chadwick Garden, 193, 217

Unterman, Patricia, 35, 90, 159, 189

Upson, Bill, 279

Urasawa, 314

Valentino, 55, 89, 94, 111–12, 184. See also Selvaggio, Piero

Van Den Broeck, Herman, 204

Vanessi's, 18, 161

Vann, Mark, 255

vegetarian cookbooks and restaurants, 43–44

Vegetarian Epicure (Thomas), 43

Vella, Tom and Ig, 246

Vella Cheese Company, 246, 247, 250

Ventana Inn, 32

Verdi Ristorante di Musica, 94

Verdon, René, 76

Vergé, Roger, 20, 273, 274

Veritable Vegetable, 199, 208, 215

Villaine, Aubert de, 294

Villetta, 305

Vincenti, Mauro, 39, 111, 115. See also Rex il Ristorante

Virbila, S. Irene (Sherry), 17, 41, 47–48, 118

Voltaggio, Michael, 308

Vossen, Paul, 260

Vowell, Sarah, 224

Vranian, Steven, 164, 177, 178–79

Waks, Bob, 112

Walker, Peter, 286, 289

Walton, Steve, 6, 205, 206. See also GreenLeaf Produce

Washburne Culinary Institute, 118

Washington, Doug, 184, 185

Washington Square Bar and Grill, 61

Watchorn, Michael, 237

Waterfront, 107

Water Grill, 307

Waters, Alice, 27, 32, 42–43, 152, 177, 258, 282, 303; background and influences, 17, 64, 67, 92; and Chez Panisse Café oven, 182; and Chez Panisse gardens/farm, 194, 195; and Chez Panisse remodeling, 162; impact and influence of, 41, 42, 43, 67, 85, 132, 134; and ingredients revolution, 42, 43, 189, 194, 198, 215, 216–17; and Paul Bertolli, 112, 113; and Laura Chenel, 7; and Joyce Goldstein, 62; and Mark Miller, 58, 59; and Phelps wines, 265–66; and Judy Rodgers, 98, 99;

Waters, Alice *(continued)*
  and Lindsey Shere, 91–92; and Jeremiah
  Tower, 32; and Jonathan Waxman, 175;
  Victoria Wise on, 242; and women cooks,
  85, 98; working style, 98, 102. *See also* Chez
  Panisse *entries*
Watson, Don, 229–31, 239
Waxman, Jonathan, 50, 52, 167, 175–77, 225,
  284
Webber, Tracy, 135–36
Weber, Kathleen, 252, 255–56
Weber, Marian, 227. *See also* Star Route Farms
Weber, Warren, 6, 49–50, 141, 197–99, 200,
  215, 216–17, 218, 227. *See also* Star Route
  Farms
Weiner, Joe, 210
Weinzweig, Ari, 250
Weiss, Dennis, 208
Wente, Carolyn, 282
Wente Vineyards, 282
Werlin, Laura, 6, 246–47
West, Billy, 100, 182
West Beach Café, 28, 31, 156, *157 fig*
West Central Wholesale Produce, 208
Whealy, Kent, 201
Whitmer, Brian, 89
Wild, Michael, 67, 143, 189, 226, 245, 254. *See
  also* Bay Wolf
Wilkinson, Bill, 206, 207, 273. *See also*
  GreenLeaf Produce
Williams Center for Flavor Discovery, 291
Williams-Sonoma, 17
Willinger, Faith, 95
Willis, Paul, 227
Windisch, Patricia, 91
wine, 262, 313–14; California cuisine's impact
  on wine styles, 292–93; California wineries
  before the 1970s, 263; new artisanal
  winemakers, 263–64, 296–98; restaurant
  wine lists, 264–69, 270–71; wine and food
  education, 271, 272–77, 282–90, 313–14;
  wines by the glass, 270, 272
Wine, Food, and the Arts, 285
Wine and Cheese Center (San Francisco), 7,
  273
wine country cuisine, 278–83
Wine Forest Wild Foods, 48–49
Wine Spectator magazine, 282

Wine Spectator Restaurant, 172–73, 291
Winroth, Jon, 51
Wise, Victoria, 27, 58, 85, 192–93, 240, 242–
  43, 259. *See also* Pig-by-the-Tail
Wise Sons, 307
Wolf, Clark, 28, 223
Wolfert, Paula, 38, 179
women chefs: impact on restaurant kitch-
  ens, 98, 102–3, 105, 106–8; mentoring
  and support for, 90, 93; in Northern
  California, 90–93; obstacles faced by,
  89; sensibilities of, 84, 93–94, 96–97;
  in Southern California, 89–90; today,
  303–6; traditional male-dominated culinary
  culture, 85–86, 88–89. *See also specific chefs
  and restaurants*
Women Chefs and Restaurateurs, ix, 93, 305
wood-burning ovens, 3, 9, 66, 180–83
Wooly Weeders, 229, 230
Worlds of Flavor conference, 291–92
Worlds of Healthy Flavors conference, 292
Worthington, Diane, 30–31
Worthington, Tom, 63, 235–36, 318. *See also*
  Monterey Fish
Wu, Rowena, 160, 161

Yamaguchi, Roy, 9, 70
Yanatta-Goldway, Ruth, 212
Yap, Andrew, 34
Yasuda, Glenn, 191
Yellowfingers, 100
Yoshida, Nori, 127

Zagat Guides, 122, 304, 305
Zaré, Hoss, 67, 68–69, 148
Zaré at the Fly Trap, 68–69
Zarela, 89
Zenzero, 80
Zimmerman, Linda, 167
Zinfandel Nouveau festival (Chez Panisse),
  266
Zola's, 64, 90, 111
Zuni Café, 31, 37, 96, 99, 100–102, 303, 309;
  design, 160, 162; food and menus, 100, *101
  fig*, 182–83; purveyors, 143, 149, 228, 233,
  238; winemaker dinners, 269; women cooks
  at, 102, 103; wood oven, 182–83. *See also*
  Rodgers, Judy

CALIFORNIA STUDIES IN FOOD AND CULTURE
Darra Goldstein, Editor

1 *Dangerous Tastes: The Story of Spices*, by Andrew Dalby

2 *Eating Right in the Renaissance*, by Ken Albala

3 *Food Politics: How the Food Industry Influences Nutrition and Health*, by Marion Nestle

4 *Camembert: A National Myth*, by Pierre Boisard

5 *Safe Food: The Politics of Food Safety*, by Marion Nestle

6 *Eating Apes*, by Dale Peterson

7 *Revolution at the Table: The Transformation of the American Diet*, by Harvey Levenstein

8 *Paradox of Plenty: A Social History of Eating in Modern America*, by Harvey Levenstein

9 *Encarnación's Kitchen: Mexican Recipes from Nineteenth-Century California: Selections from Encarnación Pinedo's* El cocinero español, by Encarnación Pinedo, edited and translated by Dan Strehl, with an essay by Victor Valle

10 *Zinfandel: A History of a Grape and Its Wine*, by Charles L. Sullivan, with a foreword by Paul Draper

11 *Tsukiji: The Fish Market at the Center of the World*, by Theodore C. Bestor

12 *Born Again Bodies: Flesh and Spirit in American Christianity*, by R. Marie Griffith

13 *Our Overweight Children: What Parents, Schools, and Communities Can Do to Control the Fatness Epidemic*, by Sharron Dalton

14 *The Art of Cooking: The First Modern Cookery Book*, by The Eminent Maestro Martino of Como, edited and with an introduction by Luigi Ballerini, translated and annotated by Jeremy Parzen, and with fifty modernized recipes by Stefania Barzini

15 *The Queen of Fats: Why Omega-3s Were Removed from the Western Diet and What We Can Do to Replace Them*, by Susan Allport

16 *Meals to Come: A History of the Future of Food*, by Warren Belasco

17 *The Spice Route: A History*, by John Keay

18 *Medieval Cuisine of the Islamic World: A Concise History with 174 Recipes*, by Lilia Zaouali, translated by M. B. DeBevoise, with a foreword by Charles Perry

19 *Arranging the Meal: A History of Table Service in France*, by Jean-Louis Flandrin, translated by Julie E. Johnson, with Sylvie and Antonio Roder; with a foreword to the English language edition by Beatrice Fink

20 *The Taste of Place: A Cultural Journey into Terroir*, by Amy B. Trubek

21 *Food: The History of Taste*, edited by Paul Freedman

22 *M.F.K. Fisher among the Pots and Pans: Celebrating Her Kitchens*, by Joan Reardon, with a foreword by Amanda Hesser

23 *Cooking: The Quintessential Art*, by Hervé This and Pierre Gagnaire, translated by M.B. DeBevoise

24 *Perfection Salad: Women and Cooking at the Turn of the Century*, by Laura Shapiro

25 *Of Sugar and Snow: A History of Ice Cream Making*, by Jeri Quinzio

26 *Encyclopedia of Pasta*, by Oretta Zanini De Vita, translated by Maureen B. Fant, with a foreword by Carol Field

27 *Tastes and Temptations: Food and Art in Renaissance Italy*, by John Varriano

28 *Free for All: Fixing School Food in America*, by Janet Poppendieck

29 *Breaking Bread: Recipes and Stories from Immigrant Kitchens*, by Lynne Christy Anderson, with a foreword by Corby Kummer

30 *Culinary Ephemera: An Illustrated History*, by William Woys Weaver

31 *Eating Mud Crabs in Kandahar: Stories of Food during Wartime by the World's Leading Correspondents*, edited by Matt McAllester

32 *Weighing In: Obesity, Food Justice, and the Limits of Capitalism*, by Julie Guthman

33 *Why Calories Count: From Science to Politics*, by Marion Nestle and Malden Nesheim

34 *Curried Cultures: Globalization, Food, and South Asia*, edited by Krishnendu Ray and Tulasi Srinivas

35 *The Cookbook Library: Four Centuries of the Cooks, Writers, and Recipes That Made the Modern Cookbook*, by Anne Willan, with Mark Cherniavsky and Kyri Claflin

36 *Coffee Life in Japan*, by Merry White

37 *American Tuna: The Rise and Fall of an Improbable Food*, by Andrew F. Smith

38 *A Feast of Weeds: Foraging and Cooking Wild Edible Plants*, by Luigi Ballerini, translated by Gianpiero W. Doebler

39 *The Philosophy of Food*, by David M. Kaplan

40 *Beyond Hummus and Falafel: Social and Political Aspects of Palestinian Food in Israel*, by Liora Gvion, translated by David Wesley and Elana Wesley

41 *The Life of Cheese: Crafting Food and Value in America*, by Heather Paxson

42 *The History of Cooking in Rome and Lazio: With Folklore and Recipes*, by Oretta Zanini De Vita, translated by Maureen B. Fant

43 *Cuisine and Empire: Cooking in World History*, by Rachel Laudan

44 *Inside the California Food Revolution: Thirty Years That Changed Our Culinary Consciousness*, by Joyce Goldstein, with Dore Brown